KINGDOM
in the
WEST

The Mormons and the American Frontier

Will Bagley, series editor

VOLUME 7

THE COMPANIONS OF MARSHALL

This official portrait, taken in San Francisco at the California Gold Rush Jubilee in 1898, honored the four surviving members of the LDS work crew who were present at the Coloma gold discovery in January 1848: (*left to right*) Henry W. Bigler, William Johnston, Azariah Smith, and James S. Brown. *Courtesy LDS Archives.*

Gold Rush Saints

California Mormons and the Great Rush for Riches

by
Kenneth N. Owens

THE ARTHUR H. CLARK COMPANY
Spokane, Washington
2004

LIBRARY OF CONGRESS CATALOG CARD NUMBER 2004010657
ISBN 0-87602-336-2
ISBN 0-87062-274-9 (entire series)

THE ARTHUR H. CLARK COMPANY
P.O. BOX 14707
SPOKANE, WA 99214

Library of Congress Cataloging-in-Publication Data
Owens, Kenneth N.
Gold rush saints : California Mormons and the great rush for riches / by Kenneth N. Owens.
p. cm. — (Kingdom in the West ; v. 7)
Includes bibliographical references and index.
ISBN 0-87062-336-2 (hardcover : alk. paper)
1. Mormons—California—History—19th century. [1. California—Gold discoveries. 2. California—History—1846-1850.] I. Title. II. Series.
F865.O935 2004
979.4'9504'0922--dc22

2004010657

For Sally

Contents

Illustrations

Foreword

There are few more intriguing stories in the American West than the epic rush for gold in California. It is a tale in which the members of the Church of Jesus Christ of Latter-day Saints were inextricably involved—Mormons were present at the first gold discovery, made many of the initial "strikes," and accumulated some of the first fortunes in the gold fields. And yet, with the possible exception of the Indians, none of the protagonists in this drama have been overlooked more often than the California Saints.

Scholars such as Dale L. Morgan, Brigham D. Madsen, David L. Bigler, and John Unruh have illuminated the role of the Mormon "waystation" on the wagon road to California. Madsen's *Gold Rush Sojourners in Great Salt Lake City* and Bigler's *A Winter with the Mormons* remain the best studies of the symbiotic relationship between the Utah Mormon community and the forty-niners, whose trade proved invaluable to the survival of the Latter-day Saints in the Great Basin. Now Kenneth N. Owens, a respected scholar with a lifetime of research experience on early California and western American history, brings his expertise to the neglected legacy of the gold rush Saints. His narrative chronicles a period of less than a dozen years, from 1846, when LDS church authorities dispatched colonists to northern California on the ship *Brooklyn* (hence the phrase, "Brooklyn Saints"), to 1857, when Mormon leaders called all California church members back to the embattled capital at Great Salt Lake City. But in those few years, the California gold rush transformed the American West.

The reader will quickly find gold in this collection, which includes both familiar and forgotten accounts by some of the best-known witnesses to the gold discovery and its aftermath—among them James S.

Brown, Henry W. Bigler, Azariah Smith, and the irrepressible Abner Blackburn. Following the tradition of the KINGDOM IN THE WEST series, Owens also rescues some of the West's most intriguing characters from obscurity. Among them are the marooned sailor Francis Hammond, who left Hawaii intending to return to New England but instead cast his lot with the Mormons, despite their reputation as "about the worst people on earth," and Nathan Hawk, the rider who carried the April 1848 issues of Sam Brannan's *California Star* east in his saddlebags, helping to spread the contagion of gold fever. Zadock Judd, who washed gold with "a little Indian basket or common milk pan," describes how he and fellow trail-builders used fire and water to demolish boulders that blocked their passage, creating a wagon trail down West Carson Canyon on the east slope of the Sierra Nevada.

The volume provides a host of details that dispel the romantic image of gold country created by Victorian era myth-makers like Bret Harte and Mark Twain. Little-known writers such as Thomas Morris, Goudy E. Hogan, George W. Hickerson, Solomon Chamberlain, James Sly, and Thomas Orr, Jr., testify to the hard—and often unrewarding—lives of the gold seekers. James Skinner remembers a time in his childhood, when San Francisco was a dusty trading village, when he played hooky to follow an organ grinder and his monkey through the streets. Within a few years, as Albert K. Thurber reports, the city had "gambling hells" adorned with "life size obscene pictures."

The narratives of the gold rush Saints provide a glimpse of a California before it paid the environmental cost of gold mania. Early arrivals recall haunting images of "a most lovely country—a Gods country" that was, as James Marshall recalled so aptly, "sowed with gold." "In those days," as Thomas J. Orr, Jr., later recalled, "the underbrush of the present time was conspicuous by its absence and there were no annoying small ravines or washouts."

Owens brings attention to the tremendous sacrifices of the women who made possible the Mormon settlement of the West. Among the gold rush Saints were three women: Melissa Coray, whose entire recollection of her adventures is reprinted here for the first time in a century; Mary Ann Fisher Cheney, who tells how she tried her hand at washing gold; and Emeline Lane Sirrine, whose letter home reported that the

$6,000 she and her husband had accumulated—a phenomenal "pile" in the 1850s—was "not a fortune in California." Tellingly, two of the three, Cheney and Sirrine, did not survive the hazards of childbirth on the frontier.

While the volume focuses primarily on the experiences of the California Saints, the narratives illuminate the challenges and opportunities that the gold rush posed to the Mormon colony in the Great Basin. Ambivalence characterized the relationship from the start: even before the Mormons set out for the Great Basin, church leaders considered the possibility that remote California might provide a haven for the Saints. After the discovery of gold Brigham Young feared that El Dorado might become a refuge for the disaffected and the dissolute, who could lure the faithful from the fold. Modern historians tend to forget what a tenuous hold the Latter-day Saints had on their desert kingdom during their first ten years in the West. During the grim days of famine that began in 1855, Brigham Young wrote to Apostle Amasa Lyman, "Perhaps we may have to take our line of march to your point [San Bernardino] in order to save ourselves from starvation." Young, who never saw California, quickly understood that the lure of California's climate and riches could prove fatal to his vision of building a new Zion in the mountains. Yet goods brought by the forty-niners were a godsend to the desperately poor residents of the City of the Saints after the brutal winter of 1849, and tithing from California Saints provided the church with badly needed currency. But for ordinary Mormons, the greatest windfall from the gold rush turned out to be not the precious metal retrieved from California, but the supplies that accompanied gold seekers from the East. In the cold, wet spring of 1849, a fellow apostle told Heber C. Kimball he had "burst his boiler" when he prophesied that cheap goods and wealth would soon come to the Saints in Deseret—but few predictions in American history have proved as accurate.

Owens includes narratives that address the legacy of the gold rush Saints in California, the West, and the LDS church. Among non-Mormons, California's Saints made remarkable progress in overturning the dreadful image the faith had acquired in the Midwest. On 1851 Apostles Amasa Lyman and Charles C. Rich established San Bernardino, which became the major center of Mormon power and influence in southern California, and for half a decade, their settlement was the state's second largest city. San Bernardino residents, like many other LDS pioneers, earned a reputation as stable, hardworking ranchers and farmers. As a gold rush history, this volume focuses on LDS activity in northern California, so this story is mentioned only in passing, since it would require a volume of its own to address properly.

One old gentleman in San Francisco could not believe that Albert Thurber and his companions belonged to the West's most notorious religion. "You Mormons?" said the old gent. "Why you look like other folks." After eating a bountiful free meal at Thurber's camp in the Sierra Nevada, three starving miners left the camp with tears of gratitude in their eyes, "surprised to think," Thurber recalled, that "anything good come from a Mormon."

Without openly defying Brigham Young, California Mormons maintained strongly independent views about the authority of the church leadership and the status of plural marriage as a sacrament. Many believers chose to remain in the Golden State despite orders from the hierarchy to abandon their homes in 1857 and head for Zion; others agonized before eventually making the journey east. In the long run, Owens proposes, the success of moderate leaders such as Rich and Amasa Lyman in California offers an intriguing model of what early church history might have been had Brigham Young adopted a less confrontational stance.

Why did such treasures escape the notice of the historians of the West until now, and why did Mormon chroniclers not draw extensively on the collections maintained in the archives of their church? Many of these documents were the records of "ordinary" people, so they may have been lost or overlooked in the vast collection of LDS personal and family records. Much like California's glittering gold deposits before 1848, these historical nuggets may have been hiding in plain sight. But this wealth of materials that Owens has collected from repositories in Utah should put to rest the notion that there is little to interest non-LDS researchers in the records of Mormon country. Owens, like other non-Mormon scholars such as Elliott West and William P. MacKinnon, reports receiving outstanding cooperation from the LDS church's magnificent archives. The existence of this volume should encourage more western historians to mine the rich fields of those archives.

The best new works of western history continually remind us what a diverse and dynamic society existed on the frontier. "Mormon" San Bernardino was home to freed slaves, Jewish merchants, retired trappers, and American Indians. At Mormon Island, the Natomas diggings, and dozens of other placer-mining sites in northern California, veterans of the Mormon Battalion and prospectors fresh from Deseret worked side by side with "gentiles," often in partnership arrangements, share and share alike. *Gold Rush Saints* contributes significantly to our understanding of one of the many different cultures that created the modern West and reminds us that the region's openness and ability to provide new beginnings to people from all over the world have always been among its greatest strengths.

WILL BAGLEY
Salt Lake City, Utah
April 2004

Acknowledgments

My first acquaintance with California's gold rush Saints came during the course of contract research for the U.S. Forest Service on the Carson Pass Wagon Road, a route referred to locally as the Mormon Emigrant Trail. This important trans-Sierra link in the California Trail had been opened in July and August 1848 by eastbound Mormon Battalion veterans and a few other Latter-day Saints from Samuel Brannan's *Brooklyn* colony at San Francisco. Also joining the first company of road builders was a pioneer missionary from Tahiti, the earliest Saint to return from an LDS proselytizing mission in the South Pacific. These trail-making Mormons, thirty-eight men and one woman, had enjoyed at least moderate success placer mining during the previous few months. Now, however, they were heading for Brigham Young's newly established LDS capital at Great Salt Lake City, leaving the gold fields behind even as elsewhere thousands of other adventurous men and women began hasty preparations to join the worldwide rush toward California's riches.

By no means did all California Mormons depart in 1848. Many hesitated to leave the land of gold, and other LDS adventurers soon arrived from the Great Basin settlements, coming to northern California's gold country against the strong counsel of Brigham Young and his colleagues in the Utah country. Until 1857, I came to realize, the movement back and forth between northern California and the center of western Mormonism at Salt Lake City had been constant. President Young and other church leaders were compelled to develop a California policy and, in response, the Saints of the gold country improvised their own practices for dealing with Utah church authorities and their representatives.

It became clear to me that the Mormon role in California's gold rush had been for the most part overlooked, deliberately ignored, misunderstood, or forgotten. The battalion veterans, the *Brooklyn* colonists, and later LDS participants were responsible for unique and significant contributions to California's development during the gold rush era. I was convinced that their stories were worth recalling and retelling, with utmost fidelity to the available documentary sources. I felt prepared for the project, not least because in-depth conversations with Leonard Arrington and Brigham D. Madsen years earlier had persuaded me that the study of Mormon history should not be off-limits to non-Mormons like myself.

My first effort was "Gold-Rich Saints: The Mormon Beginnings of the California Gold Rush," a talk for the California Gold Rush Sesquicentennial lecture series that appears in the University of Nebraska Press essay collection, *Riches for All, the California Gold Rush and the World.* With an abundance of newly discovered documentary materials available, however, it became apparent that only a larger work could give the gold rush Saints a proper opportunity to speak for themselves about their role in the grand drama of the California gold rush.

I was encouraged by a small cadre of historians who, as friends, colleagues, and fellow enthusiasts for documentary fidelity, have continued to give me aid and support. Chief among them is Will Bagley. As general editor of the KINGDOM IN THE WEST series, he urged me to convert my budding interests into a published volume. Will's enthusiasm for the project matched and sometimes overmatched my own. His assistance in locating original materials and supplying editorial oversight has been both expert and dependable.

From first to last, my former graduate student and excellent friend Michael N. Landon has been closely involved. During his graduate study years, Mike worked as my research assistant on the Forest Service's Mormon Emigrant Trail study. Subsequently, from his strategic post as archival specialist in the LDS Church History Department in Salt Lake City, Mike has used his expert knowledge of LDS documentary sources and his indefatigable energy to push this project forward.

It was Mike who introduced me to Will Bagley and also to David L. Bigler, whose keen understanding of LDS history has guided me through many interpretive tangles. Like both Will and Mike, Dave came to history after a successful career in another, non-academic field. A historian by conviction, with a clear sense of purpose in his writing, he ranks foremost among those shaping a strong new scholarly tradition in western Mormon historiography. His example has been inspiring, and his critiques of my work, invariably generous but acute, have strengthened it beyond measure.

Through Will Bagley, Mike Landon, and Dave Bigler, I have formed an acquaintance with many others, LDS church members and not, who are active in expanding and revising historical knowledge about the Saints in the West. It is a large (one might say ecumenical) group, whose work is creating a new golden age in historical writing about the LDS participation in the settlement of western America. An especially notable contributor is the remarkable Ardis E. Parshall, who has generously shared selections from her impressive survey and transcription of Mormon letters, journals, and newspapers. My gratitude is great as well to historian Norma B. Ricketts. She pioneered the recovery of California's Mormon history, and her work forms an essential resource. She freely shared her splendid image of a young Melissa Coray for this volume. Photo archivist William W. Slaughter helped locate outstanding items in the LDS Church History Department's pictorial collection, while Bernie Rhoades provided the only known picture of his ancestor, Thomas Rhoades. I would also like to thank the Daughters of Utah Pioneers, especially President Mary Johnson, Edith Menna, and Elma Odegard for making available the riches of their portrait collection.

I feel fortunate to have been able to call on many people not named here to expand and refine my understanding of the Latter-day Saint religion and Mormon culture. Above all others, my debt is greatest to Sally Owens, to whom this volume is dedicated. Her counsel and good advice, her editorial refinements, and her occasional gentle and sometimes not so gentle reminders that I needed to bring this project to a conclusion have been essential. Of course, all statements of fact in this work, as well as the interpretive views and conclusions advanced, are entirely my own responsibility

California's gold rush Saints transformed California—first and foremost by initiating and promoting the gold rush itself. The great rush for riches and its consequences also changed Mormonism, directly and indirectly. The LDS church and the Mormon people began to move along a different path than that intended by Brigham Young and his counselors when they first rooted Zion in the desert oasis between the Wasatch Range and the Great Salt Lake. Church authorities called on California's gold to sustain Zion, even while criticizing or repudiating some of the men who added that gold to the church treasury. Within a few years the Mormons learned, within limits, to accommodate themselves and their faith to the rich commerce and the flow of visitors who made Utah's capital a convenient supply center and way station between California and the eastern states. Spreading gradually through Mormon congregations, the spirit of accommodation fostered by the gold rush would in time remake LDS church policy and Mormon culture.

The loss of historical memory and the growth of myth in its place are hazards in every area and on every topic where past realities collide with fondly held beliefs. Gold rush California is such an area. Mormon history is such a topic. My fierce ambition for this volume is that it will help clear away a thicket of myth and accurately reclaim a lost memory. In retrospect, the gold rush Saints of California deserve to be honored with nothing more and certainly nothing less than historical truth.

Editorial Procedures

This volume seeks to represent faithfully the original records in a readable format. I have rendered the texts as close as practicable to the original handwritten manuscripts, retaining original spellings while inserting minimum punctuation (such as periods at the ends of sentences) and occasional capitalization for purposes of clarity. Capitalization follows the source except that the first letters of sentences and of personal names are capitalized. If a writer used commas in the place of periods, they have been converted to periods, but otherwise the documents preserve the punctuation (or its absence) of the original. In certain cases, I have used more literal transcriptions, using the exact capitalization and punctuation (or lack of it). In such cases, two em spaces [   ] separates sentences instead of periods.

The material is organized into chapters, sections, and documents. Each document contains an abbreviated heading that identifies the source and its location. Full citations for these items, including manuscript numbers, are found in the bibliography. I use "sic" sparingly, where the word or phrase in question is significant or could be mistaken for a typo. Brackets enclose added letters, missing words, and conjectural readings. I have dropped most superscripts and placed interlined insertions in their logical location in the text. Long, unbroken text is sometimes divided into paragraphs, while single-sentence paragraphs are occasionally combined. Underlined text is italicized, while crossed-out text is rendered as ~~strikethroughs~~.

The holdings of the extensive collections of the Archives of the Church of Jesus Christ of Latter-day Saints in the Family and Church History Department at Salt Lake City, Utah, are cited as LDS Archives. Footnotes cite published sources by author, title, and page number. The bibliography contains a complete list of all the books, articles, newspapers, journals, and manuscripts referenced in annotations. I italicize book titles and put article, thesis, and dissertation titles in quotation marks. Manuscript citations appear in plain text without quotation marks. Quoted material from the sources reproduced in this volume book is not footnoted, but the text should identify its origins.

INTRODUCTION

The Latter-day Saint presence in California began in the mid-1840s as a key element of the "Great Western Measure," a strategy that leaders of the Church of Jesus Christ of Latter-day Saints (LDS, or popularly, the Mormons) adopted to escape the political conflict and religious persecution they and their followers had experienced in Ohio, Missouri, and Illinois. They sought a place to build a new Mormon Zion, the prophesied refuge for the Latter-day Saints: a good-sized, secure, isolated place with ample farming land and other material resources somewhere beyond the borders of the American nation. California, still a province of the Mexican Republic, apparently offered decision-makers among the Saints virtually all they sought.

Led by Brigham Young, church officials in 1845 and 1846 authorized special expeditions by two separate groups that might together establish an LDS population and LDS authority in California. First was a sizeable emigration of colonists from New York by sea to the San Francisco Bay area, organized under the command of Samuel Brannan, one of the "young lions of Mormonism." Second came the enlistment of the Mormon Battalion, a unique Mexican War military unit of untrained volunteers drawn from church ranks. This hastily formed, ill-supplied unit, numbering at first 500 men and boys, marched from the LDS Missouri River refugee camps to New Mexico, with 335 battalion members continuing across Arizona to southern California as part of Col. Stephen W. Kearny's invading Army of the West.

After they reached California, the members of both groups became centrally involved in events that would have great significance not only to Mormonism but also to the broad course of history in the American West and beyond. The conquest of California, the early establishment and promotion of San Francisco as the leading U.S. port on the Pacific, the 1848 discovery of gold in northern California, the beginning of North America's first great gold rush, and the opening of three major overland routes between California, the Great Basin, and the eastern states were all due in substantial part to the California Saints. Golden-state Mormons also became instrumental in sustaining an ambitious missionary program in Hawaii and other Polynesian islands that would in time further U.S. cultural and commercial ambitions in the South Pacific.

California Saints made crucial contributions to the establishment and early growth of the LDS community in western America. Their labor, enterprise, generous financial support, and dutiful service, willingly given, immeasurably aided the survival of the Salt Lake Zion colony during its hard-pressed first years. They made California's gold rush prosperity a ready resource for Brigham Young's ambitious efforts to build his Mormon city, his Mormon temple, and his Mormon country in the valley of the Great Salt Lake. Among other accomplishments, they founded San Bernardino as a faith-based settlement and a far western staging point for LDS expansion. At San Francisco and San Bernardino, LDS settlers acted as Pacific Coast representatives of the church, and they kept open a corridor to the Pacific sea routes for the movement of missionaries and immigrant converts between the Utah center and overseas regions of Mormon activity, both in western Europe and the islands of the South Pacific. An outpost of gold rush California, Mormon Station at the eastern edge of the Sierra Nevada—the Carson Valley site later renamed Genoa—became another LDS colony and the first long-term Anglo-American settlement in what shortly became the state of Nevada.

Mormon gold seekers experienced widely differing results in their attempts to find wealth in northern California. Early mining efforts at Mormon Island and the Natomas diggings were richly rewarded, but such returns were not often replicated in later years. Never again did LDS miners have the kind of virtual monopoly on new discoveries that the Mormon Battalion veterans and *Brooklyn* colonists enjoyed during the first flush times. Moreover, every rich surface placer discovery, at Mormon Island and elsewhere, sooner or later played out. Still, at least moderate success was not unusual among the Saints who came to the gold fields during the next few years. Particularly among the inexperienced young LDS argonauts, however, it proved a challenge to hold onto hard-earned golden gains. Ill health, high prices, bad luck, and the expensive temptations of California's sin-steeped society made the gold rush for many novice miners no better than a break-even enterprise.

Northern California Saints soon found a great many moneymaking alternatives to the tough, uncertain work of placer mining. Some profited in the trading business, dealing in beef cattle and horses, groceries, whiskey, clothing, mining equipment, and other provisions. Others became innkeepers and hotel owners. A few turned to farming in northern and central California, while the astounding growth of San Francisco and Sacramento as centers of merchant enterprise enriched capable LDS businessmen.

San Francisco's position as the leading American port on the Pacific Coast also made it a gathering place and organizing point for LDS missionary activity directed toward Hawaii and other South Pacific archipelagoes. Because these early missions had vital importance to church leaders, the movement back and forth between Salt Lake City, San Bernardino, San Francisco, and distant Polynesian lands established California as a strategic crossroads, as well as a source of financial and spiritual support for the missionaries, during the formative years of overseas church activity.

A Mormon presence can be found at many places in the Mother Lode, but the northern California Saints did not often form the type of unified communities, presenting a common front under ecclesiastical leadership, that generally characterized LDS settlements elsewhere. For the Mormons, as for other distinct population groups, gold rush society was turbulent. Alone or with a few friends, people moved easily and frequently from town to town and from one mining district to another. Even for the faithful whose religious belief did not waver, church institutions had an extremely limited role in regulating morality and social behavior.

California's allure tested faith and church loyalties. Like Samuel Brannan, as Amasa Lyman and Charles C. Rich reported to Brigham Young in 1850, quite a few *Brooklyn* emigrants soon fell away from the church. Some devout battalion veterans also found life so much more attractive in the Golden State than in Utah Territory that they ignored repeated appeals to gather in Zion. As time passed, the ruling church authorities increasingly came to mistrust all California Saints. From the perspective of the Lion House in Salt Lake, the gold fields of the Sierra Nevada sheltered too many Mormon mavericks and doctrinal dissenters, not to mention avowed apostates. In Brigham Young's view, so he made clear at an early date, it was impossible to unite California's Babylon with Utah's Zion.

Two specific points of dissension emerged between even the most dutiful Saints in northern California and Utah church leaders. One was the question of theocratic authority, since the church presidency claimed power over temporal matters as well as spiritual. Brigham Young expected wealthy California Saints to support the church generously, yet from an early date he overestimated their income and the amount of tithing the church had a right to expect from their mining efforts and other enterprises. Many northern California Saints contributed substantially to the church treasury directly as well as to various church-backed projects in California, but these amounts generally fell short of the Utah leadership's expectations.

The second particularly divisive issue was the institution of plural marriage. Affirmed by doctrine and fixed in orthodox LDS practice after the church's move to the Great Basin, Mormon polygamy remained primarily a Utah institution. A few leaders lived quietly with multiple wives in San Bernardino, but most northern California Saints apparently were disinterested if not hostile toward it. Although not quarreling with the patriarchal beliefs that sustained plural marriage, gold-country Mormons remained silent observers, not practitioners. They seemed to conclude that in California, one wife was enough.

Most Mormon residents in northern California, of course, remained loyal to the church headed by Brigham Young. But on the Pacific Coast, separated from the church presidency by miles of harsh desert and high mountains, the gold rush Saints exhibited a degree of independence as well as a religious and social diversity not found in Great Salt Lake City and its immediate environs. Distant from the center of authority, the community of the faithful in northern California was decidedly a more individualistic, more complex social and spiritual entity than that taking shape in Utah. This complexity appears as a central theme in the surviving documentary record of those Saints who came to make money during the gold rush era and in some instances remained to establish their permanent homes in the land west of Zion.

By 1857 Brigham Young and his closest counselors had adopted a harshly negative view of California as a home for any faithful Saint. Just at this juncture, for reasons related to the growing sectional division between North and South, the Buchanan administration ordered a federal army to Utah, intending to force Governor Young to resign while compelling church officials to submit their theocratic independence to national authority. Faced by this crisis, the LDS leadership recalled the California Saints to Utah and essentially abandoned the Golden State. No LDS mission existed in California until the very end of the nineteenth century. In the interim, while the Salt Lake church hierarchy blandly ignored their religious needs, a fair number of Saints who remained in the California but still felt connected to Mormonism became recruits for the Missouri-based Reorganized Church of Jesus Christ of Latter Day Saints (now known as the Community of Christ).

As a result of the 1857 exodus, no visible Mormon presence remained in California when Theodore H. Hittel and Hubert Howe Bancroft led the post-gold rush generation into a detailed examination of the state's history.[1] Focused on Victorian-era concerns of priority and personal prominence, Bancroft duly acknowledged the importance of Samuel Brannan and the colony of LDS firstcomers who sailed into San Francisco Bay aboard the *Brooklyn* in 1846 as the first shipload of American colonists to reach California. He also relied on the journal furnished by Mormon Battalion veteran Henry W. Bigler, an eyewitness to events at the Coloma sawmill in the winter of 1847–1848, principally because it helped fix beyond doubt the correct date for James Marshall's initial gold discovery. But with no prominent Mormons on hand to remind them of the wider part taken by LDS pioneers in the gold rush era, Bancroft and Hittel largely ignored the contributions California's gold rush Saints made to the early development of this prosperous, dynamic American state. Taking their cue from these two historical pioneers, California historians ever since have tended to dismiss gold rush-era Mormons with only the most cursory notice.

[1]For a general historiographical overview, see Owens, "The California Gold Rush in History," in Owens, ed., *Riches for All: The California Gold Rush and the World,* 1–13.

In LDS historical circles, meanwhile, a Zioncentric perspective for many years placed the northern California Saints largely beyond the purview of those chroniclers who wrote the authorized accounts of the church's past. For more than a century after Joseph Smith founded the LDS church, Mormon historical writing, like virtually every other church activity, was intended to be faith-promoting; yet the known historical record concerning the gold rush Saints contained little that could be made to serve an obvious evangelical purpose. Hence, their story had little place in the LDS historical canon.

In 1958 Harvard University Press published Leonard J. Arrington's *Great Basin Kingdom: An Economic History of the Latter-day Saints, 1830–1900.* The appearance of this book was a crystallizing event; it promoted a new spirit of scholarly inquiry in Mormon historical writing. Originally undertaken as a doctoral dissertation at the University of North Carolina, Arrington's work demonstrated an extraordinary command of research resources. It also adhered to an interpretive approach that Arrington termed "naturalistic," not conflicting with LDS doctrine but offering historical explanations based on documentary evidence rather than inspiration. "Religion, as with all social institutions," Arrington wrote in his preface, "must be judged according to its usefulness in attacking the great problems of humanity." *Great Basin Kingdom,* as Arrington intended, demonstrated that LDS church leaders throughout the nineteenth century "attempted in a systematic way to improve the economic welfare of their followers as a group. . . ." In this first book and in other works, particularly his biography of Charles C. Rich, co-founder of the San Bernardino colony, and his masterly biography *Brigham Young: American Moses,* Arrington took notice of California's importance to the Saints' settlement of the Great Basin. But even these volumes, while they led the way in revising standards for LDS historical study, maintained a Zioncentric perspective, not really looking far beyond the concerns of the Utah Saints. To this day, the traditional Utah-based historical vision has not substantially altered in works dealing with the Saints anywhere else in the American West.

This volume has a distinctly different perspective. It regards the early Mormon experience in northern California as a significant episode in the history of western America, including but by no means exclusively relating to the establishment of the Latter-day Saints' Zion in the Great Basin. It provides a full documentary record of Mormon activities in this most interesting part of the West between 1846 and 1857, revising and expanding the cursory accounts found alike in LDS historical writing and in standard California and western histories. Without attempting to glorify the role of LDS church members, it gives fresh emphasis to their importance in the early phases of the California gold rush.

Implicitly, it also examines whether northern California's Mormon pioneers developed a set of interests that tended to separate their economic welfare, as well as their religious and moral status, from the concerns that predominated in Utah's LDS heartland. Conflicts over divergent cultural values; a tension between individual initiatives and institutional claims of devotion and duty; attachments to place in competition with allegiance to distant church authorities; a struggle to reconcile ambitions for a better life in this world with devout hopes for eternal bliss: all these themes are evident throughout Mormon history in northern California, even down to the present.

Gold Rush Saints attempts to break new ground in two ways. It brings to light previously unknown or neglected documentary sources about the Mormons who first came to northern California, and it follows these sources toward revisionist conclusions. That the California Saints had major importance as history makers and shapers in western America during the late 1840s and early 1850s is one of those conclusions. The closeness of the interface between Mormon Utah and the California gold country—and its substantial significance to both regions—is a second. Despite the growing differences between church authorities and the gold rush Saints, California's Babylon and Utah's Zion developed side by side. These two regions were not united, but they were inescapably interrelated. In large ways and small, they each came to depend on the other.

A third conclusion deals with issues of faith and institutional allegiance. Especially for those Saints who were critical of church authorities in Utah, California came to be a refuge—a hospitable Mormon middle ground where toleration rather than conformity was the rule. Life there could be comfortable for converts who found themselves somewhere between zealous belief and confirmed disbelief, or between unquestioning devotion to the church hierarchy and outright rebellion.

Just as Frederick Jackson Turner claimed that the frontier's free lands offered an outlet for economic and social unrest in America's older settled regions, so migration to California provided a safety valve for discontented Great Basin Saints. Since it was always possible to move west of the Sierra Nevada with reasonable prospects for economic security, California's proximity relieved pressures generated by discord among the Utah faithful. The connections between Zion and Babylon, in other words, extended also to matters of Latter-day Saint belief and practice. Meanwhile, the negative example of California's cross-grained LDS society helped Brigham Young and other church leaders define and promote a vividly clear image of righteous behavior for the observant Saints whose moral compasses pointed to Salt Lake.

Now that the LDS church is once again a strong presence in California, with rapidly growing, diverse congregations that reflect the state's cultural landscape, it is appropriate to reexamine the historical underpinnings of California Mormonism. The church members of the gold rush era tried to gain a share of the world's riches, and they just as surely pioneered a frontier in faith. Not least because Brigham Young was then directing his most devoted followers into a new territory of church doctrine and practice, markedly separate from the broadly shared American Protestant consensus, the gold rush Saints found themselves increasingly set apart both from Utah Mormonism and from California's rapidly developing, radically changing secular society. Too long marginalized in California's historical texts, too long ignored in the authorized record of LDS achievements, their ventures deserve our respect and a good, fair measure of historical appreciation.

Chapter I

"For the Coming of the Church"
The *Brooklyn* Saints Arrive in California

Latter-day Saint leaders began the initial movement of Mormons to California in 1846 as part of their strategy to seek security and freedom for their followers beyond the boundaries of the United States. Early church attempts to establish a faith-based community of devout Saints—first in Ohio, then in Missouri and western Illinois—had encountered virulent hostility and militant opposition. As LDS believers increased in numbers and prosperity in their headquarters city of Nauvoo, Illinois, they faced a growing campaign of anti-Mormon terrorism, culminating in the murder of church founder Joseph Smith and his brother Hyrum by a wrathful mob at Carthage, Illinois, in 1844.

After the Smiths' martyrdom, Brigham Young assumed leadership of a religious and social movement deep in crisis. Young and his closest advisers faced sharp factional dissension within the LDS community and increasingly violent mob-led attacks from without. Threatened by Illinois state authorities and facing federal indictment, the church leaders decided to abandon Nauvoo and seek a new gathering place for the Saints where Joseph Smith had once prophesied they would find it: somewhere in the Far West. Safely beyond the Rocky Mountains (then the western boundary of the United States), they hoped to settle their people in a refuge that could support the faithful until, as devout Mormons confidently believed, the Second Coming of Christ should bring an end to the present era. As Brigham Young declared to his vanguard company while traveling west in May 1847, "we are going to look out a home for the Saints, a resting place, a place of peace, where we can build up the Kingdom and bid the nations welcome, without a low, mean, dirty, trifling, covetous, wicked spirit dwelling in our bosoms. . . ."[1] Along with the Bear Lake and Salt Lake Valley regions in the Great Basin and possibly Texas or Oregon or Vancouver Island, California ranked high on the short list of alternatives.[2] What church officials then regarded as California, however, was not entirely clear.[3]

SAMUEL C. DAMON: CALIFORNIA IS NOW TO BE THE GRAND CENTRAL RENDEZVOUS

By late August 1845, Brigham Young and his closest advisers in Nauvoo had decided to relocate their people at least temporarily to the Great Basin, though this decision did not become general knowledge among the church's rank and file for nearly a year. In New York City, meanwhile, Samuel Brannan, an energetic, extremely ambitious LDS lecturer, promoter, and newspaper editor, received encouragement from Young to establish a colony of Mormon converts on the Pacific Coast in northern California. "I wish you together with your . . . paper and ten thousand of the brethren," Young wrote Brannan in September 1845, "were now in California at the Bay of San Francisco, and if you can clear yourself and go there do so and we will meet you there."[4]

Acting on Brigham Young's letter of counsel and the instructions of other church leaders, Brannan organized a colonizing expedition of 240 men, women, and children. With the men "all armed to the teeth" with

---

[1]Egan, ed., *Pioneering the West, 1846–1878: Major Howard Egan's Diary*, 54–57, quoted in Slaughter and Landon, *Trail of Hope*, 61.

[2]For Mormon goals and the decision to move west, see Arrington and Bitton, *The Mormon Experience*, 2nd ed., 83, 93–96; Arrington, *Brigham Young: American Moses*, 123–29; and above all the outstanding recent work by David L. Bigler, *Forgotten Kingdom: Mormon Theocracy in the American West, 1847–1896*, 24–30, 34–41. Also informative is the discussion in Bagley, ed., *The Pioneer Camp of the Saints: The 1846 and 1847 Mormon Trail Journals of Thomas Bullock*, 45–50.

[3]At that time the Mexican province of Alta California was a vast territory with unmarked, ill-defined boundaries, still only partially explored. It could be vaguely described as a region south of Oregon, west of the Rocky Mountains, and north of New Mexico and Baja California that extended from the Great Basin (so named in 1844 by John Charles Frémont) to the Pacific Ocean. In Appendix 3 of *The Journals of George Q. Cannon*, vol. 1, *To California in '49*, editor Michael N. Landon has assembled an array of period maps that illustrate contemporary geographical conceptions of Alta California.

[4]Young to Brannan, 15 September 1845, in Bagley, ed., *Scoundrel's Tale*, 91–92. Evidence regarding Brannan's instructions from LDS authorities starts on page 100. Bagley's "Lansford W. Hastings: Scoundrel or Visionary?" and "'Every Thing Is Favourable! And God Is On Our Side': Samuel Brannan and the Conquest of California" present circumstantial detail on several schemes to seize California that involved Brannan with the machinations of various non-Mormon politicians and speculators.

HEBER KIMBALL, BRIGHAM YOUNG, AND WILFORD WOODRUFF
Taken in the studio of Mahonri Young in 1947, this photograph shows the commemorative statues of the Mormon leaders that now stand atop the "This is the Place Monument" overlooking the Salt Lake Valley.
Courtesy LDS Archives.

rifles, pistols, and Bowie knives, the members of this colonizing venture sailed from New York harbor aboard the ship *Brooklyn* in early February 1846. Their goal, as Brannan described it to Young just before their departure, was to establish LDS primacy in California. With the aid of such notable California promoters as John Sutter and Lansford Hastings, Brannan claimed, the LDS colonists could win over the native Californians; and then, he declared, "no mistake the country is ours." As a result, he added, "we shall have a strong and ruling party in this country that will back us, politically and commercially." Showing his hazy knowledge of northern California's geography, Brannan promised that he would "select the most suitable spot on the Bay of Francisco for the location of a Commercial City," which he thought necessary to assure LDS dominance. Their ultimate goal, Brannan's colonists well understood, would be to prepare the way for successive groups of Mormon refugees who would—as they had every reason to believe—soon be coming to California under Brigham Young's leadership.[5]

Coincidentally, the *Brooklyn* put to sea on the same day the first contingent of Nauvoo Saints left Illinois, ferried across the Mississippi River, and headed westward, struggling along the frozen trails of Iowa toward a temporary haven near the Missouri River in the region centered on Council Bluffs.[6] While the evacuation from Nauvoo continued, Brannan and his colonists sailed around Cape Horn and into the Pacific, stopping for a week to take on wood, water, and a supply of freshly caught fish at the island of Juan Fernandez. Then, like most California-bound ships during the 1840s, the *Brooklyn* sailed for the Sandwich Islands (as the Hawaiian Islands were known at the time) to reprovision before heading eastward to the California coast on the prevailing winds.[7] During the few days that the *Brooklyn* lay at anchor off Oahu, the identity of her passengers and the nature of their voyage stirred great interest in the American colony at Honolulu. As Rev. Samuel C. Damon, editor of the town's leading newspaper, the *Friend*, stated, "California is now to be the grand central rendezvous, while the region around San Francisco is the chosen spot where the Latter Day Saints propose to settle."

Commodore Robert Stockton was already in port at Honolulu aboard the frigate *Congress*. He was the first to inform the *Brooklyn* company that war existed between the U.S. and Mexico. (Some sources say Stockton provided the *Brooklyn* colonists with an additional 150 muskets.[8]) The LDS leaders, passenger Edward C. Kemble recalled, "learned with blank displeasure that the seizure of California was contemplated by the United States," for "such a possible obstruction of their plans of sovereignty . . . had never been imagined by the *Brooklyn* colonists."

---

[5]Brannan to Young, 26 January 1846, in Bagley, ed., *Scoundrel's Tale*, 122–24. Until the war against Mexico ended these plans, eastern LDS church leaders Jesse Little and William Appleby intended to charter another ship and follow Brannan to San Francisco with a second colonizing expedition, "to get beyond the reach of persecution and oppression," as Appleby wrote. Once the war began, Little received instructions from LDS authorities to have emigrants "go by land, as fast as they can."

[6]For this migration and the camps on the Missouri, see Slaughter and Landon, *Trail of Hope*, 40–48; Bennett, *Mormons at the Missouri*, 1846–1852; and Arrington, *Brigham Young*, 126–29.

[7]The *Brooklyn* voyage is thoroughly documented in Lorin Hansen's "Voyage of the *Brooklyn*," 46–72; and Bagley, ed., *Scoundrel's Tale*, 131–68.

[8]*The Annals of San Francisco* reported in 1854 that Brannan purchased "one hundred and fifty stand of arms" to supplement the twenty-four muskets already on board the *Brooklyn*. A recollection attributed to John Eagar claimed Stockton inspected the ship "and advised the passengers to procure arms on account of the unsettled state of California; the ship's company accordingly bought condemned muskets at $3 and $4 each." See Bagley, ed., *Scoundrel's Tale*, 26, 140.

Stockton received the *Brooklyn* Saints graciously, while informing them that "they would be expected to render assistance in the conquest of the country." The Mormons were armed and ready to make "any needful acquisitions under the banner of the church. But to help establish the authority of the United States again over themselves was a wide departure from their original plans."[9]

William Glover: We Thanked God for What We Had

Narratives of the *Brooklyn* voyage and the establishment of the LDS settlement on San Francisco Bay are few. Unlike their co-religionists from New England, the upper Midwest, or Utah in later years, the *Brooklyn* Saints as a group were not devoted to keeping journals or diary records of their travel adventures. The rare accounts that have survived to provide details of the enterprise are reminiscences, mostly set down at the urging of LDS church officials for the use of Hubert Howe Bancroft, California's entrepreneurial pioneer historian. Prominent among these chronicles is the recollection of William Glover, written in 1884 in response to Bancroft's request. Lacking a journal record, Glover wrote from memory, noting that "thirty eight years is a long time to stretch the mind over," but his memory generally served him well. Glover's narrative fits into the category of "faith-promoting" literature, offering testimony to the religious devotion and sense of mission that motivated these California pioneers. This account also reflects his close alliance with Sam Brannan, who soon became the target of criticism from the *Brooklyn* Saints for his high living while others struggled. Brannan, his critics agreed, guided the colony's communal business activities in ways that primarily benefited his personal fortune. The following section from Glover's memoir describes the coming of the Saints into San Francisco Bay and their efforts to survive during the early months of settlement there.

William Glover, The Mormons in California, Bancroft Library.

The Ship Brooklin left New York on the 4th of Feb 1846 with 170 emigrants, 65 of that number being men, with Samuel Brannan President, E. Ward Pell and Isaac Rob[b]ins his counsellors.[10] Nothing out of the ordi-

---

[9]Kemble, *A Kemble Reader*, 23–24.

[10]The actual number of passengers was about 234, a few of whom were non-Mormons. See Hansen, "Voyage of the *Brooklyn*," 52, 69–72. Glover (or a clerk in the LDS Church Historian's Office) derived the number 170 from inaccurate 1846 newspaper reports.

nary way of seafaring transpired till the 8th when we encountered a very heavy storm that did not sub side till the 12th. All aboard were very sea sick—There was none well to wait on the sick. Some that were more resolute than others struggled to the deck to behold the sublime grandeur of the scene, to hear the dismal howl of the winds and to see the ship with helm lashed pitching, rolling, dipping in the troughs of the sea and then tossed on the highest billow. These are sights once beheld are never to be forgotten. It was only by realizing the Lord has said He holds the waters in his hand that we could have faith to be delivered from our perilous condition. There were some that were fearful, but the greatest part had their abiding faith and trust in God that all would be well, so much so that some of the smaller ones, that were not quite so sick as others, were singing the song "We are going to California," when Captain Richardson came below to tell us to prepare for the worst as he had done all he could and there was but little hope of saving the ship. He thought it was marvelous that any could sing while in such peril, and that we ought to be praying and preparing for death; but we felt we knew our Father was at the Helm. He stared at me when I answered and told him I was going to California. When the storm was past the Captain with spy-glass could see Cape Verd[e] Islands near the African coast.

In a few days the people were called together and organized, and an agreement drawn up and signed by all of the men, 65 in number, that they would work together as a company to clear the debt of the ship and make all the preparations they could for the coming of the Church.[11] We had some sickness. Brother Ensign and daughter Eliza were the first that died; afterwards six small children, Silas Aldrich and Sister [Laura] Goodwin, the latter we buried on the Island of Juan Fernandes.

Our voyage was prosperous till within three days of our landing. At this point our water and fuel were getting short. It was thought best to go to Valperasa [Valparaiso, Chile] to replenish the ship for the rest of the voyage. There arose a heavy storm of wind, blowing from the land. After trying for three days to go in to Port Valperasa without success we were forced to go to the Island of Juan Fernandes. There we got all the wood, water and fish we wanted, with out price, whereas, if we had gone into Valperaso it would have cost us thousands of dollars, thus showing to us the hand of the Lord and His overruling Providence and care for the His people.

There were two brethren, Robert Smith, and Samuel Ladd that understood military tactics. Brannan thought the brethren had better learn them, as they did'nt have much else to do, and besides, we did'nt know under what

[11]This common-stock company was named "S. Brannan & Co." Members promised to turn "the proceeds of their labor for the next three years into a common fund from which all were to draw their living," instituting "a limited communism" for the company's "convenience and protection." See Crocheron, "The Ship *Brooklyn*," 83.

conditions we could land. Accordingly we were called out every day to drill and go through the exercises of war discipline till Captain Richardson became alarmed and ordered it to be stopped. We afterwards learned he feared we would become mutineers. We were becalmed a few days near the Equator. Nothing transpired worthy of note till we landed at Wauhooane [Oahu], off the Sandwich Islands, where we had some freight to deliver, and get some more fresh water, which took about a week.[12]

We were there on ~~the~~ Sunday and preached the first Mormon sermon on the Island. We were four weeks going to San Francisco. When we got to San Francisco Captain Montgomery was there with the Portsmouth Sloop of war, and we were landed under her guns. We expected to fight, and would have had to if General Valyahu [Vallejo] had not been called to Santa Cruse, leaving the town unguarded. We landed, and there was no one to lift a stick or a stone against us. Our praises to God for the deliverance He had wrought out for us, and our joy to once more set our feet on tera firma, after being six months at sea, can be better imagined than described.

We had some tents, and as many went into them as could get. There were but nine houses in the place, good and bad, besides the Barracks, into which the balance crowded, such as we could get, so that all were sheltered. As soon as we dare venture out, a good number went to the Mission Delorus, three miles away, and made themselves verry comfortable. We had one month's provisions when we landed which was a great blessing to us, as we didn't dare to go verry far to find any. We owed the Captain (1,000) one thousand dollars when we landed, in payment of which he agreed to take lumber. Part of the company went to South Seleter [Sausalito], hired a sawmill, hauled the logs, sawed and delivered the lumber and paid the debt, while the balance of the company were left to protect the families, and to do whatever work they could. They took contracts to make [a]dobies, dig wells, build houses and haul wood to make money to keep up the expenses of the company. The first addition we had to our provisions was jerked beef that was nearly half spoiled, and some dirty wheat that was thrashed on the ground by oxen. We had to wash and pick it over to get the gravel out of it and ground it without bolting[. A]lthough our fare was not sumptuous, We thanked God for what we had and none went hungry or suffered for want. The landing of the Mormons was a terror to the Spaniards. Although we stood guard nights for months we were not molested.[13]

---

[12]"My company consists of a noble hearted set of men and they are all armed to the teeth and before they reach their [destination], they will have learned how to use them—" is how Brannan described his preparations for landing in California to Brigham Young. "I shall have 14 pieces of cannon at my command, that Mr. Benson sent to the Sandwich Islands about four months ago—I shall take them with me from their, as I shall stop their to discharge about $1000 worth of freigh[t]." See Brannan to Young, 26 January 1846, in Bagley, ed., *Scoundrel's Tale*, 123.

[13]Paul Bailey published Glover's narrative as *The Mormons in California*.

Edward Kemble: A New Civil and Ecclesiastical Dominion

Two published accounts by Edward Cleveland Kemble, who accompanied the Latter-day Saints to California in 1846 as a young printer's devil, are especially valuable primary sources about the *Brooklyn* expedition. Kemble always insisted he was not a Mormon, but he was reluctant to tell all he knew about the California plans of his lifelong friend Sam Brannan. Kemble was one of two men from the *Brooklyn* company who served under John C. Frémont in southern California, an experience that left him ragged and disgusted with military adventures. He went on to become editor of Brannan's *California Star* and a founder of the *Alta California* newspaper in 1849. During his later career Kemble became a noted journalist, a Union army paymaster, and an Indian agent.

When he published his first recollection of his youthful adventures, "Twenty Years Ago," in the *Sacramento Union* in 1866, Kemble provided the single best eyewitness description of the LDS arrival in the American West. Long escaping notice by scholars, a prior early narrative—written in 1858 at the end of the Utah War—provides intriguing details about the *Brooklyn* expedition and Mormon intentions that are not included in his later memoir. This account also incorporates an excerpt from a favorable contemporary description of the voyage by Samuel C. Damon, chaplain for the American Seaman's Friend Society and editor of the Honolulu *Friend.* Damon conveyed his understanding of the voyage's purpose, based in part on information quite likely supplied by Kemble and by the ship's captain, Abel W. Richardson. Together, the reports by Kemble and Damon succinctly describe the ambitions of the *Brooklyn* Saints and the great expectations Sam Brannan and his supporters carried with them to California.[14]

"Flag of the Twelve Stars," *Sacramento Daily Union*, 22 May 1858, 2/2.

In the month of July, 1846—the month in which the American flag was raised in California—an expedition sailed through the Golden Gate, whose banner, though destined never to be unfurled on these shores, bore the device of a woman crowned with stars. As the ship passed under the walls of the old

[14] "Twenty Years Ago" appears in Kemble, *A Kemble Reader*, 7–25. See also Kemble, *A History of California Newspapers.* This earlier account was discovered by David L. Bigler, who graciously provided it for this volume. See also the story from a second Honolulu newspaper, *The Polynesian*, for 27 June 1846, published in Bagley, ed., *Scoundrel's Tale*, 142–43.

fort at the mouth of the harbor, only the master on the quarter-deck and the sailors at the braces were to be seen, but before she had arrived opposite Alcatraz Island (out of reach of the supposed guns of the fort,) her decks were thronged with men, women, and children. The Commander of the United States ship Portsmouth, at anchor off the town, guarding the present site of San Francisco, saw with astonishment a strange, weather-beaten ship approaching him, whose decks appeared alive with men. Laying down his glass, he ordered his guns to be doubleshotted, the anchor hove short, and the decks cleared for action. It was not until the new arrival caught the breeze off "Washerwoman's Bay," that her flag expanding revealed the stars and stripes. A few minutes later, she was anchored under the lee of the Portsmouth.

The vessel was the ship Brooklyn, Richardson, master, 198 days from New York and 30 days from the Sandwich [Hawaiian] Islands. On board was the first company of emigrants which had ever sailed out of an Atlantic port bound for this coast. It was the expedition under the leadership of Samuel Brannan, and composed the vanguard of the large Mormon emigration, who, fleeing from their enemies in Illinois, had made California their watchword and rallying cry. The Brooklyn set sail from New York on the 6th [4th] of February, with 238 passengers, of which number about 220 were Mormons. Her departure excited no unusual interest outside the community to which her passengers mostly belonged, and the relatives and friends who assembled at the pier to bid the voyagers farewell. The expedition, collected from the neighboring New England and Middle States had been secretly formed in New York city, under directions imparted to Elder Brannan from the head of the Church, at Nauvoo, and their movements seem to have escaped the vigilance of the press, which only knew of a vessel being advertised by Benson & Co., for freight to the Sandwich Islands and Oregon. The Brooklyn steered out of the harbor on a cold winter's day, with a banner, on which was inscribed Oregon, flying at her masthead. Her real destination had even been concealed from some of those on board. Nevertheless, filled with the enthusiasm of the enterprise, and stirred by the deep solemnity of the scene, the whole company joined in one of their religious anthems, as the vessel sailed away from the pier, sending back to their friends, amid the waving of hats and handkerchiefs, the stout promise:

"Rejoice! Rejoice! The wilderness shall bloom!"

At the beautiful island of Juan Fernandez, the Brooklyn made her first halt. Here, during one week, the company and crew were occupied taking in wood and water, and in catching and salting the delicious fish with which the harbor abounds. She then filled [sailed] away for the Sandwich Islands, where she arrived in the latter part of June. Her arrival created no little interest, and from Commodore Stockton, who was waiting there in the frigate Congress, the Brooklyn company first learned the tidings that war had been declared between the United States and Mexico. The news, though not unexpected, was evidently not altogether pleasing to the Mormons, coupled, as it was, with the intimation that the land to which they were going might shortly be brought under the great guns of the frigate whose dimensions they were admiring from their vessel's deck. Commodore Stockton took an interest in their expedition, and counseled them to perfect the military organization and discipline which they had commenced after leaving New York, and which they did, so far as it was in their power, by daily muster and drill, while on their way from Honolulu to this coast. The Sandwich Islands papers spoke kindly of the expedition from one of which (the *Friend*) we make the following extracts:

Before closing our remarks, we feel ourselves in duty bound to give publicity to the testimony of Capt. Richardson, master of the Brooklyn, in regard to the general character of the emigrants, as it has been developed during a long passage around Cape Horn. Of their general character and behavior he speaks in the most favorable manner. They have lived in peace together, and uniformly appeared to be quiet and orderly. They are going with the full determination of making a settlement, and have brought plows, carts, scythes and all kinds of husbandry implements, and tools for house and ship building. Nor have they lost sight of the means of promoting education and common schools.

During the passage of the Brooklyn, there have occurred ten deaths (four adults and six children) and two births. A male child born before doubling the Cape, was called Atlantic, and a female born this side is called Pacific.[15] So far as we are able to learn, California is now to be the grand central rendezvous, while the beautiful region around San Francisco Bay is the chosen spot where the Latter Day Saints propose to settle. The natural facilities of the country and the bay conspire to render it certain that many years cannot elapse before flourishing villages and cities will diversify the scene.

The watchword of the Mormons now is, "California." The few score of emigrants on board the ship Brooklyn are but a fraction of the immense numbers already on their way thither. From various reports, we conclude that about 25,000 have left Nauvoo and other parts of the State for California; while the report has reached us that a vessel, with Mormon emigrants, has left Liverpool and that others will soon follow, all bound for California.[16]

The Brooklyn had been some minutes at anchor off the town, which formed the nucleus of the present City, before her captain, or any of those on board observed that the American flag was flying in the Plaza, on shore. An officer from the Portsmouth first made them acquainted with the capture

[15]The children were John Atlantic Burr, later a well-known southern Utah cattleman, and Georgiana Pacific Robbins, who became a musician in Salt Lake City.

[16]This article appeared in *The Friend*, 1 July 1846, 100–2. For additional text, see Bagley, ed., *Scoundrel's Tale*, 144–48.

of the principal ports on the coast; and when the news spread from one to the other that they were again under the flag of their native country, but which, according to their view, had proven so incapable to protect them, it was difficult to say whether regret, or joy at the reunion predominated. From this hour, however, the hopes of a separate civil establishment appear to have been at an end among the Brooklyn Mormons. Though they were afterwards charged by their enemies at San Francisco with an intent to raise a new flag and rebel against the United States Government, it is to be doubted that such a purpose was meditated. That they had such a banner among them, is a well remembered fact. It was composed of white silk, and in the center was the Virgin and twelve stars. The standard was carefully put away out of sight, but it was manifestly the design of the leaders of the Church, which had dispatched this colony to the Pacific to establish a civil and ecclesiastical government on this coast, and plant this banner on the soil of California.[17]

The Mormons landed and pitched their tents in an open space not far from what is now the rear of City Hall. After seeing their wives and goods safely bestowed (and if we remember rightly, the married portion of the Brooklyn community were no richer in the first named commodity than other wedded people,) the emigrants proceeded to form a Labor and Trading Association, of which Brannan was the President, and a Board, consisting of six or seven elders and laymen elected by the company, the managing officers. Through these, contracts for labor and for the sale of such articles as were to be manufactured by the company were made, and parties dispatched into the country or out upon the bay, in the different capacities of woodmen, launchmen, dairymen, millers, etc. A settlement [New Hope] was meantime established on the Stanislaus [River], to which a number of the families were removed, and when the rising of the native Californians in the south summoned the Americans to the field, several of the Brooklyn people enrolled under Fremont and served during the campaign. But as other immigrants began to arrive and settle in the country, and the opportunities for individual enterprise and skill were opened, the Mormon Company, which had barely held together, amid frequent ruptures and secessions, dissolved, no one, out of the Church, knows how, and probably some of its members are ignorant to this day. The Brooklyn Company then scattered, and those who composed it went off, either to join their brethren at Salt Lake, or serve in various occupations as farmers, herdsmen, woodmen, and mechanics, throughout the length and breadth of California.

Thus began and ended the movement which, in 1846, looked to the establishment of a new civil and ecclesiastical dominion on the shores of the Pacific. The banner of the Prophet, which was to be planted in California, is now trailing in the dust, and a new Hegira has begun among the simple-

[17]For a picture of the flag that appeared in the *San Francisco Chronicle*, see ibid, 156.

minded and credulous disciples of Smith, from the borders of Salt Lake. Where it will end, cannot now be foreseen, but it has seemed appropriate to the occasion of their recent disgrace and flight to recall the period of their first arrival west of the Rocky Mountains, their lofty hopes, and deep laid plans, under the flag of the twelve stars.[18]

James Skinner: There was Plenty for All, But the Big Fish Got It

The *Brooklyn* arrived in San Francisco Bay at the very end of July 1846, taking just over six months for the entire voyage. When the weather-beaten ship cleared Fort Point and came in view of the straggling little town of Yerba Buena, those aboard were startled to see a U.S. warship in the harbor and the Stars and Stripes waving from a flagstaff in the central plaza. Legend says that when Brannan saw the American ensign flying over San Francisco, he exclaimed in disgust "There's that damned flag again."[19]

As Commodore Stockton had first informed the Saints in Honolulu, the situation in northern California now was quite different than when Brannan and Young had made their plans the previous fall. Two and a half months before the *Brooklyn*'s arrival, the Polk administration carried the nation into war against Mexico, fully determined to acquire California and New Mexico as part of the anticipated spoils of victory. While the Bear Flag irregulars and Capt. John Charles Frémont's small military force campaigned about the country, news of the fighting in Mexico brought Commander John Montgomery and his ship, the U.S. sloop-of-war *Portsmouth*, into San Francisco Bay. Meeting no opposition, Montgomery, his sailors, and marines made themselves masters of the situation. They took formal possession of the customs house and the town on 9 July, hoisted the American flag over the town square, and thus effectively preempted Brannan's grandiose plans for establishing an LDS dominion on San Francisco Bay.[20]

---

[18]The "recent disgrace and flight" referred to the Utah War and Brigham Young's dramatic "move south" to Utah Valley in spring 1858.

[19]Bagley, ed., *Scoundrel's Tale*, 166–67; Bancroft, *History of California*, 5:550.

[20]Harlow, *California Conquered*, 126–27, describes Commander Montgomery's ceremony of possession at Yerba Buena. For eyewitness Joseph T. Downey's entertaining account of these events, see Lamar, ed., *Cruise of the Portsmouth*, 127–54; and Rogers, ed., *Filings from an Old Saw*, 35–54.

Commander Montgomery realized that Brannan's colonists could be important allies in shifting the local balance of power from the Hispanic *Californios* to the Anglo-Americans. He immediately sought to ensure a cordial relationship with Brannan and other prominent men among the *Brooklyn* group, visiting them aboard their ship, then hosting them at a conference aboard the *Portsmouth*. According to the description of one young female Saint, Montgomery also made less formal efforts to establish ties with the newcomers. "The American officers," she wrote home to her family, "were so pleased to see so many immigrants . . . that they gave a festival at the tavern. Invited us all to attend. A great number attended. Plenty of cakes and wines, music, and Spanish dancing." Her description ended on an intriguing cultural note: "I wish you could see them dance what they called a Spandango."[21]

Other members of the colony told a story about the Saints' struggle for survival during the early months of their settlement that was significantly different from the pretty tale related by William Glover. James Skinner was only four years old when the *Brooklyn* reached San Francisco Bay, but his autobiography, written in 1915, demonstrated a vivid recall of those distant events. Very likely Skinner's account reflected not only his personal experiences but the sentiments of a well-remembered family tradition hostile to the leadership of Samuel Brannan.

JAMES SKINNER, AUTOBIOGRAPHY, LDS ARCHIVES.

We arrived in what is now known as San Francisco, California, then known as Yerba Buena (Good Herb) on the last day of July, 1846, to find a country then at War with Mexico. A country deserted and dreary, not like the California of today. As I remember where San Francisco now stands was covered with chaparral manzanetta, Poison Ivy, etc. Miscete [mesquite], etc., with very little fresh water.

Before we had time to get settled or anyway fixed to live Father and Mr. [Julius] Austin, with most of the men of our company, were called to go up the Sacramento River to load the ship with Redwood, hides and tallow for her return trip to New York. While they were gone their families were to draw rations from the stock that was brought with them from home, but what they got was something scandelous, not enough to hardly keep life in their bodies, not but what there was plenty for all, but the Big Fish got it, as they almost always have or will—and still do. The President of the Com-

[21]Mary Holland Sparks to Maria and Holly Clark, 15 November 1846, in Bagley, ed., *Scoundrel's Tale*, 158–62.

pany, Sam Brannon, he and his family lived high at the expense of the poor and needy, the widows and orphans. What he didn't need [he] sold, which laid the foundation for wealth that he afterwards accumulated. But tribulation and sorrow overtook him in after years. For he lost his Fortune, Family, and Friends and at last died a miserable death without a friendly white person to comfort him in his last hours. . . .

Soon after Father and Bro. Austin left, Mother and sister Austin, with their families, and what food they could get, moved to the Mission Delorus, some 3 miles from San Francisco. And to try and help make a living for themselves and children with what they had or could get in the way of food, opened a small eating house. The Spanish Women helped them what they could with milk, beef, chickens, Eggs, onions, Beans, etc., after they got acquainted with them and found that the Mormons were friends, not enimies.

You must remember the United States was at war with Spain [Mexico]. We were right in the midst of War, but as providence would have it, there was peace around where we were. For which we were very thankful. . . .

Mother and Mrs. Austin some way got hold of a bushel or more of wheat that had been thrashed with horses on the ground. They cleaned and washed and dried it good. Then took it to be ground. The Spaniards had rig[g]ed up a pair of burrs (stones) that they used [for grinding wheat] by hitching a mule to a sweep or pole. The women took me along to feed the mill; for the mule power, the women was the propeling power. I fed the grain. The 2 women turned [the mill], and hard work it was you better believe. These were 2 very tired women when the job was done, but they had some good Flour after it was si[e]ved and made in to Bread. It would have been much better if there had been less grit mixed with it. . . .

While living here, (Deloris) I witnessed four or five bull fights. In fact the ring was in front of where we were living. One fight as I well remember well, the bull broke out just in front of our door. The path was packed with men, women and children. They opened a path for him to pass through. He passed close enough to me that I could have touched him. He passed through that crowd without hurting a person, but as soon as he reached the street he began to hook every person that he could get at. He was soon caught and brought back to finish his work, which was to kill a horse or two or perchance kill an Indian or two who had been made drunk for that special purpose. Blood was what they wanted to see fly, nothing else would satisfy them: A bull fight without blood and death was not a fight. They are a cruel, treacherous, people: be good to your face, and stick a dagger in your back at the first good chance.

A Mr. [William Leidesdorff], [was] a native of Russia [*sic*], and a very wealthy man for those days, owning lots of property in San Francisco. Among the rest was the Big Hotell, called the City Hotell. He used to come out often to the Mission with his Friends, and would allways stop and order Lunch, he was a great spender. He took quite a liking to Father and Mother—Father had returned from loading the ship—and offered them a good salary to take charge of the Hotell and run it for him. They accepted his offer and moved back again to the City, which had grown like a mushroom by this time.[22]

William Glover: There Was Continual Improvement in the City

According to historian Hubert Howe Bancroft, Yerba Buena (officially renamed San Francisco in January 1847) became an LDS outpost on the Pacific for a year or more.[23] Despite growing differences between Brannan and other *Brooklyn* Saints over his management of the group's business affairs, many colonists turned to the work of settlement. They claimed land, put up tents and houses, and began building a Yankee-style trading town around the Mexican plaza, now called Portsmouth Square, while the American flag continued to wave in the bay breezes. William Glover's autobiographical memoir provides a succinct account of the development of Mormon San Francisco amid the American conquest of California. He highlights the mistrust between the Saints and the troops commanded by John Charles Frémont, leader of the Bear Flag irregulars. Already a famed western explorer, Frémont was not incidentally the son-in-law of powerful Missouri senator Thomas Hart Benton, who Brigham Young frequently castigated as an anti-Mormon extremist.[24]

---

[22]William Alexander Leidesdorff, born in the Virgin Islands to a Danish sugar planter and a mulatto mother, was San Francisco's leading merchant in 1846 and an admired community leader. He died at age thirty-eight in 1848. See Cowan, "The Leidesdorff-Folsom Estate," 7–105.

[23]Bancroft, *History of California*, 5:551.

[24]Prominent among the Bear Flag irregulars who made common cause with Frémont was William Brown Ide, an 1845 overland emigrant to California identified by local historian S. Dennis Holland as the head of California's first Mormon family. A native of Massachusetts, Ide and his wife Susan Haskell Ide had joined the LDS church in Ohio. He was a presiding elder of a church branch in Sangamon County, Illinois, but in 1837 became inactive because of his opposition to risky business practices that led to the failure of the Kirtland bank in the Panic of 1837. Due to the influence of his friend Parley P. Pratt, Holland states, Ide rejoined the LDS fellowship in 1844, but after the death of Joseph and Hyrum Smith he sold his farm in Springfield, Illinois, and in April 1845 started by wagon for Oregon with his wife and five children. At Fort Hall the Ides changed their destination to Sutter's Fort, where they arrived in mid-October 1845. They moved north to Peter Lassen's ranch, then to the Thomes ranch near Red Bluff on the Sacramento River. Ide became a leader in the American emigrants' Bear Flag revolt at Sonoma, issuing the proclamation that declared California an independent republic. When some Bear Flaggers began to rethink their loyalties, Ide made a stirring speech that reunited the rebels, who then declared him president of the new republic. After Captain Frémont and his U.S. troops arrived, Ide and the other Bear Flaggers joined his command as the California Battalion. After the war, Ide and his sons went digging for quick riches. With $25,000 (*continued*)

William Glover, *The Mormons in California*, Bancroft Library.

When Col. Freemont came with his volunteer company he brought the bear Flag, and he wanted Brannan and the Company to join and go with him. The most of the Company were willing to go, but I rebelled and told them I would not go. I thought we didn't want anything to do with the Missouri mob[b]ers, as there were many in Freemont's Company [and] that turned the scale. They all back[ed] out but two. They returned without any pay and almost without clothes.[25]

Col. Stephenson brought seven hundred volunteers from New York and landed them along the coast in different places, but all was peace.[26] They had nothing to do. The city was surveyed and many bought lots and build themselves comfortable houses. There was continual improvement in the city, almost from the day of our landing. Our next move was to sellect part of the Company to go to the San Jo[a]quin Valley to make preparations for the coming of the Church. We bought a lounch [launch], oxen and seed wheat to send with this company that cost a good deal of money. They went up there and put in grain, built some houses and did all they could to provide for the wants of the Saints when they would come. There was a few that withdrew from the company, but nearly all clung together till the Spring of '47 when Brannan was fitted out with mules, provisions for himself and a man by the name of Charles Smith to go and meet the Church and pilot them through.[27]

Addison Pratt: There Was Much Dissatisfaction Among the *Brooklyn* Brethren

As Glover briefly related, a dozen or more *Brooklyn* colonists ventured inland by boat, intending to start an agricultural colony and raise the

(*continued*) profit from gold mining, he purchased the Mexican land grant property *Rancho de la Barranca Coloradea*, the Red Bluff ranch, which became his settled home. He established the Adobe Ferry across the Sacramento River and served until his death in 1857 as county judge and in other local offices. There is no record that Ide became an active participant in LDS church activities in California. See Holland, *Sierra Saints*, 2–5.

[25]For Edward C. Kemble's hilarious 1871 account of marching with Frémont, see Kemble, *A Kemble Reader*, 83–109.

[26]New York City ward-politician Jonathan Stevenson allegedly conceived the idea of sending a regiment of New York volunteers, which he eventually commanded, to counterbalance LDS influence in California while discussing the enlistment of the Mormon Battalion with former Postmaster General Amos Kendall. See Bancroft, *History of California*, 5:472, 501.

[27]Distantly related to the Prophet Joseph Smith, Charles C. Smith had associated with some of Nauvoo's most notorious characters before traveling overland to Oregon in 1845. On the eve of the gold rush he founded a store at Sutter's Fort with Samuel Brannan. Smith was last seen late in 1848 sailing to Hawaii with a considerable fortune.

crops—principally wheat and potatoes—that would feed the main body of Nauvoo Saints when they reached northern California. At a poorly chosen location in the San Joaquin delta, on the north bank of the Stanislaus River less than two miles upstream from its confluence with the San Joaquin, they selected a town site that they named New Hope. Here they began plowing, planting, and building fences and shelters, eventually putting in three hundred acres of wheat. The New Hope enterprise was formally established under the ownership of Samuel Brannan and Company. This arrangement soon became a cause of controversy because Brannan's personal business interests appeared more and more to conflict with his role as a spiritual leader.

Among those involved with the New Hope venture for a brief time was Addison Pratt, who in mid-1847 was returning from the first LDS mission to the Hawaiian Islands and Tahiti by way of San Francisco Bay. Pratt's autobiographical account describes his June arrival among the *Brooklyn* Saints, where he found that Brannan had headed east to meet Brigham Young and the vanguard of the Mormon migration as they journeyed west from the Missouri River. Immediately, Pratt was drawn into the growing controversy centered on Brannan.

> I soon found there was much dissatisfaction among the *Brooklyn* brethren as to Brannan's proceedings while on board the *Brooklyn,* and several of them proposed to me to take charge of the spiritual affairs among them. But I told them it was not my place to meddle with their affairs in any wise as Brannan was the man that was appointed by the church to look after them, and my mission was to another part of the world altogether.[28]

Apparently to distance himself from the local quarrels, Pratt volunteered to help with the wheat harvest at New Hope. He and four others made the trip from San Francisco to the San Joaquin River in an open launch. On the third day of travel they went ashore and began a sixteen-mile walk to reach the New Hope settlement. This proved to be a dry, hot journey across open prairie. Pratt had not traveled so far by foot for more than a year. Two miles before reaching the little settlement he virtually collapsed, but one of his companions went on ahead, returning with water, a jug of milk, and some bread. "I thought [this] one of the greatest repasts I ever enjoyed." Pratt recalled.

---

[28]Ellsworth, ed., *The Journals of Addison Pratt,* 330.

The newcomer was welcomed at New Hope by Thomas King Tompkins and his family, with whom he boarded during his stay. Quickly, as he relates in his autobiography, Pratt discovered the site's main drawback for settlement.

ELLSWORTH, ED., *THE JOURNALS OF ADDISON PRATT*, 333–34.

Here was a lovely situation and everything seemed pleasant, but when the sun was nearing the western hills, the musketoes began to gather in such multitudes that they seem'd to threaten a compleete extraction of all our blood, when we commenced beating, threshing and smoaking to drive them away. But to little purpose, and in spite of our best efforts they kept us awake nearly all night, and the kiotes or prairie wolves, and a variety of owls, together with the buzzing of musketoes kept up a clamor of discordant sounds that seem'd to well befit the din of the infernal regions.

In the morning we commenced preparations for the harvest [of wheat] which was already white. But at noon, I went out and took a nap under the shade of an oak and this I continued to do from day to day, and it was all the rest I could get during the 24 hours. The spring floods had drownded out a part of their wheat crop and had left innumerable stagnant ponds where those muketoes bred. Had it not been for the musketoes, I should have enjoyed myself well there, as there was an abundance of wild game, such as elk, wild-cats, hares, skunks, a great variety of wild ducks and a plenty of California quails, a variety of other animals too tedious to mention, besides a good supply of rattlesnakes, and in the rivers were an abundance of fish.

I staid here some six weeks and returned to San Francisco in the first boat that came down.

Despite its once promising prospects, the New Hope settlement ended in complete failure. Floods, mosquitoes and endemic malaria, and quarrels over Brannan's attempts to impose communal ownership all handicapped the venture. The last of the New Hope colonists, however, did not abandon the site until September 1847, when they learned for certain that there was no longer any reason to prepare for the church's coming to California.[29]

Isaac Leigh: Aplenty of First Rate Beef Stake

A few *Brooklyn* Saints had already left San Francisco and Brannan's sphere of influence by the summer of 1847. Among the first to strike out on their own were Isaac Leigh and his wife, who took up residence

[29]Bagley, ed., *Scoundrel's Tale*, 234.

across San Francisco Bay. Perhaps they made their home on the lordly Sonoma estate of Mariano Guadalupe Vallejo, the former Mexican commander of California's northern frontier who in 1850 would be elected as a delegate to the California constitutional convention. Leigh's recently discovered letter, directed to his family in Princeton, New Jersey, describes his situation in less than glowing terms, but emphasizes the cordial relationship between the LDS emigrants and Hispanic *Californios*. He provides a unique depiction of ordinary life for a hard-working family man whose experiences with a grasshopper infestation proved less providential than those of the Mormons in Salt Lake that summer. Apparently someone traveling from west to east on the California Trail in the summer of 1847 carried Leigh's letter, since it was postmarked St. Joseph, Missouri, 30 October.[30]

ISAAC LEIGH TO SAMUEL LEE, 1 JULY 1847,
PIONEER LETTER FILE, CALIFORNIA STATE LIBRARY.

July the first 1847

Dear friends

I take this opportunity to wright to you and to let you know that we are well and in good helth and hopeing these lines may find you the same. I should like to here from you very mutch as I have never hird a word from one of you since we left you whitch is know [now] about eighteen months. I hope you are all well and doing well and I hope to see you all again but I don't expect any of you will ever come out here. For my part I would not advise you to come out here know [now] fore the best of the land will soon be taken up as there is a great emigration to California. And the grasshoppers are so numeres in the most part of California that they destroy the most part of the vegetation. This is about the sixth or seventh year that they have been here and still get worse. This year they are very bad, some farms they have destroyed everything. I have planted considerable this year wich is know [now] nearly all eat off close to the ground except the wheat whitch is good altho not a leaf of it & scarce a beard. We had a good many peas and potatoes and turnips which we just began to pick and pull when the Chappoolies, as the Spanyards call them, began too and they distroyed the most of them with our later planting.

Commodore Stocton left her[e] this morning on his way some forty or fifty miles above us to purchase a large farm or ranch as the Spanyards calls them and in about a weak he leaves here for New Jersey by land. We are still liveing with a Spanyard whoo has ever been very fine and cliver to us. We

[30]Researcher and *Brooklyn* descendant Richard H. Bullock located this letter and published it in "A Second Discovery," *The Brooklyn Banner* 3:1 (July 2002), 6–7. The letter is broken into paragraphs for readability.

have been with him about a year. He sais we had beter stay with him two or three years till we get some stock together and we have no rent to pay fore house nor land and he sais we shal never want as long as we stay with him. As beef is the prinsuple part of the living here we never have been without aplenty of first rate beef stake wich never costs me one cent.

We have a comfortable house and live on the east of San Francisco Bay at Suneta [Sonoma?] about fourteen miles from Urbuano [Yerba Buena] by water or one hundred and sixty by land. Urbuano is quite a town. It contains two printing ofises and many stores and taverns, in all about one hundred houses. The Spanyards are very liberal people and very kind to the farmers. I can talk a good deal of Spanish there is no American lives nearer us than Urbuano. The rany season is over as we have had no rain of any acount since April and don't expect any more till October or November. Everything is very down here know [now] horses from five to fifty dollars, cattle from five to twelve dollars, sheap from one and a half to two dollars, wheat about one dollar abushel, beans from two to three dollars, peas the same, potatoes fore cents a pound, onions eight, chickens one dollar apare, butter fifty cents apound, eggs three cents apeace. I have three horses and two cow and calf.

We had a light shock of and [an] earthquak fore days ago are [or] a turabalum [temblor de tierra?] as the Spanyards call them. Eight years ago there was one here that jared down a great many houses. As the ware [war] is not settled with Mexico we have no laws here yet but I think it will soon be settled know [now] fore the Americans have taken all the princple ports.

Tell William Stouts folks that they are well and doing well. I expect you have received our leters too. Nothing more at present, only give my best respects to all inquireing friends and tell tem we are wel and tel them to wright to California San Francisco Bay Urbuano ware I shall be very glad to hear fro them. Know wright soon as I shall loock for leters all the time. Excuse my bad wrightting. I remain yours, direct your letters to Yerba Buana.

[Signed] Isaac Leigh

Brigham Young: We Have No Business in San Francisco

For a year after their arrival, Samuel Brannan and the other *Brooklyn* Saints continued to believe Brigham Young would lead the Nauvoo refugees to their zone of LDS influence in northern California. In September 1846, Apostle Orson Hyde, writing from New York, reaffirmed this intention. In a letter to Brannan, he related that the main body of the church, the "Camp of Israel" as it was termed, was going into winter quarters at Council Bluffs and along the Platte River. Then, Hyde

[31]Bagley, ed., *Scoundrel's Tale*, 157.

declared, "in the spring, just as soon as grass shall start so as to sustain our teams, we shall start en masse for California."[31]

In all likelihood Brannan received Hyde's letter, sent by ship to San Francisco, in March or April 1847. In late April, despite the deep snow that still covered the Sierra Nevada high country, he and two or three companions took the established trail route eastward—passing along the way the grisly site of the Donner party remains—to find the migrating Nauvoo Saints and guide them to northern California.[32] The small party met Brigham Young's advance expedition on 30 June where the overland trail crossed the Green River, west of South Pass in the modern state of Wyoming. At once Brannan entered into earnest and vigorous discussions with Young and his closest advisers, extolling the advantages of California as the site for the LDS Zion. A few days later Young sent him to guide a party of Mormon Battalion veterans coming to join the pioneer camp from their winter quarters at Pueblo on the Arkansas River. Early on 27 July, three days after Young's arrival in the Salt Lake Valley with the last wagons of the pioneer company, Brannan reappeared, then immediately joined Young and other church leaders on an exploring excursion to the Great Salt Lake.[33]

Late in the afternoon of the following day, 28 July, Young assembled a general congregation of the LDS pioneers at the site of the future Salt Lake City temple. Cutting off further controversy, the church president struck the ground with his cane and proclaimed that this would be the spot—a moment memorialized by a bronze statue of Young that now stands nearby, alongside Temple Square. Without a dissenting voice, though Brannan was standing close at hand, the Saints passed a motion to "locate in this valley for the present, and lay out a city at this place."[34] According to one later report, Young turned to Brannan and declared "We have no business in San Francisco; the Gentiles will be there pretty soon."[35]

The heat of the argument between Young and Brannan is emphasized

[32]Ibid., 204–5, prints Brannan's description of the journey across the Sierra, written from Fort Hall in mid-June and originally published in the *Latter-day Saints' Millennial Star,* 15 October 1847.

[33]Bagley, ed., *Scoundrel's Tale,* 208–12. Bagley points out that Young's actions in sending Brannan "on a variety of odd errands" suggest that the church president was not fond of Brannan's company, "but there is no direct evidence that relations between the two men were strained."

[34]Egan, *Pioneering the West, 1846 to 1848,* 111.

[35]Brown, "An Evidence of Inspiration," *Juvenile Instructor* 16 (1881), 269.

in the recollections of another well-placed witness to this scene. Wilford Woodruff remembered that Brannan saw at the Salt Lake City site only "desolation and barrenness, and tried with all the power he had to persuade President Young not to stop here, but to go on to California." It was then, Woodruff recalled, that Young struck the soil with his cane and answered "No, sir; I am going to stop right here. I am going to build a city here. I am going to build a temple here, and I am going to build a country here."[36] His stubborn determination, all agree, was one of the great strengths of Brigham Young's leadership.

William Glover: The Company Was Broken Up

Deeply disappointed but still hopeful that he might in time bring the church authorities to his way of thinking, Brannan headed back to California. By his own account years later, before leaving Salt Lake he denounced polygamy to Brigham Young and Heber Kimball, or told them at least that "Women are the mothers of great men & Nations, and should be looked up at instead of down."[37] But this statement, if he actually made it, by no means marked a decisive break between Brannan and the church.

Brannan returned from Salt Lake with Brigham Young's "Epistle of the Council of Twelve Apostles of the Church of Jesus Christ of Latter-day Saints to the Saints in California." The letter appointed Brannan president of the California church while noting his mistakes—particularly in advocating and attempting to practice the common ownership of property. In addition to a lengthy narrative of the church's tribulations and a description of the coming of the pioneers to Salt Lake, President Young took note of reports that some of the *Brooklyn* colonists at San Francisco had abandoned their obligations to the LDS community in pursuit of wealth. Here Young dictated words of advice that ring across the years: "Get rich, for the Lord designs that his should be the richest people on earth. . . ."[38] Did these words later came to mind when Brannan first learned of the gold discovery on the American River? If so, one must wonder how carefully he read and remembered the rest of Young's

[36]Woodruff, *The Discourses of Wilford Woodruff*, 322–23.

[37]Brannan to Jesse Little, 24 December 1886, in Bagley, ed., *Scoundrel's Tale*, 396–97.

[38]Young to the Saints in California, 7 August 1847, in ibid., 219.

message: "Get your riches honestly, and close not your ears, neither tie up your purse strings against the cries of the widow, the fatherless, the poor, and especially of the household of the faith."

During Brannan's absence from San Francisco, William Glover had charge of the LDS colony's affairs and its business. Considering his early allegiance to Brannan, Glover's recollections of the period following Brannan's return indicates that sharp divisions had grown among the *Brooklyn* Saints. The dissatisfaction with Brannan's leadership, despite Brigham Young's counsel that the California Saints should continue to recognize his authority, was aggravated by the foundering of S. Brannan & Co., the communal enterprise at San Francisco and New Hope. Immediately on Brannan's return in September 1847 the company was dissolved and its holdings offered for sale. But, as Glover bitterly remembered, most of the remaining assets found their way into Brannan's personal ownership:

> When Brannan returned and told the Company that the Church would stop at Salt Lake, you can imagine our disappointment. The Company was broken up and everyone went to work for themselves, to make a fit out to go to the [Salt Lake] Valley, as best we could. Most of those that kept together till the last have come to Salt Lake. The land, the oxen, the crop, the houses, tools, and lounch, all went into Brannan's hands, and the Company that did the work never got anything for their labor. While the brethren labored in the Company they and their families had sometimes nothing to eat, but boiled wheat and molasses, until their wives began to take in washing from the sailors and supported themselves and their husbands.[39]

Francis Hammond: I Did Not Feel It My Duty to Remain There and Go into Speculations

The force of Brannan's appeal to Young and the disappointment that he carried back to northern California are reflected in the reminiscences of Francis A. Hammond. A New York-born sailor, Hammond had been disabled aboard a whaling ship and then stranded in Hawaii. Intending to return home, he sailed to San Francisco Bay in October 1847, duly warned by Honolulu friends to avoid contact with the dreadful Mormons. But, as his published autobiographical memoir relates in detail, by

[39] William Glover, *The Mormons in California*, Bancroft Library.

accident he became acquainted with William Glover and other devout Saints and found them not at all the strange beings he had been cautioned against. Two months later, after lengthy study and intense religious discussion with various members of the LDS community, Hammond converted to the LDS faith. Although he wrote vividly about the prejudices prevailing against Mormons in the ante-bellum West, by the time of his conversion Hammond had come to believe totally in the inspired vision of Brigham Young.

In this further brief section of his memoir, Hammond relates his impression of Samuel Brannan and describes the situation at San Francisco following Brannan's return from the Great Basin.

FRANCIS ASBURY HAMMOND,
"IN EARLY DAYS: MY INTRODUCTION TO MORMONISM,"
PUBLISHED SERIALLY IN *THE JUVENILE INSTRUCTOR*, JUNE–SEPTEMBER 1894.

> Brannan was President over all the Churches on the Pacific Coast at that time. He was a very eloquent preacher, and more than average in general intelligence. He was a very ambitious man, and sought honor of men. He came a long journey in company, I believe, with Captain James Brown and some of his sons, at least part of the way, and met President Brigham Young and [the] pioneers on Green River, or some distance east of Salt Lake, and in council did all he could to have President Young travel on to the coast and locate the Saints in California. He did not succeed. President Young could not be turned away from settling the Saints in the Great Basin in the tops of the mountains, in the midst of the great highway of the nations, as it has proved to be. The Lord had shown in vision, the place where His Prophet Brigham was to locate His people, and all the power of the world could not turn him aside from his purpose.
>
> Elder Brannan was not pleased with the outcome of his trip: he returned and ever after his course was such that he lost the spirit of his calling and finally become alienated in his feelings from the Church. During the golden days that soon followed he became very wealthy and went into great speculations.

Hammond added further detail about Brannan's activities and the advice he offered to Mormons in the months before the gold discoveries on the American River. Hammond's recollections, like Glover's reminiscences, demonstrate that many in the *Brooklyn* colony had begun at an early date to plan an eastward exodus to join their friends and co-religionists in the Salt Lake Valley. While Brannan, by Young's appointment, might remain president of the church in California, that church would soon be abandoned by many of its most substantial members.

> My business prospered during the winter [of 1847–48] and I was enabled to add considerable to the means I brought with me from the Sandwich Islands. During the winter I loaned to President Samuel Brannan some $500 which he invested in goods and fitted out a pack train and sent it into Lower California on a trading expedition among the Spaniards and Mexicans. The venture did not prove very successful and I had much trouble to get my means back from him and took part of it in horses and pack saddles. I mention this circumstance to show that Brother Brannan was not blessed at this time with much wealth, although in a few months from this period he was a very wealthy man. He advised me to go into partnership with him in buying up real estate which, at this time, was very low in San Francisco. City lots could be purchased for from $10 to $50 per lot, that is, out on the sand hills and in the business portion they could be bought from $100 to $250. I told Brother Brannan that I did not feel it my duty to remain there and go into speculations; that I had agreed to start for Salt Lake with a company in July and gather with the heads of the Church. He did all he could to dissuade me from my purpose, intimating that the Church would be obliged to abandon that desert country where they had settled and emigrate to California, for he did not believe they could sustain themselves in the Rocky Mountains; therefore what a nice thing it would be for me to invest in real estate and have some to sell when the emigrants should come.
>
> Thus was I tempted to remain in that land and wait for the Church to come to me. The Lord blessed me, however, with a great desire to gather with the people of God who had been driven many times from their homes among Christians and now had been led by the inspiration of the Lord and His Prophet Brigham, to pitch their tents in the midst of the Rocky Mountains, as far removed as possible from their former Christian neighbors and red hot persecutors, where they could live in peace in the midst of hostile Indians, rather than among so-called Christians.

While Hammond and most *Brooklyn* Saints remained at San Francisco, by late 1847, significantly, many former New Hope settlers and a few others had gravitated inland in search of employment, toward John Sutter's New Helvetia operation near the confluence of the Sacramento and the American rivers. There they would soon meet their co-religionists from the Mormon Battalion, who had also reached California in a daring venture meant to prepare the way for the church's reestablishment in the West.

Samuel Brannan

Leader of the 1846 *Brooklyn* expedition and a founder of both San Francisco and Sacramento, Samuel Brannan appears here at about age 40, after he had begun circulating an exaggerated story regarding his break with Brigham Young and the LDS church. *From Shuck, ed.,* Representative and Leading Men of the Pacific Coast.

Chapter 2

"Return to California and Go to Work"
The Battalion Veterans Follow Church Counsel

The second contingent of LDS pioneers to reach California were the men of the Mormon Battalion—the "battalion boys," as they frequently called themselves. A few wives accompanied this extraordinary military force, as did several teenage boys who went along as officers' aides. The battalion's origin dates to the middle of 1846, after President James Polk and his cabinet convinced Congress to declare war on Mexico. By this time the main body of Nauvoo Saints had left Illinois and found refuge in temporary camps along the Missouri River, where they would remain, with growing numbers of sick and destitute, until the following spring. Early in June, President Polk authorized the U.S. Army to enlist five hundred men from the refugee camps into a special force, the Mormon Battalion. Led by company officers selected by Brigham Young, these men marched with Col. Stephen Watts Kearny's Army of the West to carry out the American conquest of New Mexico and the occupation of California.

For Brigham Young and his counselors, President Polk's offer was not entirely unexpected, since they had earlier petitioned for federal assistance in moving the LDS faithful to some unspecified place in the West.[1] Church officials welcomed the opportunity presented by Polk and urged able-bodied men to volunteer. Many Mormon refugees were suspicious of the U.S. authorities, and they feared for the well-being of the families they left behind. But to the LDS leaders, the creation of the battalion appeared

---

[1]The most recent account of the Mormon Battalion is Bigler and Bagley, eds., *Army of Israel: Mormon Battalion Narratives.* For a clear summary of the circumstances that led the Polk administration to authorize enlistment of the battalion, see pages 19–22 and 31–42.

to be an act of God, since it promised a much-needed infusion of cash. Each man would receive a clothing allowance of $42, paid on enlistment, in addition to their regular army pay of $7 a month. Brigham Young expected—too optimistically as it turned out—that the volunteers would cheerfully turn over all clothing funds to the church to help feed the impoverished families and outfit them for the move westward.[2] In addition, as the battalion volunteers understood when they departed from the Missouri River camps, by marching to California with Colonel Kearny's forces they would prepare the way for the main body of their co-religionists, who would be joining them in the West within a short time.

The march of the Mormon Battalion from Fort Leavenworth to Santa Fé, then across the Arizona desert to San Diego and Los Angeles, is an epic of endurance and fortitude. One of the longest infantry marches in history, it was carried out by poorly supplied recruits with no military experience—ragged, often hungry, and many barefoot by the end of their ordeal. Nevertheless, the expedition had important direct results for the future of California. Although the battalion boys fought no battles, they surveyed and constructed a wagon road from New Mexico across the southern Arizona desert to San Diego. With few changes their road became the main southern overland route, the critical line of communication and emigration that helped end southern California's longstanding geographical isolation. Moreover, when the battalion reached California in late January 1847, rumors of renewed Mexican resistance were causing concern among U.S. military officers; the Mormon Battalion, numbering about 335 men at this point, briefly became the largest army unit in California. Given supplies and a month's training in close-order drill and then posted at San Diego and Los Angeles, the LDS troops provided a margin of safety for U.S. authorities in securing southern California for the American nation.[3]

---

[2]The ensuing controversy about the volunteers' reluctance to hand over their cash clothing allocation to the church is thoroughly examined in Bigler and Bagley, eds., *Army of Israel*, 78–84. Brigham Young was mightily vexed that the battalion enlistees donated only $5,860 of the total payment of $21,000, while his subsequent failure to support their families adequately "was a constant bone of contention for the next two years and would leave a bitter legacy." Federal authorities granted the Saints another much-needed boon as a result of the battalion's enlistment—permission for the Mormon refugees to settle temporarily on Indian tribal lands west of the Missouri River.

[3]Ibid., 51 and note 14. As Bigler also points out, Jefferson Hunt's open practice of plural marriage as a battalion captain predated by five years the public avowal of "the principle" announced in 1852 at Great Salt Lake City.

JEFFERSON HUNT: WE ARE A MUCH SUPERIOR RACE TO THE AMERICANS

Capt. Jefferson Hunt's May 1847 letter appears to have been the first report to reach Brigham Young concerning battalion affairs in California. President Young had named Hunt, the commander of Company A, the senior captain when the battalion organized in Council Bluffs. A tall Kentuckian with a stern look and a commanding, patriarchal appearance, Hunt had set out with his entire family, including two wives, two sons enlisted in his company, four other sons, and three daughters, but only his son Marshall accompanied him to the Pacific.[4] Hunt's letter summarized the battalion's relations with regular army officials in California and indicated the general opinion among the men that they did not want to re-enlist in the federal service. Hunt advised Young that, despite the calumnies against the Saints spread by Colonel Frémont and the Missourians in his command, the battalion boys had made a strong positive impression on the Californians as well as the army leadership. Significant for the future, Hunt told Young about the excellent terms he had been offered to purchase a large interior valley for a Mormon colony in southern California. As the future showed, Captain Hunt was quite ready to make his home on the Pacific Coast.

JEFFERSON HUNT *ET AL.* TO PRESIDENT BRIGHAM YOUNG,
14 MAY 1847, BRIGHAM YOUNG COLLECTION, LDS ARCHIVES.

Head Qrs Mormon Battalion
Camp by the town of the Angles
May 14th 1847

To President Brigham Young
Dear Brother

I embrace the present opportunity of sending you a few lines to let you know a little of the movements of the battalion. I have seen Genl. Kearney; he has seen the battalion, and has given them a very excellent character. I have had a ~~very excellen~~ good deal of Conversation with him in regard to the future disposal of the battalion. We are now about 500 miles South of Monterey. He told me that it was altogether probable we Should Stay here till our time expired and here be discharged. He manifested a great anxiety to have the battalion mustered for another year or, at least, the young men of it. All the men are against it.

[4]Larson, *A Database of the Mormon Battalion*, 135–39.

Since we Started, all the officers, with one or two exceptions have been well united: nor would there have been anything but union amongst us, had not a few unquiet Spirits stirred up mal-contentment and dissension through the battalion, of Course aiming their weightiest blows at me. This has caused me much anxiety and trouble. I have all the time done the best I knew, and used every endeavor to console the men and make the burthens laid on them by the officers of the regular army as light as I could; but every good intention was construed into evil, and of all characters I was the most vile.

As to the history of our march [illegible strikeout] Brother [Jeremiah] Willey, who will be one of an escort of thirteen men to go with Gen Kearny to the States can give it you in detail.[5]

An excitement has lately been got up in the battalion in regard to the terms of our discharge. A number State that they heard Col Allen Say that, at our discharge, we Should not only get our equippage as a present, but we Should be paid for the time it might take for us to go back as other troops are.[6] The letter with instructions from Genl Kearny to Col Allen was produced; nothing to that amount was contained therein. It said we Should be discharged in California and have our arms be given to us as a present. How glad I should be to have instructions from you Soon how to proceed with matters.

When we got into the country we found that Fremont in connexion with our old Missouri friends had been giving the Californians a character of the Mormons; They told them we were barbarous, robbers, and no Americans. The inhabitants however are joyfully disappointed. They find that we are a much Superior race to the Americans. Everywhere we have been we have left a good impression upon the minds of the people. I hope it may continue. Not only this but when anything of importance has to be done the Government officers seem to give our battalion the preference. Our fame is spreading far and near.

Col. Cooke will accompany the General.[7] Col Stevenson of the New York Volunteers will succeed him in Command of the district and post and I in

[5]For details of this assignment, which had fifteen battalion members escorting General Kearny to Ft. Leavenworth to start court-martial proceedings against Frémont for his defiance of Kearny's orders, see Ricketts, *Mormon Battalion,* 161–68. Kearny's "Lifeguards" reached the Parting of the Ways near South Pass on 24 July 1847 and so missed Brigham Young's Pioneer Company, but Jeremiah Willey probably gave the letter to the westbound Mormon wagon companies that Kearny's men met at Fort Laramie. If so, Young would have received the letter about 3 September after meeting the westbound parties near South Pass.

[6]Capt. James Allen of the First Dragoons had been the popular first commander of the Mormon Battalion, beginning with the battalion's enlistment at Council Bluffs. His death at Ft. Leavenworth soon after the unit's departure left the LDS enlistees saddened and in a difficult situation when dealing with other, less sympathetic regular army officers.

[7]Capt. Philip St. George Cooke of the Second Dragoons had succeeded to the command of the Mormon Battalion at Santa Fé in mid-October 1846. A tall, straight-backed Virginian with West Point training and two decades of experience in the frontier army, Cooke was known as a hard-swearing *(continued)*

command of the battalion.[8] Two Companies of the New York regiment are Stationed here with us. They don't Seem to be liked much. Many of them have deserted Since they came to the country.

We are in perfect suspense here. In two months we look for a discharge and know not whether to stick our course. We have a very good offer to purchase a large valley sufficient to support 50,000 families, connected with other excellent country which might be obtained. The rancho connected with the valley is about thirty miles from this place and about twenty miles from a good ship landing. We may have the land and Stock, consisting of eight thousand head of cattle, the increase of which was three thousand last year and [strikeout] an immense quantity of horses by paying 300 dollars down and taking our own time to pay the remainder if we had only the privilege to buy it. There are excellent water privileges in it.[9]

Give ~~my~~ our respects to your quorum and all friends. Wishing you every comfort in life I remain

Your obt. Servant and Brother
Jefferson Hunt
P. C. Merrill
D. C. Davis
Lorenzo Clark[10]

Zadock Judd: I Wanted to Get Home or Back to the Church

After months of garrison duty, the battalion veterans were discharged at Los Angeles on 16 July 1847, the anniversary of their enlistment. At

(*continued*) disciplinarian with a strict sense of military propriety—traits that did not immediately endear him to the untrained battalion volunteers. By the time the unit reached California, however, mutual respect and appreciation had replaced the earlier suspicions and shaped a bond of high regard and even affection between Cooke and most of the LDS soldiers.

[8] A regiment of New York Volunteers commanded by Col. Jonathan Stevenson arrived at San Francisco in four ships between early March and early April 1847. Four companies went to Monterey and two subsequently sailed to Los Angeles, arriving there in early May with General Kearny, who was then attempting to quiet rumors in southern California of a Mexican invasion.

[9] Isaac Williams offered Jefferson Hunt the vast Rancho Santa Anna del Chino, but he set the price at $150,000 when Mormons discussed purchasing it in December 1850. See Arrington, *Charles C. Rich: Mormon General and Western Frontiersman,* 155, 162.

[10] Lt. Philemon C. Merrill had been the battalion's adjutant from Santa Fé to Los Angeles. Capt. Daniel C. Davis commanded Company E. Lorenzo Clark was the second lieutenant of Company A. These three men apparently added their signatures after Hunt had completed the letter. Despite Hunt's opposition to reenlistment, Davis subsequently commanded the Mormon Volunteers, a company of eighty-two men mustered into U.S. service on 20 July 1847 to serve an additional six months. On the Volunteers, see Ricketts, *Mormon Battalion,* 261–67; and Bigler and Bagley, eds., *Army of Israel,* 267–76.

once they set out to find the Camp of Israel, the traveling main body of the LDS church, which according to vague reports was somewhere east of the Sierra Nevada in the Great Basin. While one party marched north toward San Francisco, a larger group (numbering 163 veterans by their captain's count) took an inland route through the stifling heat of the San Joaquin Valley, heading for Sutter's Fort. Both companies intended to cross the Sierra Nevada by the Donner Pass route, then the only well-known trail connection with the Great Basin. While the inland contingent camped on the Mokelumne River in late August, a messenger brought word that Brigham Young's pioneer party of Nauvoo refugees had reached Salt Lake. The main body of Saints was expected there by the end of the summer, this report continued, and the Salt Lake Valley was where the church would stay.

With this news, the veterans moved northward to the American River, camped two miles from Sutter's Fort, and paused to consider their options. Short of funds, many of the men lacked the provisions, equipment, and animals necessary for the trip across the Sierra, and this group (forty to sixty of the veterans according to the later statement of James S. Brown) favored remaining in northern California to replenish supplies. They appointed a committee to approach John Sutter with an offer to work for him. "The committee," Brown recalled, "informed Mr. Sutter that we had carpenters, blacksmiths, wheelwrights, millwrights, farmers and common laborers, and that we should want horses, cattle, and a general outfit for crossing the plains early the next summer, and if we could not get all money, we could and would take a part of our pay in the above mentioned stock and supplies." Sutter, with two major construction projects waiting, liked these conditions, Brown stated, "as he had an abundance of the above mentioned property . . . [and] the greatest obstacle that confronted him had been removed by the propositions that our committee had made to him."[11]

While Brown and his comrades began working for John Sutter on the terms they had negotiated, the remaining veterans, anxious to be reunited with families and friends, paused only to have their horses shod at Sutter's Fort before starting across the Sierra. Beyond Donner Pass at Truckee Meadows, near where the town of Reno stands today, they met

[11]Brown, *California Gold—An Authentic History of the First Find, With the Names of Those Interested in the Discovery*, 9.

Samuel Brannan returning to California from the newly founded Great Salt Lake City. Just behind him came a small company led by battalion captain James Brown, who carried a further message to the returning veterans from President Brigham Young. In a letter addressed to "Capt. Jefferson Hunt & the officers & soldiers of the Mormon Battalion," Young urged the soldiers to join him and the Camp of Israel as soon as possible. "Come then and see us," he wrote, "and we will do you good, and we will show you a location which can not be beat upon the Pacific Ocean, and you shall have an inheritance in this goodly land."[12]

But apparently a second thought had altered Young's message to the battalion veterans before he sent Captain Brown on his way. On behalf of Young, Brown advised all the men who had no families needing their support to return to California and work there until the following year. Provisions were scarce at Salt Lake, he stated, and there was no food to spare for unattached former soldiers. "It would be wisdom," continued Brown's version of Young's counsel, for those without dependents ". . . to return to California and go to work and fit themselves out with plenty of clothing, stock, provision, etc., and come up the next season to the valley."[13]

Among those who heard and heeded this message was Zadock Judd. Eighteen years old and in frail health when he enlisted along with his older brother at Council Bluffs, Judd had served as a private in Company E. His concise recollections of his military experience and subsequent sojourn in California convey the sentiments of a young man certain of his duty, who was sometimes awed by the sights and amazed at the events he witnessed and yet anxious for this adventure to end. Judd's description of the meeting with Brannan at Truckee Meadows well summarizes the message that sent many of these men back to California, while his subsequent difficulties in finding work point up the precarious state of the California economy in the fall and winter of 1847.

ZADOCK KNAPP JUDD, REMINISCENCES OF ZADOCK KNAPP JUDD, UTAH STATE HISTORICAL SOCIETY.

Our time of discharge was now drawing nigh. We were allowed to buy horses or mules or anything for our outfit for home. Good horses could be

---

[12]Young to Hunt and Battalion, 7 August 1857, Journal History, in Bigler and Bagley, eds., *Army of Israel*, 355–57.

[13]Gudde, ed., *Bigler's Chronicle of the American West*, 78–79. See also Bigler, ed., *The Gold Discovery Journal of Azariah Smith*, 8 September 1847, 102; and Bagley, ed., *Scoundrel's Tale*, 221–23.

bought for from $3 to $5, beeves from $2 to $3 per head. In the meantime it was considered our discharge was going to leave the country too weak and we were earnestly requested to enlist again and a few did enlist again and were sent to Santiage [San Diego] to strengthen that place, but I thought we had done all we were sent to do and I wanted to get home or back to the Church. So, my brother Hyrum and I, with a number of others of the same mind, (from forty to one hundred men), prepared ourselves for the journey toward home.

We travelled up the west coast until we came to Sutter's Fort, about east of San Francisco. From here we started over the mountains on the wagon road. When we arrived at the Truckee River we met Samuel Brannan and others, just from Salt Lake, bringing word from the Quorum of the Twelve, which was then the ruling authority of the church, advising all who had not provisions enough to last them until the next harvest to return to California unless they expected to go right through to Winter Quarters, for provisions were scarce in Salt Lake. Therefore, I, with a number of others, returned to California. I went to San Francisco and looked for work at the tailoring business. I remained there a few days but not finding work that suited, I went to Monterey. Here I found a chance to work in a tailor shop. I worked for a few weeks. In the meantime many of my comrades had stopped at Sutter's and were digging a mill race for Sutter.

James and William Pace: We Parted with Those Returning to Calafornia

Among those who did not turn back at Truckee Meadows was James Pace, Jr. As he relates, Pace was the elected captain of the main veterans' contingent that reached Sutter's Fort in late August 1847. A Tennessean by birth and thirty-six years old in 1847, he had been a member of the LDS church since 1840. While farming at Nauvoo, Pace had also served on the city police force and as part of the personal security force for Joseph Smith and later Brigham Young. Following the evacuation from Illinois, he joined the Mormon Battalion with the rank of lieutenant, accompanied by his youngest son, William Byram Pace, who served as his father's aide.

The elder Pace began his travel memoir with the battalion's discharge in Los Angeles, and he trenchantly remarked, "At a distance of 2500 miles from our place of Enlistment, Which I traveled on foot and under the most Heart rending circumstances that an Army was ever called to march, being placed on Short rations and required to make forced marches through Deserts and mountain regions that never [had] been traveled by white man." From the outset the two Paces were determined to return to the refugee camps at Council Bluffs, where their closest family members were living in straitened circumstances. Well outfitted for the trip by the time they left Sutter's Fort, they would be foremost among the returning veterans who reached the Salt Lake settlement from northern California in late 1847.

JAMES PACE, AUTOBIOGRAPHICAL SKETCH, LDS ARCHIVES.

A number of us amediately commenced fitting up for Home and on the 23rd [of July 1847] we organised our company of 163 men, I being elected Captain.

On the 24th we set out on our Journey through the Great San Joaquin Valley (to Sutters Fort thence via Fort Hall) Homeward bound, with pack animals.

On arriving at Sutters Fort, on the 26th of August a number of our brethren were compelled to stop through the Winter, for want of sufficient outfit to take them through to the states.

On the 27th [of August 1847] after purc[h]asing a fresh supply of provisions, and exchanging some of our poorest animals we set out again, crossing the great Sierra Nevada Mountains on the Truckey River Route passing the remains of a camp of Missourians that had perished there during the Fall of 46 subsisting on Human flesh until there number were reduced to some four or five before assistance came to there relief, which was in accordance with the predictions made by the Prophet Joseph while in Missouri.[14]

On the 7th of September we met Captain James Brown with an Epistle from Prest. Young and Council also letters from families and friends. From this Epistle we learned the location made by them in the Great Salt Lake Valley, and the consequent scarcity of provisions, That would probably be during the Winter coming, in consequence of which many of our young men and such as could not go through to the States for want of an outfit returned back to Calafornia to work over Winter.

On the morning of the 8th we parted with those returning to Calafornia, and proceeded [on] our way to the great Salt Lake Valley Where we arrived on the 16th of October. Here we met with many of our brethren that we has associated [with] in troublesome times in Nauvoo, and other places, also that portion of the mormon Battalion that returned from Santafee to Peublo and Wintered they having been met by General Kerney and discharged previous to their arrival in g[r]eat Salt Lake Valley.

[14]The tradition that the Donner disaster was an act of God's retribution for the wrongs Mormons suffered in Missouri began as soon as Samuel Brannan told the pioneer company about it in June 1847, but only two of the party's families were from Missouri.

William Byram Pace, the sixteen-year-old son of James Pace, also kept a travel diary while serving as his father's assistant.[15] The two Pace accounts form a unique father-and-son record of their adventures. This excerpt describes the journey as far as Truckee Meadows, where the party divided, with the Pace contingent continuing eastward while the returning veterans headed back to Sutter's Fort.

WILLIAM B. PACE, JOURNALS 1847–1857, LDS ARCHIVES.

17th [August 1847] Cooler past another dry creek within 12 miles traveled ten miles further to Another on the 18th weather cooler traveled 20 miles or'e rocky ridges and gravly planes to another river encamped within one mile of a large Indian Town the Indians was friendly and brought us melons and green corn

19th Crost the river traveled ten miles to another River [Tuolumne River] and encamped Near another town.

20th left camp early traveled the nine miles down this river then turned north for the next wich was nine miles further we made in all eighteen miles travel there we came to the 3rd tribe of Indians

21st left the river traveled twelve miles to another small stream.

22nd this morn'g Alred, Bennett, Tuttle & House left, for fort sutters in search of more provisions[16] after this was done we left traveled north twelve miles to a creek found some cattle and grass

24th traveled North west course twenty miles found an old settlement formerly from mosouri[17] Here we rested until the 26th bought some peas on the 25 the Pioners went on to the fort to get the use of a Blacksmith shop for to shoe some horses that was tenderfooted

26th [August 1847] we left this settlement traveled a north-west course about twenty miles there we came up with the Pioneers they were camped on the American Fork about fifty miles East of San Francisco Bay and about two miles North of sutters Fort

on the 27th weather warm and cloudy four tenns Left for the Council Bluffs while the remainder of the company were left one day longer to Shoe their horses & mules that were tender footed this day we traveled about 18

[15]William Pace later continued his family's military tradition, seeing hard service during Utah's Black Hawk War and writing the Nauvoo Legion's handbook on infantry and artillery tactics. A brigadier general in the Utah militia, Pace died in Provo, Utah, on 18 June 1907.

[16]There were four Allreds in the battalion, but Sgt. Reddick Newton Allred led this party. "Bennett" was probably John Wesley Binley, a former private in Company E who settled in Salt Lake County. "House" was Alpheus Peter Haws, a sergeant in Company D who was suspected of "White Indian" depredations on the Humboldt River during the 1850s. Luther T. Tuttle was also a sergeant in Company D, a future mayor of Manti, Utah, and Haws's brother-in-law.

[17]Murphy's Ranch, home of Martin Murphy, Jr.

miles up the Sacramento Valley and encamped in a deep ravine where we found a little water by digging for it.

28th left camp early traveled about eighteen miles encamped on the River Near Mr. Johnsons[18]

29th we left the last California Settlements that was on the road traveled over the Hills 18 miles encamped at a place called the mule springs[19] grass scearce but water plenty and cold

30th warm and rainy traveled fifteen miles good camping water plenty to the right of the road at about ½ miles

31st Cool we crost some lofty mountains and through some very heavy Pine timber about fifteen miles encamped at a large cold spring on the right of the road

on the 1st of September traveled ten miles encamped at the head [of] little Bear River Valley plenty of grass and good cool water found plenty of Huckle Berrys on top of the mountains

2nd lay by to rest our animals we Had a small shower of rain in the afternoon

on the 3rd weather pleasent crost a number of rocky ridges and encamped on a small river

4th this day we crost several ridges and passed several nice Lakes of considerable size encamped at a Large cold spring at the left of the road

on the 5th we crost the main Backbone or dividing ridge of the California Mountains traveled twenty miles passed the cabbins where the Emigrants Perished in the Fall of '46 encamped on a branch of Truckeys River plenty of grass

on the morning of the 6th we left our camp early traveled about two miles met Samuel Brannon from the Great Salt Lake Valley he told us that Cpt. Brown was on his way to California with a company of twelve or fifteen men and would likely meet us at the Truckey Branch within a day or two if we would return back to it as the grass was scarce ahead[20] we returned back to our old camp ground on the Truckey Branch they sent two men to meet the Cpt. and also one to go back and meet Levi Hancock & Andrew Little's company.[21]

---

[18]Johnson's Ranch on Bear River.

[19]Pace has mistakenly identified Mule Spring. The actual Mule Spring was fifty miles from Donner Lake and was as far as the Donner rescue parties could take pack animals. Levi Hancock camped at the actual Mule Spring on 2 September and found a tree with the names of Kearny's Lifeguards, the battalion veterans who escorted the general back east earlier in the summer, on one side and "on the other side was Capt Pace with 50 men camped August 31 – 1847."

[20]Brown's party had grown from the nine or ten men who left the Salt Lake Valley for Monterey on 7 August. Presumably, several men joined the party at Fort Hall, possibly including the guide whom Abner Blackburn called Lou Devon. For the only firsthand account of Brown's journey, see Bagley, ed., *Frontiersman: Abner Blackburn's Narrative,* 57–102.

[21]For Levi Hancock's account of this journey, see Bigler and Bagley, eds., *Army of Israel,* 338–54. Andrew Lytle had been a lieutenant in Company E and later settled in San Bernardino.

morning of the 7th about ten oclock the Captains arrived at our camp with a large amount of letters for the Battalion Boys in the afternoon the company that was in our rear arrived which were glad to meet the Captain and to hear from their friends. Lieut. Little's while on company said while they were on their way to overtake our company Henry P. Hoit Died very suden after an illness of a few hours[22] their company being principle ahead the man was buried in a deep ravine instead of a grave in consequence of having no spades or tools for that purpose, the ground being very Hard & rocky he was covered mostly with Stones which was very hard.

on the morning of the 8th we parted with a number of the Boys that were obliged to return back to California to work and stay over winter inconsequense of their animals & provissions not being suffisient to carry them to the Council Bluffs the remainder of our company left for the vally of the Salt Lake or to Council Bluffs this day we traveled fifteen miles and encamped on a small creek here we left another division of our company as a part thought it best as they were expecting only to go to Salt Lake Valley to make up a company and stop back and take there time & let those that wished to go to the Council Bluffs push through as we had about eight Hundred miles farther to go to get to the Bluffs[23]

Samuel Miles: Here We Found our Brethren and Employment

Samuel Miles, twenty-one years old in 1847, had served in Company B under Capt. Jesse Hunter. After the battalion's discharge he marched northward through the San Joaquin Valley with the overland contingent led by James Pace, then remained with Pace and the smaller group that immediately left Sutter's Fort for the Great Basin. His autobiographical account tells of Miles's dismay at coming across the unburied remains of the Donner party, the meeting with Sam Brannan and Capt. James Brown, and his return to California to search for work. Like the recollections of his friend Zadock Judd and the journal of John Borrowman, Miles's brief narrative illustrates the varied fortunes of these young men during the fall and winter of 1847–1848. For Miles, as for Borrowman

[22]New Yorker Henry Pike Hoyt died 3 September 1847. He had been a private in Company A with his brother, Timothy Sabin Hoyt.

[23]The younger Pace's journal of his party's nearly fatal winter trip from Fort Hall to Winter Quarters on the Missouri River is in Bigler and Bagley, eds., *Army of Israel*, 370–75.

and a good number of other discharged battalion members, the San Francisco colony of *Brooklyn* Saints provided vital social and material support.

SAMUEL MILES, AUTOBIOGRAPHY, LDS ARCHIVES.

We reached Sutters Fort after traveling through a wild and seldom traveled region crossing large streams with rafts. We now added to our store of provisions and started to cross the Sierra Nevada Mountains by the Emigrant wagon road. While in the mountains I was taken with the chills and fever which caused me much distress to travel and attend to my animals. I requested the brethren to administer to me which they did and I was healed not having another chill.

We passed the camps of the immigrants who were caught in the mountains the previous winter where many perished by starvation, the remains of some were still in view. After passing over the mountains we met Samuel Brannan returning to California. He having gone out to meet the Pioneers with Pres. Young and [we] were shortly [afterward] met by Capt. Brown of the Pueblo detachment going to California to draw their pay. He brought word from Pres. Young and the authorities in Salt Lake that on account of the scarcity of provisions at the valley that those not having families there or not intending to go through to the states to winter had better remain in California for the winter. This word caused about half of our company to return.

We of the return company made our way immediately to Sutters Fort, where most of the brethren obtained work from Capt. Sutter. Bro. Zadok Judd and myself made our way on horseback to San Francisco most of the way being an unsettled part of the country. On our way we passed through a settlement [New Hope] on the San Joachum [San Joaquin] River made by some of the Saints who came to California in the ship Brooklin with Samuel Brannan as their leader in 1846–47. They were among the first families of Americans to colonize California and built the city of San Francisco. Here we found our brethren and employment. I remained here about two months chopping wood on the Sand Hills near the town and other labor. There were others of the discharged members of the Battalion here who had made their way up the coast. I now obtained employment as clerk in a store in Benecia on the Bay through a reccommend from Samuel Brannan to Mr. [Edward] Von Phister, the owner, who came to California in the Ship Brooklyn as a passenger with the Saints. Most of the customers being native Californians I had a good opportunity to add to [my] understanding of the Spanish language both in the store and in traveling around among the customers on the borders of the Swesum [Suisun] Bay and vicinity to collect grain, sent by launches to the San Francisco Market.

Brigham Young: Not that We Wish to Depopulate California of All the Saints

Once he fixed on Utah as the site for the LDS Zion, the focus of President Young's concern became the survival of the Mormon people and their future prosperity in the Great Basin. Still, the church leaders could not ignore California. In addition to the instructions he sent to the battalion veterans in August 1847, Young dispatched a lengthy letter to "the Saints in California under the Presidency of Elder Samuel Brannan" describing the trek to Utah and the founding there of a city at a site "which for beauty & convenience we have never before seen equalled." With an uncharacteristic concern for harmonious community relations, he advised that for the time being California Mormons should avoid calling public attention to their religious affiliation and practices.

> We do not desire much public preaching, or any noise or confusion concerning us, or our religion, in California at the present time; for the elements in which you live are in confusion, as it were, & the waters are troubled; therefore, be wise; meet together often; you who have the opportunity, in your still & quiet habitations; pray with & for each other; exhort each other; instruct each other; & do each other all the good you can. . . .

Young told how the church had been driven from civilization "& hurled as it were like a stone from a sling" but had landed "just where the Lord wants his people to gather unto." While he assured the *Brooklyn* colonists they would be welcomed if they decided to join the Salt Lake settlement, he also declared that they might remain in California. There, he assured them, they could help build a stronghold of the faith.

> we say to you all, & to all the saints in California, you are in a goodly land; & if you choose to tarry where you are, you are at liberty so to do; & if you choose to come to this place, you are at liberty to come, & we shall be happy to receive you, & give you an inheritance in our midst; And if any emigrants should arrive upon the Western Shores, let no one discourage them from coming to this place, if they wish to so do; not that we wish to depopulate California of all the Saints, but that we wish to make this a Stronghold, a rallying point, a more immediate gathering place than any other; & from hence let the work go out, & in [the] process of time the Shores of the Pacific may be overlooked from the Temple of the Lord. It is desirable that there should be a stoping place, a resting place for the Saints on the west of the mountains, where those who arrive from the Western Ocean can locate

> if they chose, or stop awhile, & recruit, prepare for their journey hither. We know not but your Settlement on the San Joaquin is the best location for this purpose that you can find, if so, it is the right place for you to labor upon to make a stronghold for the present.[24]

Elder Brannan, Brigham Young wrote, "returns to you, by our council," as president of the California Saints. It was soon obvious that this decision made no one happy.

JOHN BORROWMAN: ELDER BRANNAN DELIVERED A LECTURE

Like Samuel Miles, Scottish-born John Borrowman had served with Company B alongside Henry Bigler and Sidney and Ira Willes, foremost among LDS veterans who would become directly involved in the Mormon beginnings of the California gold rush. Rather than join either group trekking overland to northern California after the battalion's discharge in Los Angeles, Borrowman and his messmate James Park worked their passage aboard a small schooner that sailed up the coast to San Francisco Bay. The two young men introduced themselves to the *Brooklyn* Saints and began searching for ways to support themselves. Borrowman's journal relates not only his work life doing manual labor but sketches his engagement with San Francisco's LDS religious community during the months between his arrival and the start of the gold excitement the following spring. Borrowman's journal makes clear that despite the divisions among the Mormon residents, Samuel Brannan continued to lead the LDS congregation whenever he was in town. This excerpt, which begins with the conclusion of Borrowman's voyage up the coast from San Pedro, illustrates his rapid integration in San Francisco's Mormon community.

JOHN BORROWMAN, JOURNAL, LDS ARCHIVES.

> Thursday, 23rd [September, 1847]. This morning we found the mouth of the [San Francisco] bay and turned into it about 6 in the morning and at about 11 we came to anchor before the town of San Francisco but were not permitted by the mate to go on shore till we discharged the lumber we had taken on board.
>
> Friday, 24th. In consequence of some change in the mind of the Captain the lumber was not put ashore today and we were permitted to leave the ves-

[24]For Young's complete 7 August 1847 letter, see Bagley, ed., *Scoundrel's Tale*, 215–20.

sel and so we went into the town and found several of the brethren and stopped over night with Brother [George W.] Sirrine.

Saturday, 25th. Went in search of work and finally concluded to work for Brother [William] Glover who offered us 2 dollars a day and we find [feed] ourselves.

Sunday, 26th. Visited several of the brethren and went with some of them to a prayer meeting at night. I commenced to board at Brother [William] Kittleman's.

Monday, 27th. Went to work at putting up posts for a butcher to tie up his beef cattle to.

Tuesday, 28th. Went to the same man that I was with yesterday but he did not need me. I then went to Mr. Glover's but he was so engaged that he could not set me to work.

Wednesday 29th. Worked ¾ of a day at digging a well in the employ of Brother Glover.

Thursday, 30th. Worked all day at the well.

Friday, October 1st, 1847. Worked all day in the well.

Saturday, 2nd. Worked half the day.

Sunday, 3rd. Spend most of the day in conversation with the brethren and went and heard Brother Brannan preach in the evening.

Monday, 4th. Worked at digging the well. I also bought a book of Doctrine and Covenants from Brother Brannan today.

Tuesday, 5th. Worked at well digging.

Wednesday, 6th. Worked still at the well. This evening I went to Brother Perat [Addison Pratt] and received a lesson in Kanaka [Hawaiian].

Thursday, 7th. Worked in the well. . . .

Sunday, 10th [October 1847]. This day I received a letter from pioneer James Craig [at Salt Lake] dated August 8 and was glad to hear from the Church. We had preaching today by Elder Pratt at 11 and also meeting in the evening. . . .

Sunday, 17th. Went to meeting and was called on by Elder Pratt to preach which I did in the best way I could under existing circumstances.

The young veteran continued this pattern of casual work until spring, with the tedium of his daily activities offset by his social and religious connections with other Saints in the small settlement. This section of Borrowman's journal records the organization of the "San Francisco branch of the Church" on 2 December 1847, nearly eighteen months after the arrival of the *Brooklyn*. Borrowman also demonstrates the important role that Addison Pratt had come to take as a religious leader for the Bay area Saints.

Monday, [November] 29th. Worked at digging.

Tuesday, 20th. Bought 24 yards of muslin for shirts and garments and paid 4 dollars and 7 reals for it, 1 bolt of tape and 2 spools of thread included.

Wednesday, December 1st, 1847. Took my cloth to a woman to have her make me some shirts. This evening I went to Mr. [William] Hood for the pay for digging the foundation of his house but he refused to pay saying it was not done according to the contract which it was.

Thursday, 2nd. I took the remainder of my cloth [to] Sister [Hannah] Reid to make me two garments. In the afternoon I worked with Brother [David] Clark. This evening I went to meeting and the San Francisco branch of the Church was organized. . . .

Sunday, 5th. Had meeting in forenoon, preaching by Pratt. In the afternoon sacrament was dispensed by Pratt. . . .

Sunday, 12th. Went to meeting and preached on the universal salvation in the morning, and in the evening attended a business meeting. This evening Brother Austin presented me with a sixshooter pistol. . . .

Sunday, 19th. Went to meeting and preached on the gathering of Israel. . . .

Sunday, 26th. Attended meeting twice.

Monday, 27th. Drove team. I would just mention here that on the 24th Brother Robins presented me with a ram-rod and powder flask for my pistol.

Tuesday, 28th, Wednesday, 29th, Thursday, 30th, Friday, 31st, worked for Mr. Sullivan.

Saturday, January 1st, 1848. This day I was thrown out of work, it being New Year's day and I spent most of the day reading.

Sunday, 2nd. Went to meeting. Brother Brannan preached. In the afternoon had sacrament administered by Pratt. . . .

Borrowman continued this uneventful way of life through the first months of 1848. Early in April he briefly mentioned receiving a letter from his friend Henry Bigler. By way of Sutter's Fort, the letter came from Coloma, on the South Fork of the American River, where since October Bigler and a few other battalion veterans had been constructing a sawmill under the direction of James Marshall, John Sutter's partner. Borrowman gave no indication in his journal about the substance of Bigler's letter. He was more candid, however, in recording the critical state of affairs concerning President Brannan and other San Francisco church members.

Monday, [April] 3rd. Worked at digging the foundation of a house for Mr. Glover. . . .

> Saturday, 8th. . . . This day I received a letter from Henry Bigler.[25]
> Sunday, 9th. Had no meeting and spent the day visiting the brethren. . . .
> Sunday, 16th. Wrote a letter to Henry Bigler and attended meeting in the evening. . . .
> Sunday, 23rd. Had meeting in the afternoon. . . .
> Sunday, 30th. Attended meeting. Elder Brannan delivered a lecture on the disaffection that existed in the branch and called for those that found fault with him to bring forth their charges. . . .

Immediately after this confrontational church meeting, Brannan left for New Helvetia, to investigate firsthand the excited rumors that were reaching San Francisco about gold discoveries on the American River. A little more than a week later, on 10 May 1847, Brannan returned from his hurried reconnaissance trip. He had not reached Coloma, but he had inspected the gold diggings at Mormon Island, located twenty miles east of Sutter's Fort near the confluence of the American River's South Fork and Middle Fork. At this site two other B Company veterans, coached by Henry Bigler and following his example, had uncovered exceedingly rich placer gold deposits a month earlier. The news Brannan brought would send Borrowman and a large part of San Francisco's LDS settlers rushing away, many never to return to the Bay area.

Bring With You All That You Can of Things That Will Be of Value

At the end of August 1847, Brigham Young left Great Salt Lake City with 106 men, returning east to Winter Quarters to help prepare some two thousand Saints for travel west the next spring. In his absence the management of the new settlement was in the hands of a presidency headed by John A. Smith, Joseph Smith's uncle, aided by Charles C. Rich and John Young as chief counselors, and a stake high council of twelve

[25]As described in Chapter 3, Bigler was present when James Marshall discovered gold on 24 January 1848. Bigler's journal indicates he wrote to Borrowman about the success of his efforts and those of other Mormon workers at finding gold on their own. Bigler later told Hubert Howe Bancroft that on about 20 February he wrote to three battalion friends then working on Sutter's grist mill project, Jesse Martin, Ephraim Green, and Israel Evans, with news of the successful gold hunting at Coloma, urging them to keep the matter confidential. Bigler must have written Borrowman at about the same time. See Gudde, ed., *Bigler's Chronicle of the West,* 103. Borrowman did not react to Bigler's information until the news was confirmed by the gold Samuel Brannan brought back from the American River.

men. No more than two months after Young's departure these leaders adopted Capt. Jefferson Hunt's proposal to send a select small company to southern California to purchase "cows, mules, mares, wheat, and seeds" for the struggling colony. To make this wintertime journey, the company under Hunt's guidance would head south from Great Salt Lake City, connecting with the Spanish Trail to cross the desert to Las Vegas and Los Angeles, the only feasible route at that time of year. The High Council authorized three men to direct this expedition: Asahel Lathrop and Elijah Fuller, both captains in the 1847 migration to Salt Lake, and the famed Orrin Porter Rockwell, known as a fearless and militant agent of the LDS church leadership.[26]

The Salt Lake council drafted two letters for Lathrop to carry to southern California. The first introduced the expedition's leaders to rancher William Workman, a prominent settler.[27] The second, addressed to former Mormon Battalion members who had re-enlisted in the Mormon Volunteers or gone to work for local ranchers, embodied a different set of instructions than Brigham Young had sent to the *Brooklyn* Saints three months earlier. With the infant Salt Lake settlement experiencing want and the prospect of further difficulties, the council appealed to the veterans to assist their colony's survival. At the same time, the council discouraged the battalion boys from re-enlisting in the federal military service.[28]

---

[26]The legendary Orrin Porter Rockwell had been a close associate of Joseph Smith since the earliest days of the LDS faith. Rockwell had gained particular attention for his attempt to assassinate Missouri governor Lilburn Boggs in 1842, for killing an anti-Mormon extremist near Nauvoo following the murder of Joseph and Hyrum Smith, and for various shady activities including a campaign of thievery against Mormon enemies and the passing of "bogus" counterfeit coins in Illinois. Described by one acquaintance as a diamond in the rough, by 1847 Rockwell was a trusted confidant of Brigham Young. Western Saints generally admired him for his services as a frontier scout during the move to Winter Quarters and the Great Basin. Along with his comrade William Hickman, Rockwell became known as a violent enforcer of church dictates and a terror to enemies of the Mormon faith. His career, including his time in relative seclusion in California, is fully described in the exemplary biography by Harold Schindler, *Orrin Porter Rockwell: Man of God, Son of Thunder.*

[27]Englishman William Workman left Taos, New Mexico, for Los Angeles in 1841 with John Rowland. They became naturalized Mexican citizens and established extensive ranching operations on a huge land grant in the San Gabriel Valley. See Rowland, *John Rowland and William Workman: Southern California Pioneers of 1841.* A Mormon Battalion detachment under Lt. James Pace camped at Workman's ranch in April 1846.

[28]A summary of this letter taken from the Journal History appeared in Schindler, *Orrin Porter Rockwell,* 170–71, but apparently the complete text has never been published. Oddly, "Proceedings of Stake Presidency and High Council in Executive, Legislative and Judicial Capacity, Great Salt Lake Stake 1847–48," in Carter, comp., *Our Pioneer Heritage,* 17:89–112, omitted the letters entirely.

SALT LAKE STAKE HIGH COUNCIL MINUTES,
16 NOVEMBER 1847, LDS ARCHIVES.

Great Salt Lake City, Great Basin, N. A.
November 16, 1847.

To Mr. Workman and his friends in California,
and to all whom it may concern, greeting.

Though we write to you as strangers, we feel, from all we have heard of you and your friends and countrymen, by our brethren of the Mormon Battalion, to do it frankly and as of one friend and well wisher of the human family would to another. We therefore hereby and herein recommend as worthy and upright men and due all confidence, the bearers of this, vs. Asahel A. Lathrop, Orrin P. Rockwell, and Elijah K. Fuller, and fully authorize and empower said above named persons to trade, and make all contracts at their discretion, in our behalf and in the behalf of this people, while they are in California, with you; and we, in their behalf and ours, ask it as a favor of much worth to us, that you will be so kind as to facilitate their movements in the purchase of cows, mules, mares, wheat, seeds of all kinds etc., etc., for cash and other means down, as far as the same may go, and in a credit of one year, as far as said means may fall short, for the payment of which, when it may become due, we herein pledge and obligate ourselves individually and collectively and in the behalf of this people.

And we do feel assured that a compliance with the above by all concerned, will be of great and mutual and lasting benefit.

We subscribe ourselves your well wishers, and the wellwishers of the human family and as the Presidency and High Council of Great Salt Lake City.[29]

Great Salt Lake City, Great Basin, N. A.
November 16, 1847

Epistle of the Presidency and High Council of this Stake
of Zion, to the Saints in California, greeting:

Beloved Brethren:

It seemeth good unto us to write you a few words of counsel and advice, by our trusty and confidential Bros. Asahel A. Lathrop, Orrin P. Rockwell and Elijah K. Fuller, who, in company with others, are going to California this winter to obtain seeds and animals to bring to this, our city.

For a better description of this our beautiful location and our numbers and circumstances, than we can write, we refer you to our above named brethren and those who accompany them, and shall simply state that our location has been pointed out to us by the Spirit of the Lord, through His

[29]A signature block identical to the letter to the Saints in California, below, has been omitted.

servants the Twelve, and is truly delightful and desirable, for beauty, for richness of soil, mildness of climate, and above all for rest and peace unto us, who have been driven before our enemies like a rolling stone, lo! these many years; and the command of the Lord unto us, and our desires and determination are, to build here a city unto the most High God, that shall be holy, and a place of refuge for the oppressed and for all who delight in equal rights and in the protection of equal and wholesome laws.

The covenant we all made at Nauvoo, to use ourselves and our means to the uttermost for removing this people from that region,[30] is probably fresh in your recollection, and your hearts and hands are warm and ready to fulfill the same, and your desires are simply to know where and how; we therefore, according to you and your circumstances and to the whisperings of the Spirit in us, would hereby counsel and advise one and all of you to consentrate all your means, knowledge and efforts as much as possible for the purchasing and bringing to this place good likely young cows to a considerable number, and as far as may be with their calves or with calf; seed wheat, and seed grain of every description that would be valuable to us, potatoes, and every kind of valuable root, grape cuttings and every kind of fruit seed; mules, mares and such animals as you may deem best, together with such a proportion of beef cattle as may be thought proper, and for the regulation and comparative demand and necessity of the above named articles and such others as you think are wise to transport, both as to their several quantities and numbers, you will be advised and counseled by our trusty and confidential brothers, Asahel A. Lathrop, Orrin P. Rockwell and Elijah K. Fuller (and no others except through them) whom we hereby and herein authorize and fully empower, as our representatives, to trade and make all contract at their discretion, in our behalf, and in behalf of this people for our mutual benefit and prosperity, according to the letter and tenure of this our epistle, and we counsel and advise that in the purchase of stock of all kinds, or any purchase that requires much means, you consecrate your means, for reasons that will be made known to you by our above named brethren. We counsel all of you not to reenlist as soldiers under any government whatever, but as fast as you are liberated from your previous engagements, and as your circumstances will permit, repair to this place, bringing with you all you can that will be of value; and we wish as many of you as can consistently to come with the company now going from here, to aid them in the transportation of property and assist us in raising grain the coming season, as there will be a large emigration to this place next year, and we wish to raise all the grain and other sustenance that we can to supply our wants. We counsel our Bro. Jesse D. Hunter to retain his Indian agency as long as possible;

[30]At LDS church conference on 6 October 1845, Brigham Young proposed, "That we take all the saints with us, to the extent of our ability, that is, our influence and property." Many Mormons had sworn to share their "last cent" until the entire church reached Zion.

and in case he wishes to come to this place, let him appoint a subagent during his absence.[31] Some of your families are now here, and we in conjunction with our brethren at Winter Quarters, shall use every effort to transport the remainder to this place the next season and raise grain etc. for their sustenance, which will require our time, teams and wagons and means and as far as this may fall short of compensating you for any assistance you render us, you shall be amply rewarded and by so doing we will mutually fulfill our covenants. We furthermore wish you to use your influence and skill to assist the above named brethren to make any purchase at their discretion, or on a credit as far as their means may fall short of procuring what they may be able to transport. The length of the credit we shall wish if any is, for one year, as we expect by that time to be abundantly able to meet any demand that they may be required through lack of means on hand, as our crops will have been harvested and our money on hand from the coming season, which will be large and many of them abundantly able [*sic*?]. We also authorize and request Asahel A. Lathrop to take one or more copies of this our epistle, and circulate the same among our brethren in California. The names of the families who are here and their husbands in California, you will learn from Bro. Lathrop or some of his associates. We would say to Capts. David [Daniel] C. Davis and Jesse D. Hunter that we feel to desire them to use all their influence in carrying out the letter and spirit of this our epistle and to make no delay in assisting our brethren to return to this place as soon as possible.

Praying God the Eternal Father in the name of Jesus Christ to bless you all and those going to California, with all needful blessings, we remain your brethren in the New and Everlasting covenant.

High Councillors. John Smith, president.

Henry G. Sherwood	Ira Eldredge	Charles C. Rich
Thos. Grover	Edsen Whipple	John Young

Counselors

Levi Jackman	Shadrach Roundy	Albert Carrington,
John Murdock	John Vance clerk	Daniel Spencer
Willard Snow	Lewis Abbott	Abraham O. Smoot

Led by Jefferson Hunt, nineteen men on horseback rode south from Great Salt Lake City on 18 November 1847, packing supplies for one month. Exhausted and starving, they reached the Rancho Santa Ana del Chino, near the future site of San Bernardino, forty-five days later on Christmas Eve. Ranch owner Isaac Williams, a former Rocky Mountain

[31]Former battalion captain Jesse D. Hunter served as the military government's Indian agent at San Luis Rey Mission, but he left the position to work in the gold fields. Hunter never visited Utah.

fur trader who had moved to southern California in 1832, taken Mexican citizenship, and married the daughter of Antonio María Lugo, welcomed the suffering men and offered his generous hospitality while they recuperated from their desert ordeal.[32]

While he and his companions regained their health, Lathrop negotiated with Williams for the purchase of cows, pack mules, mares, and bulls. Williams sold the cows for six dollars a head, hardly more than their hides were worth in the California trade, and he offered to let Lathrop have without charge "all the bulls you can drive off." With Hunt again guiding, the company started back in mid-February, herding two hundred cows and forty bulls. Three months later they reached Salt Lake City with only a remnant of their stock. According to the report of Lathrop and Fuller summarized in the church's unpublished Journal History, one-fifth of the cows and all but one of the bulls had died, principally from thirst. Indians had harassed the expedition, and once more hunger made the trip a painful memory for expedition members.[33]

Porter Rockwell did not return to Salt Lake with Lathrop and Fuller. Instead, according to a letter written from Los Angeles by William A. Kennedy in early April 1848, he was one of four Saints—the other three all ranking members of the recently discharged Mormon Volunteers—arrested for passing counterfeit gold coin in five-, eight-, and sixteen-dollar denominations. The fraud was detected, Kennedy reported, because "the 16 is too large and the 5 & 8 too Rough."[34] In their defense, Kennedy reported that one of the men, Mormon Volunteer Sgt. Samuel Myers, claimed he had received the gold from the army paymas-

[32]For Joseph S. Woods's sketch of Williams's life, see Hafen, ed., *The Mountain Men and the Fur Trade*, 7:371–79.

[33]Journal History, 15 May 1858, LDS Archives.

[34]W. A. Kennedy to James Ferguson, 2 April 1848, Ciudad Los Angeles, LDS Archives, in Bagley, ed., *Scoundrel's Tale*, 404–5. Unfortunately, J. Kenneth Davies apparently confused the identity of the sender and the recipient of this letter. Since it was addressed to Ferguson at "the Adobe Store, San Francisco," Davies supposed erroneously that the letter provided evidence that Rockwell had traveled to northern California, where he might have learned of the Coloma gold discovery and perhaps subsequently relayed it to Brigham Young. See Davies, *Mormon Gold*, 53–55. Ferguson was a former battalion sergeant and "arguably the most literate man in the Mormon Battalion." For a summary of his career, see Bagley, ed., *Scoundrel's Tale*, 251. Kennedy was not a Mormon. He had come to California with the New York Volunteers and was also waiting in Los Angeles for his company's discharge.

[35]This claim had added credence because the other two men arrested with Rockwell and Myers, according to Kennedy's letter, were 1st Lt. Cyrus Canfield and 2nd Lt. Ruel Barris of the Mormon Volunteers. The Volunteers had drawn their pay and been disbanded in San Diego on 14 March 1848. See Ricketts, *Mormon Battalion*, 264.

ter.[35] At any rate, Rockwell was soon set free. The three former Mormon Volunteer officers, C. C. Canfield, Samuel Myers, and Ruel Barrus, however, were tried by a jury in Los Angeles with approval of the military governor, Col. Richard B. Mason. The veterans were charged with passing counterfeit gold coins and each had their own jury trial in April 1848 before a special court consisting of Stephen C. Foster, a former Mormon Battalion scout, and Los Angeles land baron and merchant Abel Stearns. Although Canfield and Myers were acquitted, Barrus confessed "that he had played at monte with counterfeit money," and in May the jury found him guilty and the court sentenced him to five years in prison at hard labor. Colonel Mason, on recommendation of the court, subsequently reduced the sentence to one year, "because of palliating circumstances which appeared upon the trial, as well as the youth of the prisoner."[36]

While the three veterans faced trial in Los Angeles, Rockwell returned to Rancho El Chino. There he and James Snow agreed to serve as guides for thirty-five recently discharged Mormon Volunteers, along with the wife and young son of Capt. Daniel C. Davis, who were preparing to make the journey to Salt Lake City. This company left El Chino on 12 April 1848, accompanied by one wagon and 135 horses and mules. Rockwell and Snow led the way along the Spanish Trail past Las Vegas, then pioneered a new route northward to the Salt Lake Valley, where they arrived without mishap by 5 June.[37]

Three weeks after their arrival, another explanation of Rockwell's troubles in California came to light at a Salt Lake church meeting. According to the minutes of the Salt Lake stake, Elder John Taylor called for the Saints to stop "practicing inequities" upon the gentiles, and "spoke warmly against the matter of sending counterfeit money to Calif[orni]a—." At this point, well beyond the reach of California authorities, Rockwell made a candid admission concerning his brief career in passing bogus coin.

---

[36]Bancroft, *History of California*, 5:610–11; and Sec. of State H. W. Halleck to J. D. Stevenson and S. C. Foster, 20 July 1848, "California and New Mexico," House Exec. Doc. 17 (31-1), 1850, Serial 673, 571, reprinted in Bigler and Bagley, eds., *Army of Israel*, 407. Bigler and Bagley summarize the history of "bogus" coinage charges that were associated with LDS church members in Illinois, Iowa, New York, and California.

[37]Ricketts, *Mormon Battalion*, 265; Schindler, *Orrin Porter Rockwell*, 173; and Journal History, 5 June 1848, 6.

SALT LAKE STAKE MINUTES, 25 JUNE 1848, LDS ARCHIVES.

O P Rockwell came on the stand & sd he had a stamering tongue but a heart turned to his friends, sd what he had heard to day was good & he would like to live by it, & sd he tried to do good, & was ready to die for his friends, sd the little counterfeit gold he passed let go in Califa was the first & it had hurt nobody, sd he never passed counterfeit money any where sd let justice be administered equaly, sd he was ceased [seized] in Califa for a little bogus & they had got it but if he had consulted his own feelings they would not have got it, when they got it they got drunk & gambled & got put in jail—sd he was willing to do any thing the people required—was ready to answer for all his own wrongs,—sd he never dealt in bogus,—Elder Taylor rose & sd I believe as Porter says he would give his life for his friends, he has proven that before often, I am sorry he has had anything to do with this money—sd he was at the defiance of the whole world to prove his ever having passed counterfeit, had always believed Porter to be a person of integrity & truth & did yet.

HENRY W. BIGLER: WE MADE A BARGAIN WITH SUTTER

Of all the battalion boys who reached California, no one put on paper a more carefully detailed record of daily events than Henry William Bigler. Thirty-three years old in the late summer of 1847, Bigler had served with Zadock Judd, Samuel Miles, and John Borrowman in Company B, helping to garrison San Diego. After the battalion's discharge he marched northward with Captain Pace through the San Joaquin Valley to Sutter's Fort.[38] Unfortunately, the original of Bigler's Mormon Battalion and gold rush journal has never come to light. Only a small remnant is preserved: two manuscript pages concerning the gold discovery at Coloma that Bigler tore from his journal and sent in 1888 to California historian John S. Hittell. This fragment is now part of the collections of the California Pioneer Society in San Francisco.[39] But in his later years, aware of a growing historical interest in the events he had witnessed in California, Bigler transcribed three slightly different versions of his journal that have been preserved.

---

[38]M. Guy Bishop's fine biography, *Henry William Bigler: Soldier, Gold Miner, Missionary, Chronicler, 1815–1900*, accurately portrays Bigler as a common man who became involved with events that brought him uncommon fame.

[39]A transcription of Bigler's journal pages at the California Pioneer Society covering the Coloma gold discovery appears in Paul, ed., *The California Gold Discovery*, 61–62.

One version Bigler sent in a series of letters to California businessman, collector, and historian Hubert Howe Bancroft between May and August 1872. This manuscript now reposes in the Bancroft Library at the University of California, Berkeley. It is this earliest transcription that Erwin G. Gudde edited, making a substantial number of unmarked interpolations, and published as *Bigler's Chronicle of the West.* The second version was transcribed about 1898—the grandly celebrated jubilee year of the California gold discovery—in a large blank journal volume sent to Bigler by Hittell. This manuscript is now in the collections of the LDS Church Archives in Salt Lake City. A third version is found at the Henry E. Huntington Library in San Marino, California. It consists of what is apparently Bigler's most literal, unmodified transcription of entries from 1846 to 1898, accompanied by an autobiography. Additionally, the Huntington materials include three Bigler daybooks (labeled books B, D, and G) that cover portions of the period from October 1849 (after Bigler reached Utah) to January 1859, and still another daybook for 1892–1893.

One more Bigler account of his California experiences has recently come to light. Appearing in the *Juvenile Instructor,* a periodical for Mormon young people published in Salt Lake City, this narrative was featured in two installments in December 1886. For purposes of publication, Bigler half-humorously assumed the pen name Henele Pikale, a transliterated Hawaiian version of his name that he brought back from missionary service in the Sandwich Islands. The *Juvenile Instructor* narrative is obviously based on his journal record, but Bigler added details and retrospective explanations that are missing in his other, more literal transcriptions. This excerpt describes the trek of his contingent of battalion veterans to Sutter's Fort, over the Sierra to the meeting with Sam Brannan and Capt. James Brown, and back again to accept employment with Captain Sutter. It reveals more fully than any other account the events of this journey and the circumstances surrounding the agreement between Sutter and the battalion boys.

HENELE PIKALE [HENRY W. BIGLER], "RECOLLECTIONS OF THE PAST," *JUVENILE INSTRUCTOR* 21 (1, 15 DECEMBER 1886).

On the evening of the 20th [of August 1847] we camped near a river, where we were visited by some Indians, who sold us corn and melons. They told us of some Americans living down the river about nine miles. We were of the opinion that they were some of our brethren, and the next morning Brother Andrew Lytle and two others set out to visit them and find out who they were.

On the 24th these brethren overtook us. They stated that they had found some of our people at the settlement down the river. This same day we arrived at a place where some white settlers had located. We were told by these people that the Twelve Apostles, with a number of pioneers, had reached Salt Lake Valley and that five hundred wagons were close behind. This to us was glorious news, and the first we had heard definitely concerning the location of the body of the Church or the pioneers.

[Inexplicably, at this point Bigler omits any account of the battalion veterans' first visit to Sutter's Fort. To remedy this lack, here are the appropriate entries from the Bancroft Library version of his journal, edited by Gudde and printed in *Bigler's Chronicle of the West*, 70.]

August 25. This morning we got a few bushels wheat for one dollar per bushel. The Spanish phrase and price was two dollars per fanega. Our course today was northwest across a large plain for twenty miles and we encamped on the north side of the American River about one mile and [a] half from Sutter's Fort.

August 26. Laid by while some visited the Fort, where there was a blacksmith's shop, and got their animals shod, as some of them were tender footed. The price of shoeing was one dollar for each shoe made and nailed on. We learned here was plenty of grass and unbolted flour and peas to be had. Unbolted flour (which was all the kind in California those days) was worth eight dollars per sack, peas one dollar and half per bushel. Captain Sutter seemed to have plenty of everything in the shape of cattle, horses and mules, grain etc. Several of our boys concluded to stop here and go to work for Sutter, as he was wanting to hire and was offering pretty fair wages, as the boys thought, and fit themselves up and come on the next spring.

On the twenty-seventh the pioneers struck out leaving behind the greater part of the camp, who expected to stop another day and more fully complete their outfit for the journey. At 2:00 P.M. we camped, making about eighteen miles in a northeast direction.

[Here Bigler's *Juvenile Instructor* narrative resumes.]

On the 28th we camped on Bear Creek, where there were a few white families residing.

On the 29th we began to penetrate the great Sierras, covered with oak and pine. At 2 o'clock, P.M., we halted for the purpose of making camp for the night. At evening we had a prayer meeting.

On Wednesday, September 1st, we camped in a valley in the mountains. Pea vines were found here so high as a man's head. The valley is surrounded by high California mountains, densely covered with pine timber. The trunks of many of the trees measured ten feet in diameter and more than two hundred feet in height. Near our camp were two wagons left by emigrants. We were told at Sutter's Fort that a company of ninety emigrants were overtaken by a snow storm the previous Fall, while crossing the mountains. The snow fell ten feet deep and fifty of the company perished through starvation and otherwise.

September 2nd, 1847, we lay by to let our animals rest, and to feed on pea vines. I took my gun and left camp to hunt a little, but was soon obliged to give it up because of the hard traveling over and among so many rocks.

On the 3rd, we crossed a lofty mountain, camping at 2 P.M. on a creek where we found a grave. On the head-board was the name: "Smith, died October 7th, 1846."

We passed a wagon, in the box of which were tin pans and some clothing. This seemed to show there were no Indians around. Our camp was surrounded by high mountains covered with a heavy forest of pine, balsam and redwood timber so dense and luxuriant as to cause the whole surroundings to have a dark and dismal appearance, and I thought if there was any truth in the existence of hob-goblins they surely lived in these mountains.

On the 4th, we passed several small lakes or ponds near the top of the mountains, with no outlets and said to have plenty of fish in them. At 12 o'clock, we camped by one of the coldest springs I ever saw. There was plenty of green grass, while at no great distance on the side of the mountains were great banks of snow.

The next day we reached the summit of the main chain of the Sierra Nevadas, where we found a windlass some emigrants had made to haul their wagons up over a very steep ascent from the east side. Passing down to the Truckee River we camped for the night. We passed a cabin, in and about which we found the skeletons of several human beings. Among them was a woman's hand, nearly whole, though partly burned. The little finger was not hurt but the flesh was completely dried. The shanty was partly destroyed by fire. Some thought Indians were the cause of this disaster; but we hardly believed it as we had passed several broken-down wagons containing boxes, trunks and clothing, which would not have been left had the Indians perpetrated this horrible deed.

September 6th, at 7 A.M., we broke camp and had not proceeded far when we met Sam Brannan. He told us that Captain Brown was just behind with his detachment on their way to Monterey, California, to get their discharge, and that the captain had a package of letters and an epistle from President Young and the Twelve to the boys of the battalion. This began to wake us up with anxiety to hear the news, and as there was poor camp ground at hand we at once returned to the place we had left that morning to await the arrival of our company, whom we had left at Sutter's Fort. Captain Brown was also likely to arrive about the same time, when all would be together to share the news from the Church. Brannan halted an hour to let his animal feed and to take a little refreshment himself. He was alone. He and Captain Brown had left Salt Lake together, but on account of some misunderstanding and sharp words between them that morning, Brannan had left and proceeded on his journey homeward alone. He gave a glowing account of the Salt Lake country, but thought it no place to live in, as according to all accounts from the mountaineers it was too cold a country. Nothing would grow, and he believed the Church would have to come to California.

In the afternoon of the 7th the rear of our company came up. Captain Brown had already arrived and nearly every man received a letter from his family or a friend; and truly we had a time of rejoicing together in the mountains, although a few had news of sadness—they had either lost a dear wife or child or an affectionate parent. Captain Brown then read the epistle, which was to the effect that all who had no families in Salt Lake, and had not plenty of provisions, would do better to return to California and go to work and fit themselves out with plenty and come on in the Spring. Provisions were very scarce both in Salt Lake and Fort Hall, and they had already sent out a hunting party to kill buffalo.

A letter from Brother George A. Smith informed me that my folks were all well. My sister, Emeline, and husband (John W. Hess) were in the valley, having arrived from Pueblo in Captain Brown's detachment on the 29th of July; and that President Young, with a company of 143 pioneers arrived in the great basin July 24th. Since then they had been busy plowing and planting seeds and potatoes. A number of men were at work making adobies for building houses. The whole face of the country was covered with large, black crickets. Salt Lake Valley was surrounded by high mountains, some of which were capped with snow. There were nice streams of water running from them, the greater number being so situated as to be easily made to irrigate the land. Provisions were scarce and the Saints were living on half rations. The valley would be organized into a Stake of Zion and Father Smith appointed to preside; and that President Young and the Twelve would soon return to Winter Quarters.

While some of the battalion boys were out hunting they reported having found a shanty and several dead bodies. Some of them had been cut up; men and women with their legs cut off, their ribs sawed from their bodies and their skulls sawed open and their brains taken out. From the best information we could procure we learned that they were Missourians emigrating to California, about ninety in number. They disagreed among themselves and split up into different companies. The strongest moved forward, leaving the weak behind with little or no provisions. A bed of snow falling ten feet deep prevented travel; and being out of food the most of them perished. When help from the settlements reached them those who were alive had been living on the dead; and it was said that children ate and lived on the dead bodies of their parents.

On the morning of the 8th, thirty of our number, myself included, gave our brethren the parting hand with blessings on each other's heads, they to continue their journey to Salt Lake, we to return to California. We divided provisions, scarcely reserving enough to last us to the settlements, 150 miles distant. It was hard parting; but all knew it was best to obey the counsel of the servants of God. It was stated in the epistle that the Lord would be with those who went back.

On the 11th, we passed a little grave which had been opened by wild beasts; the coffin was broken and the feathers out of the pillow or bed were scattered all around. On one side lay the skull of a child. I was moved with pity at the sight. Near the place was another grave and on the head-board the name: "Ann West, aged 62 years."

We passed Brother Henry Hoyt's grave. He was burried so shallow that the air got to his remains. He was in the rear company at the time he died and the pioneers, who were two days in advance, had all the tools for digging, so the men had nothing but a hatchet or two with which to dig his grave. He was buried high up on the side of a mountain, under a low-spreading oak. He was a good man and, I might say, died a martyr.

On the 14th, about 1 P.M., we arrived at our old camp ground near Sutter's Fort. After eating dinner three of our men went to see Captain Sutter. When they returned that evening they reported having seen the captain and had a talk with him and that he was willing to hire the whole of our number either by the month or by the job. He would pay one-half in cash and the other in trade; and that he was wanting to build a [grist] mill and wanted mill timbers got out and a race dug three miles long. He promised to pay twenty-five dollars per month for working on the race, or twelve and one-half cents per yard.

The next morning we made a bargain with Sutter, this time he agreed to pay all money. He was to furnish us provisions, but we were to do our own cooking. Our animals could run with his band of horses free of charge and they would be driven up by his *vaquero* (horse-herder) every night and corraled. This we took as being very kind in the captain. In the afternoon we moved on to the ground where the work was to be performed and found a very good adobe house to occupy.

Sutter furnished all the tools and teams to be used on the ditch, and on Friday morning, the 17th of September, all hands except our cooks were on the race with ox teams, plows, scrapers, spades, shovels and picks. We earned one dollar and fifty cents per day all around to the man. Our hands were tender and soon became very sore. Some of our men were taken sick with chills and scurvy.

The rate of pay promised by Sutter, $1.50 a day per man, was reasonable but not exceptionally generous for northern California in 1847, even considering that provisions, rudimentary housing, and horse pasturage were added to the bargain. When they were ready to leave Sutter's employment, however, Bigler and his companions would find it difficult to collect. In a cash-shy frontier economy, Captain Sutter had repeatedly financed his operations by securing generous credit from anyone who might be in a position to assist him, his loans backed only by his grandiose, seldom-fulfilled promises. This practice had already cost him friends, but the battalion veterans were unfamiliar with Sutter's habitual inclination to promise more than he could deliver. They needed the work, and they brought to their tasks a degree of skilled expertise and a willingness to labor, accompanied by a habit of sobriety, that was scarce on northern California's interior frontier in 1847. For them, as for John Sutter, the arrangement seemed perfect.

Robert Pixton: We Couldn't Help Each Other to a Drink of Water

Sore hands and hard work could seem relatively minor inconveniences to the veterans after the hardships they had suffered in the United States military. But they encountered a new and unexpected danger at Sutter's Fort: malaria, a disease that had become endemic in the lower Sacramento Valley since its advent in 1832–1833.[40] In his autobiography, Robert Pixton, a Company E veteran, summarized his experiences after leaving Los Angeles and told of a severe episode of "bilious fever," a common term for malaria, which put him and two of his comrades temporarily out of commission while they were digging the millrace for Sutter's gristmill.

Robert Pixton, Autobiography, LDS Archives.

We travelled down the Tulare to Sacramento, about 800 miles away. I got a fine mare and a Spanish pet. We travelled on to Mr. Sutter's Fort at Sacramento where we got a fresh supply of provisions. Daniel Browett, Robert Harris, Henderson Cox, Len Roberts, Richard Slater and Robert Pixton

[40]Concerning malaria in the lower Sacramento Valley, see "Begun by Gold: Sacramento and the Gold Rush Legacy after 150 Years," in Owens, ed., *Riches for All*, 330–31.

ROBERT PIXTON
A veteran of the Mormon Battalion who went to work building a grist mill for John Sutter in the fall of 1848, then mined briefly at Mormon Island, Pixton had become a stage actor in Salt Lake City at the time he sat for this dramatic portrait. *Courtesy Pioneer Memorial Museum, International Society, Daughters of Utah Pioneers.*

messed together all the way from Council Bluffs, I being the cook for the mess. We travelled by the way of the Truckee River, after crossing the Sierra Nevada Mountains, and had passed the place where the Donner Party was overtaken in the snow. . . . The brethren found one body that had been buried in the snow.

After travelling over the mountains one day we met with some of the brethren from the [Salt Lake] Valley. This was a time of rejoicing. Captain Brown who left us at Santa Fe with the sick which went by the way of Fort Kearney [*sic*] and a few brethren with him from the Valley, brought news that we were not to go to the Valley, and told us we had better stay another year in California. So the company divided right where we met each other; some went on to Winter Quarters, some to the Valley, and some turned back. Daniel Browett, Slater, Cox, Levi Roberts and myself turned back to Sacramento and went to work for Mr. Sutter who treated us very kind. I sent a mule to my wife with Brother [Robert] Harris, which she got. . . .

We all went to work at the same place for Captain Sutter. We took the work of cutting a millrace. Brother Browett went to work with the millwright, this was in September and later on in the fall, I and two others took sick with the bilious fever. We were so sick we couldn't help each other to a drink of water. We lay under some ties and had to crawl around with the sun to keep from making us chill. . . . Our appetites were very poor, and our food was flour, water and squash. Had it not been for the thoughts of my wife and family I could have died, but we all three recovered after awhile and went to work on the millrace again and worked all winter. Sometime in the winter two of the brethren who was working for Mr. Sutter in the mountains found gold in a tailrace they were making. Mr. Sutter let me see the first gold they found before sending it to San Francisco to get it tested.

JOHN A. SUTTER: THE MORMONS ARE THE BEST WORKERS I HAVE

The site where Pixton and his LDS comrades set to work is located about four miles upstream from Sutter's Fort on the south bank of the American River, near the present campus of California State University, Sacramento. The river flow was subject to substantial seasonal fluctuations, with unpredictable flooding episodes that could easily tear apart any structure situated within the stream's natural levees. Nonetheless, in his usual way, Sutter assumed that nothing would go wrong. His Saint-built gristmill, he was certain, would finally enable him to grind his wheat into flour efficiently and to sell similar services to neighboring farmers. With a large supply of flour to trade, Sutter was confident that he would at last be able to pay off his outstanding debt to the Russian-American Company, whose property at Fort Ross on the Mendocino coast he had purchased on credit for $30,000 in 1841.

The availability of an LDS workforce brought Sutter the promise of other lucrative projects. He began a tannery, where he expected to process hundreds of hides from his cattle that roamed the countryside all but untended. He also acted on plans to build a water-powered sawmill in the mountains, where yellow pine was abundant at elevations over 3,000 feet. An earlier sawmill venture on the Cosumnes River had failed, but Sutter clearly saw the need for sawed lumber to supply his and his neighbors' building efforts. All potential sawmill sites were a long distance from Sutter's Fort, well outside the boundaries of his Mexican land grants; but at this point neither the military government nor any other official body commanded the authority or showed a desire to regulate land use and ownership. Now that he had experienced, reliable men to do the work, Sutter felt confident in going ahead with this venture.

Very soon Sutter was bragging about the accomplishments of his LDS workmen. Writing in mid-October to Mariano Vallejo, his *Californio* rival and occasional business associate at Sonoma, Sutter said that both the sawmill and the large flour mill would be finished in a month or two because of the skilled labor of the battalion boys. "The Mormons," he stated, "are the best workers I have, without them the mills could not be made." He also offered to send Vallejo various items that his LDS employees were turning out in the workshops at Sutter's Fort. "If you need strong shoes for your vaqueros I can send them to you, for I have good shoemakers—all Mormons," he told Vallejo.[41] Two weeks later Sutter wrote proudly to his friend Thomas Larkin, the leading merchant and former U.S. consul at Monterey, about his turn of fortune. "My tannyard is now [for] once carried out well. I have about 1500 hides to tann. I have two tannery [workers] and 3 shoemakers (Mormons) all the hands on my mills are Mormons, and [they are] the best people which ever I has had employed." Sutter compared his new workers with the other non-Native employees he had hired in the past: "If I would have had Mormons 4 or 5 years past," he told Larkin, "I would have a fortune, but so long [as] I am here I has had only a few good men, the balance was a bad kind of people."[42]

The battalion veterans, working for Sutter's promises, now appeared to be the long-sought solution for his financial problems. While we have no evidence that he ever reflected on the reason for his good fortune, Captain Sutter might well have thanked Brigham Young for sending him the men he needed to make New Helvetia profitable at last. "I hope now that when this gristmill, sawmill & tannery are going well on," he confided to Larkin, "I will soon be out of my difficultys."[43] Then came the Coloma gold discovery, and everything changed.

---

[41]Sutter to Vallejo, 21 October 1847, New Helvetia, Sutter Collection, Box 312, folder 10, California State Library. Translation from Spanish by Nellie Van de Grift Sanchez. The original letter, written in Sutter's rudimentary Spanish, is in Mariano G. Vallejo, *Documentos para la historia de California, Tomo XII,* 1844–48, Manuscript 315, Bancroft Library.

[42]Sutter to Larkin, 28 October 1847, in Hammond, ed., *The Larkin Papers,* 7:47.

[43]Ibid. Dillon, *Fool's Gold: The Decline and Fall of Captain John Sutter,* is the standard account of Sutter's American career. Owens, ed., *John Sutter and a Wider West,* reappraises Sutter's historical role in the American West and contains Sutter's self-serving 1856 recollections of the gold rush, while a longer "Personal Reminiscences" prepared for H. H. Bancroft is now at the Bancroft Library. Edited freely by Erwin G. Gudde, this latter work reached print as *Sutter's Own Story.* Brief mention of the battalion veterans' activities at Sutter's Fort appears in Sutter *et al., New Helvetia Diary,* 113–14.

Chapter 3

"Gold, Boys, Gold!" Mormon Beginnings of the California Gold Rush

As he told the story much later, John Bidwell let slide a splendid opportunity to become the premier *empresario* of gold mining in northern California four years before James Marshall's discovery at the Coloma sawmill. The New York-born Bidwell had traveled overland to California in 1841 as a member of the first American wagon train from Missouri to reach the Pacific Coast. While he was working as superintendent of John Sutter's Hock Farm on the Feather River in March 1844, one of his employees, a Mexican named Pablo Gutierrez, told Bidwell "there surely is gold on Bear River in the mountains." Gutierrez explained that he had gone to the mountains to find his missing Native wife, and on the Bear River he had seen clear signs of gold. A few days later Bidwell traveled into the mountains a short distance with Gutierrez, who showed him a location that he knew must have gold deposits. But he couldn't find any of the gold now, Gutierrez said, because he lacked the necessary equipment: a *batea* such as Mexican miners used in their gold washing operations. No one in Alta California had one or could fashion one for him, he told Bidwell; he would have to make a trip to the placer mining region in northern Mexico to bring back a *batea*. Ignorant of the fact that a *batea* was nothing more than a shallow wooden bowl, Bidwell proposed that the two men save enough money to travel together to Boston, where the "very ingenious" Yankees could make anything, even a *batea*. Meanwhile they pledged to keep the whole matter a secret.

Circumstances repeatedly delayed these plans. In 1845 came the *Californio* revolt against Governor Micheltorena, and Bidwell took up other duties. He joined Sutter in a brief, ill-starred military campaign as an

JAMES W. MARSHALL
Commissioned by the California state legislature in 1883, this bronze memorial statue towers over Marshall's grave on a hillside in Coloma, with a gesture that points perpetually toward the nearby site where Marshall made the initial gold discovery on the South Fork of the American River, 24 January 1848. *Courtesy California State Library.*

ally of Governor Micheltorena. Subsequently he went to work at Sutter's Fort as New Helvetia's bookkeeper and business manager. He "still had it in my mind to try to find gold," Bidwell recalled, but what with one thing and another, including the death of Gutierrez, the takeover of Sutter's Fort by John C. Frémont and his Bear Flag irregulars, and the subsequent American conquest of California, the entire matter slipped by. Then in late January 1848, James Marshall came to the fort with the first small pieces of gold from Sutter and Marshall's sawmill site on the American River's South Fork.[1]

[1]Bidwell's account appears in *Life in California Before the Gold Discovery*, reprinting a section of his memoirs first published in *The Century Magazine* in 1890 and 1891. After Marshall's discovery, Bidwell improved on his missed opportunity when he located an extremely rich placer in July 1848 on the south fork of the Feather River that became known as Bidwell's Bar. Directing the labor of as many as one hundred Indian workers, he secured enough gold to purchase two Mexican land grants in the Sacramento Valley, which he combined into Rancho Chico, a prosperous 26,000-acre farming estate. Rockwell Hunt's *John Bidwell, Prince of California Pioneers*, is a detailed biographical study. An outstanding recent reexamination of Bidwell's career with a substantial selection of his writings and correspondence (but lacking this recollection of his missed gold discovery opportunity) is Gillis and Magliari, *John Bidwell and California: The Life and Writings of a Pioneer.*

John Sutter: Made a Contract and Entered into Partnership with Marshall

In August 1847, when the first contingent of Mormon Battalion veterans arrived at Sutter's Fort, John Sutter's sawmill venture was well along in the planning stage. Earlier that year Sutter had sent out various small parties to look for a possible mill site somewhere along the western slope of the Sierra Nevada, both in the American River and the Feather River drainages. One group led by his general manager at the fort, Samuel Kyburz, reported the discovery of a promising location in a little valley along the south fork of the American River, close to a Nissenan Indian village at a place the Nissenan called Cullomah. In mid-May Sutter's most adept carpenter and mechanical craftsman, James W. Marshall, headed another small expedition to examine this area.

After he returned to the fort, Marshall told Sutter that the Coloma site was a good one. It had abundant timber; the river was strong enough to power a mill, and the nearby Nissenan settlement offered a potential supply of Native workers. Most important, he pointed out, it could be reached by wagon without great difficulty. But it was not until three months later, on 27 August, after a committee of LDS veterans had come to negotiate for employment, that Sutter wrote in his journal record of affairs at the fort, the New Helvetia Diary, "Made a contract and entered into partnership with Marshall for a sawmill to be build on the Amer: fork."[2] In this contract, written by Bidwell and witnessed by Kyburz, Marshall agreed to construct and operate the mill. Sutter would furnish the necessary workers along with tools, materials, and equipment, and the two men were to divide equally the mill's output of finished lumber.

---

[2]The full entry reads: "Friday, Aug. 27th 1847/ A good Many of the Mormons here, to get some Blacksmith work done, & to buy some provisions. Made a contract and entered into partnership with Marshall for a sawmill to be build on the Amer: fork." *New Helvetia Diary*, 113. The best description of events leading to the siting of the mill is in Theressa Gay's thorough and perceptive work, *James W. Marshall, The Discoverer of Gold*. Notable earlier studies are Heizer, Fenenga, and Neasham, *California Gold Discovery: Centennial Papers*; and Paul, ed., *The California Gold Discovery*. None of these authors point out the obvious chronological link between the arrival of the battalion veterans and the negotiation of the mill contract. Before he signed the contract, Marshall evidently preferred a site on Butte Creek in the Feather River country, close to his own ranch.

James S. Brown: The Great and Memorable Discovery of the California Gold

For years firsthand authentication of the Coloma gold discovery has been based on two contemporary records, each set down by a Mormon Battalion veteran who was part of the work force at the sawmill. Of prime importance is the diary of Henry W. Bigler, in particular the two pages recording the gold discovery now preserved in the holdings of the California Pioneer Society.[3] Second is the journal kept by Azariah Smith. While Smith's relatives often made this source available to scholars in a typescript copy, recently his great-nephew, David L. Bigler, published *The Gold Discovery Journal of Azariah Smith,* a meticulous edition of the manuscript. Frequently consulted also is a third account, written a few years after the event: a gold discovery narrative that James Marshall dictated to James M. Hutchings in the summer of 1857, and which appeared in *Hutchings' Illustrated California Magazine* that November. These three sources, supplemented by Bigler's transcriptions of his journal, have provided basic documentation for every scholarly reexamination of the gold discovery story since 1887–1888, when historian John S. Hittell relied on the Bigler and Smith records to demonstrate beyond doubt that the discovery date was January 24th, instead of "on or about January 19th" as Marshall had frequently asserted.[4]

Less well known are three other eyewitness accounts that provide further details and help clarify lingering questions about the course of events at the Coloma sawmill. Earliest in origin is a descriptive narrative dictated in 1850 or 1851 by James Marshall and written down by

---

[3]Based on Erwin Gudde's assumptions, historians long believed Bigler's original daybook had vanished, but Juanita Brooks located Bigler's manuscript journals in southern Utah, including "a large record giving the march of the Mormon Battalion day by day, except that eight leaves recording the discovery of gold have been cut out." Bigler's daughter used the diary as a scrapbook, pasting newspapers over every page, "so that some pages are spoiled." See Brooks to LeRoy (Uncle Roy) Hafen, 12 October 1936, Hafen Papers, Utah State Historical Society. Brooks gave the diary to the Huntington Library, where it is now identified as "Book A." This, according to historian Guy Bishop, "is *the* original Gold Discovery journal."

[4]The question of the exact date preoccupied many writers until John S. Hittell settled it in two *Overland Monthly* articles published in September 1887 and February 1888. Richard H. Dillon summarized the controversy, with emphasis placed on Hittell's accomplishment, in his introduction to *The Discovery of Gold in California* by John S. Hittell, James W. Marshall, and Edwin G. Waite. See also Paul, ed., *The California Gold Discovery*; and Bigler, ed., *The Gold Discovery Journal of Azariah Smith,* 108n39. Another early controversy arose regarding Marshall's claim to be the first discoverer. Hittell also effectively put this issue to rest, although other versions of the discovery story, undocumented or fancifully documented, have continued to appear from time to time.

Charles B. Gillespie, who was mining near Coloma. It was not published until 1891, when it appeared in *The Century Illustrated Monthly Magazine.*[5] While the publication has a Pennsylvania provenance, which might raise doubts about the authenticity of the Marshall account, critical evaluation proves its validity. Gillespie had no discernable motive for fraud. Although he could not have seen Sutter's New Helvetia Diary or any of the Mormon accounts, his version of Marshall's story is factually accurate at every verifiable point, and it is remarkably consistent with statements made by Marshall at later dates.

Henry W. Bigler, as previously noted, contributed another important though long-neglected account, the narrative published in the *Juvenile Instructor* in 1886, which remained unknown to scholarship until recently. Like Bigler's better known descriptions of his adventures, this one has a precision of recall that shows its debt to the diary the author had yet in his possession when he wrote it. But in this version Bigler allowed himself to expand on the diary record with a freer reliance on his still trustworthy memory, adding explanatory detail and reflections not present in his other accounts.

Filling out this group of comparatively neglected documentary sources is the autobiographical memoir of Mormon Battalion veteran James Stephens Brown.[6] Apparently Brown kept no journal of his military experiences, but on the forty-sixth anniversary of the Coloma gold discovery he set down his recollections of this event and the circumstances that led to it. With his retelling no doubt polished by the passage of time, he intended to add to the record a statement about his own part in "the great and memorable discovery of the California gold [that] was made at Capt. John A. Sutter and James W. Marshall's sawmill, on the American Fork River, California." Moreover, as he made quite plain, Brown was intent on claiming for the battalion veterans the credit he believed should rightly be theirs for their central role in beginning the California gold rush.

[5]The account appears in Paul, ed., *The California Gold Discovery,* 197–201. It was subsequently republished as "Marshall's Narrative" in Hittell, Marshall, and Waite, *The Discovery of Gold in California.*

[6]Brown's little volume was reprinted in 1933 by New York publisher William Abbatt, which is the edition now most commonly available. The section dealing with the controversy over the discovery date appears also in Paul, ed., *The California Gold Discovery,* 169–73. James Stephens Brown should not be confused with Capt. James Brown, who led the battalion detachment of dependents and disabled men that wintered at Pueblo in 1846–1847, and who later started for California to collect the mustering-out pay for the Pueblo detachment from the U.S. Army commander at Monterey.

Placed side by side, these three versions of the same story do more than simply add detail to the gold discovery narrative. They complement, clarify, and reinforce one another in sometimes surprising ways. Each provides context for the other two. Each reflects the experiences of one person, but considered together they shift our eyes from a narrow focus on James Marshall and John Sutter to a wide-lens examination of the total interplay of people and events in the small community that came together, however briefly, at Coloma. The result is a multi-dimensional historical perspective that greatly enhances our understanding of the importance of the LDS veterans to the discovery itself, then to the slowly growing realization of its significance, and finally to the developments that grew from the discovery. An essentially haphazard search for bits of placer gold in January and February, they demonstrate, led the California Saints in short order to systematic large-scale mining and the start of the California gold rush.

In contrast to the traditional, myth-reinforced story, in which Sutter and Marshall appear as chosen agents to push forward the inevitable progress of American Manifest Destiny, these autobiographical narratives make clear that the Coloma gold discovery was a peculiar historical accident, contingent on a unique alignment of circumstances within northern California's remote frontier borderland. John Sutter's precarious economic situation and his imprudent speculative behavior had left him heavily in debt, short of capital and short also of experienced, reliable workers. His vaulting ambition for wealth and respectability led the émigré Swiss adventurer to subsidize the sawmill construction at Coloma as yet another risky new speculation. At the same time, James Marshall was in financial distress, caused by the neglect of his Feather River ranch property during the war with Mexico. Marshall's knowledge of the country, his cordial relationship with Sutter, his mechanical talents, and his quirky interest in precious metals all helped place him in the Coloma millrace on 24 January 1848. The willingness of some Coloma-area Nissenan to work for Sutter and Marshall, intensified by the great interest in Euro-American ways shown by a few of these Natives, also formed part of the gold discovery scenario.

These circumstances converged because Sutter was able to enlist from among the Mormon Battalion veterans a skilled labor force, willing to trust his recklessly optimistic pledge of future payment. Prompted by Brigham Young's message, these men had turned back to California with a two-part agenda: they had a temporary need to make a living, and they were determined to travel to the Great Basin the following summer with livestock, supplies, and equipment to assist their church's newly established Zion colony. There is no better illustration of the accident factor in history, nor, from the very different perspectives of John Sutter and Brigham Young, of the doctrine of unintended consequences.

James S. Brown: To Wait Upon Mr. Sutter

In the fall of 1847 James Stephens Brown was nineteen years old, a Mormon Battalion veteran traveling with his thirty-three-year-old uncle, Alexander Stephens. In his autobiographical memoir Brown tells us that he remained at Sutter's Fort in August while the detachment including Bigler and Smith headed into the Sierra and met Samuel Brannan and Capt. James Brown. The opening section of his account describes the August separation at Sutter's Fort and the negotiations that led to Sutter's initial employment of the battalion boys. Sutter's decision to build the Coloma sawmill as well as the gristmill just upriver from Sutter's Fort, as Brown remembered it, proceeded from his discussions with a committee representing the LDS veterans. The Saints' terms of employment were fixed during this meeting according to a proposition their committee made to Sutter. Given Sutter's lack of ready money, a critically important point was the willingness of the Saints to work until spring without pay and then to take part of their earnings in horses, cattle, and supplies for the trip eastward to join the church.

James S. Brown, *California Gold—An Authentic History of the First Find, With the Names of Those Interested in the Discovery*, 8–9.

Now to give a clear conception of that most notable event, we must go back to the time when the project of building the mill was first conceived by Messrs. Sutter and Marshall, which was on or near the 1st of June, 1847. But, for want of skilled labor, the matter was delayed for a time, as the class of white men that was to be hired could not be trusted so as to justify a man in the undertaking of an enterprise of such importance as building a gristmill, which he already had under contemplation, and a sawmill forty miles away, in an Indian country; and again, the unsettled condition of the country as it was, so soon after the war, and considering the scarcity of money, caused Mr. Sutter to hesitate until a detachment of 150 men of the Mormon Battalion came up, August 26, and camped on the American Fork River about two miles from Sutter's Fort. After they had a short consultation it was decided that about one hundred of the party would remain over till the next year, and seek employment as best they could.[7] Accordingly, a committee was appointed to wait upon Mr. Sutter, to learn from him what the prospect for employment was. The committee informed Mr. Sutter that we had carpenters, blacksmiths, wheelwrights, millwrights, farmers and common laborers, and that we should want horses, cattle, and a general outfit for crossing the plains early the next summer, and if we could not get all money, we could and would take a part of our pay in the above mentioned stock and supplies. This proposition seemed to meet with favor from the Captain, as he had an abundance of the above mentioned property, and, if my memory is not at fault, he told the committee to call again, or for the men to come in two or three days, and he would speak further with them.

I understood then that in two or three days he decided to construct the two mills above mentioned, for the greatest obstacle that confronted him had been removed by the propositions that our committee had made to him. I have not heard the foregoing statement denied, therefore it is confirmed in my mind that had it not been for this opportunity the sawmill at least would not have been built, nor the discovery of gold made at that time. The State of California would have waited indefinitely to have been developed and to be christened the "Golden State," and that entrance to San Francisco Bay might never have received the title of the "Golden Gate."[8]

Quite a number, say from forty to sixty of us, called on Mr. Sutter between August 29 and September 5th. Some were employed to work on the gristmill, others took contracts on the mill race of that mill, the race was seven or eight miles long and was also designed for irrigation.

By the time Bigler, Smith, and their comrades returned from meeting Brannan and Captain Brown at Truckee Meadows, young James S. Brown was part of a large LDS crew already hard at work on Sutter's projects. Planning to go to Salt Lake as soon as the passes across the Sierra Nevada opened in the spring, they were making use of Sutter's situation for their own purposes.

---

[7]According to Henry Bigler, many men decided to remain in California at this point on the recommendation of Levi Hancock, the highest-ranking LDS church official in the battalion, who had assumed authority after the battalion disbanded and who led the company on the march from Los Angeles through the San Joaquin Valley to Sutter's Fort.

[8]John C. Frémont had in fact named the Golden Gate in January 1846. See Spence and Jackson, eds., *The Expeditions of John Charles Frémont*, 2:45n27.

JAMES W. MARSHALL: MY MEN WERE GREAT WITH THE AX

Because he later gave an incorrect date for the actual first gold discovery, and perhaps also because his reputation was tarnished by personal idiosyncrasies and his repeated failures as a businessman and mine developer during the balance of his life, historians have tended to give scant attention to James Marshall's account of the proceedings at Coloma.[9] Yet, the issue of the discovery date aside, Marshall's recollections of his own activities were vivid and remain historically valuable. In this version of his story, Marshall recounted his experience after returning from his site inspection and then beginning the mill project with the help of a few battalion veterans and one or two other workers from Sutter's Fort.

JAMES W. MARSHALL,
"MARSHALL'S OWN ACCOUNT OF THE GOLD DISCOVERY,"
THE CENTURY ILLUSTRATED MONTHLY MAGAZINE (FEBRUARY 1891).

You may be sure Mr. Sutter was pleased when I reported my success [in locating a mill site]. We entered into partnership; I was to build the mill, and he was to find provisions, teams, tools, and to pay a portion of the men's wages. I believe I was at that time the only millwright in the whole country. In August, everything being ready, we freighted two wagons with tools and provisions, and accompanied by six men I left the fort, and after a good deal of difficulty reached this place [Coloma] one beautiful afternoon and formed our camp on yon little rise of ground right above the town.

Our first business was to put up log houses, as we intended remaining here all winter. This was done in less than no time, for my men were great with the ax. We then cut timber, and fell to work hewing it for the framework of the mill. The Indians gathered about us in great numbers. I employed about forty of them to assist us with the dam, which we put up in a kind of way in about four weeks.

When Henry Bigler and his comrades returned to Sutter's Fort in September 1847 after their trip into the Sierra, they discovered their battalion companions already working in Sutter's tanyard, at the shops at the fort, and digging a millrace and putting in foundations for a grist-

[9]Curiously, the post mortem neglect of Marshall as an authority on the gold discovery coincided with a developing public adulation of a mythical, non-historical Marshall. The uncritical reverence for an imaginary Marshall is best exemplified by the heroic bronze gold discovery statue of a supposed Marshall figure, commissioned by the California state legislature, which can be seen today on the Coloma hillside. Gay's detailed biography of Marshall provides a substantial measure of even-handed historical justice to this man, however delayed.

mill on the lower American River. Bigler joined the digging crew and found the task hard, with the malaria danger added to the ordinary perils of physical labor. He soon learned that a small number of men including his friends Ira and Sidney Willes and Ephraim Pearson, all from Bigler's Company B of the battalion, had gone into the mountains with James Marshall to start construction of a sawmill. When the opportunity came ten days later for him to change jobs by joining Marshall's project, he showed no hesitation.

HENELE PIKALE [HENRY W. BIGLER], "RECOLLECTIONS OF THE PAST," *JUVENILE INSTRUCTOR* 21 (1, 15 DECEMBER 1886).

We earned one dollar and fifty cents per day all around to the man. Our hands were tender and soon became very sore. Some of our men were taken sick with chills and scurvy.

While at dinner on the 27th [of September 1847], a man entered our quarters dressed in buckskin, and said Captain Sutter wanted four men from our company to go up into the mountains about thirty miles to help build a saw-mill on the south fork of the American River. He said that he and Sutter were partners in building the mill and that he had been up there with a few hands and had done a little work, but some of them were expecting to leave soon, hence they wanted more help. This man was James Wilson Marshall. In the afternoon Israel Evans, Azariah Smith, William Johnston and myself started with Mr. Marshall, accompanied by Charles Bennet, late from Oregon.[10] Marshall took an ox team and wagon loaded with provisions, and a few tools. We arrived at the mill site in the evening of the 29th, where we found several of the battalion boys who, by the advice of Levi W. Hancock, had stopped at Sutter's at the time we passed there in August.

To me the surrounding country looked wild and lonesome. We were surrounded by high mountains, more or less covered with a heavy growth of pine, balsam, redwood, pinion pine and oak timber. The place was infested with wolves, grizzly bears and Indians. Before our arrival at the mill site, Marshall and the brethren had built a nice double log cabin about one-fourth of a mile from the mill. In one part of the house lived a family. The man's name was Peter L. Wemer, whose wife was to be cook for the mill hands.[11]

---

[10]A veteran of the First Dragoons, Charles Bennett had emigrated to Oregon in 1844. After his gold rush experience in California, he returned to Oregon. He joined the Oregon Volunteers during the Cayuse War and died in 1855 at the Battle of Walla Walla. His death came before Bennett recorded any account of the gold discovery.

[11]Peter L. Wimmer came overland in 1846 with his wife, Elizabeth Jane "Jennie" Wimmer, and their seven children from previous marriages. Until Christmas 1847, the couple shared a double-log house with the battalion veterans.

On the night of the 3rd of October all hands were aroused from slumber by the cry from our tame Indians: *"Marlohinty! Marlohinty!"* meaning there were bad Indians around; but we could see none and soon retired. The next evening we were awakened again by the same cry from our Indians. This time some of our men said they saw one. We could hear them walking, but they kept themselves in the dark and behind trees. We called to them but they would not speak. Up to this time we had not thought of much danger. There were ten white men and only four guns, as the most of the boys had left their muskets below. We forthwith chose guards and kept watch for some time, but were never disturbed afterwards, the enemy finding out, perhaps, that we had something else to defend ourselves with besides bows and arrows.

Nothing of note took place from this time on until the following 24th of January. We continued to work on the sawmill. Sometimes it happened that Sutter neglected to send up provisions to the mill, when we would be on short rations. At such times Marshall detailed me to be hunter, as the black-tailed deer was quite plentiful. He owned a good rifle and this I used, taking with me one of the tame Indians to help carry in the venison. This suited me full as well as using an ax or shovel about the mill, for I was paid just as much.

For writers attempting to allocate proper credit, typical of a nineteenth-century antiquarian attitude toward history, it became a matter of great concern to construct an accurate list of the men working at Coloma at the time of the gold discovery. This task became more urgent as various pretenders circulated their claims to have taken part. Modern scholars are less likely to become fixated on the issue, but it remains difficult to reconcile the various eyewitness accounts. Both James Brown and Henry Bigler made obvious errors when attempting to set the record straight. The best source appears to be James Marshall's 1857 dictation to James Hutchings. Though Marshall had trouble getting the names of the battalion boys exactly right, the Hutchings dictation was his first recorded attempt to lay the matter to rest. This extract begins with Marshall's departure for Coloma after signing the mill contract with John Sutter.

JAMES W. MARSHALL, "THE DISCOVERY OF GOLD IN CALIFORNIA," *HUTCHINGS ILLUSTRATED CALIFORNIA MAGAZINE*, II (NOVEMBER 1857).

On the third day (I think) afterwards, I set out, with two wagons, and was accompanied by the following persons, employed by the firm of Sutter & Marshall, viz: P. L. Wimmer and family, James [William H.] Barger, Ira Willis [Willes], Sidney Willis [Willes], Alex. Stephens, Wm. Conce [Coons], James Brown, and Ezekiah Persons [Ephraim Pearson, Jr.].

> On our arrival in the Valley we first built the double log cabin, afterwards known as Hastings & Co.'s store. About the last of September, as Capt. Sutter wanted a couple of capable men to construct a dam across the American river at the grist-mill . . . I sent the two Willis', as the most capable; (Wm. Cunce being in feeble health, left about the same time;) and I received Henry Bigler, Israel [Azariah] Smith, Wm. Johnson [Johnston] and [Israel] Evans in return; and shortly afterwards I employed Charles Bennet and Wm. Scott, both carpenters. The above named individuals, with some ten Indians, constituted my whole force.

Taking Marshall's testimony as accurate, we can form a rudimentary demographic profile of the battalion veterans in the Coloma workforce. The first contingent included Ephraim Pearson, Jr., and the brothers Sidney and Ira Willes from Company B, along with Alexander Stephens, his nephew James S. Brown, William H. Barger, and William Coons, all from Company D. Coons and Barger had served as corporals, the others as privates. The second contingent included former privates Henry Bigler, Azariah Smith, and Israel Evans of Company B and William Johnston of Company C. With the departure of Coons and the Willes brothers for Sutter's Fort, the LDS cohort at Coloma numbered four Company B men (Pearson, Bigler, Smith, and Evans), three Company D men (Stephens, Brown, and Barger), and Johnston as the sole veteran of Company C. Apparently all these men were unmarried. At thirty-eight years of age, Barger was senior; Bigler and Brown were five years younger, and the other five ranged in age from nineteen to twenty-three. Except for Barger's duties as a corporal, none had experienced the responsibilities of military command. If the thought had occurred, doubtless these LDS veterans would have counted themselves among the ordinary men of their generation. When setting to work under the direction of James Marshall, also single, thirty-eight years old, and much given to spiritualist religious musings, they had no reason to think they might soon be touched by fame.

James S. Brown: He Was Rather a Notional Man

As Sutter and Marshall had expected, the veterans at Coloma proved to be a hard-working crew. While Henry Bigler gladly took every opportunity to go deer hunting rather than labor with a shovel or ax in his hands, all the men applied themselves to building the mill with energy

JAMES S. BROWN
A Battalion veteran who worked for Sutter and Marshall at Coloma when he was nineteen years old, Brown later served missions in Tahiti and Great Britain. This portrait shows him at about age thirty, before he penned his reminiscences of the Coloma gold discovery. *Courtesy Pioneer Memorial Museum, International Society, Daughters of Utah Pioneers.*

and a decided interest in the progress of the project. Under Marshall's loose guidance, each focused on specific tasks. Brown and Barger were felling timber, dragging it to the mill yard with oxen, and, aided by Native workmen, they whipsawed the logs into rough lumber. Stephens was hewing logs to fit the mill's design, while Johnston assisted Charles Bennett and William Scott in assembling the structural framework for the mill. Bigler and Smith were mostly occupied with digging and blasting boulders from the raceway channel. Peter Wimmer, a non-Mormon who had been at Coloma since the start of the project, had charge of Indians excavating the raceway as the boulders were blasted away.

The only recorded disagreement in that small community came when Elizabeth Jane Wimmer, cooking for the whole camp, complained sharply about the tardiness of the Mormon workers in coming to the table. Apparently none too pleased with her cooking, the battalion boys responded by forming their own mess, as they had been accustomed to do in their military days, and building themselves a separate cabin. We can suppose this arrangement worked out well. It meant less work for Mrs. Wimmer, and it provided the veterans with a greater degree of privacy and distance from potential annoyances by the lively Wimmer children.

Recalling the exact circumstances of the first gold discovery, James Brown explained that James Marshall anticipated the event based on his rudimentary knowledge of minerals and his book-gained belief that quartz rock was "blossom of gold," a strong indicator that gold might be present. Marshall's anticipation, Brown acknowledges, only brought a derisive smile to the faces of the LDS veterans.

JAMES S. BROWN, *CALIFORNIA GOLD*, 10–12.

Now the work commenced in earnest; the cabin was pushed, and a second room put on in true frontier style. Some finished up the cabin, others worked at getting out timbers and preparing for the erection of the mill. The site chosen for the mill was at a point where the river made considerable of a bend, and just in the bank of what appeared to be the old bed of the river, which was lowered to carry the water from the mill.[12]

Sometime between the 15th and 20th of January the mill was started up, and it was found that it had been set too low and the race would not carry off the water, but that it would drown or kill the flutter wheel. To avoid this difficulty several new pieces of timber had to be got out, and as there was found suitable timber within ten or fifteen rods from where the tail race entered the river, all hands were set to work getting out the timber at that place.

It had been customary to hoist the gates of the fore bay when we quit work in the evening, letting the water through the race to wash away the loosened sand and gravel, then close them down early in the morning, and a gang of Digger Indians had been employed to dig and cast out the cable [cobble] rock, such as was not moved by the water.

I, having picked up sufficient of the Indian dialect to direct the Indians in that labor, was set to look after that work, and as all hands were getting out timber so near the race, I had stepped away from them and was with the white men when Mr. Marshall came down to look after the work in general. Having talked a few moments, he stepped away to where the race entered the river. He discovered a bed of rock that had been exposed to view by the water the night before; the rock that was in sight was in the bottom of the race and was from three to six feet wide and fifteen to twenty feet long. It

[12]Marshall's map of the mill site, which is in the collections of the California State Library, is the key document in fixing the location of the mill and the millrace.

appeared to be granite, but so soft that it might be scaled up with a pick, yet too solid to be carried away by the water.

I, being an all-around worker, [was] sometimes called from one thing to another, and the Indians did not require my whole attention. Mr. Marshall called me to come to him. I went, and found him examining the bed rock. He said, "This is a curious rock, I am afraid it will give us trouble," and as he probed it a little further, he said "I believe that it contains minerals of some kind, and I believe there is gold in these hills." Said I to him, "What makes you think so?" He said he had seen the blossom of gold, and I asked what that was, and he told me that it was the white quartz scattered over the hills. I, being no better informed, asked what quartz was. He answered that it was the white flint-like rock that was so plentiful on the hills. I told him that it was flint rock, but he said no, that it was called quartz in some book that he had read, and that it was an indication of gold. He then sent me to the cabin to bring a pan so that we could wash some of the sand and gravel to see what we could find. (It is well to say here that Alexander Stephens, H. W. Bigler, James [W.m H.] Berger, Azariah Smith, W. Johnson and the writer had built a cabin near the site of the mill and were doing our own cooking, and it was to this cabin I was sent.)[13] On my return we washed some of the sand and gravel and also some of the bed rock that we scaled up with a pick. As we had no idea of the appearance of gold in its natural state, our search was unsuccessful. Then he said, "Well, we will hoist the gates and turn in all the water that we can to-night, and tomorrow morning we will shut it off and come down here, and I believe we will find gold or some kind of mineral here."

As he was rather a notional man, I had but little thought of what he said; so [do] not think I even mentioned it to the other men. We each went our way and did not see each other till the next morning. We in the cabin, at a very unusually early hour, heard a pounding at the mill, and someone said "Who is that pounding so early?" Some one of the party looked out and said it was Marshall shutting the gates of the fore bay down. This brought to my mind what he had said the evening before about finding gold, and I said, "Oh, he is going to find a gold mine, this morning."

Nothing but a smile of derision stole over the faces of the parties present. We ate our breakfast and went to work. James Berger and myself went to the whipsaw, and the rest of the men some eight or ten rods off from the mill. I was close to the mill and saw pit, but was also close to the tail race where I could direct the Indians that were there. This was January 24, 1848.

---

[13]Both Bigler and Smith mention the dispute that led the veterans to build their own cabin and free themselves from the tyranny of Jennie Wimmer: see Bigler, ed., *The Gold Discovery Journal of Azariah Smith*, 108; and Gudde, ed., *Bigler's Chronicle of the West*, 84. These accounts do not mention Evans and Pearson as part of the Mormon cabin society.

Henry W. Bigler: His Eye Caught the Glimmer of Something

The events of 24 January 1848 have been told and retold countless times, with the most trustworthy evidence (as John Hittell first demonstrated) coming from Henry Bigler's diary and the journal kept by Azariah Smith. These source documents are terse, sparing in details. Bigler wrote "Monday 24th this day some kind of mettle was ~~discover~~ was found in the tail race ~~that~~ that looks like goald." At an unknown later time he added these words, interlining his diary: "first discovered by James Martial, the Boss of the Mill." Azariah Smith had formed the habit of updating his journal every Sunday. The pertinent entry appears as part of his weekly summary under date of Sunday, January 30th, 1848: "This week Mon. the 24th Mr. Marshall found some pieces of (as we suppose) Gold, and he has gone to the Fort, for the Purpose of finding out."[14]

When he wrote for the *Juvenile Instructor,* Bigler found it appropriate "to give a somewhat detailed account" of the discovery that went beyond his other versions of the story.

Henele Pikale [Henry W. Bigler], "Recollections of the Past," *Juvenile Instructor* 21 (1, 15 December 1886).

In the afternoon of the 24th of January, 1848, gold was found in California, and it may not be out of place to give a somewhat detailed account of how it was discovered.

The names of the men who were at work at the saw mill at the time of the discovery were Alexander Stevens, James S. Brown, James [Wm. H.] Barger, William Johnston, Azariah Smith and myself, of the battalion, James W. Marshall, the superintendent, Peter L. Wemer, Charles Bennett and William Scott, who were not member of the battalion nor members of the Church. By New Year's day we had the dam in and the tail race nearly completed. Mr. Wemer had charge of some tame Indians and was at work in the ditch. Marshall had been in the habit of going down every afternoon to see how they were progressing, for they had struck bed-rock, though it was mostly of rotten granite. Yet the work on the ditch was slow; but this time

[14]The exact page in Bigler's diary, now in the collections of the California Pioneer Society, is conveniently reproduced in facsimile in Paul, ed., *The Discovery of Gold in California,* 27. Azariah Smith's entry is in Bigler, ed., *The Gold Discovery Journal of Azariah Smith,* 108–9.

when he went down to the lower end of the race his eye caught the glimmer of something that lay in a crevice on the base or bed-rock a few inches under the water. He sent a young Indian to Brown, who was at work in the mill yard whip-sawing, to send him a plate. Brown was the top sawyer. He jumped down from the saw-pit remarking:

"I wonder what Marshall wants with a tin plate!"

He walked to our shanty and gave the Indian a plate. Just before we ceased work for the day Marshall came up from the tail race and said he believed he had found a gold mine. Some one merely remarked:

"I reckon there is no such good luck."

Nothing more was said then, but just before going to bed Marshall came in and said he believed he had found a gold mine near the lower end of the race; and it strikes me strongly that he said he had been trying to melt some of the particles but could not. Before leaving he said:

"Brown, I want you and Bigler, in the morning to shut down the head-gate, throw in some saw-dust, rotten leaves and dirt, make it all tight and to-morrow I'll see what there is there."

Accordingly, the next morning we did as directed, after which we went into breakfast. We saw Marshall going down the race after breakfast and before we had scarcely commenced work in the mill yard. I was busy preparing to put a blast of powder into a boulder that lay in the tail race near where the flutter wheel was when Marshall came, carrying in his arms an old white hat, looking very good-natured and pleasant, and said "Boys, I believe I have found a gold mine," at the same time putting his hat on the work bench that stood in the mill yard. In an instant all hands gathered around and sure enough in the top of his hat crown (the crown being knocked in a little) lay the pure metal. How much I know not, perhaps an ounce. The pieces varied in size from small particles up to the size of a grain of wheat; the most, however, being in thin scales. The coarse pieces were in little cubes and other shapes.

Azariah Smith took from his pocket a five-dollar gold piece and we compared the two metals. We could plainly see a difference in the looks which was due to the alloy in the coin.

All were satisfied it was the pure virgin gold, although not one in the crowd has ever seen gold before in its natural state. We were invited by Marshall to accompany him back to the spot where he had found it, where we saw other particles in the seams and crevices of the base rock. The gold fever at once set in. Marshall enjoined it on the mill hands not to say much about the discovery until we ascertained how extensive the mine was. We only spent a short time prospecting, when every man returned to his usual labor; but gold was the chief topic of our conversation.

James W. Marshall: They Were All a Good Deal Excited

Without stating specifically his belief that quartz was an indication of gold, Marshall's dictation leaves no doubt that he recognized the millrace as a likely site for a mineral discovery. He also indicates that no one at the sawmill had any idea that their first discoveries were more than a random fluke of nature.

James W. Marshall,
"Marshall's Own Account of the Gold Discovery,"
The Century Illustrated Monthly Magazine, February 1891.

In digging the foundation of the mill we cut some distance into the soft granite; we opened the forebay and then I left for the fort, giving orders to Mr. Weimar to have a ditch cut through the bar in the rear of the mill, and after quitting work in the evening to raise the gate and let the water run all night, as it would assist us very much in deepening and widening the tail-race.

I returned in a few days, and found everything favorable, all the men being at work in the ditch. When the channel was opened it was my custom every evening to raise the gate and let the water wash out as much sand and gravel through the night as possible; and in the morning, while the men were getting breakfast, I would walk down, and, shutting off the water, look along the race and see what was to be done, so that I might tell Mr. Weimar, who had charge of the Indians, at what particular point to set them to work for the day. As I was the only millwright present, all of my time was employed upon the framework and the machinery.

One morning in January,—it was a clear, cold morning; I shall never forget that morning,—as I was taking my usual walk along the race after shutting off the water, my eye was caught with the glimpse of something shining in the bottom of the ditch. There was about a foot of water running then. I reached my hand down and picked it up; it made my heart thump, for I was certain it was gold. The piece was about half the size and the shape of a pea. Then I saw another piece in the water. After taking it out I sat down and began to think right hard. I thought it was gold, and yet it did not seem to be of the right color: all the gold coin I had seen was of a reddish tinge; this looked more like brass. I recalled to mind all the metals I had ever seen or heard of, but I could find none that resembled this. Suddenly the idea flashed across my mind that it might be iron pyrites. I trembled to think of it! This question could soon be determined. Putting one of the pieces on a hard river stone, I took another and commenced hammering it. It was soft, and didn't break; it therefore must be gold, but largely mixed with some other metal, very likely silver; for pure gold, I thought, would certainly have a brighter color.

When I returned to our cabin for breakfast I showed the two pieces to my men. They were all a good deal excited, and had they not thought that the gold only existed in small quantities they would have abandoned everything and left me to finish my job alone. However, to satisfy them, I told them that as soon as we had the mill finished we would devote a week or two to gold hunting and see what we could make out of it.

While we were working in the race after this discovery we always kept a sharp lookout, and in the course of three or four days we had picked up about three ounces—our work still progressing as lively as ever, for none of us imagined at that time that the whole country was sowed with gold.

The recollections of James Brown add more detail in reconstructing events surrounding the gold discovery. He describes the LDS veterans' efforts to find more gold in the millrace on each of the following mornings, and he mentions as well their decision to put their small discoveries into Marshall's safekeeping. His testimony reinforces Marshall's statement that no one then had any thought "that the whole country was sowed with gold."

JAMES S. BROWN, *CALIFORNIA GOLD*, 12–13.

Just when we had got partly to work, here came Mr. Marshall with his old wool hat in hand, and stopped within six or eight yards of the saw pit, and exclaimed, "Boys, I have got her now." I, being the nearest to him, and having more curiosity than the rest of the men, jumped up from the pit and stepped to him, and looking in his hat discovered say ten or twelve pieces of small scales of what proved to be gold. I picked up the largest piece, worth about fifty cents, and tested it with my teeth, and as it did not give, I held it aloft and exclaimed, "gold, boys, gold!" At that they all dropped their tools and gathered around Mr. Marshall. Now, having made the first test and proclamation of that very important fact, I stepped to the workbench and put it to the second with the hammer. While doing that it occurred to me that while in the Mormon Battalion in Mexico, we came to some timber called manzanita. Our guides and interpreters said that wood was what the Mexicans smelted their gold and silver ores with. It is a hard wood and makes a very hot fire and also lasts a long time. Remembering that we had left a very hot bed of these coals in the fireplace of the cabin, I hurried off and made the third test by placing it upon the point of an old shovel blade, and then inserted it in among the coals, and blew the coals until I was blind for the moment, in trying to burn or melt the particles; and although it was plated almost as thin as a sheet of note paper, the heat did not change its appearance in the least. I remembered hearing that gold could not be burned up, so I arose from this third test confident that it was gold. Then running out to the party who were grouped together, made the second proclamation, saying "gold! gold!"

At this juncture all was excitement, and all repaired to the lower end of the tail race, where we found from three to six inches of water flowing over the bed of rock, in which there were crevices and little pockets, over which the water rippled in the glare of the sunlight as it shone over the mountain peaks. James Berger was the first man to spy a scale of the metal. He stooped to pick it up, but found some difficulty in getting hold of it as his fingers would blur the water, though he finally succeeded. The next man to find a piece was H. W. Bigler; he used his jackknife, getting it on the point of the blade, then, getting his forefinger over it, placed it in his left hand. And as we soon learned how to look for it, as it glittered under the water and in the rays of the sun, we were all rewarded with a few scales. Each put his mite into a small vial that was provided by Marshall, and we made him the custodian. We repeated our visits for three or four mornings to the tail race, each time collecting some more of the precious metal, until we had gathered somewhere between three and four ounces.

Henry W. Bigler: O Boys, It Is the Pure Stuff!

The testing done by young James Brown strongly reinforced Marshall's original belief that he had discovered gold, but none of the men at Coloma could yet be absolutely certain about the nature of the mineral in the millrace. Although they continued to gather flakes and small pieces as opportunity arose, Marshall came to suspect they were dealing with some alloy, perhaps a mixture of gold with silver or another metal. His dictation also indicates that the matter was not yet important enough to disrupt the work schedule at the mill site. Only when he needed to make the day-long trip downstream to Sutter's Fort for some other reason—to replenish their provisions according to Henry Bigler—did he trouble to show John Sutter in secret what he and the others had found. Sutter's excitement and, after various tests, their joint conclusion that the mineral was indeed pure gold led Marshall and Sutter to decide to keep the whole matter quiet until the mill, still their top priority, was completed.

JAMES W. MARSHALL,
"MARSHALL'S OWN ACCOUNT OF THE GOLD DISCOVERY,"
THE CENTURY ILLUSTRATED MONTHLY MAGAZINE (FEBRUARY 1891).

In about a week's time after the discovery I had to take another trip to the fort; and, to gain what information I could respecting the real value of the metal, took all that we had collected with me and showed it to Mr. Sutter, who at once declared it was gold; but thought with me that it was greatly mixed with some other metal. It puzzled us a good deal to hit upon the means of telling the exact quantity of gold contained in the alloy; however, we at last stumbled on an old American cyclopedia, where we saw the specific gravity of all the metals, and rules given to find the quantity of each in a given bulk. After hunting over the whole fort and borrowing from some of the men, we got three dollars and a half in silver, and with a small pair of scales we soon ciphered it out that there was no silver nor copper in the gold, but that it was entirely pure.

This fact being ascertained, we thought it our best policy to keep it as quiet as possible till we should have finished our mill.

Marshall returned to Coloma convinced that he and his work crew had found gold in its pure form. According to Bigler's account, he described to the men all the particulars of his meeting with Sutter and shared with them his renewed excitement about the discovery.

Three or four days afterwards we began to be in want of provisions, for Sutter had neglected to send up supplies. Marshall said he would go down to the fort and see what was the matter and take our gold and have it tested. If I remember right, he was gone four days, and when he returned and was asked what it was, he said: "O boys, it is the pure stuff!" Giving emphasis to his remark by an oath. Continuing, he said: "I and the old Cap. locked ourselves up in a room and were half the day trying it; and the regulars down there wondered what in h–ll was up, and surmised I had found a quicksilver mine; for, you see, there is a quicksilver mine found by a woman down towards Monterey. But we let them sweat. We found it agreed with the encyclopedia and we applied *aqua fortis* and it had nothing to do with it. We then weighed it in water by balancing the dust against silver on a pair of scales held up in the air. We let the scales down and when it came in contact with the water the gold went down and the silver up; and that told the story that it was the pure stuff."[15]

Under the federal government's Preemption Act of 1841, any settler who was head of a family, a single adult male, or a widow, and who was either a U.S. citizen or had filed a declaration of intent to gain citizen-

[15]Pikale [Bigler], "Recollections of the Past," *Juvenile Instructor* 21 (1, 15 December 1886).

ship, could establish a preemption claim to a quarter section (160 acres) of unoccupied public land. To make the preemption claim good, an eligible settler must inhabit and improve the land, put a dwelling on it, and at the proper time pay the General Land Office the government's minimum price of $1.25 an acre. Settlers claiming land not yet offered for sale were required to prove their claim and pay for their land at the opening of the public sale period. But in 1848 federal law did not sanction any settlement or any preemption claims on unsurveyed federal lands.

On 2 February 1848, just about the time Marshall returned to Coloma from Sutter's Fort, the Treaty of Guadalupe Hidalgo made California a possession of the United States. All California lands not subject to prior claim through Spanish or Mexican land grants now became part of the unsurveyed U.S. public domain. Strictly speaking, therefore, in the Coloma area there could be neither any legal settlement nor any legitimate preemption claims until Congress acted to settle preexisting land title issues and then authorized a land survey and sale under U.S. law.[16]

The complexities of federal land law were not well understood at Sutter's Fort. When Marshall returned from meeting Sutter, James Brown remembered his first concern was to establish preemption claims for Sutter and himself at the Coloma site, roughly following the requirements of a law he knew imperfectly. Then, assuming that his actions would be validated in time, he bargained with the LDS workmen to stay on the job while offering them a privilege of mining on condition that they cooperate with him and Sutter by remaining quiet about the discovery of gold in the millrace.

JAMES S. BROWN, *CALIFORNIA GOLD*, 13–14.

> The next move was to step and stake off two quarter sections beginning at the mill, one running down the river and the other up. Then we cut and hauled logs and laid the foundation of a cabin on each of them; one was for Sutter, the other for Marshall. Now, this matter being finished, Mr. Marshall was prepared to dictate terms to us, for every tool and all the provisions in that part of the country belonged to Capt. Sutter and Mr. Marshall, and they had full control, and we were depending on the completion of the

[16]Gates, *History of Public Land Law Development*, 238–40. In 1853, Congress took the first step to resolve the problem by authorizing preemption of unsurveyed lands in California for one year, a privilege that was extended for two additional years in 1854 and applied as well to other specifically designated trans-Mississippi territories and states. The preemption privilege became a general provision of U.S. land law in 1862, at the same time Congress approved the homestead privilege on surveyed public lands. See ibid., 244.

mill for our pay. He said if we would stay by him until the mill was completed and well stocked with logs, he would supply us with provisions and tools and the first right to work on their gold claims.

So we all agreed to his proposition, and also that we would not disclose our secret of the gold discovery until we learned more about it and had made good our claims. Not having the remotest idea of its extent, we pushed the mill as rapidly as possible, for as yet we had not received one dollar's pay for our four months' labor.

HENRY W. BIGLER: BY JOE! IT IS RICH!

After Marshall headed back to Coloma, John Sutter made plans to take his first trip to the sawmill site and see for himself the source of the gold Marshall had shown him. The story of Sutter's visit is best told in Henry Bigler's narrative, which goes far to explain an enduring tradition among Wimmer family descendants that it was the Wimmer children who actually made the first gold discovery. Bigler also summarizes the attempt of Sutter and Marshall to secure land title for themselves under U.S. law by negotiating (and predating) a private treaty with the Yalisumni Nissenan. This purported treaty, called an indenture in the document, allowed the two partners a twenty-year lease on the Coloma area, with rights to farm, cut timber, build a sawmill, and carry out other unspecified operations. By special messenger Sutter sent it to the military governor at Monterey, Col. Richard B. Mason, for approval. As Bigler mentions, Governor Mason very properly refused to sanction this agreement, which was patently illegal under a provision of the U.S. Constitution that reserves treaty-making powers exclusively to the federal government.[17]

HENELE PIKALE [HENRY W. BIGLER], "RECOLLECTIONS OF THE PAST," *JUVENILE INSTRUCTOR* 21 (1, 15 DECEMBER 1886).

[Marshall] said Sutter would be up in a few days and see for himself and to learn how the work on the mill was progressing, etc. A few evenings after this Marshall came into our shanty and said Sutter had arrived and that he was up at the other house.

---

[17]Gudde, ed., *Bigler's Chronicle*, 92–94; Bigler, ed., *The Gold Discovery Journal of Azariah Smith*, 108–10; Sutter to Mason, 22 February 1848, with enclosure dated 1 January 1848, Box 236, George McKinstry Collection, California State Library; Col. Richard B. Mason to John Sutter, 5 March 1848, in Paul, ed., *The California Gold Discovery*, 81–82. Hurtado, *Indian Survival on the California Frontier*, 102–3, takes up the issue of whether Sutter and Marshall were being additionally duplicitous by negotiating with the Yalisumni for rights on land that properly was within the customary jurisdiction of another people, the Kolomas.

"And now boys," said he, "we have all got a little gold. I motion we give Henry [myself] some gold, and in the morning when you shut off the water, let him go down and sprinkle it all over the base rock; but not let on to the old gentleman and it will so excite him that he will set out his bottle and treat, for he always carried his bottle with him."

This caused a hearty laugh; so early next morning we did as Marshall proposed. Just as we finished breakfast we saw the old gentleman coming hobbling along with his cane, Mr. Marshall one side and Mr. Wemer on the other. As they neared our shanty we went out and met them. After shaking hands and passing the common salutations we were all invited to go along and have a general time prospecting for gold; but at this juncture one of Wemer's little boys ran past us down into the tail race, where he picked up nearly every particle and came running back almost out of breath to meet us. He reached out his hand and exclaimed:

"See what I have got!" having in his hand for aught I know, to the value of fifty dollars or more. We did not dare to say a word lest the joke be turned and we lose our expected treat. As soon as the captain saw what the boy had he thrust his cane into the ground, saying:

"By Joe! It is rich!"

All hands went into the race and spent an hour, where the captain had the pleasure of picking up a few particles the boy had overlooked and from that day forward gold was found in the tail race. I advised Marshall to marry the woman who found the quicksilver mine if she was like himself, not married, saying to him:

"If this is what the tail turns out, I wonder what the head will do?"

The next move of Sutter and Marshall was to call in the owners of the land—the Indians—and lease a large tract, ten or twelve miles square, for three years, for which they paid some shirts and handkerchiefs, a few knives, some meat, unbolted flour and peas, giving a promise to pay so much every year until the lease expired. Afterwards they sent Charles Bennett to Monterey to see Governor Mason to have the land secured on mill, pasturage and mineral privileges, as it bore strong indications of containing silver and lead. They said nothing about gold. But his excellency told Mr. Bennett that as California affairs were still unsettled between Mexico and our government, he could do nothing for them.

Without intruding on the preemption claims adjacent to the sawmill that he had helped stake out for Marshall and Sutter, Henry Bigler began prospecting for gold on his own time during the weeks following Sutter's visit. As he explained in the account he sent to Hubert Howe Bancroft, "I seemed to be the only one in the crowd that had gold badly on the brain. . . ."[18] Certainly at that time he was the only one willing to brave the extreme discomforts of wading naked across the river in winter, apparently oblivious to rain and snow, and spend hours crouched at the water's edge picking out with the point of his knife small fragments of mineral from the bedrock.

> On Sunday, February 6th, Barger and I went over the river opposite the saw-mill to look for gold. I found six dollars' worth and Barger about two-thirds as much.
>
> Six days later I borrowed Brown's gun and went down the river to hunt ducks, as was supposed, but in reality to prospect for gold. When about a half mile below the mill I saw on the opposite side of the river bare rocks of the same kind as were in the tail race, looking as though there had been a land slide, leaving the base rock to view. It struck me so forcibly that there might be gold, I pulled off my clothing and waded over, and sure enough I found it, and picked up to the amount of one dollar and fifty cents.
>
> Saying nothing to the boys of my discovery, I returned the next day and found eight dollars' worth, or half an ounce. We had already made a light pair of wooden scales to weigh our gold, using a silver dollar for an ounce, worth sixteen dollars, and a half dollar was equal in value to eight dollars, and so on down in proportion.
>
> On Monday, February 14th, it rained so that we did not work and I spent the forenoon in mending my pants. In the afternoon I went to my gold mine and picked up seven dollars worth, and on visiting it six days later I got seventeen dollars worth, or thereabouts.
>
> On February 22nd the ground was white with snow, which prevented our working at the mill. I therefore set out to hunt for deer, but soon changed my mind and went to my mine. I waded the river as usual, after removing every stitch of my clothing. The river was rising and the water was almost as cold as ice itself. It was also deep and swift, and I was scarcely able to walk. When I got over my feet were very cold. I tried to strike fire, but my hands were so benumbed with cold I could not hold my flint and steel. I tried to catch fire from my gun but [it] being wet I could not fire it, and at last I was forced to dance, jump and run over the rocks until I got warmed up and went to work, having nothing but my pocket knife to work with. Since the morning the weather had moderated and a heavy, misty rain had set in, causing the snow to soon disappear. I searched closely every crevice and finally went down near the water's edge in the sand, where I began to find it more plentifully though in very fine particles, except one piece of pure gold nearly round like a bullet, worth between five and six dollars. I almost felt I had found a fortune on picking it out of the sand.

[18]Gudde, ed., *Bigler's Chronicle*, 99.

> At this spot I sat in one position all bent over for hours, picking up the valuable particles. All at once I could not see, and as I arose to my feet I yelled with pain; I reeled and staggered and it seemed as though my back was broken, but after a few severe groans I was at ease. Night had set in so I made my way up the river over rocks and through brush until arriving at our mill dam, I called for Brown, who brought over the raft (three pine logs pinned together) and took me across.
>
> On reaching the shanty the boys began to quiz me and wanted to know what luck, where my game was, why out so late, and why I did not cross at the dam that morning, etc. They had suspected at last. I called for the scales and found twenty-two and a half dollars' worth of clean gold as the result of my day's hunt. The secret now being out I told them, of course, all about my discovery.
>
> The mill hands came very near deserting their employer and turning their attention to hunting gold, but on second consideration thought it a pity to leave before the mill was finished. Another thing they took into consideration was the uncertainty of doing any better than they were. Fair wages were given them for their labor and their pay was sure, while by leaving they might lose in the long run more than they would make.

Bigler's discoveries were pivotal in the sequence of events that led to the California gold rush. In his recollections, James Brown described Bigler's return from his surreptitious prospecting effort on 22 February and the Mormon veterans' decision to keep to themselves the news of additional discoveries outside the bounds of Sutter's preemption claim. Brown indicates his suspicion that it was William Johnston, the sole Company C veteran at Coloma, who let the story slip to other former battalion members when he visited their camp near Sutter's Fort a few days later.

JAMES S. BROWN, *CALIFORNIA GOLD—AN AUTHENTIC HISTORY OF THE FIRST FIND, WITH THE NAMES OF THOSE INTERESTED IN THE DISCOVERY*, 14–15.

> There came a rainy day, it was too wet to work; H. W. Bigler thought it was a good day to hunt ducks, so he got on an old coat, and was gone all day. When he returned, we said "Where are your ducks?" He said, "Wait awhile, I will show you; I have got them all right." Finally he drew an old cotton handkerchief from his pocket, in a corner of which he had at least half an ounce of gold tied up. For a while all were excited, and he was asked a great many questions like the following: "Did you find it on Sutter's claim along the river?" "How far is it from here?" "All in one place?" "Is there any more?" "How did you get it, you had not pick nor shovel?" "Can you find

> the place again?" He said that he had found it down below Sutter's claim, along the river where the bed rock crops out along the bank, and in little rills that come down the hills to the river, and everywhere that he found the bed rock cropping out. "Then you found it in more than one place?"—"Yes, more than a dozen." It was now proposed that we keep this discovery a secret, as the discovery in the race had been kept. So the mill work was pushed with vigor to completion. But in the meantime Marshall felt it had become his duty to inform his partner of the discovery. Accordingly he wrote a letter stating the facts, and sent me out to find a strange Indian that would take it to Capt. Sutter, fearing that if he sent it by someone that was acquainted with the facts, the secret might leak out. Just about this time W. Johnson found that he had some urgent business below and he must go, and he did; he went to the gristmill and along the camps on that mill race. And somehow or other the bag came untied and our old cat and all the kittens ran out, and to the camps they went, until everybody heard them. But, like all great truths, people were slow to believe the story.[19]

To Henry Bigler, the spread of information about the newer Coloma gold discoveries, outside Sutter's preemption claim, was no mystery. He shared the news with some of his best friends from the battalion in a letter, most likely sent down to Sutter's Fort with either James Marshall or William Johnston, and these friends in turn told others. In response, on the following Sunday evening three men came into camp from the LDS workforce down below. Guiding the other two was Sidney Willes, who had worked at the Coloma site before Bigler's arrival. Marshall, as Bigler explains, was in his usual expansive mood. After talking for some time that Sunday evening with the newcomers, he readily granted their request for mining privileges in the millrace. Their results the following day or two, accompanied no doubt by further discussions with Bigler and the other neophyte miners at Coloma, inspired Willes and his two companions to begin a wider search for gold on their return trip downstream toward Sutter's Fort.

HENELE PIKALE [HENRY W. BIGLER], "RECOLLECTIONS OF THE PAST," *JUVENILE INSTRUCTOR* 21 (1, 15 DECEMBER 1886).

> About this time I wrote a few lines in a confidential way to the boys who were my messmates in the battalion, then at work below on Sutter's flouring mill, that we had found gold up at the saw-mill.
>
> On [Sunday] the 27th of February I piloted the boys to my gold mine but

[19]Brown, *California Gold—An Authentic History of the First Find,* 14.

WILFORD HUDSON
A Battalion veteran and a member of the Holmes-Thompson party, Hudson carved the inscription honoring the Mormon scouts who died at Tragedy Spring. He sat for this photograph many years later, when he had become a substantial family man and Utah citizen. *Courtesy Pioneer Memorial Museum, International Society, Daughters of Utah Pioneers.*

the river had risen so high that the spot where I had found it so plentifully on the 22nd was under water and the river still on the rise. However, among the five of us we found about thirty-three dollars, of which I was the finder of eleven dollars. [William Harrison] Barger declared I could see gold and pick it up where there was none, or in other words, they were not permitted to find it so readily.

That evening three of the battalion boys arrived at our shanty, they having learned through my letter to my messmates that we had found gold, and they had come up to learn the truth for themselves. It happened that Marshall was in and sat till a later hour talking. Being in a fine humor, as he most always was, just before he left for his own quarters on the hill, Hudson asked for the privilege of prospecting in the tail race, which request was readily granted. Accordingly the next morning the three men, Sidney Willis, Wilford Hudson and [Levi] Fifield, went into the tail race when Hudson with his butcher knife picked out a nugget worth nearly six dollars. They tarried with us until the morning of the second of March, when they left to return below. They followed the river and prospected. At a certain place, afterwards known as "Mormon" Island, they found a few particles, but not enough to induce them to remain and hunt for more.

SAMUEL BRANNAN: I HEAR YOU ARE FINDING GOLD

James Brown's account of these events demonstrates that he knew nothing about Bigler's letter to his friends at the gristmill. Brown's narrative, however, describes well the sequence of events after the visiting battalion veterans left Coloma a little more than a month following the original Coloma discovery.

JAMES S. BROWN, *CALIFORNIA GOLD*, 14–15.

Sidney Willis and Wilford Hudson began to feel that they would like a little venison, and with that for an excuse took their guns and set out on foot, having been assured that by following up the river they would come to the sawmill, which they succeeded in doing the first day. I think that it was only thirty-five miles distant. I think that they stayed one day and two nights with us, then after a thorough examination of the bed rock, sand and gravel, and the surroundings, they gathered a few specimens among which was one nugget worth about five dollars, the largest by odds that had been discovered up to that time.

As they passed down on their way home they discovered a small ravine or creek in which there was some of the same kind of bed rock that they had seen at the mill race, and by picking around in the sand and gravel they discovered quite a rich prospect that was just opposite what was afterwards called Mormon Island, about twelve or fifteen miles above the gristmill and about the same distance below the sawmill. Then they returned to the [grist]mill and told their story and showed the specimens to the boys. Then some went to Sutter's Fort, to a little grocery store kept by a Mormon by the name of Smith, that came around by the ship "Brooklyn." The story of the find was told to him and specimens exhibited to him, and he wrote to Saml. Brannan, who was publishing a paper in San Francisco at that time, and from that press the news went forth to the world.

When Willes, Fifield, and Hudson found gold at Mormon Island, they may not have been convinced that the new discovery was rich enough to pay for their hard labor. As Brown related, they came back downriver to the LDS work camp at the gristmill and showed their few flakes and small nuggets to friends. Their story spread at once to Sutter's Fort, where it was circulated at the store being run by Charles C. Smith, who was Samuel Brannan's partner in the enterprise. Hudson and Willes, however, did not go back to work on the gristmill. On Tuesday, 7 March, according to the record in Sutter's New Helvetia Diary, just after they had returned from Coloma "Hudson & S. Willis left for the mountains with the intention to work in a Gold Mine."[20]

Another version of Samuel Brannan's first involvement with the gold discovery excitement appeared in a 1906 *Sacramento Bee* newspaper story, reporting the account of battalion veteran Nathan Hawk, who had been working in San Francisco at the time of the Coloma discovery. Although he was eighty-two years old when he visited the *Bee* office in January 1906, Hawk described in vivid terms the story that he had apparently received from Brannan himself in 1848.

NATHAN HAWK, *THE SACRAMENTO EVENING BEE*, 4 JANUARY 1906.

Early in 1848 a party of us [Mormons] operating on the South Fork of the American River in what is now known as Coloma, discovered gold, and some of it was brought to the Fort by Marshall, who was one of those employed at the mill. When Sam Brannan came up to the Fort a few days later some of the boys told him that the mill boys had discovered gold, and showed him some of the small nuggets. Brannan owned a store right across the road from the main entrance to the Fort. He became very much excited. He took the gold over to the Fort, and marched in to where Sutter was sitting at his desk, and said:

"I hear you are finding gold up where you are building a mill."

Captain Sutter replied: "I know they are finding something that looks like gold, and we have sent some of it to Monterey to have a test made."

"I don't need any test. This is gold, and I will give goods for it out of my store at the rate of $14 per ounce," said Brannan.

Brannan procured all the "dust" he could get, and returned immediately to San Francisco. He there worked off his boom edition of the Star, and secured a number of letters for me to take East, and returned several days later. The [bundle of] papers weighed eighty pounds. They were [each] not much larger than a sheet of foolscap, but just bristled with glowing descriptions of the country which Brannan declared was the long-sought Eden.

A few months later, as described in Chapter Five, Hawk became the first person to deliver news of the California gold discovery to Brigham Young. By that time, however, he would have his own "dust" to show, taken not from Coloma but from the richer, more extensive diggings at Mormon Island, where a growing crowd of battalion veterans and *Brooklyn* Saints—following the lead of Hudson and Willes—were soon working long and hard to amass earthly treasure.

[20]*New Helvetia Diary*, 121. See also Gudde, ed., *Bigler's Chronicle*, 101.

The Coloma discoveries by Marshall and Bigler started the search for gold elsewhere in the streams and streamside gravel of the American River drainage. But the Mormon Island find by Sidney Willes and Wilford Heath Hudson did far more to incite the rush of hopeful gold seekers into the Mother Lode. When they returned to the site in early March, the two men expanded their search, finding gold deposits more extensive and more readily mined by the simplest placer methods than those at Coloma. Henry Bigler, as he relates in this excerpt, only learned about the Mormon Island discovery when he arrived at Sutter's Fort in April to settle his business affairs with Sutter and to attend a general meeting of LDS veterans as they planned their departure for the Salt Lake Valley.

HENELE PIKALE [HENRY W. BIGLER], "RECOLLECTIONS OF THE PAST," *JUVENILE INSTRUCTOR* 21 (1, 15 DECEMBER 1886).

On the 7th of April, Stevens, Brown and myself saddled our horses and set out to go below to have a settlement with Sutter, as the time was now drawing near when we would want to leave for the valleys of the mountains. We also wanted to meet with our brethren at the mill below, so as to be posted concerning the arrangements to be made for the journey up to Salt Lake. We got a late start and traveled only a few miles and camped in the mountains.

The next day we arrived at the mill below, where the boys were at work. Here we learned that Willis and Hudson had gone up the river with some of the boys to examine closely the spot where they had found the few particles of gold at the time they were returning from the saw-mill on the 2nd of March.[21]

JAMES W. MARSHALL: SOON THE WHOLE COUNTRY WAS IN A BUSTLE

As the Coloma sawmill began turning out lumber in March and April, James Marshall found himself besieged by gold seekers, with many attempting to invade the preemption claims he had marked out for

[21]As young George Q. Cannon traveled to California with Henry Bigler in October 1849, Bigler related another account of the gold discovery and subsequent events that Cannon recorded in his journal. After Sutter and Marshall agreed that Marshall had found gold, Cannon related, the LDS mill workers "then kept gathering on but still they did not quit working at the Mill, still thinking there was not much; they heard reports occasionally from people coming from below that they were making $50 & $100 a day below [at Mormon Island] but still did not believe it, until they had to go below & seen it." See Landon, ed., *The Journals of George Q. Cannon, Volume 1: To California in '49*, 17.

Sutter and himself. While he continued to believe that running the sawmill would be more profitable than gold digging, his tactic in dealing with the newcomers began building his reputation as a person with remarkable skill in pointing out good mining sites. As Marshall reveals in this section of his dictation, it was not a matter of skill. No one was more surprised than himself when it turned out that the entire western Sierra Nevada region was full of placer gold.

> But there was a great number of disbanded Mormon soldiers in and about the fort, and when they came to hear of it, why it just spread like wildfire, and soon the whole country was in a bustle. I had scarcely arrived at the mill again till several persons appeared with pans, shovels, and hoes, and those that had not iron picks had wooden ones, all anxious to fall to work and dig up our mill; but this we would not permit. As fast as one party disappeared another would arrive, and sometimes I had the greatest kind of trouble to get rid of them. I sent them all off in different directions, telling them about such and such places, where I was certain there was plenty of gold if they would only take the trouble of looking for it. At that time I never imagined that the gold was so abundant. I told them to go to such and such places, because it appeared that they would dig nowhere but in such places as I pointed out, and I believe such was their confidence in me that they would have dug on the very top of yon mountain if I had told them to do so.[22]

When he summed up the experience forty years later, James Brown was intent on claiming for himself and other Mormon Battalion veterans the credit he believed they deserved for their work that led to the California gold rush. He also pointed out, with long-nurtured resentment, that neither he nor the others had ever been paid for their services by Sutter and Marshall. Yet Brown also attempted to make a fair assessment of the consequences of the gold rush for the two men. While the world had given Sutter and Marshall full credit for the gold discovery, he stated, both had been greatly wronged and their business affairs ruined because the pandemic of gold fever had caused the collapse of all other projects.

JAMES S. BROWN, *CALIFORNIA GOLD*, 16–18.

> To Sutter's capital and enterprise and Marshall's shrewd sagacity has been given the credit of the great gold discovery of California. The facts are that James W. Marshall discovered the first color, and in less than an hour six

[22]Marshall, "Marshall's Own Account of the Gold Discovery," *The Century Illustrated Monthly Magazine* (February 1891), 538.

Mormons found color as well, and in less than six weeks had discovered it in hundreds of places that Mr. Marshall had never seen, the most notable of which was Mormon Island, to where the first rush was made, and from where the news was spread to the uttermost bounds of the everlasting hills and to all the nations of the earth.

As to Sutter's enterprise and capital, he did furnish the Graham flour[23] and mutton, wheat and peas, black coffee and brown sugar, teams and tools, while we, the members of the Mormon Battalion, did do the hard labor that discovered the metal, and it is also true that we were in Sutter's employ at that date, and that we did not get paid for our labor.

I worked 100 days for the firm, and never received one farthing for it. I heard a number of other men say that they never got their pay. Then it was our labor that developed the find, and not theirs, for many of them were never paid; and when we went for settlement we were told by Capt. Sutter that he could not settle with us for his bookkeeper had gone to the mines, and declared that he was a ruined man, that the discovery was his ruin, for it had drawn off his laborers and left everything to go to rack, and he was being robbed.

I do not wish it to be understood that I charge them with being dishonorable, for I do not, but I charge it to the general confusion of the country. I think they were honorable men in a business way. But the facts are they were perfectly overrun with all classes of people, and confused, so that the people took advantage of them, and their business affairs were undermined, and there was a general collapse of every industry and business. The cry was "gold! gold! More gold! away for the gold fields!" Every other enterprise was sacrificed at the sight of gold.

With all due respect to Capt. John A. Sutter and James W. Marshall, to whom the world has given the credit of the great find, I do believe if they had been taken out and shot to death the day of the discovery they would have suffered less, and would have met their Maker just as pure, if not more honored in this world, than to have lived and endured what they did.

As far as I am concerned, I say peace to their remains, for on this earth they have been greatly wronged, if I have read their history correctly. Like a lynching scrape when there is an outburst of the people, it is very difficult to find those who are responsible for the crime; so with the wrongs done these men, it seemed as if the whole country or people picked upon them.

The history that emerges from these documents is a complex narrative about a small, cooperative collection of people, mostly adult males,

[23]Graham flour was an unsifted and coarsely ground wheat flour, valued for its high fiber content. Promoted by Sylvester Graham, a prominent diet reformer of the pre-Civil War era, it was the basic ingredient in the original Graham crackers. What Brown and his companions received from Sutter was an unintentional form of Graham flour produced by the crude threshing and milling processes at Sutter's Fort.

who worked together under James Marshall's direction and who shared the immediate excitement of the first gold discoveries. The testimony of Marshall and the accounts that Bigler and Brown each set down in their mature years, when they had reflected at length on this highlight in their lives, allows us to perceive the origins of the gold rush as part of a unique social process. It involved interchanges among different individuals and groups, each with their own agendas, taking place at an unusual time in northern California's isolated frontier borderland. Among those most directly involved, Bigler, Smith, Brown, and their LDS companions may rightly be recognized as the main movers in transforming Marshall's single discovery into an event of worldwide significance.

We can perceive through these accounts a casebook example of historically contingent events that led to unintended consequences. For Sutter and for Marshall, as Brown remarked, the gold rush was a disaster, destroying their long-term plans and offering no real gains except the fame they would later enjoy. For the Mormon Battalion veterans and the *Brooklyn* Saints, on the other hand, all the consequences were apparently positive. As they began to gather in the riches of Mormon Island and other nearby gold strikes, the whole California experience seemed to them a blessing.

In a much wider sense, the meaning of the northern California gold discovery was admirably summed up in two stanzas of rustic verse penned by Abner Blackburn, a battalion veteran who years later retold in poetry the story of the Saints who marched as soldiers to southern California and then headed for Sutter's Fort.

> To New Helvetia we were bound
> The best place in this land.
> The gold then it was not found,
> It was buried in the sand.
>
> It slumbered quiet under ground,
> And did not know its power,
> And sho[o]k the world around and around,
> From that eventful hour.[24]

[24]"Early Dayes in California," in Bagley, ed., *Frontiersman*, 109–10. This poignant poem, which Blackburn composed about 1901, appears in full in Chapter 9.

Chapter 4

"I Certainly Never Made Money So Fast" Mining at Mormon Island and Natomas Diggings

The Mormon Island diggings, where Sidney Willes and Wilford Hudson found gold and began rudimentary placer mining operations in early April 1848, were on the South Fork of the American River close to its confluence with the Middle Fork, approximately halfway between Sutter's Fort and the Coloma sawmill. By mid-April seven Mormon Battalion veterans were working steadily at the site. Using watertight Indian baskets or tin pans to wash out the gold-bearing gravel, they were making as much as a hundred dollars each day with their crude methods. As Samuel Brannan and others spread the news, according to Azariah Smith, by mid-May "men, women and children, from the Bay and other places in California, were flocking to the gold mine, by the dozens, and by wagon loads."[1]

Nathan Hawk: It Was Mining in a Primitive Way

In late July 1849, a year after most LDS miners had left the immediate area either for Great Salt Lake City or for other mining locations, Lawson Patterson reached the Mormon Island diggings from San Francisco. A non-Mormon who was just beginning his venture into gold mining, Patterson in time became a skilled placer miner and a competent amateur geologist. His description of the diggings offers a particularly clear report on the physical setting of this remarkable California gold district,

[1]Bigler, ed., *The Gold Discovery Journal of Azariah Smith,* 115.

which was permanently flooded by the waters of Folsom Lake in the 1950s.

> This place is on the bank of the American river at the point where the foot hills of the Sierra Nevada become merged into the plains of Sacramento. It is not, in fact, an island, but a bar, the river having made a partial channel around it in time of high water; the deposits of gravel, boulders, &c., still show evidence of its connection with the banks. . . . I commenced my career as a miner here, and it was here that I first received impressions, in relation to the origin of the deposit found upon the bar. My idea was, and now is that the gold was not washed there by the operation of the river, or if so, in a very slight degree; because, where the bar was fourteen feet deep, the deposits of dirt, gravel, &c. were discolored, of an iron-rust color, with a reddish tinge in places, cemented and adhering firmly to the bed-rock. This appearance ran through the whole mass from top to bottom. In other parts, more shallow, the deposit showed a pale color, as though it had been under water. The gold found here was mostly fine. It pervaded the whole deposit, but paid best upon the bed-rock.[2]

In the latter part of May 1848 two other battalion veterans, Benjamin Hawkins and Marcus Shepherd, discovered another extremely rich placer a short distance downstream and across the river, at a location the Saints called Natomas or the Natomi mines, subsequently known as Negro Bar. Newcomers attracted to the area by the reputation of Mormon Island found the nearby Natomas diggings less crowded and equally productive.

In May John Sutter and James Marshall were still hoping to avoid publicity so they could monopolize the search for gold at Coloma, located on land to which they had no valid claim. The gold deposits there, however, were less rich and abundant than at Mormon Island and Natomas, where the LDS veterans gave the gold mining industry in western America its start.

Among the first LDS newcomers to reach Mormon Island was Nathan Hawk, another veteran of battalion Company B who, in early April 1848, was leading a small group of men on their way east with a private mail express and a special edition of Sam Brannan's newspaper, *The California Star*. This "boom edition" as Hawk called it, contained glowing stories about California's resources including its gold and quicksilver, all

---

[2]Patterson, *Twelve Years in the Mines of California*, 35–46.

meant to attract emigration to northern California.[3] Included in the letters being carried by Hawk were three from Brannan addressed to Brigham Young and another to the church leadership from battalion veteran James Ferguson, all reporting on the dissension and demoralization that had become epidemic among the *Brooklyn* Saints.[4]

Accompanied by Brannan, Hawk and seven or eight companions left San Francisco on 3 or 4 April, arriving at New Helvetia in Sutter's launch on 7 April. Brannan stayed at Sutter's Fort, but Hawk and the others proceeded to Mormon Island, where they remained a few days to try their hands at mining before departing eastward by the Donner Pass–Truckee River route. While traveling about the region sixty years later, Hawk stopped at the editorial offices of the *Sacramento Bee,* where a reporter interviewed him. In this newspaper account of his long-ago experiences in California, he provided a brief description of the Saints' elementary placer-mining techniques at the beginning of the California gold rush.

NATHAN HAWK, *THE SACRAMENTO EVENING BEE,* 4 JANUARY 1906.

I told you awhile ago that I mined a few days at Mormon Island, and it was the 'dust' that I took out of there that I carried East with me. Well, it was mining in a primitive way. We had no pans, no lumber to make rockers, and so we used Indian baskets to pan with. The Indians made a watertight willow basket that answered the place of a pan. When we would get panned down to the black sand we would dump the gold on a flour sack which we had spread out upon the grass.

In order to weigh our gold, we made a balance with two chips, a stick and a string. We imitated the scales held by Jus[t]ice. We placed the gold on one chip and [a] Mexican or Spanish gold coin on the other until they balanced; in that way we could pretty closely estimate the value of our day's work, which averaged about $20 to the man.

JAMES S. BROWN: THE SEARCH FOR GOLD WAS COMMENCED IN EARNEST

The recollections of James S. Brown reveal that experimentation characterized the earliest days of placer mining in northern California. Few,

[3]For a fuller treatment of this "express" expedition, see Ricketts, *The California Star Express,* published in pamphlet form by the Sacramento County Historical Society. As recounted in Chapter 6, Hawk brought Brigham Young the first news of the discoveries in northern California.

[4]This correspondence is reprinted in Bagley, ed., *Scoundrel's Tale,* 242–54.

if any, of the LDS veterans in northern California had mining experience. One possible exception was Alexander Stephens, who had perhaps spent time in western Georgia's placer mining districts before coming to California with the Mormon Battalion. Brown credits Stephens with the introduction of ground sluicing and the rocker, a simple-to-make device that greatly improved the efficiency of placer operations. Both these placer-mining methods would have been familiar to anyone who had been in the Georgia gold fields.

JAMES S. BROWN, *CALIFORNIA GOLD*, 15–16.

Having explained briefly the find and proclamation [at Coloma], we will return to the mill race, while from 100 to 150 Mormons flocked to Mormon Island, and then people from every part of the States followed, and the search for gold was commenced in earnest. With jack, butcher, and table knives the search was made in the crevices, after stripping the soil from the bed rock with pick and shovel. Next, we conceived the idea of washing the sand and small gravel in tin pans, but these were scarce and hard to get hold of. Alexander Stephens dug out a trough, leaving the bottom round like a log. Filling that with sand and gravel that we scraped off the bed rock, he would shake it, having arranged it so as to pour or run water in on the gravel; finally he commenced to rock the trough, which led to the idea of a rocker, which caused the gold to settle at the bottom, and he had it arranged on an incline so that it would naturally not only work to the bottom, but to the lower end of the trough, then at short intervals he would turn it into a tub of water, and at night it would be cleaned and weighed on a pair of wooden scales that he also made, using silver coins for weights, counting the silver dollar equal to one ounce of gold. The rocker above mentioned led to the renowned gold rocker; I am under the impression that Stephens did make the first rocker ever used in California. We made buckskin pouches or wallets to carry the gold in; it was not dust, nor yet nuggets, but small scales.

The next and last process that we used in gathering was to spread a sheet on the sand beach of the river, placing some big rocks on the corners and sides to keep it well stretched, then fill the rich dirt on the upper edge, then throw water on to wash the dirt down in the river, leaving the gold on the sheet, occasionally taking up the sheet and dipping it in a tub of water, thus washing the gold off the sheet into the tub, and at night clean up our day's work, averaging from $12 to $15 per hand. Our best paying dirt was carried on our shoulders from Dry Gulch all the way from fifteen to sixty rods, to where we could find water to wash it with.

David Campbell: A Hand-Saw, Draw-Knife, Hatchet, Pick and Shovel

Not all the early miners at Mormon Island, as David Campbell relates, were Mormons. Campbell had come to California in 1846, traveling overland from Missouri by wagon train two weeks ahead of the Donner party. In early 1848 he was living at San José, where he had recently begun building a sawmill, when he and his friends chanced to learn about the American River discoveries. They immediately dropped all else to investigate these reports. His reminiscences, written when Campbell was seventy-five-years-old and still living in the San José area, tell of their journey to Mormon Island, their brief mining experience there, and their departure and later return to the still newer diggings at the Placerville site. Of special interest is Campbell's description of the crude rocker he and his friends put together to work their Mormon Island claim.

David Campbell, "Pioneer of 1846: Sketch of Hardships Endured by Those Who Crossed the Plains in '46."
Porterville Recorder, 11, 12, and 13 August 1910.

In 1848 the first gold was discovered by Mr. Marshall where Captain Sutter was building a saw mill. They did not know whether it was gold or not, but thought it was something very valuable, so they sent a man in poste haste down to Monterey with it to Governor Mason to find out what it was. He told him it was gold, and he showed the sample in San Jose as he passed through and said the ground was full of it. That started the rush and the news flew fast all over the world. The San Joaquin River was so high we could not get within three miles of it, so we had to go by way of Benicia and cross the Bay on an old flat boat which was worked by oars. This boat could make but one trip a day on account of the tide being up and down, so those wishing to cross had to wait for their turn. When I reached there I was told I would have to wait three weeks before my turn would come. There were two other men with me and they were old sea captains and understood all about a boat, so we got a skiff there and put our saddles and camping outfit in the skiff, then tied two of our horses to it and the other two we held close to the boat and one of us rowed the boat across the Bay, a distance of three-quarters of a mile. We kept the horses heads out of the water and they floated over all right. This was the first time horses were ever swam across the Bay at Benecia. We then started for the Fort, crossing the Sacramento on a boat, and went to Morman Island on the American River. We found about fifty men at work with rockers.

We had with us a hand-saw, draw-knife, hatchet, pick and shovel; this was our complete outfit. We got a hollow log, cut it off about four feet long and made us a rocker and went to work on the island. One of the men did the rocking, another threw in the gravel and the third man poured in water to wash the gravel. In this way we made one and a third ounces each day as long as we stayed in the mines. The weather got so hot we concluded we would go back to San Jose and complete the saw mill I was building when the mining fever broke out. This was the first saw mill built in Santa Clara County. When we had finished the mill we went back to the mines. The first of September we went to the place which is now called Placerville. The gold here was very coarse. The only tools we used in getting it out were a pick, spoon, butcher knife and pan. I stayed there three weeks and averaged fifty dollars per day for that time.

One of our party was taken sick with the mountain fever, so I had to put him into a wagon and take him to San Jose, and when I got there I concluded to go to work in my saw mill instead of going back to the mines. I commenced making lumber and sold it at $50.00 per thousand. I kept raising on the price, and in 1849 it went up to $300.00 per thousand at the mill and everything else was high in proportion. Flour sold at $30.00 per barrel. In 1849 everything was booming in San Jose.

John Borrowman: Elder Brannan Called a Meeting and Informed Us of a Gold Mine

Mormon Island also attracted Samuel Brannan, who had spent the winter attempting to direct the LDS community in San Francisco while still locked in quarrels with many of the Saints. He had made a short visit to Sutter's Fort in early April, when the battalion boys told him about the diggings at Mormon Island, but not until the fourth of May did Brannan return and tour the site. At once he became convinced, as he later said, "there was more gold [here] than all the people of California could take out in five years."[5]

When he left the placers, Brannan took with him a gold sample in a quinine bottle. He stopped briefly to arrange construction of a warehouse and store at Sutter's embarcadero along the Sacramento river front that would become the site of Sacramento City. Then he started hastily

[5]Ibid., 265.

toward San Francisco on horseback, rather than waiting for a boat to carry him downstream through the Delta more comfortably.

As recalled years later by battalion veteran Benjamin Hawkins, and as Henry Bigler also reported, Brannan arrived in the Bay city on 10 May and acted out the scene that, after Marshall's first discovery, has become the most famous episode of the beginning California gold rush. He stepped off the ferry onto the beach, "took his hat off and swung it, shouting aloud that gold was found."[6] Two weeks earlier Edward Kemble, who now edited the *California Star* for publisher Samuel Brannan, had visited Coloma and reported that the rumors of rich gold deposits were a hoax, a humbug. But Brannan's latest report, based on his experience at Mormon Island, convinced San Francisco and soon the world that the riches were real; and so, powered by the enthusiasm of this Mormon entrepreneur, the great migration to northern California's gold fields began.

As we learn from John Borrowman, Brannan gave his flock in San Francisco vigorous encouragement to rush to the gold diggings. Still the chief figure among California's Latter-day Saints, he gathered the brethren together and urged them, one and all, to hurry to the mines and secure their share of the gold bonanza. This evening meeting proved to be the last LDS church gathering that Sam Brannan would ever attend.

At the time Borrowman was still working for William Glover, digging wells and a house foundation, and hiring out on other jobs for two dollars a day. Thirty-two years old, a Scottish-born convert who carefully kept a daily journal of his military experience and his time in California, Borrowman was not pleased with his situation in San Francisco. He was finding it difficult to get the pay he deserved for some of his work. Now Brannan's report about the placer diggings, along with the evidence of gold that he brought from Mormon Island, confirmed the news Borrowman most likely had received from his friend Henry Bigler. It convinced the young Scot to leave at once for the gold country.

JOHN BORROWMAN, JOURNAL, LDS ARCHIVES.

Wednesday, [May] 10th. I went to Origin Morey [Mowry] and requested him to pay me 8 dollars for 4 days work I done for him, the usual wages in this town for labourers, but he refused to pay me more than $1 a day saying that was sailors wages and as I had worked on a launch for him he would not

---

[6]Gudde, ed., *Bigler's Chronicles of the West,* 111; Bancroft, *History of California,* 6:56; and Bagley, ed., *Scoundrel's Tale,* 264–67.

pay any more and finally we agreed to leave it to the decision of two men but he did not appear to hear the decision. This evening Elder Brannan called a meeting and informed us of a gold mine being found by Brother Willis and gave his advice for all to go and work in it.

Thursday, 11th. This day I bought 3 yds of canvas to make a pack, also 1 yd of silk green for a particular purpose also a blank book and two sail needles at the following prices: canvas 50¢ per yd. Silk $1 book 50¢ needles 1 real for two. This evening Brothers Glover and Sirrine gave in their decision in my favor and Brother Morey agreed to settle with me.

Friday, 12th. Made my pack and prepared to start for the gold mines. This evening Brother Morey came to me and said that he was not satisfied with the decision on our difference as he was not present when it was given in and wished the case to be reconsidered which I consent to but as we could not find Brother Glover it was laid over till another time.

Saturday, 13th. This morning I took passage on board Morey's launch for Sutter's Fort and at 2 P.M. we sailed from San Francisco and came too at Marshs landing distance about 100 miles.

Sunday, 14th. At 8 we were under way. Today we got out of our course and in consequence of this we had to run through a very crooked arm of the Sacramento and was much detained with head-winds.

Monday, 15th. Had baffleing winds and had to run with oars to get along.

Tuesday, 16th. Had fair winds but light and arrived at Sutters about noon. In the afternoon we hired a team to take our baggage to the mountains where the gold mines is.

Addison Pratt: Strong Accusations Against Brannan

The general migration of the Saints from San Francisco to Mormon Island was helped along by the growing acrimony among the *Brooklyn* Saints that centered on Brannan's self-interested conduct of church affairs and high-handed management of the colonists' joint resources. Addison Pratt, who had arrived in San Francisco from a pioneer missionary assignment in the Hawaiian Islands, described the controversy and his decision to head for the diggings on his way east to Great Salt Lake City.

Ellsworth, ed., *The Journals of Addison Pratt*, 336.

With the Battalion boys and those that had come in the *Brooklyn*, there was enough at Francisco to form a large branch. A meeting of the members of the church was called by Br. Brannan, when he proposed that a branch of the church should be organized and that I should preside. To my presiding I object to strongly, but not withstanding all that, they voted me in, and I could not get rid of acting.

There were strong accusations against Brannan, by the *Brooklyn* company, that he had devised ways and means whereby he had swindled them out of their property with a pretence that he was collecting for the church. But there were two parties, one for Brannan, and the other against him, and the Battalion boys gradually began to be drawn in either on one side or the other, and party feelings were fast growing, in spite of my best efforts to keep it down. Many complaints were privately brought to me from both sides and as I made it a rule to take up in behalf of the absent party in hopes of allaying the feeling of the aggrieved ones by vindicating the cause of the absent and thereby cause a reconciliation of feeling, but it had not the desired effect, for I found in process of time that the plaintive naturally supposed I was siding against him, and by this means got both parties to think that I was against them.

And I had learned from Br. Brannan's moves, that he was calculating that I would rule the branch and that he would rule me, but when he found that I had some notions of my own, that I wish'd to have consulted also, I became verry obnoxious to him. But the time was drawing nigh that I was to start for Salt Lake, and I saw no prospect of there being any better state of things in the branch. I called a meeting of it, and presented my resignation of the presidency, and Br. [Seth S.] Lincoln was nominated I think by Br. Brannan, and chosen president of the branch.

Soon after I started with a company of gold diggers in one of the first launches that went from Francisco to the mines. We went to a place on the American Fork, known as Mormon Island.

William Glover:
All Agreed to Protect Each Other's Claims

William Glover was not long in following Addison Pratt and John Borrowman to Mormon Island. A man of property who had been Samuel Brannan's principal assistant in church and business affairs in San Francisco, Glover arrived at the diggings with his family just as a crowd of newcomers began raising questions about mining location rights. Lacking any certain precedent, those on the spot discussed the issues and adopted a simple system apparently modeled on Hispanic placer-mining practice. Each miner would be able to claim and hold a mining location eighteen feet wide, Glover relates. The claim presumably extended from the water's edge at a right angle back to the high ground. As to a means for establishing and recording these claims and enforcing their observance, neither Glover nor anyone else who took part in the early days of mining at Mormon Island left a documentary record.

WILLIAM GLOVER, THE MORMONS IN CALIFORNIA, BANCROFT LIBRARY.

The next Spring was 1848 when the gold was discovered by Hudson and Willis, two of the brethren of the Mormon Battalion. Brannan called a meeting of those who remained in San Francisco and told us of the discovery of the gold. It was the last meeting he called to my knowledge. A good many of us went to what is called the Mormon Island to dig gold. Myself and family were among the first on the ground. In a few days there was a meeting called of all those that had gathered there. I was called upon to give my opinion of how much land each man should have for a claim across the Island. It was decided that each man should have eighteen feet wide. All agreed to protect each other's claims, that no stranger could impose on us. At this time people rushed to the gold mines in such numbers that provisions became scarce. Flour sold for a dollar a pound and everything else in proportion. Clothing was not to be had, hardly, at any price. These times lasted a short time. Ships began to pour in from Chila [Chile] and Origon [Oregon] and other places loaded with provisions, groceries, clothing and merchandize till everything was down again quite reasonable. With the influx of population of all grades, nationalities, and coler came the increase of wickedness, stealing, robbing, murdering, and all manner of evil. It so often occurred that someone was robbed and their bodies thrown in the river that it became a common phrase of 'another man for breakfast.' Myself and some others thinking it was not a very safe place for wives and children, returned to San Francisco where we spent the fall and Winter.

FRANCIS A. HAMMOND: A WILD, MAD RUSH TO GET TO THE MINES

Francis Asbury Hammond was another San Francisco Saint who immediately got caught up in the scramble to reach Mormon Island. Although his recollections contain a garbled version of the origins of the gold rush reflecting his third-hand knowledge of events, he was quite accurate in describing the impact of Sam Brannan's enthusiastic promotion of the opportunities that awaited the first arrivals in the mining region.

FRANCES HAMMOND
This portrait shows the former sailor, who converted to the LDS faith in San Francisco and then endured a great trial of his beliefs before leaving the gold country. This photograph portrays Hammond many years later, after his service as a Mormon missionary and colonizer. *Courtesy Pioneer Memorial Museum, International Society, Daughters of Utah Pioneers.*

Having been left in the Hawaiian Islands after being injured while sailing aboard a whaling vessel, Hammond was now a recent convert to Mormonism. He was also a very practical businessman. His first reaction after learning about the Mormon Island placer discovery was to depart for the New Almaden quicksilver mines near San José to purchase a large supply of mercury, an element essential to many placer mining operations, which he packed to the diggings. Although, as he recalled, this enterprise proved unprofitable, his other efforts in mining and trading—especially trading with Native peoples who had started digging for gold on their own—brought Hammond the financial success he thought necessary before he could set out for the LDS colony in the Great Basin.

FRANCIS ASBURY HAMMOND,
"IN EARLY DAYS: MY INTRODUCTION TO MORMONISM,"
PUBLISHED SERIALLY IN *THE JUVENILE INSTRUCTOR*, JUNE–SEPTEMBER 1894.

In the forepart of May, 1848, if my memory is not at fault, some of the members of the Mormon Battalion, while engaged in digging out a tail race for Captain Sutter's saw mill, discovered some, to them, queer looking substance, mixed among the sand and gravel, which they were removing. A few small specimens were gathered up and sent down to San Francisco to President S. Brannan, stating in the letter, as I have the story, that "if this is good for anything there is lots of it here." Brothers Hudson and Willis and one other brother were considered during those early days as the real discoverers. This discovery caused one of the greatest revolutions or movements this generation has witnessed. Brannan obtained the credit of a firm doing business in San Francisco, and bought a big load of mixed cargo, and chartered every launch or small sloop and schooner then plying between San Francisco and Sutter's fort, some 150 miles up the Sacramento River, for twenty days, and commenced sending forward all kinds of goods to meet the great demand soon to follow, and at the expiration of his charters (twenty days) he was comparatively a rich man.

Now commenced one of the wildest scenes I ever witnessed. Everything seemed turned into the utmost confusion. All old lines of order were completely broken up, and men, and women too, became almost beside themselves, and a wild, mad rush to get to the mines seized everybody. Captains and crews deserted their ships moored in the bay, and fled helter and skelter for the region of gold. Lawyers left their offices, priests left their flocks, merchants and clerks left their business, servants and laborers left their employers, and San Francisco become almost depopulated, as it were, in a day. Commodities of all kinds immediately took a fabulous rise. You could not get service of the most ordinary kind for less than five dollars a day, and wages soon ran up to $16 or an ounce of gold dust a day.

The reader, no doubt, would like to know how this gold craze affected the writer. I must confess I too caught the fever, sold out my caboose at what would seem a fabulous price,[7] and mounted one of [my] mustang ponies and set out in haste for Santa Cruse Mountain, some sixty miles or more south of San Francisco, for the purpose of obtaining some quicksilver.[8]

There was a mine there where this article was produced. I had heard that quicksilver was necessary in the gold mines to gather the fine gold with, so

---

[7]Hammond's "caboose" was a former ship's galley that he had purchased and brought ashore to use as his store. A term of Dutch origin, caboose referred to shipboard galleys long before the term acquired a new meaning with the appearance of cooking and living cars for railroad crews.

[8]The New Almaden Quicksilver Mine, the oldest quicksilver mine in the U.S., is twelve miles from San José in the Capitancillo Hills. The Ohlones tribe used the "mahetka" rocks for decorations, but Secundino Robles found cinnabar deposits there in 1824. Mexican Army Capt. Andres Castillero filed a mining claim in November 1845 and by December had discovered quicksilver. Castillero processed some 3,000 pounds of ore by August 1846, but lacking capital and having a war to fight, he and his partners sold the mine to the firm of English speculator Alexander Forbes. It became the single most valuable mine in California history, producing some 76 million pounds of mercury before it closed in 1975. By that time the location had become a toxic waste disaster, but in February 2000 the California Environmental Protection Agency certified remedial efforts at the site, which is now a county park. See the California Department of Parks and Recreation study *Five Views: An Ethnic History Site Survey for California*, available online at http://www.cr.nps.gov/history/online_books/5views/5views5h87.htm.

I thought I would go well equipped, and make a good pile in short order. On my journey when I rested or slept I would hold fast my lariat or rope attached to my horse, for fear he would be stolen, as men in the mad rush to the mines did not scruple to seize hold of anything loose that would aid them on their journey to the land of gold.

I found the quicksilver mine situated high up on the mountain, a very rough, zig-zag road leading up to it. The metal was obtained by washing the ore in great iron pots, with heavy iron covers, oval in shape, nearly like the pot itself, under which a fire is kept, sufficient to melt out the silver, which was received into another large cast-iron pot. I purchased twenty-five pounds of quicksilver, at $2 per pound, put it into a couple of double thick glass junk bottles, and then wrapped my leggins round them, and securely hitched one on each side of the loggerhead of my saddle, as only a sailor knows how to do, and returned to San Francisco.

This journey occupied some four days. On my return I set out fixing up a pack train for the mines, and in a short time I was on the road with an outfit such as I could make up in haste, consisting of flour, bacon, tea, coffee, sugar, rice and such things as could be obtained at that time in the market. A dollar a pound for nearly everything in the way of provisions was the price. Of mining tools, I took pick-ax, shovel and some large milk pans to wash gold with. In about ten days from the date of the news of the discovery, I arrived with my outfit at Mormon Island, as it was called, situated some twenty-five miles above Sutter's Fort. Here the principal placer digging was being done at this date, as I recollect, but the whole country was full of prospectors for miles and miles around, so fast had people gathered. Mexicans in large numbers had left their ranches with crops ready for harvesting, and gathered here for the purpose of getting rich suddenly.

In company with two parties by the name of Blanchard and Goss, who were fellow passengers with me from the Islands, I took up a small claim on Mormon Island—I don't think it was over twenty-four feet square. Here I labored some thirty days washing out the gold, which was quite coarse, frequently finding nuggets worth $10 to $20; but the general dust was smaller than ordinary grains of wheat. As we would wash, we would lay the gold out on flat rocks on buckskin or cotton cloth in the sun to dry. At evening we would clean by blowing out everything we could with our breath and place it in buckskin sacks. We also did considerable trading with the Indians. They would bring in some fine specimens which they learned to find by "dry digging" as it was called. Beads, salt and sugar were the principal articles they would barter for of this early day. For these articles the poor Indian was made to pay enormous prices.

My quicksilver I took so much pains to obtain did me no good, it was not required in mining this kind of gold. People soon began to come from different parts. The news flew on the wings of the wind, and in thirty days I should judge there were some ten thousand people gathered up and down the banks of those rivers, embracing many nationalities. Stores, saloons, and all that follow in the wake of mining camps sprang up as by magic.

In the latter part of June, as near as I can remember, I quit mining and divided the results with my partners. I certainly never made money so fast as during the time I spent digging gold and trading with the Indians those few days. It was not uncommon for us to clean up from one day's work $250 to $300.

John Borrowman: Arranging Our Labour in the Mines

John Borrowman did not enjoy such splendid success at Mormon Island as Francis Hammond, but his journal offers the best record we have from any 1848 miner about day-to-day life in the diggings. Although devoid of dramatic incident, it tells the story of a hard-working man in astounding circumstances. After digging wells and house foundations for two dollars a day in San Francisco, Borrowman was making returns from the placers that were almost beyond his belief. Through his journal the reader can trace the young veteran's rising expectations. Following the enforced frugalities of his San Francisco life, he quickly and willingly adapted to the high prices for what he came to believe necessary.

Borrowman also describes a different claims system than the one sketched much later in William Glover's memoir. The battalion veterans decided on 20 April to form companies of five men each, he recorded, with each company to have an area of "5 yards square"—presumably a tract of five yards by five yards—which provides our first account of the earliest stage in organizing mining rights at Mormon Island. The plan described by Glover, with each miner claiming eighteen feet of river frontage, appears to have been a later modification based on the Hispanic system of mining claims, adopted as hundreds arrived expecting equal opportunities to dig for gold.

John Borrowman, Journal, LDS Archives..

Wednesday, 17th [May 1848]. Started for the mines and got there about sunset and found Brother Willis weighing the gold that had been dug today and there was one man had 128 dollars.

Thursday, 18th. Wrote a letter to Charles Burr this morning and then went to digging gold and together with Brother [William] Wood dug 17 dollars worth.[9]

Friday, 19th. Worked at washing gold and made 22 dollars but as Brannan & Co. requires thirty per cent my share only came to $8 as Brother Wood and I are in company.

Saturday, 20th. Worked at washing gold and made $17.75.

Sunday, 20th. Went out and shot a quail as I had no meat to eat, then returned and went to a meeting for the purpose of arranging our labour in the mines and it was agreed to form companies 5 in a company to have 5 yards square to work in and I am in Brother [James] Slys company.

Monday, 22nd. Worked and made $13.

Tuesday, 23rd. Assisted in making a raft to cross the river but failed in getting across and went to work in the afternoon and made $5.

Wednesday, 24th. Worked and made about $30.

Thursday, 25th [May 1848]. Worked and made about $30.

Friday, 26th. Worked and made about $30.

Saturday, 27th. Worked and made about $40. This day I bought a watch from Jesse Martin for 2 oz. of gold.

Sunday, 28th. Rested in camp.

Monday, 29th. Worked and made about $50.

Tuesday, 30th. It rained in the forenoon and I went prospecting. This day I have said against paying rent as I consider it an imposition. This afternoon I worked and made $25 of gold.

Wednesday, 31st. Went to hunting a new mine but did not find any. This evening I feel rather unwell in consequence of a cold I received last night.

Thursday, June 1st., 1848. Worked and made $90.

Friday, 2nd. Worked and made $40. This day I bought a belt and sheath for my knife, price $1.25.

Saturday, 3rd. Worked and made $28.

Sunday, 4th. Rested in camp.

Monday, 5th. Worked at digging trying to find the granite on which the gold is generally found but was finally compelled to quit because of the rising of the water.

Tuesday, 6th. Worked and made $32.

Wednesday, 7th. Worked and made $25.

Thursday, 8th. Worked and made $38. This day I bought a mare for $15.

Friday, 9th. Worked and made $21. This evening I bought a bridle for $4.

Saturday, 10th. Rested in camp.

Sunday, 11th. Rested in camp.

Monday, 12th. Worked and made $50.

---

[9]Charles Burr had one son die and another son born on the *Brooklyn*'s voyage to California. William Wood, a native of England, had served in the battalion in Company C. Both men settled in Utah.

Tuesday, 13th. Worked and made $21.

Wednesday, 14th. Made arrangements with Brother Hammond to get my fitout at San Francisco and weighed out $200 to him for that purpose. I also paid $40 for a rifle. In the afternoon I worked and made $23.

Thursday, 15th. Worked and made $40.

Friday, 16th. Worked and made $40.

Saturday, 17th. Worked and made $26.

Sunday, 18th. Rested in camp.

Monday, 19th. Worked and made $28. This day I bought a frying pan for $8 and a sauce pan for $4.37½.

Tuesday, 20th. Worked and made $40.

Wednesday, 21st. Worked and made $30.

Thursday, 22nd. Went in search of a waggon to buy but did not find one to suit me.

Friday, 23rd. Went again to hunt for a waggon and found one to please me but could not settle for it as the owner was not at home.

Saturday, 24th. Worked and made $50.

Sunday, 25th. Felt unwell and rested in camp. This day I bought a chain for $20.

Monday, 26th. Went to try to buy a yoke of oxen but could not find any. In the evening worked a little and made $5.

Tuesday, 27th. Worked and made $26.

Wednesday, 28th. Worked and made $36.

Thursday, 29th. Worked and made $32.

Friday, 30th. Worked and made $8.

Saturday, July 1st, 1848. I went out to a dry creek 12 miles to prospect for gold and found it but could not find water convenient to wash it in.

Sunday, 2nd. This day I paid Brother Hammond $127 for a waggon he bought for himself, Brother Wood and myself and for freight and for doing business for me at the bay.

Monday, 3rd. Attended to settling business with Brother Hammond and preparing to start for the camp in the mountains.

Tuesday, 4th. Went up the river to try to buy two yoke of oxen but could not find them, then washed about $6 of gold and returned and bought 2 yoke of oxen in company with Brothers Hammond and Wood for $170.

Addison Pratt: Enough of Brannan's Tricks

In early July, while John Borrowman was trying to find a yoke of oxen for sale, Col. Richard Mason, California's military governor, arrived at the Mormon Island diggings on a tour of inspection. He saw two or three hundred men hard at work under an intensely hot sun, living in canvas tents and brush arbors scattered thickly about the hillsides. They were washing gold, Mason reported, "some with tin pans, some with close-woven Indian baskets, but the greater part had a rude machine known as a cradle." Four men with a cradle, he stated, were averaging a hundred dollars a day. The gold they gathered, Mason added, was "in fine bright scales."[10]

Colonel Mason's adjutant, Lt. William Tecumseh Sherman, accompanied the governor on this tour. According to Sherman's recollections, Sam Brannan was also on the scene at Mormon Island, collecting tithes for the church. Sherman recalled that one of the Saints asked the governor whether Brannan had a right to claim this levy. "Brannan has a perfect right to collect the tax," the plainspoken Mason replied, "if you Mormons are fools enough to pay it."[11]

Sherman's memory was less than exact, for it was not a 10 percent tithe that Brannan claimed, but something more, as Azariah Smith tells us in his gold rush journal. Smith worked at the diggings less than two weeks between 11 and 23 May. "I got there something near three hundred dollars," he wrote. "The most I made in a day was sixty five dollars after the toll was taken out, which was thirty dollars out of a hundred, which goes to Hudson and Willis, that discovered the mine, and Brannan who is securing it for them."[12]

After his return from San Francisco, Brannan had begun managing the diggings in partnership with Hudson and Willes by collecting a toll or rent of 30 percent—10 percent for Willes and 10 percent for Hudson by right of discovery, and 10 percent for Brannan as his collection fee. According to Addison Pratt's more detailed and critical account of this business, from the beginning the question of Brannan's right to collect a 30 percent fee was a lively topic of dispute among the miners.

> This place [Mormon Island] had been discovered by two men of the Mormon Battalion by the names of Willis and Hudson. When we arrived there,

---

[10]Gudde, ed., *Bigler's Chronicles of the West,* 107–8.

[11]Sherman, *Memoirs,* 1:52–53.

[12]Entry for 26 May 1848, Bigler, ed., *The Gold Discovery Journal of Azariah Smith,* 115. On the often misunderstood question of the fee charged by Brannan, see editor David Bigler's observations, pages 115–16; Ricketts, *Mormon Battalion,* 200–1; Davies, *Mormon Gold,* 42; and Bagley, ed., *Scoundrel's Tale,* 263–64, 269–70. At Coloma, meanwhile, Marshall began taking half of the gold his workers gathered, a levy that he reduced to 30 or even 10 percent for those who came afterwards.

ZADOCK KNAPP JUDD
Judd wrote his tersely descriptive autobiography, describing his California experiences in the Mormon Battalion and as a miner and road builder, about the time this photograph was taken. *Courtesy Pioneer Memorial Museum, International Society, Daughters of Utah Pioneers.*

we found that Brannan had entered into a league with them, to make all that dug there pay them thirty percent of all that they should find there. The pretence was, that they were intending to help the church with this percentage by buying young cattle in California and sending them to Salt Lake. I had seen enough of Brannan's tricks to convince me that the church would never see any cattle brought to them through that channel. There was much dissatisfaction on the part of the brethren that went up from Francisco about it, many of them ask'd me if I intended to pay it. I told them I thought it was unjust, but still, if the church got it, I had no objections to pay it. I saw at once, that if I refused to pay it, the most of them [also] intended to [refuse], Brannan already had gathered some, and knowing his antipathies against me, that he possess'd low cunning enough, had I refused to pay, to gather up what he had and sent [it] to the church, and told [tell] them that he could have gathered a much larger amount for them had I not come out against it and put an end to his benevolent object. And I determined at once that I would give him no chance to take any twist on me, and so I readily handed over all that [I] dug to those that were appointed to take useury.

While Pratt attempted to avoid trouble by paying the 30 percent fee, the payments apparently stopped after Colonel Mason and Lieutenant Sherman visited in July. Brannan took his profits and moved to Sutter's Fort, where he pursued his expanding business affairs, which soon included a leading role in founding the city of Sacramento. In short order, through trading and real-estate speculation, he became California's first millionaire, and at no distant date Brannan became if not the first, certainly the most prominent California Mormon to fall away from the faith.[13]

Zadock Judd: A Hundred Dollars Worth of Gold, or More, in a Day

As Zadock Judd's colorful memoir and other participant accounts make clear, the battalion veterans and other northern California Saints could acquire wealth at a phenomenal rate in the diggings. Joseph W. Bates arrived at Mormon Island from Monterey in July. His brief report indicates that the returns from mining—$1,800 in four weeks—were still excellent that far along in the season.[14] He makes no mention of paying a mining fee to Brannan, presumptive evidence that the LDS miners had taken the advice of Governor Mason.

Canadian-born Zadock Judd, twenty-one years old in 1848, was another of the battalion boys who went from Monterey to the gold fields. Very likely he was a member of the company of twenty-five veterans described by Joseph Bates. Instead of digging, however, Judd worked briefly for wages near Mormon Island while others mined. His explanation for the prevailing high wage rate provides a first-rate description of the simplest method for retrieving the fine gold in the Mormon Island placers. Even though Frances Hammond had found no market for his mercury in late April, by the end of June it was in high demand. Of course, no one then understood the risks of heavy metal poisoning in the repeated handling of mercury, just as they were not at all concerned about the ravages of placer mining on the natural environment.

While Bates stayed in the diggings until August, Judd left in early July

13 Ellsworth, ed., *The Journals of Addison Pratt*, 336–37.

14 See Bates's recollection in Chapter 5.

with the Thompson-Holmes wagon company, the first LDS contingent to leave the northern California gold country and head eastward across the Sierra to Great Salt Lake City.

JUDD, REMINISCENCES OF ZADOCK KNAPP JUDD, SENIOR, UTAH STATE HISTORICAL SOCIETY.

While my companions were digging the mill race for Sutter, in which gold was discovered, I was wandering around the country trying to find work in a tailor shop. When the report reached me I was in Monterey, California, about one hundred and fifty miles away. When the report of so much gold being found reached the people they were anxious to go there. One man offered to furnish provisions, wagon and team, if men would go and work the mines and give him a portion of what they found. This company I joined, with the understanding that when my companions were ready to go home, I should go with them. We were soon on the road traveling for the mines.

I had a horse to ride, while others rode in the wagon. An intimate friend of mine took turns with me in riding the horse. One would ride while one walked. We would keep near the wagon so we could get our provisions at meal time.

In our second day's travel we came to a ranch at which I had left a horse a year previous. We got the horse so each of us had one to ride. We traveled on in this way until we came near the mines.

We came to where the road forked, one [fork] leading to the mines, the other to where my companions were. I let my friend ride the horse to the mines with the understanding that I would be up in a few days and get the horse; but when I went after the horse my friend had turned him out and could not find him, so I bade goodbye to friend, horse and mines and turned back to the camp of my companions.

They were calculating to go back home, which place was in Utah at that time.

They had got a wagon which was about one day's distance. They proposed to me that if I would go and get the wagon, I should be allowed wages for my time at the rate of one hundred dollars per day, which should be allowed on my share of the outfit they were getting up for our journey homeward. I got the wagon and brought it safe to them.

I must tell you why wages were counted one hundred dollars per day. A man would take his little Indian basket or common milk pan, go to the place where gold was found, fill it with dirt containing gold, take it to the river, sink it up until the gold was all washed away, then empty the contents of the pan onto a plate, or any tight dish, fill his pan with dirt and gold again and go through the same process of washing the dirt away, and emptying it onto

> the pile on the plate. When a quantity of this kind had accumulated, it was put into a smaller dish and [a] spoonful or two of quicksilver added to it. The quicksilver would gather all the gold and the refuse was then thrown away. Quicksilver and gold were then put into a little buckskin sack, the sack was twisted up and wrung and the quicksilver would run through like water through cloth, leaving all the gold in the buckskin sack, and the quicksilver could be used again for an indefinite number of times. In this way a man would gather a hundred dollars worth of gold, or more, in a day.

Samuel Miles, another young battalion veteran, did not join his comrades at the gold diggings. Following the battalion's discharge at Los Angeles, he had traveled north to San Francisco. There, as Miles relates in this autobiographical statement, Sam Brannan took an interest in his welfare as noted in Chapter 2. As a result, instead of going to the placers, Miles started clerking first for Capt. Edward von Phister at Benicia and then in Brannan and Smith's store at Sutter's Fort. Here he saw firsthand the material results from the diggings for his LDS brethren.

> After being here [at Benicia] about six months the gold mines just discovered at Sutters Mill caused a great rush to that part of the country and Saml. Brannan was making arrangements to sell goods at Sutters Fort. He came to Benecia and requested my employer to let me go with him to assist in the business and as Capt. Von Phister also decided to close his store and go to the mines, he gave his consent for me to go. I remained clerking in the store for Mr. Brannan about two months at Sutters Fort. The trade at the store was very large being then the only place of supplies near the placer mines lately discovered. The time had now come July 1848 for the brethren to start for the Salt Lake Valley. Most of them had done well in washing out the gold from the river sands, most of them being near the spot of the discovery. I was able to make a good fit [out] for the return home.[15]

FRANCIS A. HAMMOND: I HAD NOT LOST ALL LOVE FOR GOLD

Among those who enjoyed great success at Mormon Island was Francis Hammond, the former sailor who had converted to the LDS faith in San Francisco the previous fall. His autobiography describes this success, as well as the eagerness he felt to travel east and join the main body

[15]Samuel Miles, Autobiography, LDS Archives.

of the church. But, he was frank to confess, his faith was tested severely before he made a final determination to leave northern California. This section of his memoir takes up Hammond's story in June, just after he ended mining efforts and divided the proceeds with his partners.

FRANCIS ASBURY HAMMOND,
"IN EARLY DAYS: MY INTRODUCTION TO MORMONISM,"
THE JUVENILE INSTRUCTOR, JUNE–SEPTEMBER 1894.

I returned to San Francisco, and purchased an outfit for the journey to Great Salt Lake. I loaded up a seventy hundred government wagon, drawn by four yoke of beautiful oxen, with everything I could think of which would be needed in a new country, not forgetting a small stock of leather. My freight consisted of dry goods, some ready-made clothing, tea, coffee, sugar, rice, flour, bacon, etc.

I was so full now of the spirit of gathering that I did not regard gold at all, but my trial and temptation was to come. I was now engaged in carrying out the promise I made during the winter that I would be ready to join a company in July, ready for the journey to the "valley." After spending a few days in San Francisco I returned with my outfit to the diggings, and pitched my tent on the banks of the river opposite Mormon Island. I soon found that I had not lost all love for gold or the wealth of this world. Goods of the class I had in my wagon were in great demand, and I was offered great profits on my stock; from 200 to 500 per cent, was I offered. It fairly made my head swim, and I began to waver in my feelings as to my keeping my word and start for the valley in July, so I vacillated and went about looking for the best offer for my goods. Satan whispered in my ear, "Why not remain another year, and trade and speculate and get rich; and then you can assist the poor Saints, the widow, and the orphan, and take them up to Zion, and you will become famous on your arrival there; besides it is a new and untried country, and the people already there are hard put to sustain themselves." In this manner was I tried, and sorely too. I was in great distress of mind and could not decide; and while in this condition one night I went to my bed in great perplexity of mind, earnestly desiring to know what to do. I had scarcely fallen asleep when a personage appeared at my tent door, and calling me by name, asked me to come outside. I arose immediately and stood by his side at the tent door, when he said to me, "Look up the river." As I did so I saw instead of water, what seemed to me pitch or some black substance rolling sluggishly down the bed of the river. I beheld the multitude digging and washing gold, paying no attention to the melted pitch, and the personage said, "Look again up the river." I saw the same substance coming, but much more rapidly, as it was this time quite hot; and still the crowd kept at their labor. Again I was told to look up, when this pitch was coming down about hip deep and almost boiling hot, and the people in the diggings now seemed willing to quit if they could recover what they had spread out on rocks on their cloths or pieces of buckskin, and while searching and diving to secure these treasures I was told to look again up the river, and I saw this substance resembling pitch coming down the bed of the river in a solid mass, about fourteen feet in height and filling the river bed from bank to bank and hot as burning streams of lava that issue from volcanoes. In my fright I seemed to make a rush for the banks of the river, and caught hold of the brush which lined the banks, and thus made my escape. I also saw quite a number of brethren make their escape in the same way; but the great crowd was carried away and lost to view.

In the morning when I awoke I was much disturbed in my mind, having never experienced anything of the kind before. However, I still went about looking for a sale of my goods. Prices were increasing every day, and the temptation was growing stronger.

I went to bed at night worried and still in a quandary. The same vision was repeated, still I remained all next day in a state of unrest. Two powers seemed working with me, and each striving for the mastery.

I did very little during the day, and went to bed wondering what would become of me, for I had become almost desperate, when to my surprise the dream or vision was again given to me precisely as on the previous nights. This was the third night the dream was given to me, and when I awoke in the morning my mind was perfectly clear, and I felt to thank the Lord with all my soul that He had thus warned me, His poor servant, to flee from that land and gather with His people in the vales of Deseret, and learn to be obedient unto His commands and harken to the voice and counsels of His holy Priesthood, His Prophets and Apostles whom He has sent to lead His people.

I immediately commenced to make preparations for joining the company who were aiming to leave some time in the fore part of July, as agreed upon during the winter. I set out to hunt my oxen that had been turned out to graze in the surrounding hills. I found them all but a very fine yoke of red steers, used as my leaders. I hunted the country far and wide, but could not find them. This was a great disappointment, for I could not well move and haul my load of freight without them, and to purchase another yoke at this time was nearly impossible, for oxen were very scarce and in great demand. However, I concluded I would make one more effort to find them, and accordingly set out early in the morning on a fine, cream-colored mare, for which I had paid the sum of only eight dollars. I rode out about half a mile from camp When it was suggested to me to pray and ask the Lord to direct me that I might recover the oxen. I did so, and then remounted, and flung the bridle reins loose over the mare's neck for her to take just what course she pleased. She marched off in a direct course for about a mile, when from behind a bunch of thick brush the oxen jumped up. I was filled with rejoicing, and thanked the Lord that He had heard and answered my prayer. I returned to camp and soon had my outfit in shape for moving on the trail to the place of gathering.

After resting a few days at the place appointed for our gathering, those who were to compose the company having mostly gathered in, we made a start, having first sent a few brethren ahead as pioneers to blaze the trees through the timber and mark out the trail for the wagons to follow. This company was composed of Saints who come to California in the ship *Brooklyn,* and members of the Mormon Battalion.

JOHN BORROWMAN: A PARTY WITH PACK MULES STARTED FOR SALT LAKE

Although Francis Hammond recalled that the Lord had answered his prayers as he prepared for the journey east, John Borrowman's journal reveals that he was an unhappy partner with Hammond in a wagon and its teams. His detailed report describes one of the conflicts that plagued every wagon party ever to hit the trail. Borrowman's account begins with a precise description of how the first wagon parties and pack trains assembled in Pleasant Valley, near today's Placerville, before starting toward Carson Pass.

JOHN BORROWMAN, JOURNAL, LDS ARCHIVES.

Wednesday, 5th [July 1848]. Bought another yoke of oxen for $80. Arranged our affairs and went out 5 miles from the river and camped.

Thursday, 6th. This morning we found that we were out of our way and turned back 3 miles to find it again and traveled about 18 miles and camped for the night.

Friday, 7th. Went about 6 miles and broke the fore bolster of our wagon[16] and here we found that we were out of our way again and both Brother [William] Wood and myself had lost our saddle macheres[17] of[f] the waggon and we fixed up the waggon and returned to where we camped the night before and camped for the night.

Saturday, 8th. Started back in search of the trail and went about 6 miles and stopt to hunt it up.

---

16 This troublesome box bolster sat atop the axletree and connected the wagon bed to the front running gears. A kingpin that ran through the bolster and the axletree allowed the wagon's front wheels to turn.

17 Or *mochilas,* a type of saddle covering or saddlebag used in Hispanic California. The Pony Express later adopted the term.

Sunday, 9th. Went about 8 miles and broke our waggon bolster again and stopt to fix it again.

Monday, 10th. Started and went about 6 miles and upset our waggon and broke my rifle and several other things. Then fitted up again and went a little further and stopt for the night.

Tuesday, 11th. Went about 4 miles and in goin down a hill over a creek we broke our waggon tongue and had to stop to put in another and here Brothers Austin, Mead and Pool overtook us and Brother Austin helped us fix our waggon.[18]

Wednesday, 12th. Started and went seven miles to the camp in the mountains.

Thursday, 13th. Worked at digging gold and made $30.

Friday, 14th. This day I was unwell and stopt in camp all day.

Saturday, 15th. Rested in camp.

Sunday, 16th. Stopt in and traded with the Indians to the amount of $60.

Monday, 17th. Rested in camp and traded to the amount of 24 dollars with the Indians.

Tuesday, 18th. Stayed in camp and tried to arrange things for starting over the mountains.

Wednesday, 19th. Worked at fixing our waggon.

Thursday, 20th. . . . This day I remained in camp fixing things, and here I will just mention a case of difference that has happened between myself and Brother Hammond. When we were at the lower mines it was agreed that Hammond, Wood and myself should join together and buy a waggon and team to carry our effects over the mountains and that we should pay an equal share each for the same and in the meantime we all had to go to San Francisco to purchase our fitout. Accordingly we prepared to go there and when nearly ready to start I asked Brother Hammond if I could not send by him and let him do my business and probably I could make enough during his absence to pay his part of the waggon and mine too. Accordingly he accepted the offer and I weighed out $200 to him to trade for me which he did with the exception of $29.75 which he received in coin for me and he paid me ten of it when he returned leaving $18.75. He then informed me that he had bought a waggon and he had run in debt considerably and wanted me to pay for it and the freight of both waggon and goods. I then paid him $100 for his share of the wagon and mine and $47 dollars for the freight and $9.45 I owed him for a piece of cloth he bought for me. He had also bought several articles for both of us, my share of which came to $37. My share of the freight also only came to $28.50. This with some other little things made our affairs a little troublesome to settle and when he came to settel with me he brought me upwards of $30 in his debt. I then made up

[18]Orlando Fish Mead was a veteran of Company C, while Julius Augustus Caesar Austin and Peter John Poole were *Brooklyn* pioneers. Austin was a carpenter.

my account and made him $14 in my debt making a difference of more than $40, and when I tried to show him his mistake he would not listen to me, thinking all the while that I was wrong. I then said I would leave it to a third person to decide between us and he agreed to it and Brother [Daniel] Stark came along at the time and it was left to him and when he had reconed our accounts found I was right but Hammond would not agree to it. I then said to him if he would let it go and say no more about it I would say we were even, but he seemed much displeased and said he would have to recon it over again before he would agree to that. Then he had a crate of oil containing 12 bottles which he agreed to devide among us three, 4 bottles to a man, if we would pay him our shares of the cost, which we said we would do. He had also a large stock of sole leather and when Brother Wood and me lost our macheres [*mochilas*] he promised to let us have as much leather as would make new ones, but all these things remained unsettled for till we came here. When he found out his mistake in the account and paid me but would not acknowledge that he had done wrong and refused to let me have the oil or leather but offered it to Wood. He then wanted to buy my share of the waggon and team alledging as an excuse that he had more load than the rest of us but I would not sell it. He then offered to sell his share to me provided I would carry 300 weight which I would not do. He then offered to retain his share of the waggon and team and put 300 weight into it and he would pack the rest of his goods and let Wood and me attend to the team for him and he would give us $20. This offer I accepted but Wood would not. He then spoke very hard of us saying he could not get us to agree to anything. I then told him that he had complained a great deal of me because I gave him only fifty dollars for doing my business at San Francisco which did not take him more than one day and yet he could offer me $10 for what would take me 5 or 6 weeks and then think he had made a great offer. He then gave me a good deal of abuse and told me that he had not told me before but he would tell me now that all that he wanted was to get me out of the company and we had our provisions together and [ate] together. He wanted to have them divided and I might have my own side and he would keep his and this we have done today and thus it is with us at present.

Friday, 21st. Went a prospecting a little for gold but found very little.

Saturday, 22nd. Stopt in camp preparing to move to another camping ground.

Sunday, 23rd. Yoked up our team and went about 2 miles to another camping place.

Monday, 24th. Cut brush and fixed up a tent and here we intend to stop till we get all the company together. This evening Brother Ic [Isaac] Robins arrived in camp with his family. He is sick of fever.

Tuesday, 25th. This day I have nothing to do but lying about the camp and time passes very heavily. This day Brother [Orlando] Mead borrowed $80 of me to buy a team and left 2 mares as security. I also agreed to take the oxen provided he got a good yoke at the rate he paid for them and let him have the use of them to Salt Lake.

Wednesday, 26th. Staid in camp. This day James Clark and Brother Smith came into camp with a team.

Thursday, 27th. Spent the day in camp. This morning Brother [Julius] Austin and Timothy Hoyt came in for their oxen and I bought a pair of *macheres* from Hoyt for $7.

Friday, 28th. This morning I gave Timothy Hoyt $60 to buy a rifle and $248 lent him. He left this morning with Brother Austin for the lower mines to bring up the waggons. This morning Hoyt bought Hammond's share in our waggon and team for $115 and carries 200 weight of his goods to the Lake so today we have been arranging our affairs.

Saturday, 29th. I bought a horse from [James] Ferguson for $62.½.

Sunday, 30th. Did little else than attend to the cattle. This day a party with pack mules started for Salt Lake, I think 15 in number.

Monday, 31st. Rested in camp.

Tuesday. August 1st., 1848. I staid in camp and mended my buckskin pantaloons.

Wednesday, 2nd. I went and hunted our cattle then went to our old camp in search of gold but found none. Then returned and finished mending my pantaloons. This day [William] Prouse [Levi] Fifield and Mead came into camp from the lower mines and Brother Mead returned the $60 he borrowed from me not being able to get a team to buy.

Thursday, 3rd. This day the company bought two beef cattle and killed one of them and divided it amongst us and we cut it up and laid it out to dry.

Friday, 4th. Did little else than attend to some little affairs about the camp. This evening we held a meeting for prayer and business.

Saturday, 5th. This day Daniel [Samuel] Clark, Brother [Montgomery] Button and Brother Foulet [John S. Fowler] came into camp with their waggons.[19] This [day] I done nothing but fixed my bridle and some other little things.

[19]Fowler, who had sent his family around Cape Horn with the *Brooklyn*, came west with Brigham Young's pioneer camp. He arrived in California with Abner Blackburn and Capt. James Brown in the company that President Young dispatched to travel with Samuel Brannan to the Pacific Coast in 1847. Montgomery Button and Samuel Clark had been members of the Pueblo detachment. Although their trip is not recorded in any known document, in all likelihood they and a few other Pueblo Saints joined Brown's party as it headed west from Salt Lake. See Ricketts, *Mormon Battalion*, 255, 346; and Bagley, ed., *Frontiersman*, 57–58.

James S. Brown: A Higher Object Before Me Than Gold

A few years after publishing his account of the Coloma gold discovery, James S. Brown completed an autobiography that related his California adventures through a pleasant haze of remembrance. In this extract, his third-person memoir describes a brief, very fortunate effort at placer mining near Mormon Island the day before he and his partners set out to join the company heading to Salt Lake. His self-satisfied, sanctimonious tone in describing their decision to leave the gold country despite easy mining success—sharply contrasting with Francis Hammond's spiritual trial—may be an artifact of Brown's old age rather than the authentic sentiments of the young man who traveled east with his uncle and older friends. Yet Brown's statement testifies to the extraordinary sense shared by many LDS veterans in northern California that their duty to family, community, and church came before personal enrichment.

> The day before starting from the gold diggings on our journey was kind of an off-day, in which the writer had some spare time and wandered off from camp, with pick and shovel, up into a dry gulch, where he soon struck a very rich prospect of gold, about a quarter of a mile from water. This was about 11 o'clock A.M. By sundown he had carried the rich dirt down in his pantaloons, and washed out forty-nine dollars and fifty cents in gold; yet kind reader, strange as it may appear, he, with his partners, hitched up and rolled out the next morning, and joined the main camp at what we called Pleasant Valley, but now I think, known as Dutch Flat. I have never seen that rich spot of earth since; nor do I regret it, for there always has been a higher object before me than gold. We had covenanted to move together under certain conditions, and those conditions existing we were honor bound to move the next day. We did move, leaving that rich prospect without ever sticking a stake in the gulch, but abandoning it to those who might follow. Some may think we were blind to our own interests; but after more than forty years we look back without regrets, although we did see fortunes in the land, and had many inducements to stay. People said, "Here is gold on the bedrock, gold on the hills, gold in the rills, gold everywhere, gold to spend, gold to lend, gold for all that will delve, and soon you can make an independent fortune." We could realize all that. Still duty called, our honor was at stake, we had covenanted with each other, there was a principle involved; for with us it was God and His kingdom first. We had friends and relatives in the wilderness, yea, in an untried, desert land, and who knew their condition? We did not. So it was duty before pleasure, before wealth, and with this prompting we rolled out and joined our comrades in Pleasant Valley.[20]

[20]Brown, *Life of a Pioneer*, 108–9.

Elijah Elmer: Gold Is Not A Going to Stop Me

The last battalion veterans to reach the American River diggings in 1848 were the Saints of the Monterey contingent. Although the mining excitement had reached the former Mexican capital by early May, these men remained at work there until June, when they left in a company to begin the trip eastward toward Salt Lake. One member was Elijah Elmer, a former sergeant in Company C who had traveled with Jefferson Hunt's party from Los Angeles up the coastal route the previous August, then found Monterey to his liking. In this section of his journal, Elmer describes his June departure with other battalion veterans and their march inland to Mormon Island and Pleasant Valley. As soon as these men got on the road, they organized themselves in military fashion, making battalion lieutenant Samuel Thompson their captain and sergeant Ebenezer Brown the second in command. Elmer's account of the trip through the San Joaquin delta, with intensely hot weather and the "everlasting thick" clouds of mosquitoes, gives further graphic testimony to the difficulties of travel across the California landscape in 1848.

Elijah Elmer Journal,
Crossroads: Utah Crossroads Quarterly Newsletter (September 1993).

Left monterey monday the fifth of June 1848 for Salt Lake by way of the gold mines C[o]untry is in a Considerable of an up roar on account of gold as hole towns are desea[r]ted and all kinds of Business Stop pretty much traveled 16 miles to day and Camp 4 miles on the north Side of the Salemus [Salinas] River no wood at all here Chuseing a Capt here By Ballot [Samuel] Thompson is our Capt. And Ebenezer Brown our Lieutenant.

June 6 12 yoak of our oxen got away from the gard last knight we found them this morning with some trouble Started on our Journey this moning the Road Purty Level for 8 miles then we Came to the Salemnus mountains Crossed them and Camp for the knight tied them [oxen] in Camp so that they was not so much trouble for the gard to keep them.

7 Left Camp this morning and finished Crossing the mountain about 10 o'clock To day Roads Verry Rough over this mountain Passed St Johns [San José] mission to day Considerable of a creek in this valley about 4 roads [rods] wide on the Bed of the Stream Camp to knight [where the stream is] about half as wide traveled ab[o]ut 20 miles yesterday and about 18 to day Country all most entirely Covered with oak some white oak timber in the vally and Sickamore rodys[?] about 10 or 12 feet long. . . .

17 Started out this morning and went 1½ miles and Camp againe went to work to making Tuly Boats to Cross the [San Joaquin] river in Six

of [us] Joined together and made one Large Enough to take two of our Loads on at once and took them down the river 6 miles and then went up a Slew Some 400 yards and then we had to Carry our Loading about 50 yards further on to dry ground Been in the water up to the waist for 3 days and not done yet have got to Load up and unload twice more in a mile and a half

19 took our animals accross the river to day the weather verry hot here and the musketoes Everlasting thick and not Bashfull at all knight nor day Saw one man to day that had 27 ounces of gold dust that he got in 6 day[s] the San Walkeen river is 150 or 200 rods wide at this time with in the Banks

20 [June 1848] finished Crossing the river to day and loaded up after Crossing the Slew which was verry bad and went ¾ of a mile and unloaded againe and Swame our Load over another Slewe 150 yards wide

21 Loded up againe this morning and Left our troubles of water Behind us for the presant traveled 15 miles to day Land sandy and rough not much grass on it timber when you got to it is shruby and not fit for much but the fire

22 Laying in the Camp do day Some of the Boys went out and killed 10 Elk they are verry thick

23 Still in Camp got our meet boture [butchered] and drying of[f] so we can take it with us on the Road

24 Started out this [morning] againe and travelled 24 miles C[o]untry brown and dray and Sandy Camp on the McCalomus [Mokelumne] River to knight on the River the timber is about 15 miles the [illegible] I do not know But it is not fit for much But the fire

25 Crossed the river this morning all got over Safe about 2 o'clock we crossed in a Canoe traveled 8 miles

26 traveled 25 miles to day Country all Burnt over no timber of Consequence till we Camp on the river here is a mill[21] McCrosmy [Cosumnes] is the name of this river.

27 Crossed over hills and dale to day with out any road Traveled 25 miles to day and Camp

28 went to the Camp in the mines to day to see what the prospect was for money we found it good and back to Camp at knight and made preparation for to go to work

[21]Jared Sheldon in 1846–1847 built a grist mill on the Cosumnes River within Rancho Omochumnes, a Mexican land grant owned by Sheldon and his partner William Daylor, both formerly in John Sutter's employ. In 1851 Sheldon and two of his workers were killed nearby in a gun battle as they tried to prevent an angry group of gold miners from breaking down a dam that Sheldon had built to assure his mill an adequate summer water supply, but which was flooding the miners' claims. The mill site is about one mile southeast of Slough House on Meiss Road off State Route 16, the Sacramento-Jackson Highway. It is listed as State Registered Landmark 439. See Hoover *et al., Historic Spots in California,* rev. Douglas E. Kyle, 288–90.

> 29 [June 1848] Moved in to town (as it is Called) this morning and unyoke our Cattle and then we found a Company ready to start over the mountains we yoaked up our oxen and started on 10 miles and left the gold Behind us the rest of our Company Stoped but [myself and] Hyatt [William Hyde] we Started for holme and gold is not a going to stop me nor Thompson the Evrage [average] [return from mining] is about 32 dollars a day Some as high as 104 a day

Mormon Island and the Natomas diggings had drawn nearly all the California Saints by the end of June. Working for a month or two, or in some cases just for a few weeks, most became gold-rich according to their lights. They were the first successful fortune seekers in the northern California placer diggings.

While we can glean some information from the statements of individual miners and observers like Samuel Miles, direct evidence of the returns from Mormon gold mining in 1848 is scattered and sparse. The indirect evidence of Brigham Young's Gold Account records, according to historian J. Kenneth Davies, indicates that at least $19,103 in gold dust and coins came into the Salt Lake Valley from California sources between October 1848 and June 1849, principally representing the accumulated treasure of church members who had been in the mines. Saints known to have come from California in 1848 deposited into the Gold Account a total of about $6,561.00, for an average of $102.50 per depositor.[22] The battalion veterans and some of the *Brooklyn* Saints of course spent a substantial part of their mining profits in California, outfitting themselves and purchasing stock and equipment to take to the Salt Lake Valley. Yet, as Henry Bigler subsequently wrote, where the Mormon miners got one dollar in the gold fields in 1848, other, more experienced miners "could later get hundreds."[23]

---

[22]Davies, *Mormon Gold,* 88.

[23]Gudde, ed., *Bigler's Chronicles of the West,* 109.

This contemporary photo of West Pass shows the terrain that was negotiated by emigrants both arriving in and departing from California via the Carson Pass route. *Courtesy Frank Tortorich.*

Chapter 5

"We Left the Gold Fields of California"
Opening the Carson Pass Wagon Road

In early April 1848, just as news of the gold discoveries at Coloma and Mormon Island began to circulate, the Mormon Battalion veterans working for John Sutter met to plan their trip eastward to join Brigham Young's colony in Utah's desert country. Samuel Hollister Rogers recorded the gathering in a diary entry for Sunday, 9 April. "We held a meeting to consider upon the best means to proceed to Salt Lake, Where upon we agread to search out a new pass to Marys [Humboldt] river, To start the first of June. A good spirit was manifested. Samuel Branon attended the meeting and gave some instructions regarding the road."[1]

These men faced a daunting challenge. The established route led northeast from Sutter's Fort to the last outpost on the trail at Johnson's Ranch, up the Bear River drainage, then across the snow-covered Sierra Nevada summit to the Truckee River. Even under ideal conditions, the passes over the Sierra were difficult for horses and mules, and all but impassible for ox-drawn wagons. Best known was Donner Pass, a name that served as a constant reminder of the tragic fate of the group snowbound there late in 1846. Once over the summit, the spring runoff in the Truckee River would be another obstacle. Moving back and forth between the high walls of Truckee Canyon, the trail required no less than twenty-seven river crossings. Then came the extreme conditions of the Forty-mile Desert: a bleak stretch with no water or grass that challenged eastbound travelers before they reached the sink of the Humboldt River.

Sam Brannan, Charles C. Smith, and two companions had traveled this way on horseback in spring 1847, and James Pace's group of battal-

[1] Samuel Hollister Rogers, Diary, 9 April 1848, LDS Archives.

ion veterans, likewise on horses and without wagons, had followed the same route to the Humboldt in September. Many of the veterans had accompanied Pace as far as Truckee Meadows, and they were aware of the difficulties along this line of travel, especially if they tried to make the crossing early in the season, when snow banks might still block their way through the high country. But as yet no one had discovered a better route across the Sierra.

The April gathering was recalled years later by James S. Brown, who had come to Sutter's Fort with Henry Bigler to load up provisions for the sawmill work crew at Coloma. "This assemblage was preparatory to crossing the Sierra Nevada mountains at or near the head of the American River," Brown stated, "for we had learned that it was next to impossible to take wagons at this time of the year by what was called the Truckee route, and as we had become accustomed to pioneer life it was thought we could find a better route, so it was proposed to open up one by the way stated."[2] The veterans made plans to look for a new trail, one that could be made into a wagon road that would allow them to reach Salt Lake with a full cargo of supplies and tools. Their confidence in their own abilities, summed up by Brown, was bolstered by religious belief. Devout in the LDS faith, they shared a deep conviction that God would continue to guide their steps.

The survey and construction of the Carson Pass Wagon Road—commonly known today as the Mormon–Carson Pass Emigrant Trail or simply the Mormon Emigrant Trail—was an accomplishment that demonstrated skill, determination, and great fortitude. The LDS trail-makers, equipped with only the most basic hand tools—axes, picks, and shovels—built this road from west to east. Their western approach proved to be a tremendous advantage, since they began at the foot of the ridges and, as Samuel Rogers observed, "traveled up the main divide" between the American and Cosumnes rivers, which took them directly through the mountain barrier. Westbound explorers crossing the Sierra—including such early travelers as Joseph R. Walker's trappers, the Bidwell-Bartleson emigrant party of 1841, and John C. Frémont's Second Expedition—repeatedly followed ridges that ended in precipitous drops or impenetrable canyons.

---

[2]Brown, *Life of a Pioneer,* 107.

A pioneering party of forty-five men (accompanied by the wife of one) did the heaviest work during July and August 1848. Under the leadership of Samuel Thompson and Jonathan Holmes, the company took seventeen heavily loaded wagons across the Sierra, pulled by docile, slow-moving oxen. With the wagons came a herd of at least 150 horses and a larger number of cattle, tended by mounted herdsmen who had adopted the colorful vaquero costume of the Hispanic *Californios.*[3] Two more groups, numbering about twenty men and one woman, followed the pioneer Holmes-Thompson company with pack animals, while yet one more contingent of forty-five men and women with their pack animals and wagons left the placer diggings later in the season to take the same route eastward.[4]

The trip was not a carefree excursion, as shown by the battering the company's wagons sustained as they lurched and jolted over the new road. The route crossed West Pass, a ridge of 9,550 feet: the highest point for North American wagon roads in general use during the nineteenth century.[5] Carson Pass to the east was just a few hundred feet lower. Just beyond Carson Pass, marking the eastern rampart of the Sierra, was a sharply pitched, mile-long slope that later travelers to California would call ruefully the Devil's Ladder. A little farther along, the trail makers headed downstream through the boulder-strewn canyon of

[3]Most writers have adopted Henry Bigler's figures for the size of the Holmes-Thompson expedition: "Forty-five men and one women (Sergeant Wm. Coray's wife) two small brass pieces bought of Sutter, seventeen wagons, one hundred fifty horses and about the same of cattle, and I believe every man had a musket." See Gudde, ed., *Bigler's Chronicles of the West,* 114. Other sources give slightly different figures: Ellsworth, ed., *The Journals of Addison Pratt,* 342; May, "A Sketch of a Migrating Family to California," Bancroft Library; Judd, "Reminiscences of Zadok Knapp Judd, Senior," Utah State Historical Society. Ricketts, ed., *The Mormon Battalion,* 222, provides a roster for the Holmes-Thompson company with the names of thirty-nine battalion veterans. If we add the five company members who had not served in the Mormon Battalion, the total is forty-four individuals, excluding Melissa Coray and the three missing scouts.

[4]Bigler, ed., *The Gold Discovery Journal of Azariah Smith,* 134–35; Ellsworth, ed., *The Journals of Addison Pratt,* 348; John Borrowman, "Journal from Dec. 23, 1846 to Mar. 1870, with Lapses of Several Years," LDS Archives; and May, "Sketch of a Migrating Family," Bancroft Library. Ricketts, *Mormon Battalion,* 221–27, provides rosters of these groups.

[5]On the Overland Trails e-mail list, Bob Carter pointed out in a message of 1 July 1997 that another route, the Walker River-Sonora trail, reached two passes higher than West Pass. This wagon road crossed the Sierra Nevada range a few miles south of Sonora Pass, just north of Yosemite Park near Grizzly Peak, connecting Nevada's Antelope Valley and the town of Sonora. Little Emigrant Pass (at the head of the next canyon to the north of present-day Emigrant Pass on State Highway 108) and Brown Bear Pass, about three miles to the west, are both over 9,700 feet elevation. The merchants of Sonora promoted this route, but it did not become popular and never received such steady use as the Carson Pass Wagon Road. This road's history is summarized in Davis, "The Walker River-Sonora Crossing," *Overland Journal* (Fall 1988).

the Carson River's West Fork, a seven-mile ordeal labeled by many who came this way as the worst stretch of road anywhere between Missouri and the Sacramento Valley.

Even so, the Carson Pass Wagon Road was shorter and less difficult than the Truckee route or any other wagon road that brought overland emigrants across the Sierra during the early years of the California gold rush. It became the most heavily used branch of the California Trail from 1849 to 1851, carrying tens of thousands of gold seekers directly into the heart of the northern mines. The route lost popularity during the 1852 travel season when John Calhoun "Cock-Eye" Johnson, an enterprising surveyor, opened a shorter and less arduous wagon road that skirted the south shore of Lake Tahoe and descended into the Mother Lode region along the drainage of the American River's South Fork. But this newer route was a toll road, and the toll-free Carson Pass Wagon Road continued in heavy use during the 1860s for emigrants, freight wagons, and drovers taking cattle and sheep eastward from northern California to the Comstock Lode mining district.

Most of the Carson Pass Wagon Road has been included in the modern-day highway that links Placerville and Pollock Pines, California, with Genoa, Nevada, providing access to ski resorts and summer recreational sites in the Carson Pass area. The segment through the Eldorado National Forest between Sly Park and Iron Mountain, not kept open during the winter, now is designated by the state department of transportation as the Mormon Emigrant Trail. The original trail through Rock Valley and up Squaw Ridge to West Pass, Emigrant Meadows, and Carson Pass is no longer open to travel, but the continuation between Carson Pass and Carson Valley parallels today's State Highway 88.

Samuel H. Rogers: The Snow Falling Fast, We Turned Back and Camped

After their April conference, the battalion veterans who had worked for Sutter came to settle accounts with him, a process that continued sporadically until the end of May according to his New Helvetia journal record. Sutter wrote a last entry regarding the LDS workmen on 28 May: "Paid off all the Mormons which have been employed by me in building these mills and other mechanical trades, all of them made their pile and some of them became very rich and wealthy but all of them are bound to the Great Salt Lake and [will] spend their fortunes there to the glory and honor of the Lord."[6]

Following the terms of their agreement with Sutter, the veterans bargained for the value of their wages in wagons, draft oxen, horses, mules, cows and calves, a large variety of tools, and seeds and plant cuttings to aid their brethren at Salt Lake. They also fancied two small brass cannons, a four-pounder and a six-pounder.[7] Acting as chief organizer for the upcoming expedition, Daniel Browett, a Company E sergeant who had taken a leadership role in the veterans' march from Los Angeles the previous August, negotiated with Sutter for the cannons and took up a collection among his comrades to cover the cost. As Zadock Judd

[6]*New Helvetia Diary*, 18, 28 April, and 1, 6, 9, 10, 11, 28 May 1848, 129–35.

[7]The origin of these two small brass cannons has been a minor mystery. Norma Ricketts cited the authority of the late Norman Wilson, former California State archeologist, who told her Sutter's guns were "decorated parade cannons" originally brought into Russia by Napoleon's army in 1812 and abandoned during the French retreat from Moscow (*The Mormon Battalion*, 203 and note 28, page 339). Apparently this pretty story is entirely conjectural, as indicated by Sutter's reply to an 1879 inquiry from the Sacramento Society of California Pioneers. "These Guns of which your Society have two placed at the door of their Hall," Sutter stated firmly, "are not Russian guns; on my arrival in California (1839) I have brought 3 of the Smaller guns with me from the Sandwich Islands, 6 of the larger guns I have bought from the Capt. of an Italian Vessel who was a friend of mine, and brought them for me from South America, and I took them very Secretly in the Night on board of my Launch and brought them up to my fort (1841).... Some other guns I have bought from different Vessels among them two Arms of Spain—From the Russians I have got only one fine brass field piece, mounted with Caisson, they would not let me have more, this piece had been cast in St. Petersburg in 1804. And has been used in the war 1812 against Napolean [*sic*], after the War the Government have sold these Guns and small arms, to the Russian Amer. Company on the N. W. Coast of America (Sitka near Alaska)." Sutter lost his Russian gun during his ill-starred military adventure in support of Governor Micheltorena, but it reappeared during the campaigns of Frémont, Stockton, and Kearny during the American conquest. "After peace was restored," he concluded, "the Quartermaster Captain [Joseph Libbey] Folsom returned the gun to me as my property, afterwards after having been fired a many Salutes with the piece, I have presented her to the Society of Pioneers of which I am a life Member." (Sutter to A. P. Collin, 12 June 1879, John Sutter Folder, Sacramento Pioneer Association Papers, Membership, Individual, Box 1: A. Tingman, 3:03, Sacramento Archives and Museum Collection Center.)

Sutter's statement is backed up by the detailed inventory of Fort Ross property the Russians sold to him in 1841, which shows only the one cannon: Document 94, Inventory and Bill of Sale Transferring Possession of Russia's California Properties to John Sutter, in Dmytryshyn *et al.*, eds., *To Siberia and Russian America*, 3:431-42.

It appears that the cannons bought from Sutter by the battalion veterans had come from merchant shipmasters, either purchased directly by Sutter or received in trade with an intermediary such as Nathan Spear at Yerba Buena or Thomas O. Larkin in Monterey. This explanation is more credible since brass four-pounders and six-pounders were precisely the type of armament carried aboard merchant ships engaged in the California hide and tallow trade during this era.

recalled, "The cannons were bought, each boy paying a small pinch of gold to make up the price, which was about seventy five dollars apiece."[8] The deal was completed on 7 May, when Sutter delivered the guns and the veterans stored them in a wagon to take across the mountains.[9]

As these preparations moved ahead, Browett and a few others decided to make a first effort to scout out a route for their upcoming expedition. On 1 May, as Samuel Rogers recorded in his diary, at least nine men with horses and two pack mules set out to find a trail across the Sierra, only to be turned back by a late season snow storm. Rogers later concluded that Browett's party had reached West Pass, the "back bone of the Mountain," the highest crest at the summit of the Sierra Nevada.[10]

SAMUEL HOLLISTER ROGERS, 1848 DIARY, LDS ARCHIVES.

Mo 1 of May [1848]. We made preperations to go in search of a new pass over the mountains.

Tu 2 Last night rain was falling nearley all night and some this morning but the weather cleared about four oclock. We packed two Asses, then sad-deled our horses and started. Traveled twenty miles camped for the night.

We 3 Last night was verry rainey we got a therer [thorough] wetting. We sadled up. went to where the shingle makers had camped, distance 24 miles.

Th 4 We now number eight. packed up, started at near eight oclock, trav-eled up the main divide between the American and Cosma [Cosumnes] rivers most of the time. After having traveled over 20 miles we camped at about 3 oclock. A few spits of snow is seen flying in the air, some little is seen beside the trees, by going a little distance snow peaks can be seen. We past two Indians to day.

---

[8]Judd, "Recollections." Rumor has it that at least one of these guns wound up in the possession of a Nevada antique dealer, but the ultimate fate of the Mormon artillery remains a puzzle. Both may have been melted down during the scrap drives of World War II. Email communication to the editor from Glen Leonard, director of the LDS Church Museum of History and Arts, 16 March 2004. See also Ricketts, *The Mormon Battalion*, 339n28.

[9]New Helvetia Diary, 7 May 1848; and Ricketts, *The Mormon Battalion*, 205. In her outstanding work, Ricketts discusses the purchase of the cannon and provides a list of men who contributed to the purchase, listing also the amount donated by each man. Ibid., 301-2.

[10]Battalion chronicler Norma Ricketts identifies nine pioneers on this preliminary scouting expedition, including Daniel Browett, captain, Ira J. Willes, James C. Sly, Israel Evans, Jacob G. Truman, Ezra Allen, James R. Allred, Henderson Cox, and Robert Pixton. See Ricketts, *The Mormon Battalion*, 203. Samuel Rogers needs to be added to this accounting. Three of these men—Willes, Sly, and Evans—had been in Company B with Rogers. Cox and Pixton had served in Company E with Browett and had been part of his mess: see Robert Pixton Autobiography, LDS Archives. Rogers realized the group's mistake in identifying "the back bone" when the Holmes-Thompson company moved beyond West Pass and Carson Pass to make camp at Red Lake: see his diary for 29 July 1848.

Fr 5 We packed as usual, traveled 20 miles, up the divide. Through a heavy forrest of pine, read wood and fir, after which we camped at two oclock P.M.

Sa 6 Last night snow fell all night and this morning, untill the snow became 3 inches deep at 8 oclock. cleared up. We started as usual. Traveled 6 miles when we came to the oald snow. We past on to the back bone of the Mountain when the snow became softer than what the horses ware able to travel on, it being 4 miles from the edge of the old snow. The snow falling fast, we turned back and camped where we left this morning.

Su 7 We continued our journey down the mountain, for 32 miles. Camped in a small valley.

Mo 8 We prosecuted our journey for 40 miles, when we came to a gold mine that is worked by W S Willis [Sidney Willes] and W[ilford] Hudson and S Branon [Samuel Brannan], it having been discovered by the first named above. They are doing well.

Tu 9 We arrived at the house on the [mill] race distance 15 miles, when I found that a pair of shoes had been sent up to me from sutters, price three Dollars. I also found that Brother [George] Kelly had sent 600 pounds of flour for Brother [David] Moss and my self. for which we let him have a pair of oxen, that we bought the other day. I got an order of Brother Willis to the amount of 4 Dollars.

By the time Browett, Rogers, and their companions returned to Sutter's Fort and reported on their scouting efforts, preparations for the expedition were proceeding vigorously. One member of the party, Robert Pixton, recalled that he "stopped at what we called the Mormon Island, where there was some of the brethren at work getting gold. Brother Sidney Willis and his brother, also Brother Hudson. I stayed here for a short time and got some gold."[11]

In his diary Samuel Rogers described a round of activities during the following weeks: mining at the Natomas diggings, completing the ditch construction for Sutter's grist mill, making ox bows and ox yokes, and negotiating the purchase of animals and supplies. Captain Sutter and the resources of his establishment at the fort were the prime source of provisions and supplies of many kinds for the battalion veterans as they accumulated their "fit out" for the trip eastward.

Rogers recorded that he and his compatriots from the battalion held another meeting on 11 June, "takeing in to consideration the time and manner of our starting from here where we concluded That some start

[11]Robert Pixton Autobiography, LDS Archives.

this week."[12] With a starting time now in mind, the tempo of trading preparations increased. While a series of delays held back his actual departure, Rogers noted in his diary a few final purchases at Sutter's Fort, and on 20 June the first ox-drawn wagons set out across the Sierra for Great Salt Lake City. But his own departure remained in doubt for another few days, as first one problem and then another kept him from joining the expedition.

> Mo 19 [June 1848] I bought a horse of Sutter price 35 Dollars. I gave an order on Sutter for one Dollar to Holt [Timothy Hoyt] yestoday I bought nearley a barrel of Potatoes, for which I pade 25 Dollars in goald two thirds of which J Duglass [James Douglas] and A[zariah] Smith agrees to take and pay me for.
>
> Tu 20 Some of the men started with their teames for the mountains and there to camp for a while.
>
> We 21 Some more of the men with their teames start to day. I sent to the Fort bought a stew kettle price 5 Dollars. Smith takes 5 Dollars worth of Potatoes of me but Duglass takes none.
>
> Tu 22 I went after my cow at St. Clares.[13]
>
> Fr. 23 We made ready to start for the camp to morrow.
>
> Sa 24 All not being ready we still tarry but camped out.
>
> Su 25 some not yet being ready we still remain on the ground. I bought two Dollars worth of tallow. with a can to put it in. I bought a two inch orger [auger] for two Dollars.

[12]On this same date Rogers noted that "Thomas Weare [Weir] has been deranged from the beginning of last week he is still deranged." Addison Pratt ascribed the mental problems of his friend Weir to gold. Weir had been up to the mines, Pratt explained, "and being naturally very avaricious and a little dishonest with all, and when he saw the gold in such quantities his feeling were wrought up to such a pitch that he became insane." His comrades, Pratt added, had confined the unfortunate man in the flume at Sutter's gristmill. When given his freedom a short time each day, "he would perform a variety of ludicrous tricks, such as, mount the mill frame which was two stories high, and dance back and forth on the ridgepole, &c." After some discussion, Pratt and John Eager agreed to take charge of Weir for the trip to Salt Lake City, escorting him and carrying 150 pounds of his luggage in their wagon in exchange for the use of two oxen owned by Weir. "It was generally believed," Pratt wrote in his journal, "that the journey would restore him to sanity, as he had already began to mend a little." See Ellsworth, ed., *The Journals of Addison Pratt*, 339–40.

[13]John Sinclair, a Scotsman, was one of the earliest settlers along the lower American River following Sutter's arrival. By 1841 he had established himself with his Native wife on the north side of the American River about two and a half miles upstream from Sutter's Fort. This property became part of Rancho del Paso, granted in absentia to Elijah Grimes in December 1844 while Sinclair managed the property. Like Sutter, Sinclair became known for his friendliness to newcomers. He served under Mexican law as the alcalde for the Sacramento district and became one of the first miners on the North Fork of the American River. In spring and summer 1848 he was working a claim at what became known as Beal's Bar with a force of fifty Indians. On his tour of inspection in July, Governor Mason reported that Sinclair and his Indian crew had taken out about $16,000 worth of gold. See Hoover, *et al.*, *Historic Spots in California*, rev. Kyle, 260, 288; and Bancroft, *History of California*, 6:14, 15.

Mo 26 We made a start for the camp in the mountains, but my tire proved to be loose. For which reason I went to the mines to get [the] tire set. where we camped.

Tu 27 We changed work with brother Blancherd he weldid our wagon tire we worked in the mines.

We 28 We worked half of the day in the mines for brother [Mervin] Blancherd while he set the tire. In the PM we started for the camp. When we got about one half of a miles brother Pratt broke his wagon tung when we camped we repaird the wagon. I paid 14 Dollars for the use of the tools.

Tu 29 We hitched up when we ware detained wating for some others untill noon when we started. traveled to the shingle road then camped. . . .

30 Started out this morning in Company with [Addison] Pratt and [Samuel] Rogers and John Eager [Eagar][14] things go Better now Where one is hard up all Stop untill he is Loose and Ready to go againe this is what Suits me. I do not Like to be Left and I am willing to Stop for others So that we may all be together and help one another.

July the 1 [1848] started this morning in good Spirets for the Camp in the mountains. After going 2 or 3 miles Brother Pratt Broke out an axeltree out of his waggon fix up in a Short time and started againe [but] had not gone far Before he Broke a gaine Stoped and put in a new one It was not long Before we was on the rode agane got in to Camp about sun down

2 in Camp to day fixing our waggons, seting tires and so forth 4 waggons started on this morning with two Cannon to Break the way. Good white pine here and oak and good water and good Land We fine [find] it is a good valley This is 40 miles from the top of the California mountains

Robert Pixton: Someone Should Go Ahead and Look Out a Road

The camp that Rogers, Pratt, and Eagar had reached on 1 July was the rendezvous site for the LDS travelers that Henry Bigler and two companions had found two weeks earlier. On horseback, the three men had scouted for a likely location in the foothills where the Saints could rally. A day's trip southeast of Coloma they came across this gentle valley with abundant grass and water. Located south of modern Highway 50 and ten miles southeast of Placerville, it is still called Pleasant Valley, the name conferred on it by Bigler and his comrades. After arriving on 18

[14]John Eagar was a young *Brooklyn* colonist who had served as Sam Brannan's clerk and worked as an associate editor of the *California Star*. To reach Salt Lake, he joined returning missionary Addison Pratt in San Francisco. He was the only *Brooklyn* Saint to become a member of the Holmes-Thompson company. See Ellsworth, ed., *The Journals of Addison Pratt*, 337, 546n19.

June, as Bigler recounts, the men built corrals and waited for the others to gather. Three days later the Mormon vaqueros arrived with their horse herd, and on the twenty-second the first wagons rolled into camp, followed by more herdsmen with cows and calves.

This version of Bigler's account is based on the manuscript transcription of his 1848 daybook that Bigler sent to Hubert Howe Bancroft in a series of letters written in 1872 from his home in Brigham City, Utah. Bigler told Bancroft that it was a literal transcription, but with explanatory remarks added. Years later, as already noted, Erwin G. Gudde prepared his own transcript of Bigler's record based on these letters and published it as *Bigler's Chronicle of the West*. Comparison demonstrates that Gudde altered Henry Bigler's text extensively. He often silently corrected Bigler's grammar, spelling, and punctuation, deleted words, occasionally rendered a misreading of Bigler's handwriting, and in various places without notice inserted his own historical explanations. A literal transcription of Bigler's original manuscript version contained in his letters to Bancroft, not Gudde's published version, is given here.

HENRY WILLIAM BIGLER, DAYBOOK OF 1848, BANCROFT LIBRARY.

> Sat. June 17th [1848]. This morning myself and 2 others set out a horse back from where Brighton now stands, takeing our blankets a little grub and our axes to go in to the mountains or rather into the foothills to find a suitable place to Rally to, from which point all who were intending to go up to the Great Salt Lake would start from and the nex[t] day the 18th we found a spot we thought would do a distance as we thought a bout 45 miles from the flouring mill the place we left the day before and I Should conclude from what I have heard that this place was not far from Placerville—We gave the name of our little valley, 'pleasant Valley.' Here we fell pine timber and built a large Correl. On the 21st some of the boys arrived with our band of loose horses and the 22nd Wagons began to roal in, mostly drawn by oxen followed by our cows and calves.

While they waited at Pleasant Valley for latecomers, the veterans, as expected, elected Daniel Browett to be the president of their company. Exercising his authority, Browett announced immediately that he, Ezra H. Allen, and Henderson Cox would go ahead to search out a pass, looking for a good route across the mountains. Anxious to be on their way, restless and perhaps bored with camp life, the men ignored the warnings of their friends about the dangers of mountain travel for so small a company. As he stated in his autobiography, Robert Pixton, who as Browett's messmate in Company E had traveled with him from Missouri, was especially concerned because Browett left without the protection of his sacred priesthood underclothing, which Mormons call garments.

ROBERT PIXTON, AUTOBIOGRAPHY, LDS ARCHIVES.

> In June we called a council of brethren together and concluded to start on our journey home. We gathered to a place in the mountains called Pleasant Valley. We stayed here until all had gathered, and we chose Brother Daniel Browett as president of the company. Brother Browett thought it best that someone should go ahead and look out a road; himself, Brother Allen and Henderson Cox started, each riding a horse and leading a pack mule. I asked Brother Browett if he had his garments on; he said, "no." I advised him to put them on, but he took no notice of it. We waited for them to come back and began to feel uneasy as some of the brethren said they had seen an Indian pass through the timber with a red shirt on. After waiting until we thought they had time to come back, we started with our wagons and stock on the 27th of June [and] we stopped and camped on the divide to see if we could find the brethren. We had two small cannons that we had bought from Mr. Sutter. Two of the brethren and myself loaded them and fired them off but to no use as they did not come.

Confidently, Browett, Allen, and Cox set out on 25 June with horses and two mules packing food and camp gear. All three had been in the earlier scouting party described by Samuel Rogers. They anticipated that they would travel fast and return in just a few days. Their continued absence, mentioned in every contemporary account, had become a matter of great concern for the entire camp by 2 July, when the main party left Pleasant Valley to begin the trek across the Sierra.

Henry Bigler and a few others remained behind in Pleasant Valley for a day, hunting for strayed oxen. They caught up with the camp on July 4th, guided by the sound of a cannon being fired to celebrate the national holiday—and, as Pixton related, in hopes that the lost scouts would respond to the signal. The following day the company reached another small valley with grass and water located a mile downhill on the south side of their ridge route. Sly's Park they called it, honoring James Sly, who had discovered the site. Here they decided to make another stop. Uncertain about what was ahead, they sent out a new search party composed of ten men who they hoped would find the missing scouts and bring back word of a good route across the mountains. Leaving their wagons along the ridge above, the remaining company members took their oxen, horses, and cows down into the park to while away the time as they waited.

HENRY WILLIAM BIGLER, DAYBOOK OF 1848, BANCROFT LIBRARY.

The gathering continued until the 2 of July and on the morning of the 3d a general move was made except myself and a few others who were detained in finding our oxen when on the 4th a bout 11 A.M. we roaled out after the camp takeing the divide between the American River and the Moccozumy [Cosumnes]. We made a bout 10 miles and just as we began to prepare for camping we he[a]rd the Cannon from the front camp and was reminded that this was the birth day of American independence.

The 5th made an early start still keeping [to] the divide and by 9 A.M. we roaled up to the front Camp. Here they had concluded to stop a few days as they had found a nice little valley (though a bout 2 miles to the South on the waters of the Moccozumny four our stock, an[d] send out some men to examine the route and look for three of our company viz. Browett, Allen & Cox who had left our camp on the 25th of June to look out a pass while the company was gathering and as yet we had not heard any thing from them and the Camp began to feel uneasy a bout them. Accordeingly we sent out ten men to look for them while the rest of us took the stock down in to the little valley which we called Slys Park after one of our men who found it and there built a couple Correls and awaited the return of the ten men who returned on the 14th of July and reported they seen nothing of the 3 men neither any signs after passing a sertaine point. They had discovered a pass but it would have to be worked.

SAMUEL ROGERS: THEY WARE TAKEN BY SURPRISE—TRAGEDY SPRING

The April scouting party had set out on a line of march along the divide separating the watershed of American River's South Fork on the north from the Cosumnes River watershed on the south. Because they would be driving ox-drawn wagons across the Sierra, the men realized they needed to avoid steep "side hills." Sloping terrain might be quite passable for horses and mules, but wagons could slip and veer downhill, a maneuver called "sidling" that every wagon driver hoped to avoid. For this reason the LDS road makers attempted to stay atop the ridge of the divide. Traveling high above the creek and riverbeds meant they could also avoid crossing swollen streams, and they were less likely to confront canyon walls or precipitous drop-offs that might force them to backtrack. These advantages were offset by the increased difficulty of finding adequate sources of water and forage for their stock along the ridges. The dual demands of road building and keeping their animals healthy dictated a slow rate of travel through the mountains.

During their stay at the Sly's Park campsite, the company made decisions by general consensus at occasional informal meetings. Although Jonathan Holmes does not mention it in the sparse entries in his trail diary, Samuel Rogers reported that Holmes was taking charge of these meetings, a natural development in light of his position of influence among the LDS brethren. All expected that Daniel Browett would lead the company when he and his two companions returned. With their hard-won skills in trail making and travel through unknown territory, the veterans believed themselves equal to the challenges of the country ahead; yet by this point everyone in camp feared the worst for the missing scouts. As Azariah Smith remarked, "they all ag[reed] to be cheerful, and are waiting with anxiety for those to come back that went ahead."[15] According to Rogers' diary, "the Pioneers who started on the fifth returned, and reported that a road is found over the mountains but it requires some labor to render it passable but the three men who started first they had no news of. We expect to leave here to morrow." The news from the scouting party was the encouragement everyone needed to get the wagons moving forward again.

After leaving Sly's Park, the company fell into a work routine for blazing the mountain section of the road. A few men who were not driving wagons, usually with Henry Bigler and Francis Hammond among them, moved in front of the column to mark out the route and clear away brush and rocks.[16] The wagons and teams followed, and after them came the cattle and horse herds. With frequent stops to repair broken wagons, it was a good day's work to make eight or ten miles up the mountain ridge.

[15]Bigler, ed., *The Gold Discovery Journal of Azariah Smith*, 14 July 1848, 126.

[16]Hammond had used his mining profits to buy a fine outfit to take across the Sierra and the desert beyond: a heavy government freight wagon fully loaded with dry goods and food staples, drawn by four yoke of oxen. But he was the least experienced of these overland travelers, for his sailor's life had given him no training in handling ox teams. He quickly realized his wagon-driving skills left much to be desired. After a first calamity, Hammond made an arrangement with Timothy Hoyt to buy his wagon and team and haul his goods for him. Once across the Sierra, Hammond put together a pack outfit and joined others in striking out for Great Salt Lake City ahead of the wagon teams.

When Sly's Park was three days behind, the company members reached another choice stopping place on 17 July that they named Leek Spring. A small valley with a natural spring, wild onions or leeks, and grass, it offered brief ease and refreshment for the travelers and their animals. Elijah Elmer explained the special attraction of this site in his journal: "traveled 10 miles to[day] and camp in Leack Vally it deserves its name from the great Quantity of Leackes that grow in it. We had a good supper out of them at knight the first time I have Eat any thing green in so long a time that I cannot remember."[17]

The next morning, as the wagons and herds stopped for a day, the road-clearing crew again went ahead. According to Azariah Smith, that afternoon these pioneers saw some Indians "with clothing on which resembled those of Brothers Browett, Allen and Cox."[18] As they headed back to Leek Spring at dusk, the trail blazers came across a natural camping spot with the remains of an old fire and an area of freshly disturbed ground nearby. It looked alarmingly like it could be the grave of the missing men. Henry Bigler's account provides details of the discovery and briefly describes the scene when the entire company reached this place the following day.

HENRY WILLIAM BIGLER, DAYBOOK OF 1848, BANCROFT LIBRARY.

July 15th, This morning myself and 3 others went a head with axes to cut brush and roal rocks out of the way for our wagons & packs for my journal supposes a wagon never had been here before since theese mountains were made and for aught I know not even a white man. Our Camp made a bout 8 miles and encampted on the top of the divide a bout 1 mile from water.

16th Cutting our way as yesterday. The road very bad [—] broke a coupling pole to one of the wagons. Made a bout 8 mi. and encampted on the waters of the MocZumy [Cosumnes River]. This we called Camp Creek.[19]

17th to day we had bad road and a great deal of brush to cut. Broke an axiltree—made 8 or 10 miles and campt at leak Spring a fine spring with plenty of leeks and grass a bout it.

---

[17]Bagley, ed., "'To the Tops of the California Mountains': The 1848 Carson Pass Journal of Elijah Elmer," 5. A photocopy of the original journal is at the Lee Library, Brigham Young University, apparently donated about 1980 by family members.

[18]Bigler, ed., *The Gold Discovery Journal of Azariah Smith*, 127.

[19]Camp Creek, a tributary of the Cosumnes, lies south of Iron Mountain and the modern Mormon Emigrant Trail road. Later travelers continued to use the path down to this small stream, necessary for the sake of the animals. The Camp Creek section of the trail remained obscure until it was rediscovered by trail buff Tom Mahach in 1990 with the help of participant journals. It has now been placed in a protected status by the Historic Preservation staff of Eldorado National Forest

Tues. 18th. Camp laid by to hunt some stock that was lost out of the herd yesterday. While myself and 4 others went to work the road which we did for a bout ten miles and as we were returning to Camp we found where we supposed our 3 pioneers had campt by a large spring running from the mountains in to the MocZumy and near where they had their fire was the appearance of a fresh grave some of us thought it mite be an Indian grave as near it was old wickey up, but the more we looked at it the more we felt there lay the 3 men. When we got back to Camp all the lost stock was found and we made a report of the road and the grave &c. That evening the camp was called to gether and organized more perfectly by appointing Captains of tens and also appointed Lieut. Thompson Capt. over the whole camp in case there should be any fighting to do—that night for the first [time] we put out Camp guard. Our numbers were as follows, 45 men and one women (Serge[a]nt Wm. Corys wife) 2 small brass pieces bought of Sutter and I believe every man had a musket. 17 wagons, 150 horses and about the same of Cattle.

The 19th Roaled out from leek spring [—] had hard heavy pulling [—] the road very rocky in places. Broke our new axiltree and in passing over a Snowbank Mr. J. Ho[l]me's wagon broke down making only 5 or 6 miles and encampt at the Spring near the fresh grave. Determining to satisy ourselves it was soon opened. We were shocked at the sight. There lay the three murdered men robbed of every stitch of clothing lieing promiscuously in one hole about a foot deep. Two of them were lieing on their faces. Allen was lieing on his back and had the appearance that an ax had been stuck into his face and shot in the eye. The blows seemed fresh still oozeing from their wounds. When we came to examine a round and about we found arrows lieing plentifully on the ground many of them bloody and broken. Examining still closer the Rocks were stained with blood and Mr. Allens purse of gold dust lieing a bout a rod from the grave. The gold was still in the sack it was known by several of the boys who had seen him make it. He had attached a buckskin string of sufficient length so as to put it over his head and around his neck and letting the purse hang in his bosome inside of his cloethes.[20] Some though[t] their [guns] and Saddles mite be in their grave with them for they had set out leaving the camp having each a wrideing animal and a pack mule. At the time they left Camp they were advised not to go but wait until all the Camp was ready for a start but they seemed restless and anxious to be on the move towards home and so left saying they would travel slowly and hunt out the best way a cross the Sierra Nevada and would meet us some where in the mountains.

---

[20]Wilford Hudson carried the pouch of gold worth $120 to Kanesville, Iowa, and delivered it to Allen's widow. "There were marks of blood on upon it," Sarah Fiske Allen Ricks later recalled, "and it seemed to me the price of his life." She had a wedding band crafted from part of the gold and used the rest to migrate to Utah with her two small children. See Norma Baldwin Ricketts's powerful recounting of this story in *Tragedy Spring and the Pouch of Gold*, 28–29.

Samuel Rogers was also in the work party that came across the gravesite and led the company back to this location the following day. His account matches Bigler's description in recreating the group's shock and sorrow at the sight of their comrades' mutilated corpses.

SAMUEL HOLLISTER ROGERS, 1848 DIARY, MS LDS ARCHIVES.

Tu 18 Some men went back in search of the cows and horses that ware lost. Five of us went ahead to cut out the road. I being one of the number whilst the remainder taried in the camp. We found the place where the three brethering had camped who went first to search out the road. By a spring of water, there was a grave. Some think that it is the grave of the three Brethren. This evening the Company is organized in tens there being four of them. Samuel T[h]ompson Captain of the tens, and Jonathan H Holmes Captain of the whole.[21]

We 19 We continued our journey for 6 or 7 miles. then camped near the grave that we found yestoday. After we pitched our camp we examined the grave by diging in to it. When we found to our regreat and deep sorrow of heart the Bodies of the Three Brethren, who went in search of the road viz Daniel Browatt [Browett], Henderson Cocks [Cox] and Ezra H Allen. By the appearance and signs we could discover, they ware taken by supprise, when they ware asleep in the night. Arrows ware found round about. Allen had been struck with an axe across the mouth cutting the lower jaw in two. His purce was found which he forme[r]ly caried suspendid from his neck. The string was cut in two. Blood was on the purce. Gold dust and coin money was in it. The time they had been absent from us was twenty four days. They are supposed to have been Murdered on the 27 of June in the night. We kept a gard to protect us from the Indians.

Th 20 This morning we found that some of the cattle and horses had strayed from us some of the men are in search of them. while the remainder of us are walling the grave with stones building a yard. Others are repairing a wagon wheel for Br Holmes. We call this place Tragady springs.

The discovery at Tragedy Spring affected no one more grievously than Jonathan Holmes. As we learn from other accounts, he had been designated as the captain of the company at a meeting on the evening of 18 July, just after the work party brought back news of the probable gravesite. When the company uncovered the three bodies the next day, Holmes uncharacteristically gave expression to his deep feelings of grief,

[21] A few days later Elijah Elmer recorded the full roster of officers for the expedition: "Brother Holmes our leader and Brother Pratt with Br Rogers his Counselors Brother Samuel Thompson our Capt of 50 and Br Sly Capt. Of ten, Br Green Capt of 2 ten E Elmer of the 3 ten, B Coray of the 4 ten." See Bagley, ed., "Journal of Elijah Elmer," 5.

particularly extreme because of his long and close friendship with Daniel Browett.

JONATHAN HOLMES, 1848 JOURNAL, LDS ARCHIVES.

18 Laid in Camp & repaired wagons [In margin: Broke our wagon on the 18th of July] Some went Back & found most of the lost animels & Some went a head & looked [for] the road & found whear the 3 Brethren that went ahead was murdered But did not asertain for a sertonty

19 Started on our way traveled about 6 miles & camped & found whear those 3 Brethren ware Murdered Namely Daniel Brewett Ezra H. Allen & Henderson Cox they was murdered on the 27 of June at night while they was a Sleep. we fixed the grave as well as we could it was a Solem time when it was asertained that these men had been murderd & in so shocking a maner it was a time of Solemenity & morning to think that the man that was to Be our leader to Salt Lake was now lying Dead, he was like a father to me & we morn his loss.

20 Staid in Camp & fixt our wagon & Built a wall round the Graves of our Brethren that had Ben Murdered &t&t.

HENRY W. BIGLER: A MONUMENT TO ALL WHO MAY CHANCE TO PASS

After opening the grave of their three comrades, the camp spent an edgy, fearful evening. Just at bedtime, a disturbance in the woods greatly agitated their animals, browsing under the nearby pine trees. Henry Bigler described what followed.

> Last night just before lieing down and before the guard was posted Something or other gave our horses & Cattle a dreadful affright. Supposed to be either Grizelys or Indians. The thundering of the running stock fairly shook the ground and was like an earth quake. Lieut. Thompson ordered [us] to 'limber up a Cannon and let her speak once.' The guard was soon put out but nothing more occured. All was quiet til morning when we found more than one third of the stock missing. We lay here all day. Sent men in all directions hunting up lost stock.[22]

Whether it was a grizzly or Indians that startled their horses that night, the LDS travelers never knew for certain, although Azariah Smith stated that later "Some of the Boys came [back] with part of the horses which had been driven off [by] the Indians, but [the Indians] they could

[22]Henry W. Bigler Daybook, 20 July 1848, Bancroft Library.

not drive them off, and their [tracks] were thick all over the old camping ground, where the horses [were]."[23]

Some accounts say the stampede occurred before the cannon fired; others declare it was the booming of the cannon that scattered the animals. As James S. Brown remembered the incident, each version contained some truth.

> The night we came to Tragedy Springs was very dark, and our camp being in a dense forest of large trees, the darkness was intensified. Guards were at their posts around stock and camp, when suddenly, from some cause we never knew, the stock stampeded. This raised a great excitement, and before it subsided one of our cannon was discharged; as it belched forth its stream of fire, and the sound of the explosion echoed in forest and hills, the animals were stampeded still worse, only a few horses that had been securely tied remaining. We were compelled to lay by for two days to get things together, but we finally did so, recovering all our stock.[24]

Addison Pratt added further detail in his telling of this episode: "We hunted two days for the cattle and horses," he stated, "and found all but one leader ox in my team, him we supposed the Indians had eaten, but when the next company came on after us they brought him on to Salt Lake, and told us he came to them in Pleasant Valley, the next day after he left us."[25]

The building of a rock cairn over the gravesite at Tragedy Spring was the work of an afternoon, while the LDS herdsmen continued to search for the stampeded stock. The horror of the scene for the Mormon veterans may be judged by the comments of James S. Brown in his reminiscences. It was necessary to leave their remains where they were found, Brown related, "for the bodies were so decomposed that we could not do more."[26] In the journal transcription he sent to Hubert Howe Bancroft, Henry Bigler placed a further construction on their actions.

> In the afternoon we enclosed the grave with granite rock, to prevent wild beasts from tareing them out and to stand as a monument to all who may

[23]Bigler, ed., *The Gold Discovery Journal of Azariah Smith*, 130.

[24]Brown, *Life of a Pioneer*, 110.

[25]Ellsworth, ed., *The Journals of Addison Pratt*, 346.

[26]Brown, *Life of a Pioneer*, 110. A more detailed description, including a hypothetical recreation of the events that surrounded the killing of the three men, appears in Azariah Smith's account: Bigler, ed., *The Gold Discovery Journal of Azariah Smith*, 129.

JONATHAN HOLMES
President of the 1848 wagon train that opened the Carson Pass Wagon Road while heading from northern California gold fields to Great Salt Lake City, Holmes appears in this 1875 photograph with his third wife, Sarah Ingersoll Harvey Floyd. *Courtesy LDS Archives.*

> chance to pass that way. We judged they were killed the second night out which would make it the 24th of June. We cut the folowing inscription on a Balsome fir that stood near the grave. 'To the memory of Daniel Browett and Ezrah H. Allen, Henderson Cox who was supposed to have been murdered and buried by Indians on the night of the 27th of June, A.D. 1848.[']
> We called this place tragedy Spring.[27]

Apparent contradictions in the documentary record have caused some interpreters to doubt the unanimous conclusion by the company members, recorded in all the surviving accounts, that Indians had murdered the scouts. In particular, these few extreme skeptics have been troubled by Bigler's graphic description of the bodies of the three murdered men: "The blows seemed fresh still oozeing from their wounds." This state-

[27]Henry W. Bigler Daybook of 1848, Bancroft Library.

ment seems to call into question the hypothetical dating of the men's death to three weeks earlier. But Bigler's words must be weighed against Brown's explanation for the failure of the Saints to move and reinter the victims, which strongly suggests that Bigler mistook the nature of the physical evidence.

The context of time and place provides a strong argument for the veterans' interpretation of the killing. Native peoples on the west slope of the Sierra Nevada had experienced at least two decades of hostilities with Americans and Mexicans by 1848, dating to the murderous aggressions of Jedediah Smith and his men during their abortive attempt to cross the Sierra Nevada along the American River drainage during spring 1827.[28] Given the record of racial warfare that characterized the period, no one should find it unlikely that Native peoples attacked, killed, and robbed a small party of unidentified strangers who had come trespassing on their Sierra Nevada territory in 1848.[29]

The memorial and inscription at Tragedy Spring became one of the most frequently mentioned landmarks on the Carson Pass trail in gold rush journals. The rock cairn remains in place today, accompanied by a bronze marker installed in September 1987, when the U.S. Forest Service cooperated with the Sacramento branch of the Daughters of Utah Pioneers, the Sierra Chapter of the Sons of Utah Pioneers, and several Explorer Boy Scout groups to establish a small roadside park. The fir tree bearing the memorial inscription stood until it was damaged in winter storms in 1928–1929. A work crew headed by H. C. Petersen, then curator at Sutter's Fort State Historic Park, removed the stump with the inscription intact in August 1931 and placed this relic at Sutter's Fort. Subsequently the State Parks Department transferred it to Marshall Gold Discovery State Park at Coloma, where it is now prominently displayed.

---

[28]Brooks, ed., *The Southwest Expedition of Jedediah S. Smith*, 153–57. "I endeavored to convince them of my disposition to be friendly by every means in my power but to no purpose," Smith wrote. He picked two men ("of course not the most certain marksmen") to demonstrate the range and power of their rifles, but "both men firing at once two indians fell." Subsequent warfare between Natives and newcomers reached into this region, as summarized in Hurtado, *Indian Survival on the California Frontier*, 40–46, 50–54, 86–99.

[29]An entirely fanciful story of the murder appears in Fifield, "Wagons East Across the Sierra," 285–86. This version asserts the three men were killed by unknown Mexican outlaws (possibly including the mythical Joaquin Murieta). The author cannot claim a single piece of verifiable evidence for support.

ELIJAH ELMER: THE ROADS WORSE THAN EVER—CROSSING WEST PASS

From Tragedy Spring the Holmes-Thompson company forged ahead by slow stages, sending out well-armed, cautious work parties to clear their line of advance from day to day. As they continued their climb up the western slope of the Sierra Nevada, the LDS pioneers left behind the ridge route that had brought them into the mountains. A geographical jumble of steep hillsides, granite domes, rocky canyons, and snow-covered peaks faced them as they searched for a way across the crest of the Sierra.

After reburying their slain comrades and recovering the stock, the entire company traveled south-southeast on 21 July to a site they named Rock Creek in Rock Valley, now part of a private ranch property inside Eldorado National Forest. According to Elijah Elmer, the wagons took hard punishment on this section of road: "about 11 oclock . . . we got up our teams and Started on our Journy traveld 5 miles in to Rock Vally and camp Roads verry bad one waggon turned over and broke a tongue out of another wagon."[30]

The wagons and herds remained in Rock Valley for two days as the roadwork continued. While they waited, Samuel Rogers tells us, he made an effort to inform John Sutter, the federally appointed superintendent of Indian affairs for the region, about the Tragedy Spring affair. "I wrote a letter directed to Mr Sutter," he recorded in his journal, "giving an account of the discovery of the bodies of Browett, Allen and Cox. Allso how, as we suppose they ware murdered, which letter was buried by a tree, and a note or index on the tree directing the beholder to the place of the letter."[31] Elijah Elmer further explained the reasoning behind this action: "we wrote a letter to leave here for some indians to find and to take to some white man to read so that the news may get to Capt Sutter that they may get there punishment all the indians this side of the mountains work for the Capt Every year and he has the government of them purty much."[32]

---

[30]Bagley, ed., "Journal of Elijah Elmer," 5.

[31]Samuel Hollister Rogers, 1848 Diary, LDS Archives.

[32]Bagley, ed., "Journal of Elijah Elmer," 5. Jonathan Holmes also noted in his journal that the men "wrote a Letter to Capt Sutter Stating the Murder of our 3 Brethren wishing him to Search out the murders if possible." See Jonathan Holmes 1848 Trail Journal, LDS Archives. There is no indication in any surviving documents that this message ever reached John Sutter.

The company headed east and northeast along Squaw Ridge on 24 July, crossing the steep, treacherous slopes of West Pass on packed snow, then sinking into slush on the sunnier southeast side where the snow-drifts were thawing. Finishing a total march of six miles for the day, the main force moved down the mountain and reached a camping spot in Emigrant Meadows, today a part of the Kirkwood ski resort. Henry Bigler's daybook account provides an entertaining summary of this part of the expedition. With no wagon to drive, Bigler obviously enjoyed the scenery and the novelty of the experience.

HENRY WILLIAM BIGLER, DAYBOOK OF 1848, BANCROFT LIBRARY.

Friday 21st. Having found all our stock except 1 or 2 mules we hooked on and moved about 4 miles and campt on what we called Rock Creek and built a Correl by falling timber & pileing brush—the mountains well over laid with large masses of Rocks. In the little vallies plenty of leeks young grass and Clover with here & there a large bank of snow.

Sat. 22nd. Camp laid by while myself & 15 others worked a road to the top of the mountain. Some 6 miles from the top we saw several small lakes some of which I was told a bounded with trout. I past over snow more than 2 feet deep and saw banks ten and perhaps 50 ft. deep. This day I gathered flowers with one hand and snow with the other. There were plenty of Chickings [chickens] in the timber resembling the prairie chickings. At evening we returned to Camp tired and hungry although we carried lunch with us.

Sunday 23d. In camp all day.

Mo. 24th. Moved about 6 mi[les] and campt just over the summit. 2 wagons broke down and 2 upset. Two Indians came in to stay all night.

Tues. 25th. Laid by while some went [t]o repairing wagons others watching Stock while others again worked a road down the mountain some 2 miles.

James S. Brown's description of the struggle to get the wagons across West Pass offers a harsher, less appreciative view of that section of road.

When we reached the summit the wind blew as if it were the middle of November. As we crossed over we came to a large snowdrift; on the north side of the mountain our wagons rolled over the snow as if on marble pavement, but when we came to where the sun had shone in the latter part of the day, our wagons went down to the hub, and four were capsized and some of them badly broken. The others succeeded in reaching the bottom in safety. It took us till after dark to pick up the pieces and get them together to be ready to start the next morning.[33]

[33]Brown, *Life of a Pioneer,* 111.

Samuel Rogers described these same hardships, since he was forced to make a cold camp on the mountainside with Brown.

SAMUEL HOLLISTER ROGERS, 1848 DIARY, LDS ARCHIVES.

Mo 24 We traveled 10 miles. some of the men camped on a bench going in to the lake valley but I with some others camped on a side hill. 4 or 5 wagons a broken. We melted snow for warter.

Tu 25 I went on to the bench with those who ware with me we then repaired our wagons.

We 26 We traveled 2½ miles then camped in lake valley. Some 10 men are prepairing to go and search out the road.

While Elijah Elmer avoided the cold night on the mountainside, his account gives added details, including an explanation for Samuel Rogers's problems.

ELIJAH ELMER JOURNAL, *CROSSROADS* (SUMMER 1993), 25.

25 [July 24]— Started out againe this morning and traveled 10 miles the Roads worse than Ever Brother Rogers turned over twice and Willis Broke out a ~~tongue~~ axel tree and an other one was Broken out Steavens [Alexander Stephens] turned over the wrest of us Came on in to Camp safe or much tired Camp in Lake vally to knight Cold and frosty Some Snow here now

26 [25]— Lay still to day to fix up our waggons and to Cut Roads down to the Lake a bout 2½ miles.

More lyrical was the description provided by Addison Pratt. Despite problems with his wagon, Pratt, like Bigler, enjoyed the sights and the novel experience of mountain travel.

We drove over some snowbanks that we supposed were some 40 feet deep. In all the vallies where the snow had disappeared, the grass was young and tender, and in abundance, and the flowers, of which there was a variety, were just in blossom and notwithstanding it was the latter part of July, it seemed like April. This day we capsized two or three waggons in crossing the snowbanks. We had up to this time broken and repaired many of them in our company. One hind wheel had evry spoke broken out and it was filled again with pine, as that was the stoutest timber to be found now. This was done at Tragedy Spring. At night [we] camped near the snow, and it was so cold as to freeze over some of the streams.[34]

---

[34]Ellsworth, ed., *The Journals of Addison Pratt*, 346.

Samuel H. Rogers: Down the Back Bone—Over Carson Pass

As had been true since they left Tragedy Spring, everyone was concerned about the danger from Indians. After crossing West Pass the party camped at Emigrant Meadows where, as told by Bigler, some company members captured two Native men they found near their wagons. The Saints took custody of the Indians' bows and arrows, gave them supper, and kept them under guard until early the next morning when they fed them breakfast, returned their weapons, and set them loose. As Addison Pratt remembered, after eating and getting back their bows and arrows, the two visitors "took leave of us seemingly well pleased. It was evident that we were on the borders of a strange tribe to that that had killed our brethren, as these made signs that they were at war with those in our rear, and gave us to understand that they were bad Indians."[35]

Three days later the main company camped in a place they called Lake Valley, where a mountain meadow surrounded two small lakes, a location now flooded by Caples Lake. The animals were again resting while the men made wagon repairs and waited for an advance party to return. A large Native band came into the camp, and as Henry Bigler describes the event, they surrendered their weapons and became in effect guests of the Saints.

Henry William Bigler, Daybook of 1848, Bancroft Library.

Wed. 26th. Moved to the foot of the mountain and campt near a lake, this we call lake valley—as usual we broke down a gain an axil tree snapt in t[w]o. This afternoon we sent out ten men to explore and hunt a pass across the mountain.

Thurs. 27th. Made some Road, 20 Indians came into camp all armed with Bows & arrows but laid them by while in Camp. Late in the afternoon our ten men returned but made no new discovery.

Addison Pratt's journal offers a more detailed report of this encounter, indicating that the visit may actually have become a cordial social meeting. "Some fifteen or twenty Indians came into camp today," he wrote, "they had some beaver skin quivers, some fresh venison and a preserved buck's head with its horns on, and shewed us that they used

[35]Ibid., 346–47.

[it] to decoy, when in the chase."[36] According to Elijah Elmer, "15 Indians [came into] camp to day to 30 [of] us. They are wild though they appear friendly to us as we under stand them to say."[37]

Curious Natives apparently continued to follow the wagon train, watching its progress with attention that some company members interpreted as a threat. When work crews moved ahead, the men took along their guns and everyone was careful to stay with the group. But the LDS pioneers had no further close contact with Indians until they reached Carson Valley. There hostilities began after an expedition hunter shot an antelope. An Indian came in their camp and saw these strangers butchering the animal and dividing the meat. From that time on, remarked Addison Pratt, "they commenced stealing our horses and cattle at evry opportunity."[38]

From their stopping place in Lake Valley, the Holmes-Thompson company took another week and a half to complete their journey across the Sierra. This section of their road included two extremely difficult stretches. The first was the passage across the Carson Pass "back bone," which they accomplished just north of that geographical feature later named the Elephant's Back.[39] From the summit their roadway sharply headed down the precipitous slope later called the Devil's Ladder, reaching the Red Lake basin at the head of Hope Valley.[40] After traveling to the lower end of Hope Valley, the wagon drivers reached the second extreme obstacle, the seven-mile-long canyon of what they called Pass Creek, which we know as the West Carson River.

While camped in Lake Valley on 27 and 28 July, according to Henry

---

[36]Ibid., 347.

[37]Bagley, ed., "Journal of Elijah Elmer," 5.

[38]Ellsworth, ed., *The Journals of Addison Pratt*, 348; Brown, *Life of a Pioneer*, 111–12; and Bigler, ed., *The Gold Discovery Journal of Azariah Smith*, 134.

[39]This geographical feature, a high sloping mountain top, of course received the name because of its supposed resemblance to the back of a pachyderm. The name also recalls for later generations the wry humor with which many emigrants met and surmounted the challenge of the Sierra Nevada, having "seen the elephant" in the common phrase of the time. For the derivation and use of this phrase in the 1830s and 1840s, see Hammond, *Who Saw the Elephant? An Inquiry by a Scholar Well Acquainted with the Beast*; and Hart, *A Companion to California*, 126–27.

[40]California-bound travelers would later loop chains around stout trees upslope, hitch twelve or even more oxen to their wagons, and try to drag their wagons up this incline with the oxen pulling back downhill with all their might. Even so, the bottom of the hill became a graveyard for many of these wagons, which slipped off the track and careened to destruction. The evidence of the emigrants' struggles against gravity can still be seen on scarred trees and rust-marked boulders on this slope, which can be approached from a Forest Service viewing point south of Highway 88 just east of Carson Pass.

Bigler, the herdsmen made a corral large enough for all their stock. Some of the boys, Bigler adds, "caught a young fawn [then] they marked the youngster and let him go." On the afternoon of the 28th, he relates, "we worked and made a road a cross the mountain."[41]

Samuel Rogers made a typically understated record of the passage across the Carson Pass summit on the following day, 29 July.

> We hitched up our cattle and past down a verry steep and rocky hill. then camped near to Read [Red] Lake the distance of to days journey is 1 miles. There are numerous Lakes in this region. by pasing down the hill to day, we started down the back bone. The place that we supposed to be the back bone at the time that I went in May is not the back bone.[42]

Elijah Elmer was more graphic in describing the haul over Carson Pass and down to Red Lake.[43]

ELIJAH ELMER JOURNAL, *CROSSROADS* (SUMMER 1993).

29 [28 July]— Left Camp this morning for the back Bone of the mountain 3½ miles and Camp for the knight this we Called Summit Camp a party went to work the Road down the mountain this afternoon—about 5,000 feet down or a mile

30 [29]— Left Summit Camp this morning to Cross the Back Bone all got down safe but one waggon Brother Coxes[44] he broke both axel trees out of his waggon travelled one mile to day and Camp at the head of Read Lake this Lake is about 2 miles or 2½ long by 9 or 10 Rods wide it is not verry deep

HENRY W. BIGLER: WE BEGAN TO HAVE HOPE—INTO CARSON VALLEY

Once over Carson Pass, the road builders moved past Red Lake and downstream to the head of West Carson Canyon, where they rested their animals while most men worked on the road ahead. Their camp was "at the mouth of a Canion that is worse than any thing that we have met yet," Elijah Elmer noted. The following day, Monday, 31 July, Samuel

[41]Henry William Bigler Daybook of 1848, Bancroft Library, 27, 28 July 1848.

[42]Samuel Hollister Rogers, 1848 Diary, LDS Archives.

[43]Somehow Elmer had lost track of a day, so his journal dates must be corrected accordingly.

[44]John Cox, a native of England and former Company E private, owned this unfortunate wagon. See Ricketts, *Mormon Battalion*, 222. Of all the Thompson company journals, only Elmer's mentioned Cox.

Rogers went "with a number of others [and] worked on the road down pass creek. The canyion is verry rough and rockey." The work continued another three days, as Henry Bigler relates. He and at least a few others made time for a less strenuous activity, fishing for the cutthroat trout native to the streams of the region.

HENRY WILLIAM BIGLER, DAYBOOK OF 1848, BANCROFT LIBRARY.

Sat. 29th [July]. Moved a cross [Carson Pass] about one mile & half and campt at the head of what we called hope valley (as we began to have hope). In crossing over we broke one wagon.

Sunday 30th. Worked & made a road for a bout 2 miles and moved camp a bout 8 and encampted on what we called pass Creek at the head of a Kanyon. Here we expect to lay by for several days in order to work a road through the Cann[y]on a bout 4 miles and very bad.

Mo. 31st. A general turn out to work on the road. Making fording places to cross the Creek. Considerable dig[g]ing to do and roaling rocks out of the way.

Tues. Aug. 1st. Clear & frosty this morning. 15 turned out and worked on the road. Some went a fishing and caught a lot of trout. Here grows the first wild flax I ever seen. Some of it is in blow and some in the bowl.

Wed. 2nd. Working as yesterday in the Cann[y]on except myself who went a fishing. Caught 12 nice trout.[45]

Thurs. 3d. Road working. In the afternoon fell a little rain & Snow. We were overtaken today by 13 [14] of our boys with pack animals. They had left the mines 5 days ago. We finished our Road.

Many travelers heading for the California gold fields over the Mormon roadway in 1849 and 1850 remarked that their wagons could barely get past the tight spots in West Carson Canyon. Apparently they threaded their way through without ever marveling that the passages were *all* wide enough, if barely, for wagons. In his brief recollections of the 1848 expedition, Zadock Judd explained the ingenious though tedious technique the battalion veterans devised, using only the simplest of tools, to clear sufficient leeway and reduce to rubble the huge boulders that blocked the route.

[45]By his own account, Addison Pratt was the most successful fisherman in the company. "As I had not yet recovered sufficiently from my sickness to be thought fit for labour," he wrote, "it was recommended that I should spend the time at fishing. . . . I did so and the most that I caught in a day was thirty-five. Many others fished also, when they could be spared from the camp, but I seemed to be the most successful." See Ellsworth, ed., *The Journals of Addison Pratt,* 347.

JUDD, "REMINISCENCES OF ZADOCK KNAPP JUDD, SENIOR,"
UTAH STATE HISTORICAL SOCIETY.

We made good progress on our journey and left behind us a good road, until we got nearly across the mountains. In coming down a canyon we came to large rocks which were impassable with the wagons. They were from eight to ten feet high. We had no hammers nor drill with which we could do anything with the stone. It seemed almost an impossiblity to go farther. Finally some one suggested that we build a fire on the rocks, and as there was plenty of dry logs and brush near, there was soon a good fire blazing on each rock that lay in our way. When the fire had died down and cooled off a little, we found that as far as the heat had penetrated, the rocks were all broken in small pieces, which were soon removed with pick and shovel, and another fire built with the same result.

After building three or four fires, we found that the rocks were not much in our way, and we soon had a good wagon road right over them, and we were within a short distance of the old wagon road on Truckee River.

As the work crews were finishing the road, fourteen LDS brethren in a pack train fresh from the gold country caught up with the road builders' wagons. The new arrivals provided a timely reinforcement as the men struggled to get their wagons down West Carson Canyon. To ease the way, as Samuel Rogers recorded, the men transferred some of the wagon cargo to pack animals before starting out. "Then," Rogers added, "toock it to the lore [lower] end of the canyon then toock the remainder down in the wagons. We all got to the camp, at about 9 oclock in the eavening distance 5 miles."[46] At the end of a long, difficult day, they camped in Carson Valley near the canyon's mouth, with the snowy peaks of the Sierra now well behind them.

"Moved through the Kanyon all safe," Henry Bigler wrote with some relief on 4 August, but the trail journals and reminiscences of company members do not reflect any great sense of triumph. A long journey across the high desert country of the Great Basin still separated them from the Salt Lake colony. Yet, as Bigler's journal reflected, their accomplishment was a source of quiet satisfaction, and they must have been heartened to know, after their struggles of the previous weeks, that their path now would be easier.

---

[46]Samuel Hollister Rogers, Diary, 4 August 1848, LDS Archives.

HENRY WILLIAM BIGLER, DAYBOOK OF 1848, BANCROFT LIBRARY.

Sat. 5th of Aug. At about 7 o'clock we was on the march [—] good road [—] made about 12 miles and campt on Carson River though at the time we had no name for it only the one we gave it that was 'Pilot River.' One of our men killed a fine Antelope. Several of the natives visited our Camp. The mount[ain]s seems to be all on fire and the valley full of smoke.

Sun. 6th. Continued down Carson River past a hot spring. Campt in the bend of the River. . . .

"We now began to feel as if our fetters were broken off and that we could make good days travels," declared Addison Pratt after escaping the Sierra.[47]

Once they reached Carson Valley, there was less reason for the whole company to travel together. The fourteen packers remained with the wagons four more days while they all moved down the Carson River. The pack train moved ahead on 8 August, its strength increased by the addition of ten men from the main party, including Zadock Judd and Francis Hammond. Judd's autobiographical account provided a brief explanation for this decision.

JUDD, "REMINISCENCES OF ZADOCK KNAPP JUDD, SENIOR,"
UTAH STATE HISTORICAL SOCIETY.

While crossing over the mountains, the wagon that I was interested in broke down and was left by the roadside. We got all of our effects out of the wagon and put them on pack animals.

We now had no more road work to do, and concluded that we would divide into two companies, pack animals and wagons. I was with the company of pack animals and we could make better headway than the wagons, so we traveled ahead and left them. . . .

Nothing worthy of note happened on our journey until our arrival in Salt Lake Valley September, 1848. . . .

According to Francis Hammond, the pack trip was made memorable by a shortage of provisions, which became severe as they traveled along the Humboldt River. When the opportunity presented itself, Hammond shot an animal that he identified as a wolf, though more likely it was a coyote. "The wolf was soon skinned and dressed," Hammond related, "and we were so hungry for fresh meat that he was soon dis-

[47]Ellsworth, ed., *The Journals of Addison Pratt*, 348.

posed of by broiling or roasting him on the coals." The meal was an experience he recalled ruefully: "I have eaten a great many different kinds of animals," wrote Hammond, "but of all that I ever have tried the wolf was far the worst. I can almost taste him yet as I think of it."[48] Hurried along by their hunger, the packers reached Salt Lake City on 6 September, becoming the first of California's gold-rich Saints to reach Brigham Young's Zion in the middle of the mountains.

Richard M. May: The Glowing Stories of the Mormons of the Gold Mines

Following behind the packers, the Holmes-Thompson wagon train turned away from the Carson River on 12 August, heading northwest. After a day's march of twenty-five miles, they reached the Truckee River and the established California Trail not far from present Fernley, Nevada.[49] From that point the company's eastward journey was comparatively free from incident, except for continued problems with Indian raids on their large herds of cattle and horses. Continuing east, the wagon company contributed yet one more service to future overland travelers: marking out a new road segment from the head of the Humboldt River by way of Thousand Springs Valley and Goose Creek to join Samuel Hensley's recently explored pack trail. This road brought them safely to Bear River and Great Salt Lake City, which they reached 28 September. Their route became known as the Salt Lake Cutoff or, from Salt Lake City, the California Cutoff.[50]

Once they reached the established trail route, the eastbound LDS companies met a number of wagon trains headed for California. In friendly fashion, they advised these outfits to follow their backtrail to the new wagon road across the Sierra. They reinforced their advice with news of the discovery of gold, the first reports these 1848 overlanders received

---

[48]Hammond, "In Early Days: My Introduction to Mormonism," *The Juvenile Instructor*, June–September 1894.

[49]For discussion of the exact route, a matter in dispute, see Bigler, ed., *The Gold Discovery Journal of Azariah Smith*, 136 n36.

[50]Bigler, ed., *The Gold Discovery Journal of Azariah Smith*, 142–43; Ellsworth, ed., *The Journals of Addison Pratt*, 353–54; Gudde, ed., *Bigler's Chronicle of the West*, 123–29; Fleming and Standing, "The Road to 'Fortune': The Salt Lake Cutoff," 248–71; and Korns, ed., "The Salt Lake Cutoff," in *West from Fort Bridger*, 276–306.

about the wealth that was waiting in the rivers and streams of northern California. Offering more than just words, the Saints displayed samples of gold dust and nuggets to their astonished audiences. Judging by accounts from some travelers, the battalion veterans spun tales of easy riches that lost nothing in the telling. Upon seeing the Mormons' gold and hearing about the diggings, one elderly gentleman in the first party to meet the pack train pulled off his battered hat, flung it to the ground, jumped in the air, and exclaimed "Glory Hallelujah! I'll die a rich man yet!"[51]

A more detailed description of these encounters appears in the manuscript journal of Richard May, who was traveling along the Humboldt River with a small family group when they began meeting the LDS parties.

RICHARD MARTIN MAY,
A SKETCH OF A MIGRATING FAMILY TO CALIFORNIA, BANCROFT LIBRARY.

Friday, August 25 [1848]. We met a train of packers from California. 23 in number. Several of them had specimens of gold lately discovered in that country about 70 miles above Sutter's establishment. They represented the mines as being very rich yielding on an average of two ozs. of gold to the days labor and that one particular man had made 700 dollars in one day. The train giving this information were Mormons bound for Salt Lake Valley. . . .

Tuesday 29 Aug. Traveled 23 miles Through clouds of dust and part of the time rough road. At our encampment we met 17 Wagons from California. They had near 100 head of horses and Some fine Cattle. Bound for Salt Lake being a part of Cook's Battallion. They were returning from the Service of their Country and had with them a Small piece of Ordinance. I did not inquire but expected it was a Trophy they were carrying along won by their Arms. . . .

Wed. 30. The glowing stories of the Mormons of the gold mines nearly ran us all mad. . . .

Saturday 9th Sept. 1848. Traveled 6 miles and encamped the 19th time. We met to day another portion of Cook's [battalion.] (It will be remembered they are Mormons) Just from California. The glowing gold Stories were rehearsed and I have no doubt but fortunes are realized in verry Short time. These were packers. . . .

---

[51]Tyler, *A Concise History of the Mormon Battalion in the Mexican War, 1846–1847*, 340. Mormon reports of these meetings include Bagley, ed., *A Road from El Dorado: The 1848 Trail Journal of Ephraim Green*, 28–32; Bigler, ed., *The Gold Discovery Journal of Azariah Smith*, 135–37; Ellsworth, ed., *The Journals of Addison Pratt*, 350; and Gudde, ed., *Bigler's Chronicle of the West*, 120–23.

> Sept. 11 . . . We met too another company bound for Salt Lake. The glowing stories about the gold mines in Alta California. These wagons, 12 in number, came a new route over the mountains and represent it as much better than the old road. . . .[52]

John Borrowman: The Roughest Road I Ever Saw

As Richard May's account indicates, other Mormon parties followed the Holmes-Thompson company over the new wagon road across the Sierra and on to Salt Lake in late summer 1848. Best known is the Ebenezer Brown company. According to the roster prepared by battalion historian Norma Ricketts, twenty-four veterans were in this contingent, along with three battalion wives and one child, Ebenezer Brown's stepson. Forty-three men, women, and children from the *Brooklyn* colony accompanied the veterans, and the group also included one man who had come to California with the New York Volunteers in March 1847. The Brown company left Pleasant Valley on 12 August, nearly six weeks after the Holmes-Thompson train, and reached Great Salt Lake City on 10 October, only twelve days behind the pioneer road builders

The heretofore unpublished journal of John Borrowman gives us the fullest record of this company, the second LDS group to leave the California gold fields with wagons. Here Borrowman describes the trip from Pleasant Valley to Carson Valley and on toward Salt Lake City.

John Borrowman,
Journal from Dec. 23, 1846 to Mar. 1870, LDS Archives.

> Monday, 7th [August 1848]. Saddled my horse and started with Brothers Austin and Bore for the lower mines after some things we had left there and when we had rode about 30 miles we met the Weavers and brother Stoddard bringing our things with them so we turned back 5 miles and camped for the night.
>
> Tuesday, 8th. Started at sunrise and rode into camp where I rested the rest of the day being weary and sore with riding. This evening we held a meeting and organized ourselves according to the pattern the Lord has given to the saints to travel in, Ebenezer Brown first Captn Elijah Thomas 2 and James Park 3rd Captn.

[52]May's excellent journal has been published in two editions: *A Sketch of a Migrating Family to California in 1848*; and *The Schreek of Wagons: 1848 Diary of Richard M. May*, edited by Devere Helfrich and Trudy Ackerman.

Wednesday, 9th. Prepared to start over the mountains.

Thursday, 10th. This morning we yoked up the cattle preparing to start over the mountains but some of the cattle were found to be missing and the day was spent seeking them. Last night I stood guard for the first time on this journey. This evening the missing cattle are not yet found.

Friday, 11th. This day was spent in hunting cattle and preparing to start on the morrow. They are not yet found.

Saturday, 12th. Started and went about 5 miles when Brother [Isaac] Rob[b]ins waggon tongue broke and we had to stop and put in a new one. This day our road lay up a ridge of the mountains and was hard pulling most of the way but all got up without doubling teams except brother [Julius] Austin whose load was too heavy for his team it being weakened by the loss of one yoke of oxen & he was compelled to throw away his tool chest and many of his tools.

Sunday, 13th. This morning brother Robins threw away his tool chest and a number of his tools. This day we traveled ten miles and most all up hill and one place was so steep we all had to double teams to get up.

Monday, 14th. Rested in camp to let the animals rest and feed to prepare them for hard pulling up the mountains and 4 men were sent on to seek for the next watering place and found it about ten miles ahead. In this place there is a little valley with good grass about 2 miles down the creek where we keep our animals but all the rest of the country there is nothing but dry mountains and deep canyons and very little for the animals to eat. Last night I was on guard.

Tuesday, 15th [August 1848]. Went ten miles to the camping ground our pioneers found yesterday. Our road was up hill most all the way and on two hills we had to double our teams. Two men were sent on again today to seek another camping ground and report one ten miles ahead and worse roads than ever being rocky and steep hills.

Wednesday, 16th. We started and traveled about ten miles over a very hard road one hill was about two miles long and some of the teams had to double most of the way and all of them had to double and some of them treble in one place about 4 rods it being very steep and a flat rock so that the cattle could hardly keep their feet and when we came to the top of the ridge it was so steep on our left that we rol[l]ed a large rock over the precipice and it rol[l]ed down about a mile and then we lost sight of it among the brush.[53]

---

[53]Such "rock rolling" was an entertaining if destructive pastime on the overland trails. For other accounts by battalion veterans, see Bagley and Bigler, eds., *Army of Israel,*. 353–354; and Bagley, ed., *Abner Blackburn's Narrative,* 62. Blackburn found several large granite boulders on top of a mountain overlooking Emigration Canyon near Salt Lake "which would weigh several tons. We dug and pried them loose. Started them down the mountain. They sped through the air. Some split to peices and some held togeather and crashed down the mountain until they reached the timber line. They would strike the fir trees nearly to the top and goe right through them and start other rocks and make an awful avlanch," he recalled. "The grouse and wild animals scatterd in all directions."

At our present camping ground there is a pleasant run[n]ing stream about a rod wide in some places.

Thursday, 17th. We rested in camp and repaired our waggons.

Friday, 18th. Traveled about 15 miles mostly up hill one place about half a mile was very steep and we had to double our teams to get up. The road was full of brush and rock and very dusty which made it very bad. Brother [Albert] Knap[p] also broke one of the axls of his waggon which detained us till night before we got into camp and as the cattle had nothing to eat all day we concluded to rest in camp tomorrow. This evening we met according to order for prayer.

Saturday, 19th. We rested in camp and repaired our waggons and our pioneers went to the next camping ground distance reconed 12 miles and found the graves of our three pioneers that went out in June to search out the road and never returned. They are supposed to have been murdered and buried by the Indians.

Sunday, 20th [August 1848]. Traveled 10 or 12 miles to tragedy spring so called from our pioneers being killed there. The road was mostly up hill and some places exceeding steep and rocky insomuch that it would make one wonder that loaded waggons could come over it and not get broke. We found this evening by our camp the graves of our pioneers. There was a large pile of stones neatly built over it and on a tree at the head of the graves the following inscription was neatly cut[:] To the memory of Daniel Bruiet Ezra Allan and Henderson Cox who was supposed to have been murdered and buried by the Indians on the night of the 27 of June 1848. This was done by some of the advance company in honour of three of our brethren who died thus trying to push their way through to the Church.

Monday, 21st. Went about 6 miles. The road today was much better being mostly in a valley [Rock Valley]. After we came into camp some of the men went up the mountains and brought down handfulls of snow and I went out with two other men to hunt a little and we had not gone far till we saw two deer and went in pursuit of them but we had not gone far till several Indians made their appearance and made after us so we put about and returned to the camp and then formd a carol [corral] of our waggons to keep our oxen in for the night.

Tuesday, 22nd. We went about eight miles and camped. 3 men were sent on to seek another camping ground and returned and reported that there was an exceeding bad hill to climb and that we would have to pack our loads over it and take up our waggons empty so this evening the company were busy preparing to pack. The road we came over today was very bad being very crooked and full of large rock with several steep hills.

Wednesday, 23rd. This morning all that had animals to pack packed them and them that had none threw out about half their loads and left them under the care of some of the brethren who stopt back to fix their packs and let others have their animals to pack today. But brother [William] Wood and I thought we could take our whole load over on the waggon so we let brother Austin have our horses to take his things on. About ten o'clock we started and went 5 miles up the mountains [across West Pass] over the roughest road I ever saw to be traveled by waggons. Then we went down about 6 miles of still worse road being so steep in some places that the oxen would slide down and we had to turn so short some times between large rocks that we could hardly get through with our waggons without suffering any damage and camped in a fine valley by a lake. The snow still lies deep in places on the mountains and is so hard that the horses walked over it without sinking and hardly left a track where they went.

Thursday, 24th. I rested in camp while those that had goods left back went back and brought them on and 3 went on to see what the road was like another days journey ahead and in the evening all returned to camp safe. The pioneers reported very bad road ahead.

Friday, 25th [August 1848]. This morning we went some 3 or 4 miles of very bad road [to Carson Pass] being mostly through a wood and among large rocks and so crooked that one would wonder how we got through. Then we came to a very steep hill about half a mile long full of larg[e] rocks and in some places sidling so that it was with a great difficulty that we got down with the two hind wheels of our waggons rough locked and a man standing on one of the wheels to keep it from upsetting and after we had got down in this way we went on 4 or 5 miles further to a fine valley [Hope Valley] with a beautiful stream running through it. The road after we got over the mountain was very bad being rocky in some places and very rough and marshy in others.

Saturday, 26th. As some of the brethren who were with us were packing they wished now to go on by themselves & leave us as they could go on much faster than we with waggons so we stopt this day and killed a beef that we had along with us and the women baked sweet buisket and the men roasted the ribs of the ox and we had a general tea party and time of rejoicing. This was done that since we had to part we might part with good feeling there was also 2 Indians come into camp and shared with us. 2 men went on to look out the road and reported it still terrible but I was on guard this day.

JOSEPH BATES: REACHED SALT LAKE IN THIRTY-TWO DAYS—THE PACKERS

Joseph Bates, another battalion veteran in the Ebenezer Brown party, traveled from Monterey with the same contingent under Samuel Thompson that included Elijah Elmer. We know also from Elmer's journal that on the way to Mormon Island, former battalion lieutenant Samuel Thompson had been elected captain of the Monterey company and sergeant Ebenezer Brown his lieutenant. Thus the battalion's command structure, originally appointed by Brigham Young and then approved by the men, carried over to these later expeditions.

This reminiscent account by Bates is important because, though brief, it provides the only first-person record of the pack train that left the Brown company in Hope Valley to strike a more rapid pace.[54]

JOSEPH BATES, AUTOBIOGRAPHY, LDS ARCHIVES.

In January 1848, I with 3 others, namely S[hadrack] Holdaway, Walter Barney, and A[lbert] Knapp, went to Monterey California, and worked until July of the same year when [we learned that] gold was discovered at Sutter's Fort [Mill] on the South Fork of the American River by a company of Mormons who were digging a mill race for Mr. Sutter. Right then I started with twenty-five others for the 'Eldorado'. I stayed for four weeks panning and digging in the mines. I had $1800 that I had washed out. I then left for Salt Lake City in Ebenezer Browne's Co. We traveled over the high California mountains. There were forty-one of us. After we were safely over them we made up a little company of ten; namely, B[enjamin F.] Stewart, [John] R. Stoddard, M[iles] Weaver, C[alvin] W. Moore, J[ohn] Reed, A Breedingburgh, L[evi] Fifield, O[rlando] F. Mead, Wm. Beers, J[oseph] W. Bates, and Orrice Murdock, and came on ahead of E. Browne's Co.[55]

We had crossed the mountains on the Mormon Trail. We camped three days to rest where Carson City now stands. We left the main camp and started for the Humbolt River. We were three days in reaching the 'sinks', the fourth day we traveled to what is called the 'slough'. That night we had a fight with the Indians. Three days travel from the sloughs we met a company of emigrants on their way to California. They informed us the Indians were very bad on the road and advised us to go back with them. But we traveled and reached Salt Lake City [on 27 September] in thirty-two days from the time we left the wagons [26 August 1848].

Those who remained behind in Ebenezer Brown's party, as John Borrowman relates, still had to force their way through the narrows of West Carson Canyon before emerging in Carson Valley a few miles south of today's Genoa. Like Borrowman, many later gold rush emigrants proclaimed this stretch the worst road they ever traveled in their lives.

---

[54]Harriet May Bates Francom deposited a literal transcription of Bates's narrative in typescript at LDS Archives in 1991. My appreciation to Michael Landon for locating this item.

[55]Except for John Reed, a *Brooklyn* pioneer, these men were all battalion veterans. A. Breedingburgh is probably Benjamin Brackenbury, whose name appears as Brackenburgh on the battalion muster roles.

John Borrowman,
Journal from Dec. 23, 1846, to Mar. 1870, LDS Archives.

Sunday, 27th [August 1848]. We traveled about 9 miles 6 of which was very good and 3 [down West Carson Canyon] was the worst I ever saw being over larg[e] rocks and down hill so that it wrenched the waggons in a way that one would think that something must breake yet all passed through without injury except one that had one boun[d] brake. We camped tonight by a small river where there is very little feed for the animals. This evening we met a company of emigrants from the States consisting I believe of 19 waggons they told us that we would have 3 miles very bad road and then we would get into the plains and have good roads.[56]

Monday, 28th. The roads we had for 3 miles this morning was as bad if not worse than any we have had being a part of a canyon of the mountains. Part we came through last evening and part this morning. The mountains are very high on both sides and very steep and great rocks have rolled down from the mountains and filled the canyon with broken fragments so that one cannot get through without going over many larg[e] rocks and taking such short turns some times in narrow places between rocks that a waggon cannot get through without great difficulty. There is also a brook about 2 rods wide which we had to cross twice and being full of larg[e] rock was very bad to cross but after we got out of the canyon we had a good road in a fine larg[e] valley. This day we traveled 10 miles.

Tuesday, 29th. Went 12 miles and camped on the salmon trout river [Carson River] called by some pilot river. Here the valley widens out probably as much as from 6 to 10 miles and is called Shoshone valley.

The Holmes-Thompson company reached Salt Lake City on 28 September, twenty-two days after the pack train that had brought Zadock Judd, Francis Hammond, and their companions to the valley. If Joseph Bates is correct in his accounting of days on the trail, this second pack train arrived on 27 September, the day before the Holmes-Thompson company, although none of the trail journals mention this coincidence. The Ebenezer Brown wagon company was not far behind, with its advance elements reaching the LDS capital on 10 October and the main company arriving ten days later.

[56]This was the first of the four or five westbound wagon trains that battalion veterans encountered on their way to Salt Lake in 1848. Parties under James Clyman and Pierre Barlow Cornwall totaling about forty wagons led the way. Borrowman does not provide enough detail to identify positively which group the Brown company met on this day.

ADDISON PRATT: DANCES PROCEEDED AND CONTINUED TILL FIVE OCLOCK

The reunion of the Mormon veterans with the main body of the church became the occasion for a grand ball and banquet. A day or two after the Holmes-Thompson party reached Great Salt Lake City, Addison Pratt recorded, "The two brass cannon were now handed over by the battalion boys to the authorities as a present to the church. And as many of them had now returned, it was proposed by their officers and sanctioned by the authorities of the church, that the soldier boys should make a feast."[57] As Pratt went on to describe in some detail, this proposal set in motion a week of preparations. The grand event on 6 October mixed a celebration of the battalion veterans' arrival with Brigham Young's reconstruction of the battalion's history in a manner that would influence the future attitudes of church leaders toward those LDS brethren who remained in California.

ELLSWORTH, ED., *THE JOURNALS OF ADDISON PRATT*, 364.

Monday and Tuesday [2–3 October 1848] were spent in organizing in military style and Wednesday the cooking was to [be] done for the feast, and Thursday, the feast was to come off, but it was rainy, and conference was deferred till Sunday, and Friday was devoted to the feast.

After the people were assembled at the stand, all the officers of the Mormon Battalion with a martial band, after the tables were set under the bowery, proceeded from one side and marched around the bowery and the soldiers with their ladies fell into ranks and when they had marched once or twice around, they were marched in and seated at the tables, and what vacant seats there were left were filled up by their friends. After they had eaten, a general invitation was given, and after they [the rest of those in attendance] had eaten, the tables and benches were cleared away, and what there was of the Nauvoo band then mounted the stand after two sets of dances were drawn up, an animating tune was struck up and the dances proceeded and continued till five oclock when it was closed. The feast opened by prayer by President Young, and closed by Captain Hunt, who was the senior captain of the Battalion. After that Br. Young address'd the Battalion and commended them highly for their faithfulness as good soldiers and said their services were the temporal salvation of the church. For had they refused to turn out 500 soldiers, it is believed by the church, that the government of the United States intended to send out a force after the Mormons and exter-

[57]Ellsworth, ed., *The Journals of Addison Pratt*, 363.

minate the whole church. This plan is believed to have been concocted by Benton, the Missourian, Mormon eater, as he tried to influence the president against us as a people.[58]

This celebratory event for the LDS veterans, although it was staged a few days too early to be shared by the Ebenezer Brown wagon company, gave splendid recognition to the battalion boys' accomplishments and commemorated their safe return to families and friends. Although not recognized by church officials, the hard and dangerous work they carried out to open the Carson Pass Wagon Road across the Sierra Nevada must rank high among the feats to their credit.

A strong Mormon interest in the Carson Pass Wagon Road continued through 1849 and the next few travel seasons. Some veterans who traveled eastward in 1848 returned to California the following year, either with LDS companies or as hired guides for non-Mormon wagon trains passing through the Salt Lake City en route to northern California.[59] On one occasion a few of these men forcefully ended the attempt of an avaricious entrepreneur to charge a toll on the section of road they had built through West Carson Canyon.[60] Ira Willis prepared handwritten copies of his trail notes, which he and others sold in 1849 as a guide to westward moving parties for $1.00 per copy.[61] A more detailed *Mormon Way-Bill to the Gold Mines,* written by Joseph Cain and Ariah C. Brower, appeared as a guidebook in 1851 and remained a helpful reference for overland travelers during the next few years.[62] A steady use of the route by groups of Saints traveling both east and west can be documented through the early 1850s, but the greatest benefactors of the LDS trail builders were undoubtedly the thousands of non-Mormons who reached northern California over the Carson Pass Wagon Road in 1849 and 1850.[63] For them, the 1848 LDS wagon road toward Zion became their highway to a long-imagined land of golden wealth.

---

[58]Brigham Young's notes of a similar though less formal address to the battalion veterans two days earlier appear in the manuscript LDS Journal History for 1 October 1848, quoted at length in Chapter 6.

[59]Johnston, *Experiences of a Forty-Niner,* 184, 192, 228, 237; Sly, Journal, 1849 June–1850 March, LDS Archives; Bagley, ed., *Frontiersman,* 141 ff.

[60]Orr, Jr., *Life History of Thomas J. Orr, Jr.* , 20–21.

[61]Willis, Guide to the Gold Mines, Huntington Library. See also Paden, ed., "The Ira J. Willis Guide to the Gold Fields," 193–207.

[62]Cain and Brower, *Mormon Way-Bill to the Gold Mines from the Pacific Springs by the Northern and Southern Routes.*

[63]Owens, "Mormon-Carson Emigrant Trail," 16–19.

MELISSA BURTON CORAY
Melissa Burton Coray was the Mormon Battalion laundress who, with her husband, accompanied the Holmes-Thompson party in pioneering the Carson Pass Wagon Road. This enhanced portrait, adapted by Norma Baldwin Ricketts from a Burton family photograph, dates from about 1855. *Courtesy Norma Baldwin Ricketts.*

MELISSA CORAY: THE WORST NIGHT I EVER SPENT

Fifty-three years after she and her first husband had arrived in Great Salt Lake City with the trailblazing Thompson-Holmes party, Melissa Burton Coray Kimball—the widow of former battalion sergeant William Coray and Nauvoo Legion general William Kimball and the only woman on the Carson Pass expedition—recalled her days with the Mormon Battalion in a 1901 interview. Her recollection of exact details was less than precise, but she vividly captured the stoicism so common among her fellow covered wagon women and the emotional impact of the Tragedy Spring episode, the one event of her remarkable march that remained most firmly fixed in her memory.[64]

Although this interview dealt with far more than her experiences in the gold rush, it is published here in its entirety for the first time in more than a century in consideration of the many descendants devoted to preserving and remembering the Mormon Battalion.

[64]For an excellent biography, see Ricketts, *Melissa's Journey with the Mormon Battalion—The Western Odyssey of Melissa Burton Coray: 1846–1848.*

MELISSA BURTON CORAY KIMBALL, "UTAH WOMAN'S 2,000-MILE MARCH FIFTY-FIVE YEARS AGO," *THE SALT LAKE HERALD*, SUNDAY, 26 MAY 1901.

Comfortably seated in her home, 156 South Second West, Mrs. Kimball rocked back and forth in her chair and recalled the story of the hard march to the coast and the even harder march back across the Nevada desert to Salt Lake Valley.

"One of the hardest parts of the journey," said Mrs. Kimball, "was the starting. I had to leave my father and mother, but it was a choice between them and my husband, and I thought my duty required me to keep with my husband. I never saw my parents again.

The battalion was in command of Colonel Phillip St. George Cooke, who I believe, afterwards distinguished himself in the civil war [*sic*]. We started out for Santa Fe, but before we reached there many of the battalion were disabled. We were divided into two bodies. The sick and disabled, with nearly all the women, were sent to Pueblo, while the rest of us went on to Santa Fe and from there on to the coast. There were five of us women who made the march. We were furnished with wagons, but we did not ride in them all the way. Part of the time we rode horseback, and part of the time we walked."

Mrs. Kimball was inclined to belittle the walking she had done, although members of the battalion say she traveled on foot a large part of the 2,000 miles and of the return journey.

"I didn't mind it," she declared. "I walked because I wanted to. My husband had to walk, and I went along by his side."

From the time Santa Fe was left behind, there were hardships, and in fact, the hardships began with the march.

"We had little food and less water," said Mrs. Kimball, "but my husband and I got along pretty well. You see, many of the men in the battalion ate when they were hungry until they were satisfied. The result was that they at up their food at the start, and did not have any afterward when they needed it badly. I looked ahead and figured how many days our food would have to last, and only used so much each day. I tried to cook it to the best advantage, so that none would be wasted. The consequence was that, although we often did not have all we wanted to eat, we were never in danger of starving.

"Were we thirsty? Well, of course we often had to go many miles without water, and many of the men thought they would die with thirst, but that is something that only gets worse when you think about it. I simply did not think about it when I was thirsty, and so managed to go a long distance without feeling it much. We had a hard time in the Arizona and California deserts, but, as I said, the less we thought about what a hard time we were having the easier it was.

"We had a big scare one night in Arizona that I shall always remember.

We knew that the Mexicans were in the vicinity, and we thought we were going to be attacked. The men stayed up and were ready all night for an attack, but the Mexicans never came. That was the nearest we ever came to being in a battle with the Mexicans.

"We went on and reached San Diego in January of 1847. We stayed there some time, garrisoning the place. There the battalion broke up. My husband bought a wagon, and, in company with a few others, we started north. We had a hard trip on the way to San Francisco. Of course it was an entirely new country then, and there were no roads. We had to pick our way as best we could. In one place, I remember, we came to a gorge so narrow that we could not drive through it. We had to take our wagon apart and carry it through a piece at a time.

"We started on east to come to Salt Lake. Other members of the Mormon battalion had preceded us as far as Sutter's mills, [*sic*], and when we got there, they had found gold. We saw them washing out the gold with pans, but we did not stop there long. We were anxious to come on to Salt Lake."

The little party pressed on. It climbed the Sierra Nevada and entered the wastes of the Nevada desert.

"The worst night I ever spent was in Nevada," said Mrs. Kimball. "We had sent ahead an advance guard of five men. They were to go on and find the best route, and then send back word to us. We kept going on, and did not hear from them. We thought it strange that they did not send us any word, but we kept going on, picking our way as best we could. One night, just at dusk, we came upon the bodies of the five [three] men who had been sent out as our guides. They had been killed by the Indians, and the bodies had been thrown in a gulch and partially covered by underbrush. I do not know why they took the trouble to halfway bury the bodies. Perhaps they thought they would catch us off our guard and kill us, too. The five men had evidently been surprised, and had made a hard fight, but the Indians had been too many for them. They were killed by poisoned arrows.

"We camped on that place that night, near the bodies, which we buried. We had bought a small cannon at San Diego, and were bringing it with us. We were afraid of an attack that night, and so the cannon was fired off every little while to scare off the Indians. I lay there that night and listened to the cannon, and expected every minute to hear the Indians. It was the worst night I ever spent. The firing of the cannon may have kept the Indians away, but it did us more harm than good, for it frightened our horses to that they stampeded. We had a hard time getting them back, and some of them never came back.

"We were in danger from the Indians on all our trip, but we arrived in Salt Lake Valley safely in December of 1848, and we were glad to get here, I can tell you."

> Mrs. Kimball has spent the rest of her life here in Utah. She was honored jubilee day, riding in a carriage in the procession that day, but since then she has kept from the public view in her quiet home, and it is her purpose to do so the rest of her days.
>
> Four other women made the Journey—Mrs. Jesse D. Hunter, wife of Captain Hunter of company B, Mrs. Daniel C. Davis, wife of Captain Davis of company E, Mrs. Eleazar Davis and Mrs. Ebenezer Brown, the two last named being wives of enlisted men. Mrs. Hunter died in California before the battalion had been mustered out while the other women, except Mrs. Kimball, have since expired.

In October 1993 the United States Board of Geographic Names designated the 9,763-foot Sierra Nevada summit just north of West Pass as Melissa Coray Peak, in honor of Coray and the "thousands of emigrant women who endured similar hardships in settling the West." Several hundred people gathered on U.S. Highway 88 on 30 July 1994 to celebrate the naming of the peak at dedication ceremonies sponsored by the Sierra Chapter of the Sons of Utah Pioneers and supported by the National Society of the Sons of Utah Pioneers, the U.S. Forest Service, the Oregon-California Trail Association, and the International Society of Daughters of Utah Pioneers. Eight-year-old Melissa Richmond, a fourth-great-granddaughter of Melissa Coray, unveiled a plaque commemorating the Mormon-Carson Pass Emigrant Trail.

"As a practicing archivist, I often feel that I am charged with the responsibility of rescuing history from oblivion," said speaker Michael N. Landon, who had tracked down primary source accounts of the Carson route as a graduate student. "If the value of [these] journals can be measured by our unending fascination with the trail experience, it underscores the need to preserve these records. Identification, conservation, preservation and access to these accounts should be paramount. . . . A reading of any of these accounts causes us to re-examine our own goals, our own challenges, our own hopes and dreams and, perhaps, our own blessings."[65]

---

[65]Dockstader, "California Peak Named in Honor of Wife of Battalion Member," *LDS Church News*, 13 August 1994.

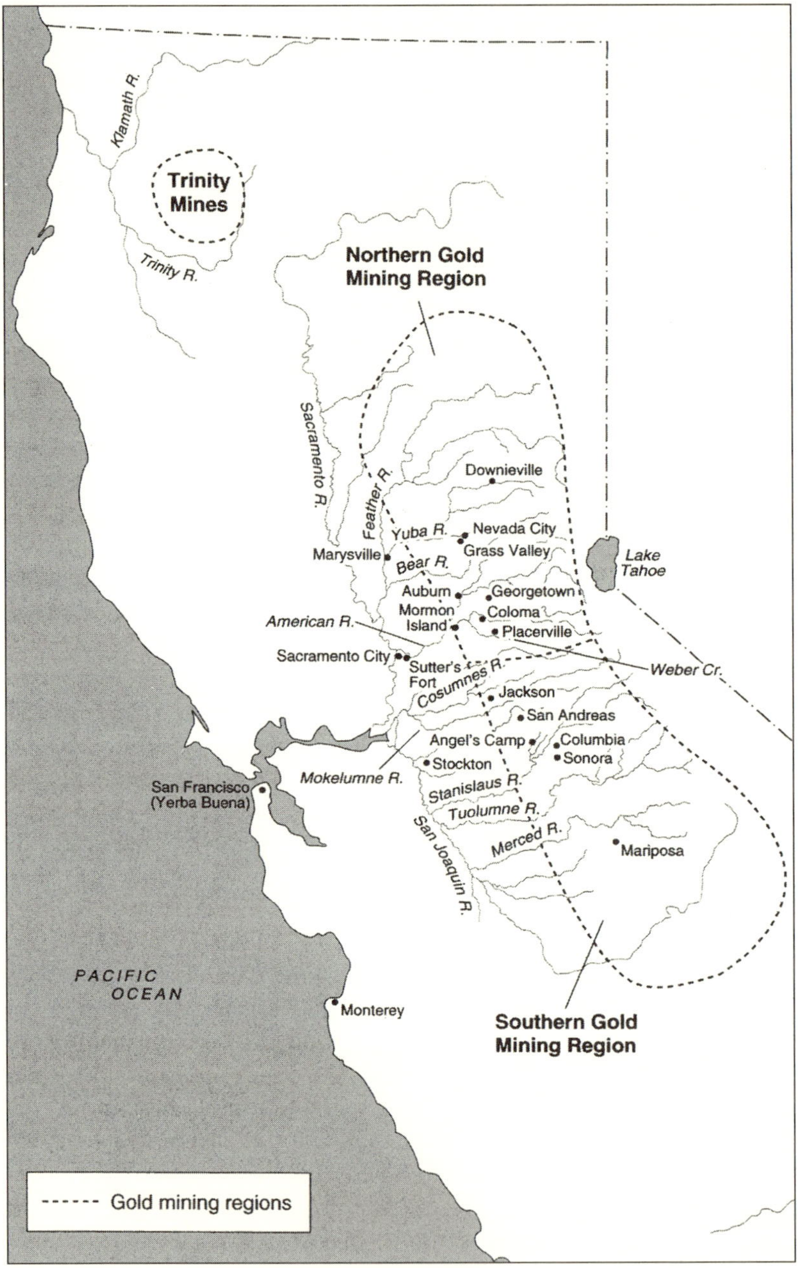

Northern California during the Gold Rush.
Reprinted from Riches for All: The California Gold Rush and the World
edited by Kenneth N. Owens by permission of the University of Nebraska Press.

Chapter 6

"Greedy After the Things of This World" Brigham Young's California Gold Rush Policy

Brigham Young never saw California. When he reached the Salt Lake Valley, Young struck the ground with his cane and announced emphatically that he would stop here, he would build a city here, he would build a temple here, and he would build a country here. Young's decision was permanent. He insisted that Zion must be isolated from all enemies of the Saints. To move onward to California, as Samuel Brannan advocated, would again place the church in a precarious situation. Surrounded by adversaries and beset by worldly temptations, believers might be seduced away from a virtuous and observant way of life. As he explained years later, Young believed the Lord had directed him to lead the Saints to the valleys of the mountains. "Why did we not go to San Francisco?" he asked rhetorically. "Because the Lord told me not: 'For there are lions in the way, and they will devour the lambs, if you take them there.'"[1]

Nathan Hawk: I Do Not Want my People to Go Digging for Their God

When did Brigham Young first learn about the northern California gold discoveries?

Battalion veteran Nathan Hawk gave the definitive answer to this question in a 1906 interview with the *Sacramento Bee.* At the head of a small party of battalion veterans in the spring of 1848, he had carried eastward the special "boom edition" of the *California Star,* dated 1 April 1848 and printed by Samuel Brannan to attract migration to San

[1]Brigham Young, "The Sufferings of the Saints," 5 January 1860, *Journal of Discourses,* 9:105.

Francisco and this newest U.S. territory.[2] Hawk had been anxious to return to his family in Missouri, he explained, and so readily agreed to take along the mail and newspaper bundles as Brannan requested. Traveling with horses and pack mules, Hawk led a group that included at least four and perhaps as many as eleven other Mormon Battalion veterans.

When Brannan published this special edition of the *Star*, neither he nor anyone else realized the amazing extent of California's gold riches. Not until a month later did he first visit Mormon Island, then hurried back to San Francisco to make his dramatic announcement about gold on the American River. The mention of gold in the *Star*'s lead story, written by Dr. Victor Fourgeaud, was quite low key, especially compared with the extravagant promotional pieces that later became commonplace. But from Hawk's own brief mining efforts at Mormon Island, he carried enough gold east to make an impressive visual addendum to Dr. Fourgeaud's restrained account. In this excerpt from the *Bee* story, Hawk summarized his journey and his trailside meeting with Brigham Young while the church president was leading the 1848 migration from Winter Quarters to Great Salt Lake City.

NATHAN HAWK, *THE SACRAMENTO EVENING BEE*, 4 JANUARY 1906.

Brannan procured [in trade at Sutter's Fort] all the 'dust' he could get, and returned immediately to San Francisco. He there worked off his boom edition of the Star, and secured a number of letters for me to take East, and returned several days later. The papers weighed eighty pounds. They were not much larger than a sheet of foolscap, but just bristled with glowing descriptions of the country which Brannan declared, was the long-sought Eden.

Brannan wanted the papers given to all immigrants [we] met, and he had packages addressed to every section of the Union. One larger than the others, I remember, was directed to the reading-room of the National Library in the City of Washington.

On our way back, there were twelve of us in the party, we met Brigham Young and his twelve trains, each one of them headed by an Apostle, in the Black Hills.

We stopped and talked with Brigham Young for quite a time. He was very anxious to find the conditions in the country we had traversed. I showed him the gold and asked if he would go on to California. He replied, 'No! I

[2]Bagley, ed., *Scoundrel's Tale*, 240–41. After reaching Missouri, Hawk persuaded his wife and her large family headed by Samuel Conrad, Hawk's father-in-law, to go with him in the spring of 1849 back to California, where they settled for life. See Ricketts, *The California Star Express*, 11–15.

hope they will never strike gold in the country where we locate, for I do not want my people to go digging for their God.'

By the way, I forgot to tell you that the gold I took with me across the plains when I carried the first news of the discovery East, was dug out by myself and three or four of my comrades at Mormon Island.

My party arrived safely in Missouri, where my family resided. My companions, who went to different sections, and the papers of Brannan's that I put in the mails and sent on to their destinations, soon spread the news, and were the cause of the heavy immigration West in 1849.

According to the record of Thomas Bullock, the official journal keeper for the church president's company during the 1847 migration and again in 1848, Hawk's meeting with Brigham Young took place on 27 July. The location was near Independence Rock along the Sweetwater River. Neither Bullock nor Hosea Stout, another journal writer with the Young party, makes mention of Hawk's report about the California gold discovery. But Abner Blackburn, who was also traveling with the wagon train, confirmed the accuracy of Hawk's recollections. While camped on the Sweetwater, Blackburn recalled, "we heard of the great gold discovery in California and manny that were going to Oregon changed their minds and went for the diggings and no one [was] going to Oregon from this [point] on."[3]

More reports of the northern California gold discoveries reached Great Salt Lake City in early September 1848, when the first contingent of California Saints arrived directly from the diggings. From this time on, the problems and opportunities created by California's gold strongly influenced the future of the Mormon people in the West. In the judgment of Leonard Arrington, dean of LDS historians, the gold rush posed one of the most critical challenges to confront Brigham Young during the Saints' early years in the Great Basin.[4] At the same time, the gold country's wealth and the hordes of gold-crazed travelers who came rushing through the Great Basin, with many of them pausing for a few days or even a few months in Salt Lake City, were potential economic resources that could, with proper management, prove vital assets for the church's survival and the future prosperity of the Latter-day Saints.

After learning about the California Saints' early mining success, Young and his colleagues began to shape a California policy that remained in

---

[3]Bagley, ed., *Frontiersman*, 131.

[4]Arrington, *American Moses*, 178–79, 183–84.

effect throughout President Young's lifetime and well beyond. Never formally codified, this policy had four main themes. First and most urgently, the church leaders united to prevent a general exodus of the faithful from the Salt Lake Valley to the gold country. Second, Young sought in a guarded, often secretive fashion to tap the riches of northern California for the benefit of the Utah settlement and its economically hard-pressed leaders. Third, until he issued a general summons for all members of the faith to gather in Utah in 1857, Young intended to maintain a Mormon presence in California despite his growing dissatisfaction with the attitudes and behavior of California Saints. Finally, as an outgrowth of his efforts to sustain the Zion settlement, by the mid-1850s he was condemning California's gold country and metropolitan culture in terms that painted this imaginary California as Babylon, the social and moral antithesis of all that Mormonism should be. Repeatedly he attempted to reinforce LDS values and patterns of behavior by pointing to California as the worst case example of what the non-Mormon world offered. Church President Brigham Young thus became the first and most earnest publicist for an anti-California ideology that has proved an enduring element of popular culture in Utah and the Rocky Mountain West.

Brigham Young: It Would Ruin Us—Brigham Young and Gold

The threat that many Saints would abandon Utah for California was the most immediate challenge faced by Young and his fellow LDS leaders. Young showed an intuitive understanding of the situation. On 1 October 1848 he gathered together the Mormon Battalion veterans who had reached Great Salt Lake City and expressed his great appreciation for their service. He explained the larger political situation that had prompted him to urge their enlistment, putting forward a unique revisionist interpretation of the political situation in 1846 that, however at odds with the historical record, would become the accepted Mormon version of these events. Young generously praised the veterans for their role in making possible the Mormon migration to the Great Basin. Finally, he emphasized that Saints must not go back to California and hunt for gold; they must not attempt to unite Babylon and Zion, for that would be their ruination.

BRIGHAM YOUNG, JOURNAL HISTORY, 1 OCTOBER 1848, LDS ARCHIVES.

I called the battalion brethren together after meeting and blessed them in the name of the Lord for their fidelity to the Kingdom of God, told them it was not generally understood why we raised the battalion. We had friends and enemies at Washington; when Pres. Polk could do us a favor he was dispo[s]ed to do it, but there were those around him who felt vindictive toward us and kept continually harping against us to him; and who thought themselves wise enough to lay plans to accomplish our destruction. The plan of raising a battalion to march to California by a call from the War department was devised with a view to the total overthrow of this kingdom and the destruction of every man, woman and child, and was hatched up by Senator Thomas H. Benton. Every day our progress was reported to Washington. Our enemies firmly believed we would refuse to respond to the call, and they told Pres. Polk this would prove to him whether we were friends to the Union; and they further advised Polk when the call would be rejected, to say to the S[t]ates of Missouri and Illinois and the mobocrats the Mormons are at your mercy. . . .

I said to the praise of the battalion that they went as honorable men doing honor to their calling and the United States, and I was satisfied with all of them; if some had done wrong and transgressed and had been out of the way, I exhorted them to refrain there from, turn unto the Lord and build up His Kingdom. Who could say he was without sin?

I felt glad that their conduct had proved to their commanders and general that they were their best and most reliable soldiers; and although there were, perhaps, no other people in the Union who would have responded to the call for men under our circumstances, still it was the best course, as a people, we could have pursued.

I further remarked that I saw the whole plan concocted [by our enemies] as plain as I see [saw] the faces then before me, and I felt within myself that my faith in God would outgeneral the wickedness of our enemies. Away went the battalion and the sword fell on the other side; if they had not gone, we would not have been in the valley now. . . .

I did not want the battalion to re-enlist for another six months. I regretted not having clothing for them; but said I would rather wear skins than go back to the United States for clothes. If we were to go to San Francisco and dig for chunks of gold, or find it here in the valley it would ruin us. Many wanted to unite Babylon and Zion; it[']s the love of money that hurts them. If we find gold and silver, we are in bondage directly. To talk of going away from this valley for anything is like vinegar to my eyes. They that love the world have not their affections placed upon the Lord.

Despite President Young's exhortations, the news from California's gold country excited many Salt Lake City Saints, just as it had excited

Abner Blackburn and his companions. After more battalion veterans arrived in the valley carrying gold dust in their baggage, the Journal History recorded in early December 1848 the observations of one diarist that the "faith of many of the Saints was sorely tried and some of them grew weak and wanted to return to the States and others wanted to go to the gold mines in California to dig gold, while many others were willing to suffer the loss of all things for the Gospel's sake and for the testimony of Jesus."[5]

Got Ready and Started for California: Levi Riter's 1848 California Trip

Apparently three small parties left Great Salt Lake City in summer 1848 to travel to the gold country.[6] Only one is well documented, the daring excursion of Levi E. Riter, who took the Truckee River–Donner Pass route across the Sierra Nevada to reach Sutter's Fort and San Francisco. Riter had been a well-to-do church member living in eastern Pennsylvania when he decided in 1846 to join the LDS hegira to the West. According to an account Riter's son wrote years later, "It was generally believed they would go to Upper California which was then a large and unknown territory west of the Rocky Mountains; a great bulk of the territory was then under Mexican dominion. As we had very indefinite knowledge of Upper California the idea was very indefinite where we were going, but it seems that the belief was general that we should go as far as the Pacific coast." Although Mormon leaders had identified the Great Basin as their destination by summer 1845, most westbound church members in 1846 believed they were heading for the Pacific Coast.[7] Based on this expectation, Riter and other prosperous eastern Mormons including John Neff and John Van Cott put a cargo of merchandise aboard the *Brooklyn* consigned to the care of Samuel Brannan, "thinking to make the trip overland and meet the other saints on the shores of the Pacific."

The Riter family united with the Nauvoo Saints at the Missouri River refugee camps. "Before we left our rendezvous on the Missouri River in the Spring of 1847," Riter's son wrote, "it was pretty generally under-

[5]Journal History, 9 December 1848, quoted in Davies, *Mormon Gold,* 80.

[6]The limited evidence for these groups is examined in Davies, *Mormon Gold,* 70–72.

[7]See Parley P. Pratt to Isaac Rogers, 6 September 1845, LDS Archives, in Bagley, ed., *Scoundrel's Tale,* 90–91.

stood that the body of the church would not go to the Pacific coast, but would locate somewhere in the Rocky Mountain region, but as to what point was wholly a matter of conjecture.—We travelled westward with only faith as a guide, to an unknown destination." They did not learn that the Salt Lake Valley was their goal until after their party reached the Sweetwater River. A few days later the Riters met Brigham Young and the returning pioneers, who confirmed the location of the LDS Zion. "We arrived here [at Salt Lake City] October 3, 1847," Riter reported, "and made the best of our surroundings during the winter of 1847–1848."

By fall 1848, the Saints from northern California had brought to Salt Lake City not only stories of their gold mining success, but also reports that Brannan was now comporting himself in a quite unsaintly manner. His reputation, in the younger Riter's words, had "commenced to suffer severely through unseemly behavior, largely caused by drink." Riter had already decided to set out for California to "take possession of his goods and either return here with them, or sell them there." The other Salt Lake Saints who had shipped goods on the *Brooklyn* made Riter their agent to handle their business affairs with Brannan. "Accordingly," his son wrote, "after harvesting our wheat crop of 1848, he got ready and started for California. . . ."[8]

When Riter met the eastbound Thompson-Holmes company in late August near the "Big Bend" of the Humboldt River, he told them he was a bishop in Great Salt Lake City and "that there was the best of grain there, and that corn grew fine, and all sorts of garden Sauce done well." Azariah Smith's journal indicates Riter was traveling with ten wagons led by California pioneer Peter Lassen, who was attempting to open a circuitous northern crossing of the Sierra to his rancho in the upper Sacramento Valley. Lassen's "cutoff" was at least two hundred miles longer than the trails over either Carson or Donner pass, and far more arduous. His pioneering company had to be rescued by a band of Oregonians heading south to the gold fields. Riter, however, seems to have continued down the Humboldt on his own when Lassen and the others headed west across the Black Rock Desert.[9]

---

[8]Statement of W. W. Riter, 10 January 1917, in Carter, *Heart Throbs of the West*, 7:402–3. Levi Riter's relationship with Brannan is noted in Bagley, ed., *Scoundrel's Tale*, 121, 131, 198. Riter's subsequent adventures in California are related in the following chapter.

[9]See the Journal History, 5 September 1848; and the 27 August 1848 entries in Bigler, ed., *Azariah Smith*, 139; and Bagley, ed., *A Road from El Dorado: The 1848 Trail Journal of Ephraim Green*, 31.

Francis A. Hammond: Against All Human Foresight

As Francis Hammond realized after reaching Salt Lake City from the gold country, the danger that Zion might be forsaken in the general rush to California was even greater because everyone in the colony was experiencing hardship from crop failures, food shortages, and a depressed, cash-shy economy. In his recollections, Hammond summarized Brigham Young's ongoing efforts to keep the faithful from running away to the mining region.

> During the winter [of 1848–1849] some became a little uneasy, in consequence of hard times, scarcity of provisions, and the general gloomy outlook. The glowing accounts which some of the Battalion boys brought in concerning the gold fields which had been discovered in California, helped to make people restless. President Young, against all human foresight, boldly counseled the Elders to stay at home and cultivate their farms, and promised that those who would do so would be able to buy those who went to the mines.[10]

By spring 1849, gold fever was threatening the Zion colony with the same sort of spontaneous exodus, led by adventure-seeking young men, that had already begun to disrupt established society in Oregon, Hawaii, northern Mexico, and Chile, and that would soon sweep over the eastern states, Canada, and many parts of Europe and South China.[11] Everywhere gold fever broke out, the contagion resulted in a massive loss of able-bodied and skilled workers, abandoned farms, shops, and stores, abruptly rising prices for food and all sorts of goods, and a growing dependent class of women, children, and old people left behind. The lure of California gold might bring social and economic calamity to the newly transplanted LDS community.

During this perilous time a minor but nevertheless remarkable episode enlivened the annals of the LDS church. At church conference in April, Heber Kimball, second in authority after Brigham Young, was moved to make a startling prediction that struck everyone, even himself, as far-fetched. "Never mind boys," he later recalled saying, "in less than one year there will be plenty of clothes and everything that we shall want

---

[10]Hammond, "In Early Days: My Introduction to Mormonism."

[11]For these impacts, see especially Malcolm J. Rohrbough's *Days of Gold: The California Gold Rush and the Nation*; and his "'We Will Make Our Fortunes—No Doubt of It': The Worldwide Rush to California," in Owens, ed., *Riches for All*, 55–70.

sold at less than St. Louis prices." George A. Smith, sitting alongside Kimball, made a fitting comment: "There, Brother Kimball, you have burst your boiler this time sure." Charles C. Rich made a similar remark. "Brother Rich," Kimball related, "told me that he thought I had done up the job at prophesying that time, but that the sequel showed the prediction to be of the Lord."[12]

In later years, the story of Kimball's amazingly accurate prophesy gained stature as one of Utah's LDS founding legends, demonstrated by its retelling in the church's biographical encyclopedia.

> When hard times pressed the Saints in Salt Lake City, and a thousand miles separated them from commercial points, President Kimball stood up in the Tabernacle and prophesied that in less than six months clothing and other goods would be sold in the streets of Great Salt Lake City cheaper than they could be bought in New York. This astonished the people. One of his brethren said to him after meeting that he did not believe it. "Neither did I," said Brother Kimball, "but I said it. It will have to go." No one saw the possibility of its verification. Six months, however, had not passed away when large companies of emigrants, burning with the gold fever from the East, came into the city, and becoming eager to reach the glittering gold fields of California, they sold their merchandise on the streets for a less price than the New York prices. They sold their large animals for pack animals, and thus more than literally fulfilled the remarkable prophecy of President Heber C. Kimball.[13]

Among those who benefited from trade with the California-bound emigrants in 1849 was Zadock Judd, who had arrived from the gold country in the Holmes-Thompson company with a few horses but otherwise little in the way of property. His autobiography describes his good fortune, which further affirmed the truth of President Kimball's prophesy.

JUDD, REMINISCENCES OF ZADOCK KNAPP JUDD, SENIOR, UTAH STATE HISTORICAL SOCIETY.

> In the meantime, the gold emmigration had begun to come in. They were going to California to gather gold that had been discovered by the Mormon Battalion, while digging Sutter's Mill Race. When they got into the Valley, they found that they had much more loading than they could manage, and

[12]Heber C. Kimball, *Journal of Discourses* 10:247, quoted in Madsen, *Gold Rush Sojourners in Great Salt Lake City*, 53.

[13]Jenson, *LDS Biographical Encyclopedia*, 1:34 .

their teams had given out, and they proposed trading oxen and wagons for horses which they could pack and go through to California.

They had many mechanical tools, and some clothing, which the people here in the Valley needed. These were sold here about as cheap as they could be bought in New York City. This fulfilled the prophecy of Heber C. Kimball, a short time previous, that merchandise would be sold here as cheap as in the eastern country.

I traded them two horses, for which I received three yoke of cattle, a good wagon, a sheet iron cook stove, a dozen shirts, a good silver watch and nearly a half a barrel of pork, some mechanical tools. They put their packs onto the horses and started for California.

Brigham Young: Go and Be Damned

With the appearance of G. W. Paul's pack train at Salt Lake on 16 June 1849, Mormon leaders informed their followers in the East that "the gold diggers began to arrive here on their way to the gold regions of California." Wagons had arrived in the valley by the 22nd, and as more than 10,000 forty-niners surged through Great Salt Lake City, their gold-induced delirium influenced many Saints.[14] Responding to the threat in July, Brigham Young made his most vigorous attempt to prevent abandonment of the infant colony by the faithful. Expressing himself forcefully, he addressed a general congregation, emphasizing the danger not only to the settlement but to the immortal soul of everyone who might leave Zion. Those church members who now went to California, he declared emphatically, were the very worst people among the Mormons; they were "hardly fit for the cellar kitchens of hell."

Brigham Young, 8 July 1849,
Manuscript History of the Church, LDS Archives.

8 July 1849

In public meeting on Sunday, the 8th, I addressed the people. The following is a portion of my remarks:—

"Those who wish to work for grain, we want them to work on the Church farm, for the same pay as in the States. I propose that wheat be $5.00 per bushel and wages $5.00 per day. Many who are going to the gold mines will have to lodge here and winter.

"If the Lord made the world out of nothing, we have got to make every-

[14] Korns, ed., *West from Fort Bridger*, 303.

thing that makes us comfortable out of nothing. If we could make worlds out of nothing we could make gold here out of nothing.

"I hope the gold mines will be no nearer here than 800 miles. There is more delusion and the people are more perfectly crazy on this continent, than ever was the case before, since the days of Columbus. If a man wants goods or clothing, a little gold is very useful. Suppose we were all to leave our harvest and dig gold, and have no food, and then the Indians were to make a break on us and drive off our animals, our gold would be a curse to us.

"What is the wealth of England? Is it gold? No, if the English had found gold, instead of stone coal, they would have been sunk in degradation. But as it is, they are the nation of nations, their flag is in every harbor. The sun never sets upon their dominions. Coal, iron, and hard labor have been the wealth, the power, and the strength of England.

"Now look at Spain, Mexico, and South America. You who have travelled in those nations, what is their society? Degradation, misery, filth. They have gone into gambling, horse racing, and all manner of iniquity. What has done it? The abundance of their gold and silver.

"We are shut of the most [miserable] part of our community, they are not fit for the society of good men, they are hardly fit for the cellar kitchens of hell. They will black boots and sweep chimneys for others in hell. This very people, after all their mobbings, and drivings, and burning, would use the gold to oppress their own brethren. It should be used to promote virtue, holiness, and intelligence, and to procure the various good things in the world. But it is employed only for corrupt purposes.

"Many people will be glad to run away from those gold mines—men who will be honest will see such a mass of corruption that they will pray to be delivered out of it. You heap up gold in the United States, and they will heap up destruction. That is all right for the Almighty has an account to settle with that nation, and as God lives it will be overthrown. At Sutter's mill they walked over the gold, they had it in their baskets and in their houses, but they never knew, until a Mormon Elder told them, that it was gold. There is no effect without a cause. The Lord revolutionizes the world at his pleasure. He takes up one kingdom and sets down another. He will cause that gold mine to be a destruction to the nation that has cast us out, and that measure will be pressed down and running over, and then the cry will be 'measure unto them double for what they have done unto my Saints.' They have been told, for the last eighteen years, that destruction would be upon this nation.

"The devil has marshaled his forces to obliterate the work of God. But it is too late in the day, gentlemen. Persecution only gave Joseph Smith power and popularity. Persecution against this people only lifts them up. The only way to destroy this people is to foster them with kindness and get the Elders of Israel to lock arms with the devil and walk into corruption, and they would be induced to walk into every dissolute hole on the earth, and the

> Priesthood would be taken away. But I thank the Lord for the persecution. We have then the greatest reason to enjoy ourselves, for all hell is boiling over. If you see mobs around you, with bowie knives and pistols, then I have no fear of danger for the Elders, for there would be war, and they would feel almighty and would have no fear. Our enemies might try to take sight at me from sunrise to sundown, and faith is that they would never see to take a good sight, for they would shoot a little higher or on one side, unless my work was fully accomplished. Were not Washington and others marked at [by their enemies]? Joseph Smith escaped many conspiracies against his life. He lived just as long as the Lord let him live. But the Lord said—'Now let my servant seal up his testimony with his blood,' and that sealed up the damnation of the United States, not of individuals, but of the nation.
>
> "Now is it for us to love gold, revellings, or drunkenness? No, gentlemen; no, Elders of Israel. Take up your cross and prepare yourselves for the regeneration. No man need think he can go through without losses and crosses. He must not have a wife, nor a child, nor gold, that he idolizes. If you Elders of Israel want to go to the gold mines, go and be damned. If you go, I would not give a picayune to keep you from damnation."

Brigham Young, as Leonard Arrington observed in his masterful biography of the Mormon leader, was a pragmatist rather than a systematic theorist. Nonetheless, in his efforts to make Mormon Utah economically self-sufficient, in later years Young pursued an economic policy that resembled a classic mercantilist prescription for the expansion of national wealth.[15] During the era of the California gold rush, however, his first efforts to forestall the people of Zion from heading farther west were buttressed by a philosophical mindset that can best be linked to the agrarian ideology of the late eighteenth and early nineteenth centuries. Like John Locke, Young held that supplies of gold and silver were not real wealth. Instead, wealth was produced by the application of human labor to raw nature. Like Thomas Jefferson, he believed it was labor devoted to the productive tasks of farming and community building that produced value and the most elemental, enduring contributions to human wellbeing, both spiritual and material. These agrarian concepts steadily sus-

[15]As the distinguished LDS historian Tom Alexander emphasizes in a recent personal communication, Young's goal was self-sufficiency for the Mormon people in the Great Basin, rather than economic isolation. He encouraged economic measures that would enable the Saints to export more than they imported, not only by promoting agricultural pursuits but by developing all other natural resources of the Utah country. Thus in time he encouraged mining for industrial metals, salt, and coal, and he also helped finance a wide variety of manufacturing and commercial enterprises. After 1870, Professor Alexander points out, President Young further revised his policy on mineral development, giving at least tacit approval for such prominent LDS authorities as John Taylor and George Q. Cannon to invest in mining.

tained his conviction that gold mining was not only economically uncertain, but that it was less socially worthwhile and risky to morality and religious duty. Faithful Saints, he steadily affirmed, would become rich and remain sure of their eternal reward by devoting themselves to the agricultural and commercial development of the Utah country.

A journal entry for September 1849, after further companies of gold-rich Saints had arrived in the Mormon capital from California, succinctly expressed this strain of Brigham Young's thought.

> The valley of the Sacramento is an unhealthy place, and the saints can be better employed in raising grain and building houses in this vicinity, than in digging gold in Sacramento, unless they are counseled to do so. . . . When the saints shall have preached the gospel, raised grain, and built up cities enough, the Lord will open up the way for a supply of gold to the perfect satisfaction of the people; until then, let them not be over-anxious for the treasures of the earth are in the Lord's storehouse, and he will open the doors thereof when and where he pleases.[16]

MYRON TANNER: THE SAINTS WHO WANDERED OFF

A native of New York state, Myron Tanner along with his parents and brothers had been members of the LDS church in Ohio, Missouri, and Illinois during his early years. He joined the Mormon Battalion at Council Bluffs, went from Santa Fé to Pueblo with Capt. James Brown's detachment to spend the winter, and reached Salt Lake City for the first time in July 1847. Subsequently he returned east to Winter Quarters and found work aboard the riverboats on the Missouri River. The following spring, when he was twenty-three years old, Tanner volunteered to return to Salt Lake as a wagon driver in a company under the direction of Apostle George A. Smith, counselor to Brigham Young, who took a strong interest in the young man's welfare. In Salt Lake he worked the family farm until his father died early in 1850, an event that freed him to leave for California. His departure put Tanner at cross purposes with Brigham Young's goals for the Saints. In his autobiographical dictation, taken down by his son, Tanner briefly described his California experience and explained his later difficulties with President Young when, for reasons of the heart, he tried to reestablish his good standing in the church community.

[16]Roberts, *A Comprehensive History of the Church of Jesus Christ of Latter-day Saints*, 3:347.

MYRON TANNER, *BIOGRAPHY OF MYRON TANNER,* 16–17.

Not long after my father's death, I made preparations to go to California. My high regard for Brother George A. [Smith], and the fact that he devoted so much of his time to the interest of the Church, were my reasons for rendering him gratuitously my services in crossing the plains and for hauling him wood with which to make his family comfortable during the winter. However, when I left him, he trusted me to a yoke of oxen and a wagon, the latter would now probably be worth $40. For this team and wagon, I sent him after my arrival in California $400 in gold.

On my arrival in California, I began work in the mines at McDowell's hill about four miles above Mormon Island. By applied industry and economy I was able in two and a half years to lay by $1,250. In the fall of '52 I went to San Bernardino. My brothers, Seth, Freeman, and Joseph had also been at work and with what we had saved we began farming, stockraising, and trading. In '56, however, my brother Seth drew out and began coal mining in San Diego.

The year before, however, in '55, I came through to Salt Lake where I became acquainted with Jane Mount who was living at the time with Henry Lawrence. Most of my boyhood days my life was separate and apart from girls in whose society I was both bashful and awkward. She was rather delicate, a very refined and intelligent woman of literary tastes and poetic instincts. Her make-up seemed just the opposite to my own rugged, untempered and uncultivated nature. However surprised others appeared by reason of her attention to me, we nevertheless became engaged.

In those days, the Saints who wandered off to, and remained in California were somewhat under the Church ban; and President Young, whose great anxiety it was to keep the Latter-day Saints within the Rocky Mountains where they might co-operatively build up exemplary communities, was often severe towards those who disregarded the counsels of the Church in that matter. Recounting his experience my father says that he called on President Young and spoke to him about his engagement to Miss Mount who he desired to marry according to the rules of the Church. "President Young," he said, "became very angry and raked me over the coals in a lively manner and explained to me the unfortunate consequences of marrying a girl and taking her off to California to live. This rebuff was too much for me and I saw that President Young was not at all likely to yield, or be in the least indulgent.

"My first thought was to turn to George A. [Smith], for I never had a truer friend than he was. His intercession on my behalf not only brought about the desired result, but brought me good counsel through which I made up my mind to leave California as soon as I could close out my interests there. Miss Mount promised to await my return to Salt Lake, and on my return in 1856 we were married on the 20th day of May."

Brigham Young: A Present of Twenty Thousand Dollars

While exerting the utmost pressure to keep the Saints from leaving Zion, Brigham Young and other church leaders by necessity looked to California in hopes that wealth from the gold fields would relieve the financial crisis in Zion. The LDS colony in 1848 was short of capital and utterly lacking in circulating coin or currency. When the first Mormon miners arrived from the placer diggings in fall 1848, their tithing contributions in some small degree helped ease the strained condition of the church treasury. More importantly, their deposits of gold dust and nuggets in a "Gold Account" established by Brigham Young, for which they were duly credited, became the basis for a church-issued currency that served effectively as a circulating medium in the region. By late 1848 church officials had set up a system for coining the dust and flakes into ten-dollar gold pieces; but in January 1849, the coinage equipment fell apart. As an expedient substitute, the Salt Lake municipal council authorized Brigham Young, Heber Kimball, and Bishop Newel Whitney to issue handwritten bills, based on the reserve deposits of gold dust.[17]

Early in March 1849, when spring weather began to break Salt Lake City's snowbound isolation, Parley Pratt as president pro tem of the Quorum of Twelve Apostles and Franklin D. Richards as clerk drafted a letter to mission president Orson Pratt and church members in the British Isles.[18] Among other news, they commented on the gold rush migration from Utah to northern California. "Many of the tares have gone to the gold mines," they wrote in biblical simile, "and some of the wheat is probably going with them." Pratt and Richards told their British brethren about the arrangements Utah authorities were making to provide for the Saints in the gold country. "Elder Amasa A. Lyman, of the Twelve," they wrote, "is appointed to go to the Pacific with the mail, and to see after the wheat which may be there or are going. Brother O. P. Rockwell is also appointed to accompany him. They may, perhaps,

[17]For discussion of the fiscal crisis in Great Salt Lake City during the early period and the LDS experience in issuing coinage, see Arrington, *Great Basin Kingdom,* 11–17, 71–72; and Davies, *Mormon Gold,* 77–98.

[18]Orson Pratt was actually the president of the Quorum at this time, and would continue in that position until 1875. Parley Pratt was evidently serving in his place until Orson returned from service as mission president in Great Britain.

return next Autumn."[19] In an addendum to this letter, dated 12 April 1849, Pratt and Richards stated that Apostle Charles C. Rich also "is appointed to take his stand in Western California, with a view to give guidance to the affairs of the Church and kingdom in that region."

The appointment of Lyman and Rockwell was made official two weeks later. Brigham Young and his counselors authorized Amasa Lyman to travel to northern California as the church's representative, with Rockwell as an escort. On this assignment, the church leaders instructed, Lyman should take an epistle to the faithful in California, and he was directed "to preach the Gospel and look after the interests of the Church and the Saints, and to return with those who might be coming to the Valley in the fall."[20] As indicated by his activities on this first California expedition, Lyman also understood that a major part of his assignment was to collect tithes and send the proceeds back to Great Salt Lake City, where they might be used to bolster the LDS coinage system.[21]

With the church leadership's letter of instruction and encouragement to the California Saints, Lyman took a personal appeal for financial support from Brigham Young to Samuel Brannan. This remarkable message combined an admonition to Brannan to do his duty, financially, to the church with a second message that implored Brannan to send Young an extremely generous gift.

> I am glad to hear you say that I "may rely upon your pushing every nerve to assist me, and sustain me to the last," for I doubt not you have been blest—abundantly and now have in your power to render most essential service, I shal[l] expect ten thousand dollars, at least, of your tithing, on return of Elder Lyman, and if you have accumulated a million to tithe, so as to send $100,000, so much the better, & may you get 2 millions next year. If you want to continue to prosper do not forget the Lords Treasury, lest he forget you, and with the liberal the Lord is liberal; and when you have settled with the treasury, I want you to remember, that, Bro Brigham has long been des-

---

[19]An Epistle of the Twelve to President Orson Pratt, and the Church of Jesus Christ of Latter-day Saints in the British Isles, 9 March 1849, Journal History, LDS Archives.

[20]Minutes of the First Presidency, 26 March 1849, Journal History, LDS Archives.

[21]Twenty men traveled with Lyman and Rockwell. Although the documents are silent as to their identity, historian J. Kenneth Davies makes the reasonable supposition that many of Lyman's companions came from the ranks of the so-called Mississippi Saints, LDS converts who had migrated as a group from that southern state to the Salt Lake Valley in 1847, guided by Lyman on the last leg of the journey. Davies, *Mormon Gold*, 110–11. This journey is summarized also in Schindler, *Orrin Porter Rockwell*, 185–86. Citing a letter from Amasa Lyman to J. H. Flanigan dated 11 April 1850 and printed in the *Millenial Star*, Schindler relates that despite deep snows, the party crossed the Sierra Nevada in four days and arrived at Sutter's Fort on 25 May.

AMASA LYMAN
In this daguerrotype portrait, the apostle is shown in his late thirties, at the time he was managing Mormon affairs in California. *Courtesy Pioneer Memorial Museum, International Society, Daughters of Utah Pioneers.*

> titute of home, and suffered heavy losses & incurred great expenses in searching out a location & planting the church in this place, & he wants you to send him a present of twenty thousand dollars in gold dust to help him in his labors. This is but a trifle, when gold is so plenty, but it will do me much good at this time.[22]

In addition to this remarkable request, Young asked Brannan to send an additional $20,000 to be divided between his counselors, Heber C. Kimball and Willard Richards. "A hint to hint to the wise is sufficient," he advised.

Some commentators have interpreted this request as an indication, however untypical, of President Young's avarice. Given the context, a more reasonable interpretation would take into account his customary tendency to mix his personal finances with the business interests of the LDS community. Young clearly seemed interested in testing the mercurial Brannan's loyalty to the church, but his central purpose for securing such a quantity of gold may have been to strengthen the newly introduced system of gold coinage he had taken under his direct management.

[22]Brigham Young to Samuel Brannan, 5 April 1849, Brigham Young Collection, LDS Archives, in Bagley, ed., *Scoundrel's Tale*, 286.

Amasa Lyman: Labor Has Been Wasted Leaving No Traces

As part of his assignment, Amasa Lyman encouraged successful Saints to leave California for Great Salt Lake City. In July he helped organize and dispatch a train led by Thomas Rhoades, Sr., who had enjoyed substantial success in placer mining. With the Rhoades company Lyman sent his own first report on his overland journey and the condition of church affairs in California. His optimism at this point would not outlast the 1849 season.

Of particular interest is Lyman's brief report of a first visit, apparently a cordial one, in San Francisco with Sam Brannan and his partner William Stout. It predates by approximately six months the much better known encounter, when Lyman allegedly told Brannan that they had "come for the Lord's money"—the tithing on Brannan's sizeable fortune due to the church. At this second meeting in January 1850, as Brannan later bragged, he supposedly told Brigham Young's emissaries, "Give me a receipt from the Lord—and you can have the money."[23] This account of his first visit demonstrates that Lyman had not hesitated to approach his old friend Brannan, but that he already recognized the need for a diplomatic course of action if Brannan was to be induced to aid the church leadership with a share of his gold rush riches.

Amasa Lyman to Young and Council, 6 July 1849, Young Papers, LDS Archives.

Sacramento July 6th 1849

Prest Young and council dear brethren I take this the earliest chance to write to you. On our leaveing the City April 11th we were prospered on our journey we had to ferry Ogdens fork and crossed the Malad by bridge. At marys river we had to ferry. The other streams we forded had plenty of feed for our animals until we came to the mountains which we comenced crossing on the 18th of May on the snow. We crossed the last divide on the 19th

---

[23]This episode is the best known legend in the history of Brannan's relations with the LDS hierarchy. In *Scoundrel's Tale*, his documentary investigation of Brannan's career, Will Bagley reviews the evidence for the "receipt signed by the Lord" story, concluding that it was originated at a later date by Brannan, "designed to distance himself from Mormonism and support his assertion that his only interest in the religion was financial." According to Amasa Lyman's manuscript journal in LDS Archives, the critical encounter took place on 8 January 1850. Schindler, *Orrin Porter Rockwell*, 187, states that Rockwell accompanied Lyman during the January meeting. Neither Schindler nor Bagley was aware of Lyman's July 1849 letter, and neither historian notes Lyman's earlier meeting with Brannan and Stout.

in the midst of the clouds the snow fast around and below us on this dreary [day]. We left a horse and a mule of which we [los]t 7 on the journey. We were about thre[e] days on the snow in which time we had no feed for our horses. We arrived at the (Sutters) fort on the 25th of May having been 45 days on the road. On our arival at the Fort I met with brother Thomas Grover who in conexion with brother [Levi] riter had the brethren generaly in notion to leeve for Salt Lake some of whom are comeing while other[s] I have advised to stay and [work] another year until I shall return and gather what means they can for the Church. The saints in Sanfrancisco still manifest a love for the truth an[d] the works of the Lord. I regret to say that many of the brethren of the Battallion who have been blessd in procuring [gold] have been as profligate in spending it. In this way thousands of dollars the fruits of their labor has been wasted leaving no trace of its having been posessed by them but their confirmed habits of profligacy and disipation. Still among them their is some who are not yet dead. Unless your word calls I shall not return until the autumn of 1850, when I hope to be able to bring some relief to the Church.

I have collected $4102 dollars tithing and donation which I send by br. Thomas Grover who is returning with the brethren. Br. Grover still loves the cause of God and his people and has exerted a good influence in this country for which may the Lord bless him and may he in nowise loose his reward. Br. I. Fowler remains here this season in consequence of the stat[e] of his means and some debts standing it out.

From all I have seen of the country and people, [I am] satisfied that a branch of the Church may be maintained who if properly guided may do well for themselves and bring help to the saints, which would hardly be realized from another qua[r]ter at present. I saw Mr. Samuel Branen, and his partner Mr. Stout. I think that Samuel will do some thing for the Church if he is let alone. I design pursuing a course with him that will alow him an opportunity to do all the good he may have the means or disposition to do.

Any instructions you may have to send by the brethren this fall will be gratefuly received by yr. brother and felow labourer in the cause of truth Amasa Lyman.

N.B. On my visit [to] Sanfrancisco I saw br. A. Badlam from Boston who had a leter of comendation from our beloved brother Wilford who is settled near that place. Brother B. proposes to tary in this country until my return and acompany me to our home in the mountains.[24]

[24]Alexander Badlam was Samuel Brannan's brother-in-law and a charter member of Joseph Smith's secretive but powerful Council of Fifty. He returned to his family in Boston via Panama, but journeyed to Utah in 1850 with Apostle Wilford Woodruff. Badlam settled in Sacramento but remained on friendly terms with church officials at Salt Lake. His son and namesake became an influential San Francisco politician and a major player in winning statehood for Utah. See Bagley, *"Cities of the Wicked": Alexander Badlam Reports on Mormon Prospects in California and China in the 1850s.*

THOMAS RHOADES
This formal portrait is the only known picture of one of the first Saints to see Utah in 1846 and the captain of the "Gold Train" from northern California in 1849. At his death in Minersville, Utah, in 1869, Rhoades left behind a legend of a "Lost Mine." *Courtesy Bernie L. Rhoades.*

The friends in francisco are anxious for preaching which I think may be don[e] to advantage if properly done.

From my observation of men and things in the country [what has] hapened to the [battalion] boys [has been] according to your sayings when they left. The [non-Mormon] company that left [Salt Lake for California] this spring with waggons have spilled out their misrepresentations as was anticipated when I left but they have no influence and prehaps by the time they dig a fortune from the Earth they may become cool.

Br. Thomas Rhoads takes charge of the [Com]pany coming to the City. Br. R. is a good man and loves the truth. I send in the care of br. Grover the funds for the Church which thoug[h] small I hope may do some good in the days of poverty and small things. The acount of tithing is in another leter.

The most of the brethren who have tithed have only tithed their money some have not tithed at all but promised to do so at the City. They will generaly have property to tithe and some money.

J. D. Hunter is here his tithing the list will show. He calculates to rema[i]n until I return which will be next year sometime probably so for the present fare the[e] well. Remember me to your family. peace be with you in the name of Jesus Amen.

Amasa Lyman

The roster of the Rhoades company is preserved in the LDS Church Archives. Thomas Rhoades, Sr., the company's leader, was a native of

Kentucky who had joined the church in Illinois in 1835 when he was forty years old, then moved to western Missouri. A large landowner and slaveholder, he remained in Missouri until 1846, when he organized family members and friends to become part of the westward migration led by Brigham Young. Apparently unaware that the Nauvoo Saints had been unable to go west in 1846, Rhoades proceeded to California with his own small wagon train, crossing the Salt Lake Valley and Great Salt Desert ahead of the Donner party, though other members of the family stayed on the California Trail via Fort Hall. Rhoades reached Sutter's Fort in early October 1846, and he and his clan settled southeast of the fort, taking up land in the Sloughhouse area and also north of Dry Creek in today's Galt, California. His older daughters married prominent non-Mormon pioneers in the area, while his sons were active in California affairs during the U.S.-Mexican War, including the rescue of the Donner party. In 1847 Rhoades became a widower. He did not take another wife until he reached Great Salt Lake City. He then entered into plural marriages, causing a long-term break with his California family.

A family tradition asserts that Thomas Rhoades and his sons discovered gold in 1847, the year before the Coloma and Mormon Island discoveries. In any case, the Rhoades family became active miners at an early point. They are associated with a site known as Rhoads' Diggings, located in an area where placer deposits were extremely rich, east of today's town of Folsom at the northeast intersection of present-day Scott Road and Highway 50.[25] The Rhoades company left California in mid-July 1849 with a great deal of gold in their wagons. Their cargo included $3,000 in gold dust and $1,280 in coin collected as tithing and contributions by Apostle Amasa Lyman, which Lyman estimated at $4,102 in his letter to Brigham Young. Rhoades himself carried a reported $17,000, while William Glover and his wife had another $3,300. Additional amounts brought along by other members of the company have not been recorded.[26]

[25]Bernie Rhoades provided updated information on his ancestors, including copies of Missouri legal documents signed by Thomas Rhoades, which confirm this spelling of his last name.

[26]The principal source of information on Thomas Rhoades and his family is Davies, "Thomas Rhoads, Forgotten Mormon Pioneer of 1846," 81–95; and *Mormon Gold,* 145–55, in which J. Kenneth Davies describes this party as the Mormon Gold Train. For Rhoads' Diggings, see Hoover *et al., Historic Spots in California,* rev. Kyle, 290.

LIST OF BRETHREN FROM CALIFORNIA, 14 JULY 1849, LDS ARCHIVES.

Sacramento City July 14th 1849

Report of the number of California Saints together with the number of Waggons, Cattle, and other property in their possession which Company was organized by Elder Amasa Lyman at Sacramento City: Thomas Rhoades was appointed Capt. by the Unanimous voice of the Company

	Ages Years	Waggons	Horses	Yokes Oxen	Cash	Cows	Mules
Thomas Rhoades	55	1	2	3			
Caleb "							
Lucinda "	4						
Sam (Indian)							
Turner Elder		1	5	2		2	
Polly "							
Martin "							
Elizabeth "							
Thomas "							
Turner "							
John "							
Nancy "							
Alondas D. L. Buckland	24	2	2	9		0	1
Nancy L "							
Alondas L. "							
Nancy L. "							
Prudence Aldredge							
Henry S. Dalton	23	2	1	5		1	4
Elizabeth G. "							
John G. "							
Daniel Henry		2					
Aaron Stow							
Wm Kittlman		2	1	5		1	
Eliza "							
James "							
Mary Ann "							
George "							
Sarah "							
Hannah M. "							
Wm Glover							
Jane "							
Jane Jr "							
Katharine "							
Joseph "							
Wm "							
Sarah "							
Zelnora Snow							
Eliza Savage							
Samuel Ladd							
Henry Hoskins	40	1					
Thomas Treat		1	2 Horses				
Ashbel Green Haskel	Desseased on the road July 27th 1849[27]						

William Glover: The Lord Put a Hook in Their Jaws

The second prominent leader in the Rhoades train was William Glover, who made the trip with his wife and six children. After his 1848 mining success at Mormon Island, Glover had gone back to San Francisco for the winter. He returned to Sacramento with his family the following July, when the Sierra passes were starting to open, and joined the Rhoades company for the trek to Great Salt Lake City. His brief account of the trip eastward is particularly notable because it tells of Amasa Lyman's early wish to recruit wealthy settlers to found a colony at San Bernardino. Glover also relates the company's experience with a menacing group that trailed them across the Sierra. Purportedly resentful because the Saints had skimmed off "the cream of the mines," these well-armed strangers threatened to attack them and take their gold.

William Glover, The Mormons in California, Bancroft Library.

In the Spring of '49 myself and a few others gathered up our effects and started for Salt Lake. While at Sacramento buying our outfit we met Amasa Lyman. He wanted me to go to San Bernardino to settle and spend my money. I told him 'no' I had started for Salt Lake and I was going. He told me then to go and I would get the [k]nots knocked off me. When we started across the mountains, the first night after we camped a company of men with pack animals, 13 in number, armed to the teeth with some picks and spades passed us, professing to be prospectors hunting for gold. They would pass and repass every day. We were meeting companies of emigrants every day and sometimes they camped with us to hear about the gold diggins. The emigrants began to warn us to be on our guard and watch those men with pack animals, and said they intended mischief. One company told us they said we had the cream of the mines and wanted them to join with them to destroy us. We took every precaution we could, not to give them any advantage of us. They turned back when they got to Carson Valley, for the emi-

---

[27]Henry S. Dalton had been a private in Company B. He married Elizabeth Kittleman of the *Brooklyn* company in January 1848 in San Francisco. Elizabeth's father, William Kittleman, with his wife and five other children joined the Rhoades company. Along with the Glovers, Prudence Aldrich, L. D. Buckland, and A. G. Haskel or Haschal had also been *Brooklyn* passengers. See Ricketts, *Mormon Battalion*, 23, 188; and Bagley, ed., *Scoundrel's Tale*, 147–48. For the gossip John Borrowman related about Susan Eliza Savage and her troubled and scandalous relationships with Samuel Brannan and then with Miles Weaver, along with her self-portrait, see ibid., 274–75. Daniel Henrie had served as a private in the battalion's Company D. At Sutter's Fort before the gold discovery, he ran a butcher shop and meat market. According to his brief biographical statement, Henrie "was in the Gold mines 11 months realized 4000$ on which I paid tithing twice after I got to Salt Lake." See Ricketts, *Mormon Battalion*, 26, 195; and "Biography &c of President Daniel Henrie," South Sanpete Stake, 48th Quorum of Seventies Records, 1857–1928, LDS Archives.

> grants were coming along so fast we could meet two or three companies a day. They had murder in their hearts, but the Lord put a hook in their jaws that they had no power to mollest us. We went our way rejoicing and praising God that he had spared our lives and the little means we had for a better purpose.
>
> When we got between the Humbolt and Goose Creek Levi Riter and Harry Green got in a hurry to reach home.[28] They started out alone and the first night they camped the Indians stole their horses and fired at them. They ran and saved their lives, but they got seperated in the darkness. The next day Harry Green came and met us and told us what had happened. We turned back ten miles to camp, and laid over the next day. Levi Riter went the other way and met a company of 18 young men. He travelled back with them to meet us. When they got where they had camped they saw some of their animals, and in trying to recover them they had quite a fight with the Indians. Two men were killed and four wounded—one died afterwards from his wounds, the balance turned back with us to Salt Lake and wintered. The Indians burned their light wagons and destroyed most of their provisions. We buried the two dead men when we came to where they were and gathered up what provisions were left, but saw no Indians.
>
> We arrived in Salt Lake on the last of September, praising God that He had preserved us through all the varied and trying scenes of a long, tedious and perilous journey, where, thank God, I have never had cause to repent my choice of identifying myself with the Latter-day Saints.

The appearance of the Rhoades company at Salt Lake in September 1849 coincided with the arrival of new coinage equipment, sent by the church's agent in St. Louis. The relative abundance of gold then made it possible for the church mint to resume operations, issuing gold pieces in denominations of $2.50, $5.00, $10.00 and $20.00. This coinage continued until early 1851, amounting to approximately $75,000 in total. The Mormon coins, designed with a variety of religious symbols and the initials "P.G." to stand for pure gold, circulated throughout the Salt Lake Valley and surrounding regions, with some returning to California. Even without a generous contribution from Brother Brannan, California's gold underwrote an era of relative financial stability and brisk trade in the Zion colony.

[28] Levi Riter's account of his California adventures and this trip back to Salt Lake appears in the following chapter. Riter's companion was most likely Henry Green, Sr., who had arrived in California early in the 1849 travel season with a pack train from Salt Lake, a party that included Abner Blackburn. Apparently Green quickly decided to return east with Riter and bring his family to California. He subsequently settled with his son and other family members in the Salmon Falls area, a center of LDS activity, where he became a partner in a hotel with Hezekiah Thatcher. See Davies, *Mormon Gold*, 222.

AMASA LYMAN: TO PROCURE GOLD REQUIRES ECONOMY AND LABOUR

After helping send off the Rhoades train with the Glover family, Amasa Lyman continued through the summer and fall months to carry out his church duties in northern California. In September, after receiving a newsy letter from Brigham Young, he replied with a report on his activities that indicated his growing dissatisfaction with the society of the gold country.

AMASA LYMAN TO BRIGHAM YOUNG,
19 SEPTEMBER 1849, BRIGHAM YOUNG COLLECTION, LDS ARCHIVES.

North Fork Sept 19th 1849

Prst Young Dear sir

I take this opportunity to write you a few lines. My health is good at present and that this [letter] ma[y] find you enjoying the same is my Daily prayr. Your favour of the 20th of June came duly to hand and was to me a great satisfaction to hear from my family and the Saints. The news from the Lake by the emigrants is truly cheering the farmers from Pensylvania to Missouri all agree that your crops are so good or beter than in the states particularly small grain and garden vegetables so I sleep quietly at night reflecting that the Saints in the mountain valy no more hunger for bread since the Lord has given another evidences that it is his buisness to provide for his saints. The latest news from the Lake was by some men who left there the last of July. Various reports have reached here about br. Rich being on the way to this country. I have concluded that he or some one else was coming or I should have received some letters by the emigrants. I am at present in the mines and shall probably remain there through the winter. When Brother Grover [Glover] left I went to Francisco and was there a few weeks during which time my health was bad but since I have been in the mines it has been good. To procure gold requires economy and labour.

While in Francisco I preached 4 times to very attentive audiences. A good field is here for labour but for me it is not home with all its gold. I long to inhale once more the pure air of the valy. That is the spirit that is breathed among the saints in but two instances has it been said to me br. Lyman will you pray my soul is pained all the day long with the coruption and depravity of manny. Coruption is corupted and sin it self is outraged. The rest let me tell when I come [back to Utah]. As to news from abroad you have more than me. I have sent a leter to br. Grouard[29] and a copy of the epistle a

[29]Benjamin P. Grouard was president of the Society Islands Mission from 1847 to 1850 and a missionary companion of Addison Pratt. Grouard settled in southern California in 1852 and even- (*continued*)

> monthly . . . I still hop[e] to be able to procure some help for the saints to bring when I return although from accounts you must be rich so say the Gentiles and have got a good country. What a Pity the fugitives should live. Time flies. I must close remember me to all my friends. Yours in the new covenent.
>
> Amasa Lyman

Henry W. Bigler: A Complete Shower of Tears

The arrival of the Rhoades train and other successful miners in Salt Lake during the summer and fall of 1849 made it even more difficult for Brigham Young to deter the faithful from venturing to northern California on their own. Then, after a reasonably bountiful harvest in 1849, President Young initiated another project to make the land of gold useful to the Great Basin Saints. In October 1849 he launched a semicovert program to tap California's treasure on behalf of a select few, all associated with the inner circle of LDS leadership in Great Salt Lake City, by sending two small companies to the placer regions with instructions to dig for gold. A favored church member in the Salt Lake Valley sponsored each prospective miner and expected to share in whatever wealth he brought back from the gold country. This enterprise, called the Gold Mission, envisioned that the miners would remain a year in California. When they returned to Zion, they would divide their gains with their sponsor, who had paid some part of their initial outfitting costs. Like the practice that became known as grubstaking in the mining regions, the Gold Mission enterprise combined speculative enthusiasm and blithe optimism with a high degree of mutual trust among those involved. In this case it required as well a due regard for confidentiality, since Brigham Young apparently intended to keep the mission and its partnership arrangements from becoming a matter of widespread public knowledge.[30]

Among the first to be recruited for this delicate assignment was

(*continued*) -tually became a Spiritualist, but Pratt adopted Frank, his son by a Polynesian woman. Frank Grouard ran away from his Utah home at age fifteen, spent six years with the Lakota, scouted for Gen. George Crook in 1876, and wrote a colorful autobiography before his death in 1905. His failure to provide accurate translations may have led to the death of Crazy Horse in 1877.

[30]The Gold Mission first received scholarly notice in Arrington, *Great Basin Kingdom*, 72–76, with an extremely helpful discussion of sources on page 440. Subsequent accounts include Arrington, *Charles C. Rich*, 138–41; and Davies, *Mormon Gold*, 109–30, 157–73.

Henry Bigler, who reluctantly agreed to return to California and again take up gold digging for the benefit of church patriarch John Smith. Essentially, Father Smith was to be Bigler's silent partner. Bigler's journal entries demonstrate his efforts to suppress his personal desires while making a few simple preparations for the unwelcome trek to California. "It fills me with sorrow to think of leaving," he confided in these pages, "for I am attached to this place and this people for they are my brethren and my friends. [It] was with considerable strugle with my feelings that I consented to go." After selling the wheat he had harvested, settling his accounts, paying a few debts, and receiving a blessing from Father Smith, he was ready to leave on the afternoon of 11 October. He revealed his further reluctance to return to California as he waited at his home for the arrival of James Keeler, his traveling companion.

> At this moment I experienced what I shall not here attempt to describe. I walked back and forth across my floor and my feelings were spent in a complete shower of tears, every thing I looked upon seemed to simpethise with me and say go in peace only be faithful and all will be right. I herd a rattling and looked up and saw the waggon a coming. I hastened to the curtings of the window and wiped a way every tear, and went out to the waggon. I was requested to get in. I refused I told Bro. Keeler I would walk as I wanted to call at the tin shop to buy me a canteen. I paid 6 bits for one & 2 bits for a quart cup. I then got in the waggon and we drove to Bro. Hales on Cottonwood about 10 miles [and] got thare in the night.[31]

While Henry Bigler knew all too well what to expect in the placer diggings, young George Q. Cannon lacked any experience with mining when he was instructed to join the 1849 Gold Mission.[32] Yet his immediate response, as he recalled it twenty years later, was not excitement but painful submission to his sense of duty to the church community. His recollections attest to the success of President Young and other LDS leaders in preventing a gold rush away from Salt Lake City by instilling

[31]Henry Bigler, Diary, 11 October 1849, Book B, Huntington Library.

[32]Davis Bitton's fine study, *George Q. Cannon: A Biography,* describes fully his youth in England, his family's conversion and 1842 voyage to join the Saints, and his activities in Nauvoo and Great Salt Lake City. As he later related, Cannon "had starved all winter" after driving a wagon from Winter Quarters in the 1847 company led by Parley P. Pratt and John Taylor, Cannon's uncle. Cannon's subsequent career as a writer, publisher, political spokesperson for the church, and member of the church presidency brought him national fame as one of the best-known representatives of Mormonism in the late nineteenth century. The journal of Cannon's 1849 trip to California is ably presented in Landon, ed. *The Journals of George Q. Cannon, Volume I: To California in '49,* which also reproduces on page 1 the following passage from Cannon's 1869 *Juvenile Instructor* account. Cannon was twenty-two years old at the time he joined the Gold Mission and headed for California.

in young men of the Zion colony a conviction that mining was a dishonorable occupation.

> There was no place I would not rather have gone to at that time than California. I heartily despised the work of digging gold. I thought it very poor business for men to be running over the country for gold. I was quite young then, and though nearly twenty years have elapsed since that time, I still think so. There is no honorable occupation that I would not rather follow than hunting and digging gold.[33]

Albert K. Thurber: Fit Us Out and Get ⅓ of What Each Made

A more willing recruit to the Gold Mission was Albert King Thurber, a young New Englander who had converted to the LDS faith in 1849 after stopping in Salt Lake on his way to California. In his autobiography, Thurber left to posterity a detailed account of his conversion, his subsequent adventures traveling and mining, and his return to the Mormon capital, where he settled for life. Thurber had departed from Boston in March 1849, one among many thousands of young men afflicted with gold fever that spring. He was then a member of a wagon company of forty-four adventurers organized under the name Congress and California Joint Stock Mining Company, all in uniform, well supplied and well armed. By the time he reached Great Salt Lake City in mid-July, the company had long since broken up and Thurber was traveling with four companions by horse and pack mule. In the city of Zion, he found himself mightily impressed by his first few religious conversations with Latter-day Saints. Quickly he made a decision: "Went into the tent and told my comrades that whenever they got ready to leave they might do so, but that I was going to learn something more about these Mormons before I left."

After making a division of property with the other four, Thurber recalled, "I found myself with a fine black coat, one pair of pants, 2 flannel shirts and a pair of 50¢ turned pumps which about constituted my wardrobe—and no money." He went to work at once for Benjamin Johnson on Mill Creek, thrashing grain with a flail. "Mormonism," he later declared, "was my study." Slowly he worked his way through the issues of

[33] Cannon, "Twenty Years Ago: A Trip to California," 13.

faith that most concerned him. He was baptized on 1 September 1849, and "a newness and peace came over me that I cannot explain."

In company with Jacob Burnham, who had performed Thurber's baptism, the young man continued to work for Benjamin Johnson until November. Then, when Johnson offered them the opportunity, he and Burnham quickly agreed to join the Gold Mission.

> The California gold mines were attracting great attention and as Johnson was of the council of 50, the president (B. Young) authorized them to send a few men, as Johnson told me, to prove them. He proposed for me and Burnham to go. We worked one week without mentioning the subject and then decided to go in a short time. Johnson was to fit us out and get ⅓ of what each made and we to receive ⅓ of what he made at home.[34]

A MAN HAVEING THE SPIRIT OF GOD IS A RARE TREAT IN CALIFORNIA

Bigler, Cannon, Thurber, and other members of the Gold Mission traveled to California in company with Charles C. Rich, the highly respected former Illinois militia leader of the Nauvoo Legion. At the LDS general conference in October 1849, Brigham Young designated Rich to join Amasa Lyman, Rich's close friend, in managing church affairs in California. Since there was no longer any regularly constituted LDS congregation in San Francisco or elsewhere in California, the two men were instructed to gather and organize the northern California Saints. Rich also brought with him a further letter of authority that empowered him to "investigate Sam Brannan, collect tithing, receive donations for the perpetual emigration fund for the gathering of the poor of the church, and not to neglect the preaching of the gospel."[35]

Rich and those traveling with him, including a large number of non-Mormon emigrants who had hired Jefferson Hunt as their guide, reached southern California in December 1849 after an arduous and extremely

[34]Thurber Journal, Bancroft Library, photocopy of typed transcript, LDS Archives.

[35]Roberts, *Comprehensive History,* 3:340, quoted in Arrington, *Charles C. Rich,* 139. The LDS church created a voluntary fund "for the laudable and benevolent purpose of facilitating the emigration of the poor" in fall 1849 but only incorporated the Perpetual Emigrating Fund Company on 14 September 1850 under the laws of the Provisional State of Deseret. The program subsidized the costs of gathering thousands of Mormons to Utah before it was dissolved by the 1887 Edmunds-Tucker Act.

CHARLES C. RICH
An early portrait of the future apostle, said to have been displayed originally in the Nauvoo Temple, this painting depicts Rich while he was a general in the Nauvoo Legion, nearly a decade before he reached California. *Courtesy Pioneer Memorial Museum, International Society, Daughters of Utah Pioneers.*

hazardous trek over the southern route from Salt Lake to Los Angeles.[36] For a month Rich and other LDS travelers in his party—the members of the Gold Mission and some (including the experienced miner James S. Brown) en route to the Pacific islands on proselytizing missions—remained at Isaac Williams's Rancho del Chino to recuperate from their trip and gather supplies. In mid-January they journeyed north toward San Francisco, where Rich and Lyman reunited and began their joint duties.[37]

The first report that Brigham Young received from the two men came in an undated letter from Rich, probably written in the late spring of 1850, that strongly argued for the purchase of the San Bernardino ranch and the establishment of an LDS settlement on this land. The San

[36]The late 1849 migration by the southern route has become famous in overland trail history for the extreme hardships encountered by the various traveling companies, Mormon and non-Mormon, and the fatal disaster that befell the party that discovered Death Valley while seeking a shortcut to the mines. The fullest account is in Hafen and Hafen, eds., *Journals of Forty-Niners, Salt Lake to Los Angeles.* For Rich's critically important leadership role in preventing disaster for the LDS travelers, see Arrington, *Charles C. Rich,* 137–52. Two other detailed accounts are Ellsworth, ed., *The Journals of Addison Pratt,* 375–412; and Landon, ed., *The Journals of George Q. Cannon, Volume 1.*

[37]The California experiences of these 1849 Gold Mission travelers to the gold fields are reviewed in the following chapter.

Bernardino project originally grew from the hopes of Col. Richard Mason, then California's military governor, to locate an LDS colony in southern California. Such a settlement, Mason conceived, would guarantee U.S. political control over the largely Hispanic population of the newly conquered territory, and it would provide a contingent of Saints for a permanent military garrison force. Capt. Jesse Hunter of the Mormon Battalion forwarded Mason's request to the church authorities, but it brought no action. Subsequently the proposal was urged again by Jefferson Hunt, Hunter's fellow officer in the battalion, when he arrived in Salt Lake from the Pacific Coast.

Despite Brigham Young's strong wish to keep any Saints from relocating outside the Great Basin, Hunt and other battalion veterans continued to nurture the plan and press it on President Young through 1848 and 1849. Such a settlement, they pointed out, would secure the western end of a winter wagon road between Salt Lake and the Pacific Coast and would provide control over a travel corridor that could bring foreign converts to Zion and carry missionaries toward their assignments overseas, particularly toward destinations in the Pacific islands.[38] Moreover, as Hunt's 1847 relief expedition had first indicated, the ranching and farming resources of the San Bernardino Valley could help sustain the Great Basin Saints during periods of hardship. To have Rich, like Lyman, back Hunt's proposal undoubtedly gave the plan greater credibility for the church authorities in Great Salt Lake City.

Throughout the spring and into the summer Lyman and Rich traveled about northern California, visiting Sacramento and the mining country from Mormon Island to Salmon Falls, Placerville, and beyond, at all those locations where groups of Saints were working in the placer diggings. In mid-July they prepared a lengthy joint report to Brigham Young and the church's governing council on their activities and the condition of church affairs in California. This crucial document informed the Salt Lake authorities about the California Saints and further shaped the attitudes that would subsequently govern relations between Brigham Young and the LDS brethren in the golden state.[39]

---

[38]The background and development of the colony proposal is summarized well in Lyman, *San Bernardino: The Rise and Fall of a California Community*, a fully drawn history of this unique LDS venture in settling beyond the borders of the Great Basin.

The first topic the two men broached was the financial condition of the church in California, which, they declared "is at a low ebb." Since the departure of the Rhoades company the previous year, California Saints had paid Lyman only one hundred dollars in tithing. "The Brethren of wealth in San Francisco have paid little or no thithing [*sic*]," they stated. "Mr. Samuel Brannan has paid nothing and now disclaims any connection or interest in the Church and the communications from the Brethren are regarded [by Brannan] rather as insults than otherwise, making drafts on him has amounted to a waste of paper and time haveing afforded him the chance to do good if he would but without effect."[40] Those Saints who claimed they might otherwise pay tithing, including those who had previously contributed the most, now said they had invested all their funds in real estate or in loans they could not sell or collect, "so in the midst of wealth they are poor."

The northern California Saints, Lyman and Rich reported, showed a general spirit of disaffection from the church. Recent emigrants from the Salt Lake colony, the two men observed, had usually remained true to the faith and continued to act as models for those who had strayed from the ways of the righteous. Yet even a few of the newcomers "have fallen into the path of the Gambler or the Drunkard." On the whole, the two church agents were more than discouraged with the situation of the Saints in northern California. "To strike hands with a man haveing the spirit of God is a rare treat in California," they ruefully remarked, "and is like a fruitfull shower in a parched land." The situation, they stated, fully proved the truth of Brigham Young's early conviction that life in California would corrupt all but the most devoted church members.

Lyman and Rich wanted to impress church leaders that riches did not come easily in California. They had remained poor, they emphasized, and had not been able to aid friends who had asked them for help in the search for wealth. "In the labor and toil of our present mission," they

[39]For the complete text of this important report, see Lyman and Rich to Brigham Young, 23 July 1850, Young Collection, LDS Archives, printed in Bagley, ed., *Scoundrel's Tale*, 292–96.

[40]Brannan's tithing contributions and his subsequent relations with the church are reviewed in detail in ibid., 281–300. By September 1853 Brannan paid all his supposed debts to church and tithing in the amount of five hundred dollars, certainly a modest valuation. Two years earlier, however, at a meeting in San Francisco led by Parley P. Pratt, Brannan's one-time friend and mentor, he was cut off from LDS fellowship for unchristian-like conduct, for neglect of duties, and for taking a leadership role in the 1851 San Francisco vigilante movement.

wryly commented, "we have found a perfect antidote to the poison of gold which consists in being taxed with the acquisition and care of the shining dust and [we] still walk hand in hand with our old acquaintance poverty. We think we shall be satisfied if we can see our homes [again] with enough to pay our debts, wood, school & other bills."

As for the organization of the church in northern California, Lyman and Rich declared it was totally impractical to gather the brethren together or establish a church structure, "especially as they are continually moving as their diggins get worked out." At the same time they set forth their conclusion that "the interests of the church require a resting place in this region for the saints, and the portion of California described by Bro Rich in his letter to you [the San Bernardino site], is the only place that is now open for settlement with all its advantages. . . ." The two men further reported that they had taken preliminary steps to start a southern California LDS settlement by sending a few reliable Saints to occupy some of the land, and to influence others to settle there "untill Bro. Rich shall be there to direct in person the settlement of those who may chose to make that country their home."[41]

Lyman and Rich intended, according to their report, to make the settlement at a southern site distinctly different from the society of the gold fields. The members of the church generally, they told the Salt Lake authorities, "as well as those cutt off and many disaffected, are all anxious that a settlement should be made, and in order that it might not be composed of a major[ity] of the disaffected class we have not urged such to hasten to the lower country." Instead, the apostles expressed their hope "that the foundation of society might be laid with better material than those who are so light that they have floated [west from Salt Lake City] over the Sierra Nevada to the gold mines."

In effect, Lyman and Rich had taken the initiative to make LDS church policy for California. "And now Brethren," they stated to their associates in Salt Lake, "if the conclusion to which we have come is right in your sight all is well, if not, the steps [we have] taken can produce no injury to individuals or the Church." They were confident in recommending a

[41]The apostles directed Jesse Hunter, Charles Crismon, and Anthony Blackburn "to locate" at San Bernardino. Hunter subsequently declined to help the apostles and settled in Los Angeles. See Bagley, ed., *Frontiersman,* 195.

course of action to President Young and his counselors. "If all is right," they wrote, "and you should send an emmigration to the lower country by the south route this fall or any other time from the Lake or any other place . . . by giving intimation of the same to Bro Rich they can be settled properly and profitably."

Despite their strong interest in establishing a southern California settlement, Lyman and Rich were not at all inclined to give California the uncritical praise that flowed from some of their contemporaries. Writing to Thomas Bullock, the church secretary in Salt Lake City, they indicated in July 1850 their personal misgivings about life in the land of gold, and they passed along realistic advice for their brethren in Great Salt Lake City about business dealing with California-bound emigrants.

CHARLES C. RICH AND AMASA LYMAN TO THOMAS BULLOCK, 22 JULY 1850, THOMAS BULLOCK PAPERS, LDS ARCHIVES.

Upper Calafornea July the 23rrd 1850

Thomas Bullock

Dear Brother Yours of June 17th come to hand this Day we was glad to hear from you and get some news from the city of the saints. we have just written Letters to the Presidency and given all the Perticalor news on what we could but to fulfil the promise I made when I Left I must say at Least a few words we trust that this will not be the Last time news from the Lake is Like a messenger from a far Country for Surely we are not fascinated with this country or the People. we think as a general thing evry Boddy will be ready to bear testimony to the [truth of the] Sayings of President young and others with regard to the best course to take I believe the Brethren that has staid in the Valley as a general thing will be better off than those that has come to this country I am aware that the Brethren will generally be astounded at Such news we will Say one thing it is not worth while for the Brethren to trust [on credit] emigrants [in Salt Lake] expecting they will Pay us [after they reach California] if they [the Saints in Salt Lake] are Disposed to give [credit] Let them give [it] but as a general thing it will be a perfect failure. This you may be assured [—] when men get in to this country you might as well find a man by saying he Lives in england we will now stop for this time hoping to hear more Soon we remain yours in the everlasting cove[nant]

Charles C. Rich
Amasa Lyman

As they traveled about northern California during 1850, Lyman and

Rich effectively brought an end to the Gold Mission. Most Saints on the mining assignment had found little gold but had suffered extreme fatigue, want, and illness, and they were more than ready to quit the placer diggings. Although the two leaders enlisted a few, including Henry Bigler, for missionary service in the Pacific islands, they encouraged the others to return to Salt Lake as soon as possible. The new convert Albert King Thurber, originally eager to reach California, was now among those who welcomed this message as deliverance from danger and unprofitable drudgery.

> Bro. A Lyman and Rich visited us, took our tithings, councilled all to go home that had not good claims or found a chance to make a lot of money in a few days. I went to them, told them my situation. Bro. Rich placed his hands on my shoulder, says he, the valleys are the place for you, go home with Bro. Amasa. This suited me as I never felt contented in the mines.

Within a short time Thurber made his preparations and joined a party heading east under Lyman's direction. After reaching Carson Valley and making a rendezvous with a larger force of Saints bound for Great Salt Lake City, the young man made a personal inventory. "I found my riches consisted of 2 mules, an old pair of boots and hat, a pair of pants and [a] flannel shirt, $4.50 in gold dust," he reported. "I felt well starting home."[42]

Brigham Young: Did You Get Rich?

Albert Thurber reached the Salt Lake Valley safely with Lyman's party in September 1850, after a journey most memorable because of an outbreak of cholera or some other intestinal affliction that claimed the life of two of his companions, Barnum Kinion and battalion veteran John C. Gould. The same illness, according to Thurber's diagnosis, killed forty-four horses in the party.[43]

Some months after his return, while accompanying a friend and his

[42]Thurber Journal, Bancroft Library, photocopy of typed transcript, LDS Archives.

[43]Modern bacteriological knowledge suggests that a form of salmonella, not cholera, was the likely disease agent. While cholera, a water-borne disease, was common in 1849 and 1850 on the overland trail from St. Louis as far west as Fort Laramie, it was seldom if ever encountered beyond that point. A deadly cholera outbreak in San Francisco and Sacramento in October 1850 was the result of its introduction by Chinese argonauts coming directly from Canton.

fiancé who were to be married by the church president, Thurber had an interview with Brigham Young. Recognizing the young man, Young asked Thurber if he had been to California as part of the Gold Mission. Thurber told him that he had. "Well, how did you do?" inquired Young. "I answered first rate, told him that I was well whilst gone and had got back all right." Young had a further query. "Did you get rich?" Thurber's reply gave the church president a candid appraisal of the Gold Mission's success. "I told him that when I got over the Sierra Nevada I had a pair of pants, a shirt and hat, pair of old boots, $4.50 in [gold] dust and provisions enough to take me home."

Young then asked him how he felt starting home in that manner. "I told him I never felt better than when I got over the mountain." Young then placed his hand on the young man's shoulder, "producing a most singular sensation to the ends of my toes," he recalled. The prophet told him "You have entered into a good work, the work of the Lord Almighty. You do not now understand what made you feel so well but be faithful and the time will come when you will understand that and 10,000 things that has not entered your imagination." Young's homily, Thurber declared, "was given in a more fatherly and paternal spirit than anything I had experienced from my earthly parents."

Asa Call: As Successful as Heart Could Desire

The return of the gold missionaries by the fall of 1850, many with their tales of hard work, meager returns from mining, and misfortune in the gold country, may have calmed somewhat the gold rush excitement in the LDS capital. Yet, according to the published report of a perceptive non-Mormon observer who wrote in September, other Saints returning from newer diggings at the eastern edge of the Sierra, adjacent to Carson Valley, were boasting of their success, and generally they could back up their boasts with a show of gold.[44]

---

[44]Asa Cyrus Call, a twenty-five-year-old gold rusher from Wisconsin, reached Great Salt Lake City in August 1850. There his Mormon relative, Anson Call, may have offered him hospitality. Asa remained through the winter, and on 1 April 1851 departed for California in the party headed by Nelson Slater. For his substantial success in the California mines and his later career, including a near escape from death when the steamer *Winfield Scott* wrecked on rocky shoals off the southern California coast, see Appendix C in Bigler, ed., *A Winter with the Mormons*. This paragraph is one small segment of a long, highly informative report on the condition of affairs in Salt Lake City that Call sent to the editor of the *The National Era* in Washington, D.C.

ASA C. CALL, "FROM UTAH. GREAT SALT LAKE CITY, SEPT. 20, 1850," *THE NATIONAL ERA* 5:212 (23 JANUARY 1851) WASHINGTON D.C., 13. TRANSCRIPTION COURTESY OF JOHN R. CALL.

GREAT SALT LAKE CITY, Sept. 20, 1850.

To the Editor of the National Era:

The Mormons who went to the mines last spring are beginning to come in, and their stories and their gold have created quite a stir here, especially among the new comers. They have nearly all been at work in the new mines on the eastern side of the Sierra Nevada mountains, and have been as successful as heart could desire. Those who went out in March last have brought home from $1,000 to $20,000 a piece. I saw one man, by the name of Carpenter, who went last spring, and returned a few days ago. I asked why he returned so soon, and he quietly replied that his provisions were about to give out, and that he had as much gold as his mule could pack, and so he thought he had better come home. I saw his "pile." It looked like about five quarts, and he said it weighed over a hundred pounds; he valued it at $20,000. But they say the miners on the western side of the mountains have not done so well this season. How it is, I do not know, as I have not been over.

BRIGHAM YOUNG: THE WISDOM OF THE LORD IN OPENING THE GOLD MINES

Every Sunday the Great Salt Lake City Saints congregated for afternoon worship service in the Old Tabernacle, as it came to be called, an adobe structure seating 2,500 people erected in 1852 on the southwest corner of Temple Square. Brigham Young presided at these services. He customarily delivered a weekly sermon, often lasting an hour or longer. His addresses, which Young gave without notes or prepared text, were taken down by stenographers, with many then being published in the *Deseret News* and others appearing in an annual compilation of church leaders' addresses titled *Journal of Discourses*. For scholars today the *Journal of Discourses* provides an unexcelled documentary source, preserving in unvarnished form the attitudes, opinions, insights, and admonitions Young pronounced from his pulpit as his principal means of guiding his followers.

Among the earliest of President Young's talks thus recorded is an April 1852 address made to a mid-week conference gathering that touched on the lure of California gold. The Lord's purpose in opening the gold mines, Young explained, was to test the Saints and separate the true believers from those who were not worthy.

> I hinted to-day at the wisdom of the Lord in opening the gold mines, and said he had one object in view, among many others,—namely, to try the faith of the Saints. By this his wisdom has been exhibited, and much accomplished by it among those also who are not Saints. Take a view of this community. A portion will not be Saints. This has always been the case when God has a Church on the earth. They are not all sheep that are in the fold, neither are they all Saints who bear the name. I wish you to understand that when the sheep are separated from the goats, they will never again bear the like afflictions they bore while they mingled with the goats, as long as the world stands; no, neither in this world or any other. Let the sheep and goats be once separated, and the master of that flock of sheep will never afflict them. When there are no goats to annoy the sheep, the latter will mingle with each other and go hand and hand in full fellowship. But when goats are among the sheep, they will besmear them with their stink, and they frisk about, and behave so as to actually turn the sheep almost into goats. They will grow short in the hair, look like goats, and stink like them. The master of the flock must therefore do something to preserve the blood of the sheep pure, lest they completely degenerate and altogether become goats. They must be chastened by persecution, to drive out the stinking goats from their midst. The Lord opened the California gold mines to lead them off; and I say to the goats, Go! I am glad of it. "But do you not think the sheep will go too?" Never mind, if they do: they will get well besmeared with the flavour of the goats, run off and wash themselves and come back again. Though I speak thus, I do not despise the goats; no, not in the least.[45]

Thus, according to President Young's reasoning at the time, only those California Saints who could cleanse themselves from the taint of the gold country and come back again to Zion were worthy of LDS fellowship and salvation. In the same talk, Young made clear his opinion of all those who went to California in search of riches, leaving behind the society of the Saints.

> If gold is a sufficient inducement to lead men off to live in the midst of that society in California, after they know and understand the condition of it, it certainly proves that they love the things of this world better than they love Christ. You may say you are poor, and wish to accumulate something to help yourself and your family. "Are you starving to death for want of food?" "No." All of you have plenty to subsist upon. If those who go to California

[45]Brigham Young, 7 April 1852, *Journal of Discourses*, 6:320.

for Gold were full of the Holy Ghost, they would clothe their wives and children with buckskin, and wear it themselves to the day of their death, rather than mingle with the wicked and be induced to leave the society of the Saints. The true cause of their taking such a course is, they do not love the Lord.

Brigham Young frequently expressed anxiety for the economic wellbeing of the Saints and the church in Utah in his public addresses. Two days after his disquisition about the lure of California's gold, he revealed his deep disappointment at the failure of gold-rich Saints to do their duty for the church.

I will now again take up the subject of tithing. The brethren have done well. They have been willing and obedient, no people could have been more so; for this I thank my Father in Heaven. I could not wish a people to work more kindly in the yoke of Jesus than this people do; the yoke grows more and more easy to them. It seems that every man will not only pay his tithing, but give all he has, if the Lord requires it. . . . Still I see wherein they may do better. . . . You may say, wherein could we have done better, for we have paid our tithing punctually? But has that brother, who sent $100 back to the East for merchandize, paid $10 of it into the tithing office? Or did the brother who has sent $500 back, let us have $50? No; these have used it themselves, and thereby involved those who bear the responsibilities of the Trust. Again, those who have not possessed sufficient money to send back for merchandize, have been necessitated to pay out what they had. Thousands of dollars have been paid here for merchandize. Has one-tenth of all that money been paid into the tithing office? It has not. And where is the tithing that should have come in from England and California? Instead of tithing their money, they have used it for other purposes, and paid it in property, with which we could not pay our debts. This is wherein we have failed to liquidate our debts. . . . The brethren in California have made no less than $100,000, the tenth of which is due this tithing office. For want of this money, we are brought into bondage; and we must now apply our faith and works to raise means to liquidate our indebtedness, which has accumulated by purchasing goods at high and extortionate prices.[46]

By early 1853 President Young's impatience with the wayward Saints in California and those who yet supposed they might relocate to the Pacific Coast, either to the gold country or to San Bernardino, had reached a breaking point. In mid-February he drafted a message that was issued as a general epistle to all Latter-day Saints from the church presidency, signed by Heber C. Kimball and Willard Richards as well as Young.

[46]Ibid., 9 April 1852, 1:51–52.

This policy statement demonstrated the deeply spiritual basis for the church president's belief that the Mormon people must remain in the Great Basin "for a season," and the expectation he shared with all devout Saints that the millennium would soon be upon the world. Those who disregarded the presidency's counsel by leaving Utah, Young made clear, placed in peril their salvation and exaltation, as promised by LDS doctrine, and the salvation of their ancestors. Those who would go or had gone to San Bernardino or elsewhere in California, unless by church direction, were following only their own desires, "through a spirit of disaffection." They would not share in the blessings that would come to the faithful in eternity.

The sentiments stated in this general epistle, it hardly need be added, represented a position that would continue to govern LDS policy so long as the church leadership adhered to the views of the founding generation.

"GENERAL EPISTLE TO ALL LATTER-DAY SAINTS,"
JOURNAL HISTORY, 19 FEBRUARY 1853, LDS ARCHIVES.

"Yes, I think I shall go south, probably to the [San Bernardino] Ranche. As I am counseled to go south, I have concluded, perhaps that this will be the best for me."

This is the story of many, as it is frequently told, and comes to my ears; and it is upon this point, that I wish to speak.

Do I counsel the brethren to go to California, south, or north. *Not unless they want to go*. If there is any man, woman, or child, who desires to go to that country, in preference to casting his or their lot among the saints,—who feels so little interest in the cause of *Truth*, as to be willing, after being delivered from the Great Babylon, to again encounter the whirlpools of sin, and wickedness for the sake of Gold,—who prefers to dwell in the tents of wickedness than to tarry among the saints,—to any, and all such persons I say; go for heaven's sake,—for our sake—and for the sake of the Gold which you desire before all other Gods, go! But to all others—to all such as have embraced the gospel, for the love of which they bear towards it,—who love righteousness and truth, and who desire the peace of Jerusalem, and the prosperity of Zion, *stay, hold*,—consider what you are doing, and remember, that *here*, in these Valleys are the chambers of the Lord for his people for a season.

"Whoso readeth, let him understand, and he that hath ears to hear, let him hear." Let no influence tempt you away, or seduce you from the path of duty. As you value your religion, which you have become the participants of, through the channel of the Holy and Eternal Priesthood of the Almighty, which in these last days he has seen fit to bestow upon mankind,—as you value the excellence, and the glory of the institutions of the people of

God,—as you value your own salvation, and exaltation and that of your kindred according to the flesh, as well, as the redemption of your dead, listen to the counselings of the servants of God, and abide among his saints,—until you are sent away to the nations, which lieth in darkness,—until you shall be chosen as Heralds of salvation, to go forth with majesty, and power of the Eternal Priesthood, remain, and assist in preparing for the great and mighty gathering of the saints,—assist in the construction of a Holy Temple, which is to be built in the tops of the mountains, to the name of the mighty God of Jacob; in which you can learn those ordinances necessary for the salvation of your dead; and can obtain your endowment, and the blessings which shall secure your exaltation in the kingdom of our God, even to a place among the Gods of Eternity.

These Valleys are the place of gathering for the saints.—This city is the place, to build a Temple unto the Lord our God, and any, and all persons who go hence, do so, without the approbation of the Presidency, except those who may be sent on missions, or business.

San Bernardino, has been selected as a place of gathering for the Pacific Islanders, Asiatics, and those who have been accustomed to tropical climates, and such as might be saved from the transient population which is continually thronging, to, and fro, through California; but was never intended for the saints coming from the East, nor any other place except those mentioned, and all who go; or have gone, with the exception of a very few, which were necessary to establish a post, have done so in answer to their own desires, through a spirit of disaffection.

Brethren, you now have my counsel, and views upon this subject, and I ask it as a favor that hereafter, I may be relieved from answering so many enquiries upon this matter. I pray God, my Heavenly Father, to inspire us all with wisdom, and intelligence, and a disposition to do his will upon the earth; and preserve all his saints in the purity of the Faith, and in the light of his countenance until his coming, which may God grant for his Son's sake, Amen.

Brigham Young
Heber C. Kimball
Willard Richards

Brigham Young: The Giddy, Vain, Foolish Vanities of the World

While he had asked not to be questioned so often on the matter of going to El Dorado, Brigham Young frequently returned to the theme that the worldly enticements of California's gold country and the San

Bernardino settlement provided a temptation to separate the worthy from the unworthy among the Saints. This example, dated only a week after the presidency's general epistle, illustrates what had become Young's unbending attitude toward those who still hoped that the church president might countenance their desire to go seek California's riches.

> Many, no doubt, would consider it a great sacrifice to be called to go on a mission a few years; to leave wife, children, friends, comfortable homes, travel perhaps on foot, encounter storms on the sea, be in perils on land among mobs, and be hated of all men. It is true we might consider this a great sacrifice, and yet men do all this, and more—they risk their own lives upon their venture to get gold, to follow the allurements of pleasure. And should not the Saints of the Most High God be more willing, more anxious to promote the cause of their holy religion, devoting themselves, their influence, property, and, if necessary, their existence, than the votaries of fashion, the devotees of wealth and pleasure, and to merely sensual, temporary objects of worldly gain or aggrandisement? Verily I say unto you, if you are not, and if you have a spirit to seek after the giddy, vain, foolish vanities of the world, the things pertaining only to the gratification of present feelings, passions, and selfish desires, and have no spirit of prayer and supplication, cannot and do not feel to exercise an interest above all others, for the cause of truth, my advice and counsel is for all such, to go straightway to the gold mines of California, and seek for gold, for rest assured, as many as have this spirit, will run as their unrighteous feelings prompt or dictate. Yes! Go to the gold region, and do not come and seek my counsel about it, whether I am willing that you should go or not, for I am not only willing that you should leave, but anxious that you may as soon as possible.[47]

In this same February 1853 address, Young again made clear that it was not merely the moral results of gold seeking but its long-term spiritual consequences that were at the root of his concern.

> Now look upon the opposite side of these principles. Suppose you say, "We will give up the pursuits of our holy religion. We are not Latter-day Saints. Let us go and seek after the things of the world, speculate, get unto ourselves riches, turn away from our duties, neglect the things pertaining to our salvation, go with the giddy, the frivolous, the seeker after gold, to California, Australia, or elsewhere, for the purpose of acquiring wealth." I tell you the result of that course. You would cease to increase in all the attributes of excellence, glory, and eternal duration, from that very moment. So soon as you conceive such ideas, they find a soil within you prepared to nurture them, and it brings forth their direful effects; from that very moment you cease to increase. The

[47]Ibid., 27 February 1853, 1:114–15, 118.

> opposite principle seizes you, fastens itself upon you, and you decrease, lessen, diminish, decay, and waste away in quality, excellence, and strength, until your organization becomes extinct, oblivion covers you, your name is blotted out from the Book of Life, from the heavens, from the earth, and from under the earth, and you will return, and sink into your natural element. . . .

Ten years later the LDS community in the Great Basin had survived its starving time. The Saints were prospering with the trade that came to them because of the overland traffic to and from California. Even though Utah's LDS leaders were facing an invasion of federal forces under Gen. Albert Sidney Johnston, who had orders to remove Brigham Young as territorial governor and end supposed Mormon resistance to federal authority, plainly President Young no longer believed that California was a major threat to Zion.

At that time, in October 1857, Brigham Young told a wonderful story about a man from Boston who once upon a time had stopped briefly in Salt Lake City before proceeding to the gold country.

> That reminds me of a circumstance that transpired here some years ago. A man from Boston, on his way to the gold diggings, stopped a few days in this city and heard me preach. Soon afterwards I met him in the street, and he asked me if I knew where hell was. I told him I thought that he was on the road to that very place; and when he crossed over the Sierra Nevada mountains into the gold diggings in California, if he discovered that he had not found hell, to come back and let me know. As I have not since heard from him, I presume he found it, which I now think a person will who goes East as well as West.[48]

Brigham Young: Poor, Ignorant Pusillanimous Creatures!

As years passed, Young toned down his exhortations to the Utah Saints to avoid California. Yet he never relaxed his animosity toward the golden state's secular society and the dangers it represented, while his remarks about those church members or apostates who remained in California became sharper over the years. As this 1858 address shows, he also kept before his Utah congregation a spirit of disapproval for those who had gone to California and then returned to Zion seeking readmission to the fellowship of the Saints.

---

[48]Ibid., 18 October 1857, 5:341.

> You may take the Latter-day Saints, as a whole and they have but very little good, sound, worldly sense. Look over this congregation, and then find thousands that, during the first four years of our settlement here, flooded these valleys with waggons and cattle, and every facility for raising what we needed. We drove in the sheep, brought the flax-seed, and this, that, and the other useful articles. But what did we see? Men, women, and children run to California to get gold. They were then told what I can now prove. "Go to California if you will; we will not curse you—we will not injure nor destroy you, but we will pity you. If you must go for gold, and that is your god, go, and I will promise you one thing: Every man that stays here and pays attention to his business will be able, within ten years, to buy out four of those who leave for the gold-mines." Since then some of those persons have come cringing back, and thinking, "O dear, I declare I wish the brethren could not know that I had been away! I want to appear as though I had not gone to California, and to be full of good works and faith." Poor, ignorant pusillanimous creatures! They come whining back and want to be considered in full fellowship, after leaving this place to which our God has led us, and after having used their means to feast and build up the Gentiles.[49]

In part, President Young used the example of California to help direct Zion's society toward righteousness, portraying the rapidly developing region beyond the Sierra Nevada as the social and moral antithesis of the LDS heartland in Utah. At the same time, particularly with reference to the San Bernardino settlement after 1851, he saw California as a refuge for dissident members of the Mormon faith and a haven for those Saints who opposed for one reason or another his management of the church. Brigham Young's Zioncentric view of California as a hellish place set a powerful precedent not only for his LDS followers but also, in later years, for others who settled the interior West and adopted a similar jaundiced, illiberal view of the diverse society and mixed cultural ways that characterized the golden state.

Nevertheless, despite repeated, powerful appeals by President Young to shun the gold fields, the documentary record demonstrates that a good many Saints—some more dutiful than others—made their way to California and shared in the quest for quick riches. The accounts they jotted down at the time and the stories they later told about their adventures demonstrate a distinctive, uniquely California Mormon perspective on the gold rush experience.

[49]Ibid., 17 January 1858, 6:172–73.

Chapter 7

"The Whole Country Was Agog With Excitement"
Mormon Mining, Farming, Trade, and Travel in the Gold Country

Even though many battalion veterans and *Brooklyn* Saints left for Salt Lake in 1848, LDS activity in northern California is well documented during the following boom years. Church members both from the battalion and from Sam Brannan's San Francisco settlement remained for an additional season or more, taking advantage of the splendid opportunities to make money. Indeed, some settled in the golden state for life despite repeated calls from Utah for all faithful Saints to gather to Zion. Beginning early in 1848 more Saints left Great Salt Lake City and came to California, either with or without Brigham Young's blessing, to seek their earthly fortunes in the diggings. Across the gold country, especially near Mormon Island and Salmon Falls, LDS miners, traders, innkeepers, and farmers were a recognizable presence among their non-Mormon contemporaries. They formed well-established enclaves, just as other gold country emigrants from one home district or native country banded together. Elsewhere California Saints lived in comparative anonymity, not drawing attention to their religious beliefs.

Very few LDS diarists and journal keepers reported incidents of anti-Mormon hostility during the gold rush years. Newspapers in the gold rush towns carried no reports of harassment of the Saints, indicating that such episodes were extremely rare before the mid-1850s. California believers recognized their common bond of fellowship and spiritual communion, but to all appearances they did not set themselves at odds with other Americans by their practices or policies. They shared in the day-to-day business and social concerns of their communities, and mostly those concerns during the flush times subordinated all else to finding gold and making money.[1] Even more clearly than other gold seekers, most California Saints regarded themselves as temporary sojourners, expecting sooner or later to leave the Pacific Coast. The faithful welcomed the prospect of rejoining the main body of the church in Zion, there to await the prophesied end of earthly time. But a few accounts demonstrate that for some Saints, from the beginning California's appeal was as strong for them as Utah's had come to be for Brigham Young and his closest advisers. Independent of the will of their leaders in Salt Lake City, these settlers rapidly made the transition from being Mormons in California to becoming Mormon Californians.

JAMES H. SKINNER: A MOST LOVELY COUNTRY—A GODS COUNTRY

The most charming of all California LDS narratives is James Skinner's recollection of his childhood in San Francisco and San José. Skinner had come to the West Coast with his family aboard the *Brooklyn* when he was four years old. As earlier noted, the Skinners lived at Mission Delores during their first year, then moved to San Francisco where James's parents managed the City Hotel for William Leidesdorff. Skinner wrote his reminiscences in 1915, when he was seventy-three and living in Utah. This excerpt begins after the American conquest, while the family was still in San Francisco.

JAMES HORACE SKINNER, REMINISCENCES, 1915, LDS ARCHIVES.

Mothers Brother came from the states soon after we got our house finished and moved in. He remained with us, as one of the Family, untill we

[1]The classic work on the California gold rush and mining country society is Rodman Paul's *California Gold: The Beginning of Mining in the Far West.* An excellent recent survey is Peter Blodgett, *Land of Dreams: California and the Gold Rush Decade, 1848–1858.* Malcolm J. Rohrbough, *Days of Gold: The California Gold Rush and the American Nation* emphasizes the social impact of the gold rush as seen through the letters and journals of those easterners who participated. J. S. Holliday's *Rush for Riches: Gold Fever and the Making of California* extols the gold rush as an era of great, daring enterprises, mostly managed by Anglo-American males. Two outstanding recent essay collections that originally appeared as special numbers of *California History,* the quarterly magazine of the California Historical Society, treat more diverse aspects of the experience: Orsi and Rawls, eds., *A Golden State: Mining and Economic Development in Gold Rush California;* and Orsi and Starr, eds., *Rooted in Barbarous Soil: People, Culture, and Community in Gold Rush California.* Social history within a wider geographical context, including the LDS experience, informs the essays in Owens, ed., *Riches for All: The California Gold Rush and the World.*

moved to Utah in 1868. He and Father worked together as pardners. Not long before our coming to Utah, he married Miss E. A. Guy, who had arrived only a few months [earlier] from Australia.

My first schooling was had in San Francisco. The first and only time I ever plaid hooky was here. In going back to school after dinner I ran across a man with a hand organ and a monkey. That afternoon I forget all about school in following the man and monkey arround. . . .

Not long after uncles arrival Father sold out and all moved to San Jose where they bought a farm of an hundred and twenty acres. I attended school again.

The school house was about two miles from home, out on the open plain. When there were no wild cattles in the way, I could make it all right, but when they were between our place and the schoolhouse I had to follow fences and under a steep bank until I got within some 30 or 40 rods then make a run for it. There was thousands of wild cattle when we first moved to San Jose valley.

Many times in going to school, a fighting cow or bull would be on one side of a wire fence, and I on the other, Hooking and bellowing, and trying to reach me. I tell you it made my hair pull more than once. Sometimes the men or Father would take me on a horse.

We had a beautiful place here. Our Farm bord[er]ed on a fresh water lake—or as it was called La Genes—Ducks and Geese by the Thousands. I knew of one man who killed 21 ducks at one shot, as I helped to pick them up with the boat. Many got away that was wounded. Wings broken. . . .

This is a most lovely country—a Gods country—to live in. Neither too hot or too cold, a live plain for miles covered with grass, and not a brush or shrub could [be seen] for miles. Grass to your knees with Flowers of all colors by the thousands, as far as the eye could see. I used to pick a Bouquet for Mother every morning early while the due was still on. In the year of 1854 we sold our Farm and moved to San Bernardino.

One Mormon Battalion veteran who delayed his departure for the Great Basin was John C. Naegle. A veteran of Company A, Naegle spent six months at San Diego serving in the U.S. Army's Mormon Volunteers. His son claimed that Naegle was digging the millrace for Sutter's American River gristmill at the time of the Coloma gold discovery, but in truth the Army did not disband the Volunteers until March 1848. Naegle then joined a company that included Ebenezer Brown and his family to go north to Sutter's Fort and the gold fields.[2] In this excerpt, which picks up the story at Mormon Island, Naegle's son relates the apparently

[2]Ricketts, *Mormon Battalion,* 223; and George C. Naegle, "Life Sketch of John C. Naegle," Brigham Young University Library.

trivial reason his father gave for not departing for Salt Lake with Brown's wagon train party in August, and explains why he remained in California for another three years.

> He washed out about $3,000 in gold dust in six weeks. He then decided to return to Utah with some of the battalion boys but he could not get any shoes that would fit him at the mines. So he went to San Francisco to get some, stayed and worked there for a short time and then went to San Jose Valley and took up a nice tract of land containing about 50 acres and went to work farming and truck gardening, and he learned to speak the Mexican Language very fluently. By that time many gold seekers had rushed to California, and he was able to get top prices for all of his produce and made thousands and thousands of dollars and made his home at San Jose. In 1853 he rented his farm and went by water to the Isthmus of Panama and crossed it and then sailed to New York and from there went to the State of Indiana to visit his parents. While there he married Mary Louise Kepple, Jan. 31, 1853 and remained there for the winter. . . .[3]

Robert Petch: A Pocket Full of Rocks

At age 50 Robert Petch had sailed aboard the *Brooklyn* with his wife and two children.[4] Called by one friend "an honest, industrious man," he and his family had previously lived in New Haven, Connecticut, for many years, where he worked for an auctioneer. Petch was also a spiritual seeker. From Methodism he had moved to Millerism and, in time, to Mormonism. In this recently discovered 1849 letter to New Haven friend William Goodwin, Petch summarized his success in California. While he continued to make his home in San Francisco, Petch reveals that he had greatly improved his fortunes on a series of trips to the gold diggings in 1848. His letter is typical of the eyewitness reports from the new El Dorado that helped fuel the gold rush frenzy that fall and the next spring. As Goodwin stated in releasing Petch's letter for publication, "When he left New Haven, he was poor, he has now got a 'pocket full of rocks.'"[5]

---

[3]George C. Naegle, "Life Sketch of John C. Naegle."

[4]Bagley, ed., *Scoundrel's Tale*, 147, 233.

[5]Researcher Richard H. Bullock located this letter and published it as "Newly Discovered Letters," *The Brooklyn Banner* 3:1 (July 2002), 4–6.

ROBERT PETCH TO WILLIAM GOODWIN, 29 OCTOBER 1848,
FROM THE *NEW HAVEN COURIER*, 19 MAY 1849,
REPRINTED IN THE *NEW YORK HERALD*, 21 MAY 1849.
COPY IN CALIFORNIA STATE LIBRARY.

San Francisco, October 29, 1848

I embrace the present moment to write a few lines, hoping that they will find yourself and family in good health, as, thank God, we are at present. My letter must be short, as the ship Flora, for New London is about to sail for that place tomorrow. I would state that I have just returned from the gold diggins, of which I will give you a brief sketch.

We live in a beautiful climate, where peace and prosperity truly abound, but where the greatest excitement revivals [prevails], in consequence of the discovery of gold mines in these parts. The mines alluded to were first discovered by the Mormon boys, in the early part of May last, near the base of the California mountains. The gold lies around the rivers and ravines of the mountain, and may be found beneath the surface of the ground from 2 inches to eight feet deep. The way we get it is by taking a pick, shovel, and a tin pan; we then fill the pan with dirt, take it to the river, and there sink it beneath the water and shake it well about. As we shake, the particles of gold being the heaviest, sink to the bottom, and as we keep sinking the pan the dirt rises, and by constantly drawing back the pan the dirt washes away, leaving the gold at the bottom.

Since our sojourn here, I have been three times to the mines. The first time, I got about $450 worth in three weeks, when I returned home, and after recruiting my strength, I went back and stayed three weeks and three days, during which time I got about $700 more. I then purchased, for the sum of $300, a house and lot, which I sold again the next day for $500, cash. On my third visit to the diggings, I dug in nine days, gold to the amount of $1250. I have now returned home, and as the rainy season is just at hand, I shall remain here until spring. We have a house worth $1200, besides $250 in gold and silver coin, and $2500 worth of gold dust; all this was made clear of expenses, in little less than five months.

San Francisco, the place of our present residence, is about 300 miles from the mines, the conveyance to which place is by water, by sloops up the Sacramento River, or round by land with pack horses, etc., it takes from two to three weeks to reach the mines. People are coming from the States, and all parts of the world, to seek their fortunes, many of whom are realizing from $5 to $15 per day. The last day I worked in the mines, myself and another man opened a hole, from which we dug out $398 worth of gold. The next day we sold our right to the hole for $150. We get here all kinds of dry goods, groceries, and provisions for gold dust, at the rate of $16 per ounce. It will be seen by the newspapers I send with this that it is [in] contemplation to have a branch mint here. We then shall get all our gold cashed ounce for ounce. Gold sells now from $8 to $10 per ounce.

This is a fine place, indeed, for merchants, clerks, and other adventurers. Any young man who is sober, steady, and industrious, may, in a very short time, become independent and rich. Should yourself and family feel disposed to join us—which I trust you will, or any friend, I would recommend that you come out with Captain Wilbur, of the bark Flora, at New London, as that gentleman expects to return very soon after his arrival at that place.

It is very probable that some of the crew may visit New Haven prior to their departure, as they promised so to do on their visiting my dwelling previous to their sailing.

[Signed] Robert Petch

Emeline Lane Sirrine: All Kinds of People Collecting Here

For historians, the dearth of personal journals kept by *Brooklyn* Saints is offset by a few family letters that relate vignettes of life in California after the gold discovery. Emeline Lane Sirrine, who Samuel Brannan had married to George Warren Sirrine a month after the *Brooklyn* arrived in California, reported from San Francisco in 1850 to her parents in Suffield, Connecticut. She summarized personal information about her married sister, Octavia Ann Austin, and other family members and friends. She also provided a concise, accurate appraisal of the impact of gold fever on California society, particularly for the Mormon settlers. Such letters, though comparatively rare, illustrate the importance of women's self-appointed task in maintaining and strengthening the social ties between relatives and friends, even those separated by the width of the continent.

Emeline Lane Sirrine to Ashbel and Ann Stoddard Lane, 10 April 1850. Copy in Possession of Richard H. Bullock.

San Francisco, April 10, 1850

Dear Father and Mother,

I now take this opportunity to write you a few lines to let you know of my welfare. My health is good at the present and I hope you are enjoying the same blessing of God. It is more than two years since I have written home. Perhaps you think I have been negligent, but it is not neglect. I have been two hundred miles from this place, where vessels do not come that are going to the States, and that is the reason I have not written.

Julius and Octavia [Austin] have gone to the Church, which is about a thousand miles from here, in the valley of the Great Salt Lake. They started the first of July 1848. We were at Santa Cruz at the time they started so we did not see them. I had not seen them for two years. They were in good health. The children have grown very much. Loesa [Louise Maria Austin] has gotten to be a great girl. Octavia was very well and in good spirits when she started away. There was a large company that went. I have heard that they got there all safe and well.[6] I have not had any letter from them yet. John S. Fowler has come across the mountains and took his family and gone to the Lake.[7] John Warner has not come, he is at Counsel Bluffs. Mrs. Warner has married to a Mr. Thorp. She has a little girl. She got tired waiting for John Warner to come to see his family. She has several letters from Salt Lake. Brother Dewey [Devy] is dead. Horace Ensign, Phoebe Train and a great many have gone back. Maries Dewey is married to John Wolley [Wooley]. They have a little boy. Ambrose Moses and family are well; his oldest daughter is married well.

We got the letter from the office that you and Julius wrote. I think it was in February. We read it, then, I shall send them to Salt Lake the first chance I have. I was glad to hear that you was able and also Julius and Caroline and much pleased to hear they have a little girl. Tell them I think my little Sarah Ann [Sirrine] will be a match for her according to Caroline's description. She is a very good looking little girl and as pleasant disposition child as ever you see. She is her father's favorite. We have been married three years the 30th of next August. Sarah will be two years old the 30th of next month. Now for the news about California. I will say there has been a great many changes in California since we first landed. I shall not give much of a description. I have but a few minutes to write, that San Francisco is as healthy as any part of California. There are several different climates in California. The seasons is wet and dry. Seldom snow falls excepting in the mountains, which fall at a great depth. The Bay is one hundred miles long and twenty wide, with good land all around it, excepting this place, which will be the greatest city in California.

I will tell you a little about the gold mines which have been discovered. It was discovered by the Mormons. It is in the mountains and valleys along the Sacramento and San Wakeesa [Joaquin] rivers. It is found in abundance. They [the rivers] are all between two hundred and three hundred miles in length. It

---

[6]John Borrowman's journal in "The Roughest Road I Ever Saw" in Chapter 6 describes the Austins' journey to Salt Lake with the Ebenezer Brown party.

[7]John S. Fowler actually stayed in California. He and Sam Brannan used the frame of Sutter's grist mill upstream from Sutter's Fort to build the City Hotel in Sacramento, where Fowler became a prominent Democratic politician.

is the richest gold mine ever discovered in the world. Thousands of people are here and thousands are coming. Money is plenty, land is raising every day, wages high. Carpenters get sixteen dollars a day. Lumber is $600 dollars a thousand. All kinds of building material in proportion. Provisions are high, of all kinds, except vegetables. Vegetables cannot be obtained. Potatoes a York shilling a pound, pork forty dollars a barrel, all kinds of eatables in proportion. I cannot write all I want to. Goods of all kinds sell at a great profit. I shall not advise anyone to come here, but do as you please. There are all kinds of people collecting here to get gold. My husband [George Warren Sirrine] is doing well. We are worth about $6000, which is not a fortune in California. He is preparing to go to the mine. He can get $16 a day [in wages] but he has a chance to go to the mines to take out a few pounds [of gold]. They get from 16 to 100 dollars a day and sometime more; it is all chance.

I was going to write another letter to Julius but I have not time. Tell him I have not any Mormon paper to send. There is none printed. The Church is going to stay where they are at the present, it will be the stronghold of Zion. I am going to write a long letter to Julius soon. I was disappointed not getting any letters by the steamer. I shall send a letter by the steamer every time they go.

Do not fail to write every chance you have to send. Tell Julius and Caroline to write. George would write, he is writing home. The mail will close in a few minutes. I want to see you and trust we shall meet before many years, if God spares our lives. We may go to the Lakes and then come home, but we cannot tell what we shall do. Do not fail to write. I would like to see you all here.

My love to all.

One more thing to father, there is plenty of wild geese here.

Yours affectionately

Emeline Lane Sirrine

Sad to relate, Emeline Lane Sirrine died the next summer in childbirth.[8]

Mary Ann Fisher Cheney: We Shall Stay Here Some Time

The Mormon settlement at San José, which attracted both the Skinner family and John Naegle, was composed principally of Saints who had arrived on the *Brooklyn*, with former New Hope colonists prominent among them. While California remained under military rule, land titles were unsettled and land tenure was in effect based on occupancy and

[8]For an 1846 letter Lane wrote from Honolulu and the memoir of her husband George, which indicates they began married life without "a dollar nor even a cent," see Bagley, ed., *Scoundrel's Tale*, 148–154.

use, modified by prior claims under the Mexican government. The San José Saints occupied a substantial tract of fertile farmland within the original boundaries of the San José mission and ranch. Located between Alameda and Mission creeks in the East Bay area, the district is part of Washington Township in modern Alameda County. Establishing himself in 1849, John Horner of the *Brooklyn* was the earliest Saint to begin farming there, but other church members soon joined him. Amasa Lyman and Charles Rich organized an LDS branch on 23 April 1850, with Daniel Baldwin as the branch president.[9]

Among the San José Saints were Zacheus Cheney, formerly a private in Company B of the battalion, and Mary Ann Fisher Cheney, his bride who had arrived on the *Brooklyn*. Their marriage was one of the few matrimonial unions that joined these two groups of California Mormons. In this 1850 letter, Mary Ann wrote to her mother and other family members in Pennsylvania, quite incidentally informing them of her marriage two years earlier and describing a way of life that combined farming with excursions to the placer diggings. The brief mention of her success at washing out gold is one of the very few accounts from a female gold miner that can be found in all California gold rush literature. Mary Ann makes the experience sound like something of a lark, undertaken to get a small souvenir sample for her family back east. More significant is the generally cheerful attitude and optimistic outlook that her words conveyed, an indication that California's flush times had greatly improved the fortunes of this young couple.

MAY ANN FISHER CHENEY TO MOTHER, SAN JOSÉ, AUGUST 21, 1850.
IN LORIN J. HANSEN AND LILA J. BRINGHURST, *LET THIS BE ZION: MORMON PIONEERS AND MODERN SAINTS IN SOUTHERN ALAMEDA CALIFORNIA*, 57–58.

> I have wrote to you about the mines several times and sent in one of the letters some of the gold dust just as I had washed it out my self—something like $2—so that you might see it. You might all have done well if you had come out here when the mines first broke out. There is still a very good chance for people that are industrious and saving. There are all sorts of people in California. The mining is not as good as it has been. We have moved from San Francisco and have been farming this summer. Things were very high last winter in this place. Potatoes were $6 and $8 a robe (that is, about

[9]The history of the San José LDS settlement and the branch is summarized in Hansen and Bringhurst, *Let this Be Zion: Mormon Pioneers and Modern Saints in Southern Alameda California*, 51–56.

> 25 pounds) cabbage $2/head and hens from $4–$6 for one. I sold eggs for $6 a doz last winter.
>
> I should like if you all were here but you must do as you think best. We think we shall stay here some time as there is still a good chance for us. I was married 2 years ago the 11th of July to Mr. Zacheus Cheny, and I have never had any cause to regret it yet. He has been a kind companion to me. We have no children yet. He has been to the mine several times. The first time he did very well. He can tell you better than I so I shall leave of[f].

She did not mention it when she wrote home, but Mary Ann Cheney was pregnant. This exuberant young woman died in December 1850, also from complications of childbirth.

Zacheus Cheney soon remarried. His new wife was Amanda Evans, another *Brooklyn* passenger, who had arrived with her mother and three younger siblings. After the church presidency directed California Mormons to gather in Salt Lake in 1857, Cheney became captain of a company with fourteen wagons, sixteen men, seven women, and fifteen children, including some of his own, that departed from Alameda and Santa Cruz.[10] As James Skinner's account tells us, some San José LDS settlers had sold out and moved to San Bernardino earlier, but the 1857 departure led by Cheney brought an end to this small Mormon enclave in the East Bay.

W. W. RITER: TURNED HIS ATTENTION TO DIGGING FOR GOLD

When he met Amasa Lyman and joined the Rhoades company at Sacramento in July 1849, Levi Riter was returning to Great Salt Lake City from a desperate attempt to rescue the investment he and other substantial Mormon businessmen had made in 1846, shipping a valuable cargo of merchandise to California aboard the *Brooklyn* under Samuel Brannan's management. As Riter's son related years later, his father went to California to secure his goods and investigate reports that Brannan had become a hard-drinking womanizer. W. W. Riter's account provided details about his father's journey to California on the northern route, a trip replete with hardship and nearly fatal calamities. He made

[10]Ricketts, *Mormon Battalion*, 226–27. Cheney's mother-in-law and his new wife's siblings were also members of this 1857 company.

the last leg of the trip accompanied by a Mexican party heading for the gold fields. This excerpt begins as the senior Riter and his companions reached the California settlements.

STATEMENT OF W. W. RITER, 10 JANUARY 1917,
IN CARTER, ED., *HEART THROBS OF THE WEST*, 7:402–6.

On crossing the Sierra Nevada the trail took them to Sutter's Fort near where Sacramento now stands. In the meanwhile he had used up all his provisions and was very scantily supplied with clothes at best, and arrived at the fort in a very destitute condition. Sutter had the reputation of being a kind-hearted man and my father applied to him for succor and gave him the Masonic sign. Sutter, being a Mason, fortunately recognized it and father immediately found a warm friend. Sutter's friendship was always a very lively matter with him, and I frequently thought I would like to have a painting of the old gentleman to hand down to posterity. He came from an immediately adjoining county in Pennsylvania, to the one from which we came, although born in Switzerland, and I think this made an additional bond of friendship between the two. In the meanwhile, just before reaching Sacramento, the news reached them that gold had been discovered, the circumstances of which are familiar to everyone.

Although when he arrived there the whole country was agog with excitement, he went on down to San Francisco, to see about his goods, and found that Brannan had practically appropriated not only his property but that of others, for which he was agent. High prices prevailing in consequence of finding of gold, enabled Brannan to realize a very large sum of money from these illegally gotten goods. Meanwhile, Brannan was drinking very heavily and could never be found in a condition to do business. There was no law in the country, the country was then passing from under Mexican rule to that of American, and it was a forlorn hope to get anything from him. My father went into Brannan's house and found that he had taken largely from father's goods to furnish his house. Father took from the house what he could identify, which was not much. The looking glass which I used is one of these things. When he returned to Salt Lake he brought them with him.

Not being able to do anything with Brannan, he then turned his attention to digging for gold, on his own account, and he mined along all those streams from the Merced to the Feather River, and in a short time was in possession of a few thousand dollars in gold-dust. I believe he made one or two other trips to San Francisco to see if he could get anything out of Brannan, but failed. This was in the spring of 1849—sometime in August [July] of that year he determined to return to Salt Lake, so joined a party of ship Brooklyn people, and possibly some members of the Mormon Battalion.

The trip was without incident until they reached the source of the Humboldt River, which was then known as the St. Mary's. He then determined to leave the party, which was traveling slowly, with a mixed equipment of oxen, horses and mules, and go on ahead on horseback with the expectation of reaching Salt Lake a few days earlier than the main body would. There was a man in the party by the name of Green, who was bringing with him some six thousand dollars in gold-dust, which had been collected from the Mormon members of the church in California as tithing.[11] Green determined also to come along and bring this gold-dust with him. They came around by old Fort Hall, up the Portneuf, past the present Pocatello.

Somewhere east and about half way between Pocatello and McCammon they were attacked by Indians. They had just gone into camp, up on the slope of a bench some distance from the river and had put their saddle and packs around them, and their horses were grazing near by (my father had three with him). Just as they were retiring, in the twilight (my father was pulling off his boots) the attack began. . . .

[*Omitted here are details of the Indian attack and subsequent flight of Riter and Green, who abandoned Riter's overcoat and watch as well as a large sack of gold they were unable to carry while making their escape. Green returned to the LDS wagon company they had left behind a few days earlier, while Riter was rescued by a party of young men on the way to California, who accompanied him back to the Rhoades company.*]

Soon after the arrival of the Mormon emigrants my father got some of them to go with him and they found the sack of gold, also his overcoat, the watch and some few other matters which the Indians had not had time to return and obtain.

In this condition they arrived [at Salt Lake] in the early part of September. . . .

Abner Blackburn: We Took Out in About Five Hours About Four Hundred Dollars in Coarse Gold

One of the first gold seekers to depart Great Salt Lake City for northern California in 1849 was Abner Blackburn. An unconventional Saint, battalion veteran, and free spirit, Blackburn had been in the battalion's Pueblo detachment headed by Capt. James Brown that wintered in 1846–47 on the upper Arkansas River in modern Colorado. He first

[11]Here W. W. Riter's rendition of his father's account contains an apparent confusion of identities. The person in the Rhoades company who had charge of the tithing was Thomas Grover, a former member of the Salt Lake Stake High Council and the father-in-law of Charles C. Rich. According to Grover's son, his father had also sent goods aboard the *Brooklyn* in the care of Brannan. See Davies, *Mormon Gold*, 71–73, 91, 148–50.

ABNER BLACKBURN
After his adventures in the California gold fields, Blackburn joined the Mormon colony in San Bernardino, where he wrote his memoirs in the late 1890s.
Courtesy Eugene Bell/Marriott Library.

reached California from Salt Lake in September 1847 as one of twelve veterans under Captain Brown, directed by Brigham Young to accompany Sam Brannan to San Francisco. Brown's small detachment met the eastward-bound battalion boys at Truckee Meadows and delivered Young's instructions to turn back to California and work until the following summer. Brown and his men then completed their assignment in California, securing official discharge for the detachment from the U.S. Army commander, collecting back pay due the veterans, and gathering further geographical information about the lands west of Zion.

Blackburn later succinctly summarized his first adventure west of the Sierra,: "We took in California with all eyes open for the grand sight." The adventurous young men made a rapid, boisterous social tour from Sutter's Fort to Monterey, Mission San José, San Francisco, New Hope, and back to Sutter's Fort. In early October Captain Brown began the return trip by the Donner Pass route with Blackburn and only four other men. "Our Boss," Blackburn explained, "thought [it] best to return soon or the dark eyed sineuretos would capture his whole outfit. There was great inducement to stay in this beautiful land." Making a dangerous late season crossing of the mountain and desert country, through a region that was home to potentially hostile natives, they drove a band of half-wild horses, carrying in their saddlebags $5,000 in Spanish doubloons and two pack loads of seed wheat for Brigham Young. It was, Blackburn declared in his autobiographical memoir, "the biggest torn fool errant that ever is known."[12]

Blackburn traveled on to Missouri in late 1847, then returned to Salt Lake the following spring with his parents and future wife. This family group accompanied Brigham Young's wagon train in the 1848 mass migration from Winter Quarters. Along the trail on the Sweetwater River, as previously related, Blackburn and the others met the express party headed by Nathan Hawk, who told them about the gold discovery and displayed samples he had panned from the Mormon Island diggings. Blackburn's trip to the gold country in 1849 was thus prompted both by his earlier California experience and by Hawk's glowing show-and-tell report of 1848 placer mining.

Blackburn joined a pack train that probably left Salt Lake in mid-March, a month before the departure of Amasa Lyman's company guided by O. P. Rockwell. Blackburn's companions included some men who had been in the mining country the previous year, almost certainly other battalion veterans. They took the newly opened Carson Pass Wagon Road across the Sierra, becoming the first forty-niners to arrive overland. In his recollections of the trip, Blackburn claimed also that he was the first person to discover gold east of the Sierra, at Gold Canyon below the site of the fabled Comstock Lode. This claim, although not free of dispute, is verified by a preponderance of evidence.[13]

Blackburn and his companions first reached the gold country near the later mining town named Hangtown or Placerville, approximately eight miles south of Coloma. Finding a few miners at work, they jumped off their horses and began following their example. "We worked around in several small gulches wi[th] our knives and bread pans for about three hours," Blackburn recalled, "and had coarse gold enough to buy some of [our] pressing needs." Moving on a few miles to Weberville, an early gold rush camp on Weber Creek (a tributary of the American River's South Fork), these pioneer California Saints of 1849 reached a store

---

[12]Bagley, ed., *Frontiersman,* 104, 108, 112.

[13]Will Bagley considers the matter, with a thorough review of the evidence, in *Frontiersman,* 132–36.

and purchased their most essential supplies: "tobacco and whiskey with some other provisions."[14]

After this brief gold digging venture, Blackburn and his companions traveled to Sutter's Fort, where he earned one ounce of gold for cutting a door with pick and ax through the adobe wall of Sutter's Fort. The men outfitted themselves well and followed a trail of rumor to the diggings at Auburn Ravine, then to the North Fork of the American River. In both locations they found the water still too high to work the gravel bars because of the springtime runoff. "The company divided up," he relates, "every one for himself."

With his friend Nathaniel Fairbanks, Blackburn set out to find a more promising placer site. What happened next was the essence of gold mining good fortune.

> Nat Fairbanks [and I] went up this river [the North Fork of the American River] to prospect. We found a little all along. Stopt in a reveine for lunch and we felt down in the mouth because we could not strike it rich and our luck had soured on us. We were sitting on a ledge of rocks in a dry reveine about twenty yards from the river. While eating, I looked down between my feet and see something yellow, about a half inch long. Picked it up [and] handed it to Nat. He sung out, "Gold! By my life!" Stopt eating just then. Searched around and found plenty more. Commenced to make the gravel fly. Kept picking up peices of gold and panning out and found a pocket or two that was rich and worked untill sundown. [We] staked off two claims and started for camp. We took out in about five hours about four hundred dollars in coarse gold. Next morning, [we] told two friends [who] staked off two more claims. We worked the raveine to the river and four of us took out two thousand five hundred dollars in eight days and we left to find other diggings.[15]

Blackburn and his companions moved on, he wrote, because "We heard they were shoveling it up rich in other places." They located a good placer at Spanish Bar on the Middle Fork of the American River where, he reported, the first miners had a bonanza. Blackburn then received a report that his family was coming to join him in California. He sold his claim and started east, soon meeting his parents and his brother "com-

[14]Ibid., 142. Weberville was located upstream from the confluence of Ringold Creek and Weber Creek in El Dorado County, where Big Cut Road now crosses Weber Creek to connect Placerville and Pleasant Valley Road.

[15]Bagley, ed., *Frontiersman*, 142–43.

ing down the mountain." After outfitting them in Sacramento, he returned with his father and brother to his old claim in Auburn ravine. The waters had receded and conditions now were good for mining. The three men, Abner later stated, "realised about eighteen hundred dollars from the place."

While their father went into business north of Auburn, opening a boarding house and "general trading station," Blackburn and his brother continued mining in the same locality. With a few other men, they worked hard for some weeks, each taking out from $80 to $150 a day in gold. "We worked as long as we could," Blackburn remarked, "but had to lay off. The excitement of mining causes one to over work themselves." At that point, they sold off their claims at a good price and gave themselves a rest. "We made a very respectable pile of the needful," he declared.

For the rest of the 1849 season, while crazed newcomers rushed to the diggings, the Blackburn brothers and three companions went rambling, treating themselves to a grand sightseeing excursion about northern California and the Mother Lode region. "We had a fine time," he recalled in describing their visit to a fandango on a *Californio* rancho. "The wine flowed freely. The Hidalgoes were verry polite and the ladys appeared to the best advantage."

Blackburn narrated further adventures on a trip that proceeded south to the Merced River, then north to the Stanislaus, the Calaveras, the Mokelumne, the Yuba, and Bear rivers. 'We started out to see all the mines," he wrote, "and did." They then returned to their original claim north of Auburn and joined a company building a diversion dam and canal to mine the riverbed. Blackburn and his brother sold out "for a good price" before the canal was finished. Apparently their partners in the business did not meet with the success they had expected. "We found out that the gold does not stop in deep places like the Bible sayes," Blackburn explained, then repeated the oldest dictum known to miners: "Gold is whear you find it."[16]

In mid-October 1849, Blackburn and his brother left the gold country with a pack train and headed east, expecting to meet other relatives coming to El Dorado. Instead, they learned these family members had

[16]Ibid., 134, 144, 147, 149, 151.

stopped to winter in the Salt Lake Valley. "I wanted to come back to California," Blackburn recalled, "[but] my brother was attracted by a girl which drew his attention." The two men continued east together "and in twelve days on our little Sonoranian mules reached our kindred in the valley. And had a splendid time with our pockets full of the needful." Among the Zion colony Saints, Blackburn remarked, "We were just as good as the Elders of Israel. At least our gold was."[17]

Blackburn spent the winter with his uncle at the Provo settlement but planned to return permanently to California, regardless of the admonitions of church leaders. "In the spring of 1850," he relates, "we made up a company to goe to California. It was not much work to find men to goe to the new Eldorado. In those times, California was the only magnet. My brother had married his girl and we were ready to leave the Saints for good."

As it turned out, they changed their plans when they reached Carson Valley and the mouth of West Carson River canyon. At this spot, where the Carson Pass Wagon Road began the sharp, treacherous climb up the east slope of the Sierra Nevada, the two Blackburn brothers with five other men decided to stop and open a trading station. They knew that tens of thousands of emigrants were coming along the overland trail behind them, and this would be the first supply point anywhere west of Fort Hall and Great Salt Lake City. Being best acquainted with the country, Abner Blackburn picked the site that became known as Mormon Station, where the town of Genoa would later be founded. "There was no better place on the river," he declared, "[with] cold water comeing out of the mountain and pine trees were plenty on the edge of the valley. There was oceans of good feed for stock. It was a choice place for our buisness. [We] built the first house for our station out of pine logs and a large log coral for stock and fixt for traffic." Blackburn took several teams and wagons across the mountains to Sacramento for supplies, carrying along a load of snow or ice that he sold at eighty dollars a ton in the hot valley metropolis. He returned with a full cargo of provisions for the trail trade, including large supplies of flour, coffee, and whiskey. He and his companions swapped their well-conditioned mules and horses to the emigrants in return for worn-out stock, two animals for

[17]Ibid., 169. Blackburn deposited $384 in the church's gold accounts on 28 October 1849 and his brother Thomas deposited $200 the following day, each receiving Mormon paper money in exchange.

one. They pastured the trail-worn animals and held them for future trade while butchering some of the newly fattened oxen for beef.

After bringing supplies from Sacramento to Mormon Station, Blackburn agreed to lead a few companions up Gold Canyon to investigate mining prospects in the locale where he had found gold the previous year. Fourteen men with two teams set out, according to Blackburn, and "worked several places with rockers and crevest [crevassed] around for a week or more and the men thought they could do better on the other side of the mountain [in northern California]." With the benefit of hindsight, knowing that later prospectors struck the famed Comstock Lode not far from this spot, Blackburn made a rueful comment on their efforts. "If we had known [about] the rich mines higher up the canion, the outcome would be different. We mist the great Bonanza and we come back to the station."

Blackburn and his companions traded at Mormon Station through the 1850 trail season, then divided the proceeds "and all were satisfied." His brother crossed the Sierra to California, where their father had remained in business. Abner meanwhile joined a party heading east to Fort Hall with livestock, which they planned to sell to emigrants the following year. Misadventure accompanied this trip. First, Blackburn became extremely ill. After a few days most of the company gave him up for dead and traveled on. He did soon recover; but while he and his two remaining companions proceeded along the Humboldt River, they were attacked by a native band that ran off nearly all their horses and seven pack animals "loaded with our outfit." With his friends both wounded, Blackburn related, and with only one horse apiece and three packs, they made their escape "more by good luck than good management." The *Deseret News* reported the men's arrival in Salt Lake at the end of October 1850, summarizing briefly their hostile encounter with "70 or 80 Boonack Indians" who drove off most their horses.[18]

After again spending the winter in Utah, Blackburn once more headed for northern California in early 1851, intending to rejoin his father and brother. Following a difficult crossing of the Sierra, he arrived in San Francisco only to learn that Indians recently had killed his father on the

[18]Ibid., 171–75. Whether this attack was carried out by Bannock tribesmen or some other force of marauders, Bagley believes the location was possibly Gravelly Ford on the Humboldt River, about fifteen miles east of present-day Battle Mountain, Nevada.

Klamath River, in the far northwestern section of the state. The elder Blackburn had been traveling upriver alone at night, intending to join his son Thomas and Thomas's wife, who were running a ferry near a newly opened mining district. The attacking natives, angry at the white invasion of their territory, killed the solitary traveler and made an unsuccessful attempt to destroy the ferry house and murder the few whites living nearby. Abner hurried up the coast and joined local miners in a homicidal revenge campaign against a native settlement in the Weitchpec area of Hupa Valley. "We made war on the savages," Blackburn wrote. "The miners had no mercy on them and cleand all the bad ones out."[19]

At this point, Abner Blackburn's personal narrative comes to a sudden end. From other sources we know that he and his brother went south to the new LDS settlement at San Bernardino, where they settled and became farmers. Writing to a Utah relative in 1894, when he was sixty-seven, Blackburn offered an apology of sorts for having been so long out of touch with his LDS kinfolk. "I would have written long ago," he explained, "but when i left Utah they cut us all off from the church. I suppose they dropt me too."[20]

Three years later, a sick and disabled pensioner, Blackburn wrote another letter from San Bernardino to explain his inability to attend a fifty-year reunion of LDS pioneers in Salt Lake City. "California is not a land of gold," he explained, "and we are nearly all poor."[21] He did make the trip, however, perhaps with the sponsoring committee's financial assistance, and he renewed a few old acquaintances. Undoubtedly he marveled at the changes that had taken place in the Mormon capital since he had last seen it.

This 1897 celebration, Will Bagley remarks, "was probably Abner Blackburn's last hurrah." While his wife Lucinda remained well enough to take part in San Bernardino's historical gatherings, his increasing debility kept Blackburn from further public outings. He died in early November 1904, remembered by an obituary writer as "a true San Bernardinoan . . . [who] rose to the front rank in this progressive community, and was ever ready with sage council and excellent example."[22]

[19]Bagley, ed., *Frontiersman*, 187. Appendix F in Bagley's volume, pages 266–70, reprints the major accounts of the senior Blackburn's death and the escape from a fierce Native attack by Thomas Blackburn and his wife. [20]Ibid., 2. [21]Ibid., 220.

[22]*San Bernardino Sun*, 3 November 1905, quoted in ibid., 223.

The local pioneer society and a committee from the Native Sons of the Golden West conducted his funeral, with a Baptist minister to preach the funeral sermon. His mortal remains were laid to rest in the San Bernardino Pioneer Memorial Cemetery, far from Zion.

JAMES SLY: ALL SORTS OF BAD LUCK ATTENDED US

Although not so adventurous as Abner Blackburn, battalion veteran James Sly was just as ready to return to northern California in 1849. He had made the trip across the Sierra to Salt Lake with the Thompson-Holmes company in 1848. The following summer he found an opportunity to work his way back, guiding a wagon train to northern California over the trail he had helped open. His manuscript journal of the 1849 trail journey sets down a rudimentary record of camping places and mileage estimates that is omitted here. In later pages Sly provides a descriptive account of his gold mining career from fall 1849 to March 1850, when the journal abruptly ends after recording the onset of scurvy for Sly and the death of a companion. In language that betrays an unschooled acquaintance with the niceties of spelling and punctuation, Sly's narrative offers a cautionary tale about the uncertainties and fatal hazards that attended the miner's life.

JAMES C. SLY, JOURNAL, JUNE 1849 TO MARCH 1850, LDS ARCHIVES.

1849 June 5th James C. Sly's Book and Jornel of life and his Travels in 1849

On the 25th of June I left the Grate Salt Lake City in Compney with father Thomas Justton and Wilmer Brunson as a guide for a Train of wagons from the united States to go to the Sacremento James Stuart Captin

[*List of camping places and mileage estimates from June 25 to July 24 are omitted.*]

on the 25th [July] at Slys park 25m
heare we Lay By two days and prospected for gold But not finding enouf to Suit us we Continud in our Jurney and
on the 28th we camped at wever Town [Weberville] 20m
on the 29th to daylys ranch 25m
Being from the Sink of Humbolt to daylys ranch 236
Makeing the distence from Graite Salt Lake City to Dalys ranch or Sacremento Citty — 810 miles—

During this Jurney i Sufferd Graitly with Canker in the mouth. I eat

Scercly Enny thing During the Jurny. On the 1st of August a Compny of nine men prevailed uppon me to go and prospect for gold and agred to Board me. I led them to a bar on the Cossumnis [Cosumnes] river to a mine that had never bin opened before where we weare giting Considerible gold but a friend of theirs having told them that on the Macalemna [Mokelumne] river about 100 miles distence was a place ware it Could be picked up in large Chuncks but that the inidiens had Killed three men that went there and no boddy dare go there. Evry one of them was up in armes to go to the place where thay Could make thier fortshun. I told them it was nothing but a gold tale and thay had better Stay weare thay weare but father Justton was a most angery and Saide i must be foolish if i wouldent go. I at last Concented to go and on the 9th of August we took up our Jurny for the grate prise and on the 10th we arived at the Big Bar 50 miles below the grate prise and i told them as we Could git no further with the wagon that if two men wuld go with me we would go and See the place. Accordingly two of them volintiered and on the 12th we Started. We followed up the river Climbed rocks and mounttains untill we Come to the Spot but to our great astonishment we found no dead men and worse than all no gold and my two friends turned about very humble and Said i wish we had takin your advice. We mite have had two or three hundred dollars in our pockets. We then Started Back and arived in Camp on the 15th after a tedious Jurney of Six days on the 20th we Started Back to the Cossumnis we arrived there on the 23d [of August 1849] and the Compney Broke up and father Justten and Willmer Brunson and my Self in Compny with two other men went to work. On Friday the 8th of September father Justton was taken Sick with a fever. On Tuesday 12th he Seemed much Better and talked of going to work But on wensday 13th he got So much worse that i Cauled a Docter and on Sunday 17th he died at 15 minits Before 3 oclock in the morning. On the 8th of octtober we left that place and moved 12 miles up the river. Willmer and my Self was taken Sick and i Began to think that all Sorts of Bad luck attended us. About the 12th of November the rainy Seison Commenced and we weare with out a tent or anny thing to Cover us. We moved down the river 15 miles and i left Willmer with Some friends and went to the Citty for a tent and our winters Provsins. It was a raw rainey time and all the Creeks weare high and after fording Some Six Streames Some of them to my waist there and Back again i arived on the Cossumnes again on the 23d of November. The rain Continued to the first of December and all the miners is idle on acount of the high water.

15 Feb [1850] We had our gol[d] Stole from us wich reduced us to poverity.

1st March I was taking with the Scurvy vary sick.

On the 12 father Bar was taking Sick and died on the 17th 1850.

JAMES S. BROWN: THEY EXPECTED TO SCOOP GOLD BY SHOVELFULS

As noted, the gold missionaries who reached California by the southern route in late 1849 did not travel by themselves. The entire body, including a large group of non-Mormon forty-niners guided by Jefferson Hunt, numbered an estimated five hundred people with one hundred ox-drawn wagons and many horse and mule pack trains. Henry Bigler, reluctantly returning to a miner's life, left only this very succinct account of his journey, making no mention of his linkup with the larger body of emigrants under Hunt's guidance.

> On the 12th of November [1849] we started, myself, J. D. Burnham and Hyrum Curtis and Wm. P. Godard, 4 yokes of oxen and 1 wagon. At Provo the co. got together and organized by appointing Simpson D. Huffaker Capt. There was 31 persons. Proceeded on to Salt creek where one foot of snow fell on us to our surprise as it was represented that [so far] south snow never fell to lay on the ground, but we were in snow from here to over the rim on the head of [Santa] Clarra [River]. There was no house south of Provo at the time. We expected to go through in 8 weeks, provisioned for that length of time. Instead of which we were three months and 5 days in getting through.[23]

To reach the gold country so late in the year, Hunt guided the company south from Utah Lake and southwest to Little Salt Lake, near modern Parowan, where they connected with the Spanish Trail between Santa Fé and Los Angeles. Following the general course of this trading track, they planned to continue southwest to Las Vegas, then make a difficult desert passage to the Mojave River, which would lead them upstream to Cajon Pass and on to Rancho Cucamonga and Isaac Williams' Rancho del Chino. Hunt had traveled over this general route in 1847 and again in 1848. Orrin Porter Rockwell and his company of battalion veterans had also traveled it successfully in the reverse direction, from Rancho del Chino to Great Salt Lake City, the previous spring.

Unfortunately for Hunt's reputation as a guide, those under his general direction soon began to dispute his commands, then divided into quarreling factions. One non-Mormon band headed into the wastes of Death Valley, with disastrous results. Although everyone suffered from

[23] Henry Bigler Diary, Book B, Huntington Library.

hunger and extreme thirst, the members of the Gold Mission and the other LDS travelers who stuck to the established trail made the trip without loss of life. Their escape from disaster was principally due to the good judgment and calming presence of Apostle Charles C. Rich, who counseled the Saints to remain on the main track rather than follow supposed shortcuts toward the gold country.

After resting and recuperating at the Williams ranch, the gold missionaries moved on to Los Angeles. Some then went to San Pedro and found ship passage to San Francisco. Others traveled overland, either by the coastal road that once linked the Franciscan missions or by inland routes to the Mariposa region in the southern mines, then farther north to Sutter's Fort, Mormon Bar, and the placer mines in the American River drainage. James Brown, briefly diverted from his Hawaiian proselytizing mission to help guide the gold missionaries, was among those who headed for the southern mines. In his autobiography Brown described the awkward initiation of the LDS greenhorns into the placer mining business.

JAMES S. BROWN, *LIFE OF A PIONEER*, 147–48.

On the third day, I think it was, we came to a small mining camp called Burns' Diggins, on the south side of the Merced River.[24] There we struck a very good prospect, and stopped until the main company came up. As it was evident we could take from twelve to fifteen dollars per day to the man, we advised the company to begin work there, as the country was so muddy and soft that we could not make much headway in traveling higher into the foot hills. They agreed to accept our advice; then came a quite laughable performance. Those who had been the very worst drones in camp were now the first with the pick and washpan. They pitched into the creek as if they expected to scoop gold by shovelfuls, leaving their teams hitched to their wagons; while those who had been on hand early and late, taking a more methodical view of things, first formed the camp, got their dinner, and then went quietly to prospecting up and down the creek. By this time our drones decided that there was no gold there, and that they would go where there was some. What a lesson we learned there of human nature! The next day, however, things settled down a little more like business, after it was ascer-

[24]Burns Camp or Burns Diggings became a well-known placer on the south side of the Merced River southwest of Hornitos. By 1851, as the surface deposits were worked out, discovery of quartz lodes brought renewed attention to this area. Mining by dredging techniques continued here until the early 1950s. See Gudde, *California Gold Camps*, 53.

tained that some had been making fifteen to twenty-five and fifty, and some even as high as one hundred dollars per day, to the man. Next day, Captain Egan and five others of our number were elected to go further up into the mountains and prospect for the company, while the others dug gold.[25] The latter were to keep an account of all they earned, and when we returned they were to give us an equal share with those who stayed and worked.

On these conditions six of us set out on horseback and with pack mules. When we got well into the mountains it began to rain and snow so that we were not able to do much but cut browse for our horses. The snow became so deep that we had to go ahead of our horses and break the road so as to get out. We were soaked to the skin, and our bedclothes were all wet. Our provisions were almost gone; so we set out for our camp, after spending ten days in a miserable condition. We traveled in snow two and a half feet deep from 2 P.M. until 6 A.M. before we succeeded in reaching camp, when we found that Apostle Rich had been there, and the men had sent every dollar's worth of gold they had dug in our absence to Stockton for supplies of provisions, clothing, tools, etc, so there was none left to pay us our proportion.

As Apostle C. C. Rich had brought word that Brother A. Pratt desired me to meet him in San Francisco by a certain date, I packed up my effects, sold my oxen to Captain Jefferson Hunt for two hundred dollars, and bade adieu to the rest of the camp, who owed me one hundred dollars, and they yet owe it.

Albert K. Thurber: The Gold Was Beautiful, Mostly Nuggets

The documentary record of the gold missionaries' California sojourn is, by LDS standards, remarkably sparse. Even Henry Bigler retired his pen after arriving in California and renewing his search for gold. His sole comment came near the end of his experience as an argonaut: "I am tired of mining and of the country and long to be at home among the Saints."[26]

While most gold missionaries wrote little or nothing about their experiences, the one notable exception was young Albert Thurber. A

[25]Born in Ireland, Howard Egan became one of the most renowned Mormon scouts. Egan served with the Nauvoo police, traveled to Santa Fé with John D. Lee in 1846 to collect the pay of the Mormon Battalion for church leaders, and journeyed to Utah with Brigham Young's 1847 pioneer company. He smuggled gunpowder to Utah in 1858 and served as a major in the short-lived Standing Army of Israel. He managed the Pony Express between Salt Lake and the central Great Basin. See Egan, *Pioneering the West, 1846–1878: Major Howard Egan's Diary*.

[26]Henry Bigler Diary, Book B, Huntington Library.

ALBERT K. THURBER
An 1849 Salt Lake City convert to Mormonism and a member of the 1849–1850 Gold Mission, Thurber became a prominent Utah cattleman and Indian interpreter after his return from California. *Courtesy LDS Archives.*

recent convert who had gladly agreed to go mining with his partner Jacob Burnham, Thurber was something of an innocent abroad. His journal provides a chatty word picture of the California he saw in the winter of 1849–1850 and his mixed fortune at placer mining until he returned to Salt Lake in summer 1850.

ALBERT KING THURBER, JOURNAL,
BANCROFT LIBRARY, UNIVERSITY OF CALIFORNIA, BERKELEY,
PHOTOCOPY OF TYPED TRANSCRIPT, LDS ARCHIVES.

After the company had all got into [Isaac Williams's Rancho del Chino] and we had rested a little, got bread by trading with the Indians and Spaniard for corn and wheat which we got ground but not bolted. We went to Los Angeles and camped a little outside of town. We had heard much of vermin as a natural companion in the California climate but had decided to keep our clothes so changed and washed that we would keep clear from them. At Los Angeles I felt my neck annoyed for two or three days and had noticed a number of the camp going through certain evolutions with the right hand as though they were mocking me. I one day went and examined my flannel shirt and in the gathers on the collar found a certain insect with heads hid in great regularity, each occupying his gather or space. I told a number of them in camp that they were lousy and when they would dispute me I would turn back their shirt collars and pick them off. The result of this was that many a good shirt and drawers were thrown away to the joy of the old Spanish women who gathered them up. Elder Amasa Lyman and Jesse D. Hunter met us here. We went to St. Pedro, engaged a passage to San Francisco on board of the 70 ton schooner Placa, old and creaky. We had a cabin for a number of days and it seemed that we would never get anywhere. Amused ourselves by [catching] little blue sharks, watch porpoises tumble, etc., when for a change we had a severe storm for a number of days. The co. were in the hold and we had to make our bed with nothing but blanket to do it with. [Our] water casques rack and rotten were filled with pis ants. The first chance the Cap. got to take an observation he said that if we wished to go to the Sandwich islands that he could take us there in 2 days. I came to the conclusion that the craft made more lee than headway and if we were in a hurry we better lay her broad side to the point we wished to make.

Got to San Francisco in 14 days, ought to have gone up in 5. A. Lyman in company with us. We presented a different appearance in our rough garb and fitouts to the citizens of San Francisco than the generality of emigrants. It was raining when we went on shore and strangers asked us what hotel we were going to stop at, which brought out a laugh from the comp., as I presume not one had thought of going to a hotel. We told them that we were going to camp on the beach, that we had been in the mountains all winter and did not know how to deport ourselves in a house. Was afraid that if we went into one that we would take cold, the usual consequence of sleeping in a house after being long accustomed to sleep in the open air. The general remark by the bystanders, them fellows will stand the mines.

Thurber and his companions were warmly received in San Francisco by a few of the Mormons who still lived there. But the young man needed desperately to find work, since he had arrived with "but a few cents in money," and that immediately went for bread and molasses. After five days of searching, he and Brother Washington Cook got work together digging out a house foundation for five dollars each per day. While at this task, Thurber recounts, they had another experience that indicated how completely their religious identity set them apart from the general population.

Whilst working at this job we were accosted by a tall man past the meridian of life. How do you do, says he. We courteously returned the salutation. How long have you been here? We told him. Where are you from? We told him our native states. What ship did you come in? We informed him of the name of the craft. He was surprised that we should come around Cape

> Horn in such a vessel. We told him we did not, but only from San Pedro but came the overland trip and had been in the mountains all winter. He became a little excited with curiosity, wanted to know if we came through Salt Lake City. Told him we did. Well, did you see any Mormons and what do they look like, how large are they and what is their color, how do they dress if at all: Said he had years ago seen one going down the Mississippi river, that he looked like other people and appeared to be a smart man. We then told him that we were Mormons and with great astonishment he arose and with wonder depicted in his countenance exclaimed, You Mormons? Why you look like other folks. We felt that certainly we were under inspection with his curious eye riveted on us. He talked with us about one hour.

Thurber described in his journal the election for sheriff in San Francisco, revealing that he and other Saints cast their ballots for Col. Jack Hayes, a former Texas Ranger who had earned great fame in the Mexican War. It was, Thurber added, "the first time I ever voted." He also wrote about the seamier aspects of gold rush social life in San Francisco.

> Gamblers held dominion and ruled the city. Saloons were open day and night where men and women were continually gambling. They were generally furnished with an orchestra of splendid music, a bar of liquors and the side walls hung with life size obscene pictures. A cargo of women from New Orleans or Sidney were sold by the capability [?] of the vessel who brought them to pay their passage. This set [up] the gamblers in a social capacity.

After working a few days and making a few dollars in San Francisco, Thurber and his companions started for the gold country. The would-be miners purchased their outfits in Sacramento and headed into the American River drainage, the central focus of early placer mining in the northern Mother Lode. As he told the story, their first success came with surprising ease.

> As we were traveling along at Greenwoods (Valley Lewisville) we calculated to go up a creek and try our luck.[27] As we passed up saw the whole bottom had been prospected and concluded it was a dull show for us. Bought a washer of Jacob Gates for $64. Five of us worked with it, first day made some $2.50 each. At night I told them there were too many with the

[27]Greenwood is the name of a creek and a town on the American River's Middle Fork in El Dorado County, five miles southwest of Georgetown. According to Erwin G. Gudde's *California Gold Camps*, 145–46, the first discoveries at Greenwood were made in 1849. The town was named Lewisville when a post office was established there in 1851, but it became Greenwood again in 1852, by which time the settlement could boast a hotel, three stores, and a half-dozen cabins. Placer and quartz mining continued actively in the district through the 1930s.

machine and we put it up at auction. I bought it with my partner Burnham, made $40 next day. We mined in this place for about one month but sent two men to find a claim for the summer. The gold was beautiful, mostly nuggets. We were very free to exhibit it to any one, supposing that we could do better anywhere else than there, as it had been all prospected over by old miners. The first thing we knew the creek bed was nearly all claimed and the place was alive with miners, leaving us small claims. It proved very rich all through that section of country.

Anxious to find a new site that might pay better, Thurber and four of his original LDS company began to travel from place to place. For more than a week they stayed on the road, heading first to Otter Creek and then moving on to Georgetown.[28] After purchasing new boots and seven or eight mules in Georgetown, the men gave up their search for richer diggings and decided to join other Mormon miners on the North Fork, where they expected to turn the river out of its course so they could excavate the riverbed, a risky strategy.

We concluded that mines were getting too thick and as soon as the water got down on the rivers started for our claim high up on the north fork of the middle fork of the American river, 30 men of us. We could not get animals within one mile of our claim on the river just below where a little stream enters in that has a beautiful cascade on it. We set to work at building a dam and making a race. The river was some 60 yards wide. We built two walls across it about 6 feet apart and packed dirt in sacks on our backs to fill in. After we got the water turned we commenced to sink a hole 30 feet across but failed to reach bed rock.

We worked here one month and got $1.50, five cts. apiece. John W. Berry was very sick at the place, [we] concluded to leave for the middle fork, previous to which the following notice was posted: This is the certify that all persons are forbid to violate the rights of a dammed claim. Got our animals packed our dunage to them packed up and started. One mule and pack rolled down the mountain a long way.

Sadly disappointed, the Mormon miners moved over to Slap Jack Bar

[28]Otter Creek is a tributary to the Middle Fork of the American River north of Bottle Hill on the trail between Georgetown and Volcano Bar, in El Dorado County. A significant quartz vein was discovered there in 1851. Georgetown, also in El Dorado County, was the business, cultural, and social center for a very rich district of placer and slate seam diggings between the Middle Fork and South Fork of the American River. Its present commercial district is distinguished by landmark historical structures, including the former U.S. Armory, the Wells Fargo office, and the Georgetown Hotel. See Gudde, ed., *California Gold Camps*, 82–83, 257; and Hoover *et al.*, *Historic Spots in California*, rev. Kyle, 83–84.

on the Middle Fork "and got at work the best we could."[29] While his friend Burnham returned to their old claim in Greenwood Valley all alone, Thurber "got to work in a hole in much water, worked 9 days and found myself a little sick."

Here Thurber relates his meeting with Charles Rich, who counseled him to give up mining and return to Utah in Amasa Lyman's company. His account continues with a detailed description of an eight-day hunt for missing mules, his own and some belonging to members of his small mining company. After two days without success, he was "astonished at this time to be invited to take animals, steal them, [his companions] told me it was right." In reply, Thurber wrote, "I told them that I was not nor did not expect to get that far into Mormonism. That I came into Cal. honest and calculated to leave so."

The final section of Thurber's journal describes his further difficulties in preparing for the return to Great Salt Lake City and the precautions he and other members of his company took for their protection. Jacob Burnham, his partner at the outset of this great adventure, decided to remain behind for a few more days mining at Greenwood, since "he wanted to make $45 in money more." Thurber urged him to return with Lyman's company, but "to no purpose." When the two friends parted, Thurber recorded, "I never saw a man look [so] lonesome." He then added a sad conclusion: "He took sick and died in about 2 weeks after."

With Amasa Lyman's encouragement, Thurber and four others started east with a train of pack mules. Their identity as Mormons apparently made them a target for dangerous men, who seemed to believe that all the Saints departing California must be both extremely rich and extremely naive. At the same time, he and his companions were generous in helping three impoverished New Yorkers who came to their camp in desperate condition from the difficulties of the overland journey to the gold country.

> Arrived at Lathrops, commenced fitting up. Did not get into a mess and having a small coffee and stew pot and fry pan I concluded to camp, mess

---

[29]Slap Jack Bar, which attracted a substantial crowd of Mormon miners in 1850, is on the American River's Middle Fork on the north, Placer County side. It is located opposite the mouth of Canyon Creek, at the extreme upper end of Rockey Chuckey (Ruck-A-Chucky rapids). According to local history specialist Melinda Peak, apparently a bridge was built there in 1853, destroyed in 1861, and so the name associated with this structure was retained in memory.

by myself. The Sierra Nevada road was infested by robbers and it was conjectured that they were watching for us as there was known to be in Lyman's hands a great amt. of tithing gold. Amasa sent me J. H. Rollins, Frank Dewey, Kiser and Isaac Brown over the mts. with 22 animals, a part of them with packs. We were very watchful and suspicious, tying up our animals and guarding them. Kiser was too lazy to tie his up one night or could not desist from eating (an occupation that he employed himself at most of the time) to do so and lost the best mule in the company. We took the pack trail west of a little lake and camped in a nice little hollow for the night. Let our animals graze and tied them up to trees close about camp.

At about 12 M 3 men came and wished the liberty of camping with us. We told them they could do so if they would put their beds between me and Rollins. They said they had camped in so cold a place that they could not stand it. We did not know but this was a ruse and with pistols handy and Bowie knives stuck in the ground within reach we guarded them all night. Up early and had breakfast cooked, invited the strangers to get up and eat. Two arose and washed themselves, said they had no money to pay for breakfast. We told them to get their partner up, when one went and after some exertion got him up but he could scarcely walk, his feet were so sore that he could not wear shoes and had them tied in rags. They set down and eat, asking many questions as to our destination and business. Said they were from Ithica, N.Y., had been of good society, started with a good fitout and at [last?] got reduced to what we saw them without one cent of money, had traveled much nights and slept days when it was warm. Had not one mouthful to eat, felt very grateful for breakfast. As they were about to leave I gave them flour enough to last them into Hangtown. They offered me their pistols. I would not accept them. Then, said they, we must know who you are and what your names are. We told them we were Mormons going to Salt Lake. They were surprised to think anything good come from a Mormon. One's name was Wells. Parted with tears of gratitude in their eyes.

Went over the summit and arrived in Carson. Struck camp about 100 yards off. . . . The next day went over to Edmunds station where the co. was to gather, it being arranged to come over the mountain in small parties. The bulk of money came in Daniel Clark['s] wagon alone. He was loaded with flour. At camp a suspicious and inquisitive individual bothered us for 2 days but he had been around about enough, took him [to] one side, told him that we understood him and that we were ready for anything and that if he wished to live to saddle his horse and leave. He was soon off. We all got together and started. . . . I felt well starting home. The company consisted of some 40 men, 8 wagons, 2 or 3 women and about 100 animals.

Thomas Morris: I Soon Possessed Myself of Five or Six Dollars, So I Was a Miner

A week or two after the Gold Mission companies had left Salt Lake City, one more group of Saints—battalion veterans and others—left for California by the southern route, intent on improving their fortunes by placer mining. They went as wagon drivers for a California-bound train of freight wagons owned by two non-Mormon Missouri merchants, the brothers Ebenezer and Thaddeus Pomeroy.

The background of this unusual company merits description. The Pomeroy brothers departed from Lexington, Missouri, early in May 1849 with 130 yoke of oxen and forty heavy freight wagons, carrying thirty tons of provisions valued at fifty thousand dollars. Originally they intended to carry this cargo to the northern California gold country, while also trading with emigrants along the way. Despite trail mishaps, when they arrived at the Mormon capital on 9 August, as LDS attorney Hosea Stout noted, the Pomeroys still commanded "a train of 34 wagons loaded with goods & groceries." They had "started for the mines," Stout added, "but fell short."[30]

At Great Salt Lake City the two merchants met a hostile reception. Mormon extremists circulated a report that in 1838 at Haun's Mill near Far West, Missouri, one of the Pomeroy brothers had taken part in the murderous attack on a camp of LDS families, an infamous incident in the Missouri Mormon War. At an open meeting the afternoon of Sunday, 12 August, Apostles John Taylor and Parley P. Pratt both vividly recalled inflammatory scenes from the event in Missouri, but reduced the charges against the Pomeroys to an assertion that they were complicit because they had not attempted to fight against the enemies of the Saints. The one brother most directly accused then rose to deny the charges. According to the eye-witness account of Pardon Dexter Tiffany, a non-Mormon forty-niner who had arrived in Salt Lake City a few days ahead of the Pomeroy train, "Then for accusation . . . all they could make out was that P was at Far West with the army & it turned out that he went there with a flag of truce to get some women who had married Mormons to leave the town before the fight."

---

[30]The appearance of the Pomeroy brothers in Great Salt Lake City is described in Madsen, *Gold Rush Sojourners in Great Salt Lake City in 1849 and 1850*, 62, from which Hosea Stout's quote is taken.

According to Tiffany's report, at this point the hearing turned sharply in favor of the Pomeroys: "After they could find no proof that P had acted against them several Mormons came out & said he had befriended the Mormons, then he [Pomeroy] called me out & I told them who he was & his standing & then I made them a speech & told them they had tried Pomeroy on [hearsay] report & condemned him & now the proof was all in his favour." The accusers also were sharply rebuffed in an attempt to introduce further hearsay testimony from Pomeroy teamsters, "The vote was then taken as to whether or [not] Pomeroy was guilty & there was a unanimous response of No from men, women, & children." Tiffany concluded his report with a wry comment: "So passed a Mormon Sabbath."[31]

Once the crisis ended, the Pomeroys found a ready sale for much of their cargo. Indeed, the arrival of their freight train was one more nearly miraculous event for Brigham Young's struggling colony; it helped rescue the Salt Lake Saints from a critical shortage of foodstuffs as another winter was approaching. But after remaining in Great Salt Lake City for nearly three months, the brothers still wanted to reach California. They had purchased stock with some of their profits, and they intended to drive their herd along with their remaining freight wagons across the desert to Las Vegas and on to Los Angeles. Since most if not all their teamsters had left their employment, they needed to recruit hired hands from among the Saints. As an inducement, the Missourians offered no wages but free transportation to wagon drivers. Fortunately for the Pomeroys, Brigham Young quietly gave his approval to their plans, clearing the way for their departure.

Leaving Salt Lake in the first week of November 1849, the Pomeroy wagon train and its cattle herd followed the same route through the desert country taken earlier by Jefferson Hunt's company. Like the Hunt company, the Pomeroys nearly met total disaster.[32] They finally managed

[31]Pardon Dexter Tiffany, Journals and Letters, 1849, 12 August 1849, Missouri Historical Society, Typescript, 99–103. Tiffany, a non-Mormon native of Maine who had practiced law in St. Louis before joining the gold rush, wrote that "a notice was given to the effect that Messers. Pomeroy had been reported as having acted against the Mormons in the Missouri War & had been ordered away with his goods but that he had appealed to people & therefore *all persons* were notified to attend at 4 o'clock to hear what could be proved against & for Mess. P[omeroy] & a decision to be given in righteousness."

[32]For the Pomeroy's expedition from Salt Lake to California, see Davies, *Mormon Gold,* 175–85; and Hafen and Hafen, eds., *Journals of the Forty-niners,* 43–44, 110, 293–305. In his account of "The Gentile Pomeroy Wagon Train," Davies claims that one hundred wagons made the trip, and supposes each wagon had as a minimum one Mormon driver. This figure, apparently derived from Goudy Hogan's (*continued*)

to reach the Williams ranch on 27 February, almost four months after their departure, having lost all their cattle and more than half their wagons. The LDS wagon drivers then moved on toward the gold fields.

Samuel Miles, one of the battalion veterans who returned to California as a wagon driver for the Pomeroys, offers a succinct summary of a difficult experience that left him and his companions wiser but not richer.

> I started on the 10th of Nov. [1849] with a company of the brethren with ox teams to the gold mines by the south route to Calif. We sold our teams here and went by water from San Pedro to San Francisco. We made our way to the mines where we worked through the season generally with very poor success. We arrived at home in the valley most of us after one years absence with pack animals [but] with little to show for our years work. I found my wife and folks well. I learned the lesson that to stay at home and help to develop the country was better than hunting gold.[33]

Thomas Morris had served with Samuel Miles in Company B of the Mormon Battalion, and he returned to California with him. Morris kept a memorandum book that served as a diary for this journey, "driving an ox team for the mines of California in company with a heavy train belonging to a Mr. Pomeroy." He continued the diary through his trip north to San Francisco, Sacramento, and the American River diggings, adding to it an increasingly sketchy record of his mining experiences over the following year. Morris also inscribed stanzas of his own poetry, lines that alternated between gloomy expressions of his loneliness and cheery affirmations of a prosperous future. This excerpt begins after the Pomeroy train had arrived in the San Bernardino area.

(*continued*) autobiography (quoted below), leads Davies to the conclusion that at least one hundred LDS men must have reached California in this fashion. Fuller documentation, including the account of Thomas Morris quoted below in full, indicates a different figure: between twenty wagons (Pettit biography in Hafen and Hafen, eds., *Journals of the Forty-niners,* 294) and fifty wagons (David Seely Sketch in ibid., 296). Each wagon, these sources agree, was drawn by two yoke of oxen with two men to each wagon. In addition, sixteen-year-old Edwin Pettit accompanied the wagons as a herder until all the cattle gave out and either died or were abandoned. At that point, at "Muddy Desert" about ninety miles east of Las Vegas, states Pettit, "our teams were so reduced and the cattle so nearly gone that we put the wagons off to one side, using them for kindling wood, and packed everything up into as few wagons as possible." This destruction of surplus wagons may account for the discrepancy in figures, with some participants recalling how many wagons began the journey and others remembering how many made the entire trip. Pettit and a few companions left the Pomeroy train at Muddy Desert and joined an independent company that went ahead to Los Angeles. Other accounts indicate that perhaps no more than twenty-one or twenty-two LDS men accompanied the Pomeroys all the way to southern California.

[33]Samuel Miles Autobiography and Diary, LDS Archives.

THOMAS MORRIS, MEMORANDUM BOOK, LDS ARCHIVES.

February 20 [1850] . . . Some of the boys are not willing to break mules. Some prefering being liberated from all former and future contracts. Mr. Pomeroy offered me and 8 others passage to Francisco on conditions that we 9 obligate ourselves in a joint note for the whole amount. This we readily did. He made our bargain with a shipmaster to take us to Francisco, $47 cash. This, with all former clauses, [including] twenty-five [dollars for] each man for the wagons we burned on Muddy to facilitate our journey, swelled the bill of obligation, food and clothing, over a thousand dollars.

Put out with a hired wagon to San Pedro, some 20 miles from De Los Angeles. Shipped on board the Brig Fremont, while Hawkins, with a company of some 12, preferred going 700 miles on foot with scarcely any money, but free from all encumbrance.[34]

Before we left the camp, I had an interview with Captain [Jesse D.] Hunter, my old Captain in the Battalion. Of him I learned that our [LDS] fraternity was about to buy the Ranch of Chaves.[35] A company of U.S. troops were being stationed at the same. The weather very wet, plenty of grass. We slept at a small house in Berkeley which Mr. Pomeroy hired for to store his goods. He treats us 9 very well and civil. Our wagons cost us for hauling to San Pedro $20.00. I had a smart walk to San Pedro. Found it nearer [nearly] 30 miles. Drank a bottle of good ale there. Get on board.

March 6 [1850]. Our anchor up. A light breeze. We are under way. Boys rather cross. Making better headway.

March 10. The wind has been making sport of our little brig, but she holds her course. She won't wait for me to get my food in comfort. One of my teeth set to achiing. Having leisure, I got the old doctor to draw it. He drew a well one, much to my sorrow, for the ill one had to be drawn after.

March 13. So up to the last our little brig has carried us safely over. We are in Francisco. I have met with Brother Prell.[36] Have seen much of Francisco, but shall speak more of it hereafter. General [Charles C.] Rich has been here and gone down the coast. I go to work and earn $13.00. The General and Captain Hunter counsel me and my party to stop one week longer.

April 9 [1850]. I have commenced again my long journey, leaving the

---

[34]Hawkins is likely Benjamin Hawkins, formerly in Company A of the battalion, who had discovered gold at Natomas Diggings—the Negro Bar site—in company with Marcus Shepherd in early summer 1848. Hawkins was the source for the often-repeated description of Sam Brannan's arrival in San Francisco on 10 May 1848 to announce the discovery of "Gold! Gold on the American River!" See Ricketts, *Mormon Battalion,* 22, 199; Davies, *Mormon Gold,* 26, 43–44, 233, 372; and Gudde, ed., *Bigler's Chronicle,* 109–10.

[35]This proposed purchase has previously escaped historians' attention. It appears that Hunter and his partners had made Julian Chavez, former alcalde of Los Angeles, an offer on his Rio de las Animas ranch, but Chavez declined to sell. See Bancroft, *History of California,* 5:627.

[36]Sam Brannan excommunicated Elder Elijah Ward Pell for "wicked and licentious conduct" on the *Brooklyn* voyage, but Pell went on to serve as sheriff of San Francisco in 1846.

forests of masts of ships of all nations in the Bay of Francisco, passing many on the Sacramento, with many a lovely scene on either side of us.

April 10. Landed in Sacramento. Nearly all under water. Ships and masts and trees all along the wharf embracing each other. Here all is bustle and life, wagons and mules going off with men and provisions every hour in the day. Everyone showing gold rings and chains. I saw no [sober?] persons, but many drunk. A Mr. [Ebenezer] Brown that was Orderly Sergeant in the Battalion supplied us. He keeps a story in Jay street. My friend, Captain Hunter, furnished me $80.00 to pay for our hauling two greasewoods. The wagoners charge us one shilling a pound for hauling 50 miles.

April 14. At Sacramento had an interview with a Brown Bosell [Abraham Boswell?], one of the Salt Lake boys who has been out one year. I am well. Got several mules. Going to town for supplies had a view of Sutter's Fort. Extensive plains. Hundreds of cattle feeding. A friend told me, a Brother Rose Crance [George W. Rosencrans], that our people had bought the Ranch of Chavez and that all of our boys who served in the Battalion two terms were entitled to two land warrants.[37] This gave me some pleasure, having served twice myself.

April 16 [1850]. Pleasant scenes and golden tales and all the way filled with miners, shady acres and lofty pines, resembling Gloucestershire more than America. Now in the area where our boys first discovered the gold. This place is called Caledonia [Coloma] or Sutter's Mills.

Greenwood Valley, April 18. Prices in the area: Boots, one pair, $60.00; Brandy, one bottle, $5.00; Pork, one pound, $6.80; Potatoes, one pound, 50¢; Onions, one pound, $1.00; Flour, one pound, 5¢. Here I see hundreds passing back and forwards. Ten thousand in readiness on the river. The water high. Mr. Hunter charged me one dollar for a quart of milk. He and his family, with many others, are camped here in the valley. Many have built houses here. Six times as large as it was in the last summer.

With pleasure or with pain
I must try my luck again
The precious metal for to find
And leave my poverty behind.

Middle Fork [American River], Sunday, April 20. I left my companions in the valley, making my way for the middle fork, having met Jeptha Condit, an old fellow soldier.[38] Placed my blankets on his mules, some stranger in the big bar having bid me $5.00 a day. My way lay over the Spanish Bar, on

[37]This report turned out not to be true.

[38]Jeptha S. Condit was a private in Company C who also served in the Mormon Volunteers. See Ricketts, *Mormon Battalion*, 24, 266, 285. He subsequently opened a tavern in the Greenwood and Salmon Falls area with William Squires as a partner. Davies, *Mormon Gold*, 119, 232, 270.

the same river that Condit was camped on. But he lost me, so having no guide, I lost my way and had to camp out all night without my blankets. But, fortunately, I fell in with Bill, the cook, who treated me well, and one of the workmen with him behaved well to me. Gave me food and money and put me on the track that soon brought me to Condit, where I dispensed with all further pursuits. Encouraged by him, I commenced work at Slapjack Bar. After a few hours I came in with gold. I soon possessed myself of five or six dollars, so I was a miner.

May 11 [1850]. Last week my income was $57.00, rather better than any before. Condit and company boards me for one ounce a week. A little while the banks of the rivers are sadly dug up nearly every stone has been tried and turned over. The weather is warm. Few care to work for less than an ounce a day, so there be many engaged in gambling with cards. Our Mormon boys do nothing else till the rivers go down, that's in the fall of the year. But some keep coming to the mines and help me with my scanty share, but generally do not stop longer than to supply their needs, then go seek for better diggings, but they never fail to take the easiest [gold] got at so leave me the worst of it. But thank fortune I can supply my wants and enjoy many luxuries even here where no harvest is.

May the 20. Sunday. Made $70.00 last week.

I have wandered far from all that's dear
Through deserts wild and filled with fear.
If pain or joy my passion move,
I have no one to return my love.

And now my story I have told.
With thousand more I am washing gold.
The loss of friends gold won't supply
That thousand know as well as I.

This golden sand doth me invite
To sweat and toil with all my might
My gathering frame doth rest refuse
The many did their spot abuse.

I am like an oyster, closed to all.
On any spot I choose to fall
My wife and children all have gone
And I am a stranger here alone.

June the 2nd [1850]. Last week made but $50.00

Hope throws her mantle and covers my gloom.
Love permeates virtue and virtue crowns love.
In the days of my youth I have traveled in the yoke
Though my labor is hard, I am used to the stroke.

Wherever I dwell, may content be my lot
  And friendship like ivy encircle my cot.
May each rosey morning be mantled in peace,
  Shed health 'round my cottage and blessings increase.
May the Sun of Prosperity ever shine on that spot,
  May Liberty's Tree ever bloom in my lot,
On my neat humble dwelling may blessings descend,
  And free from all guile have many a friend.

Goudy E. Hogan: Farewell to my Brethren on the Old Claim

Goudy Hogan, a nineteen-year-old immigrant from Norway, had been struggling to raise a crop on his family's new farm on the outskirts of Great Salt Lake City before he joined the Pomeroy wagon train. His autobiography emphasizes that departure of the LDS wagon drivers was in part a response to economic hardship caused by an infestation of Mormon crickets during the fall harvest. Moreover, Hogan attests that this venture with the Pomeroy brothers, like the Gold Mission, had the approval of Brigham Young and other church authorities.

Hogan's account of his season of gold seeking demonstrates the changes taking place in the placer mining districts by 1850. No longer could one person or a small company expect to profit by locating and working pristine claims. For the most part, success came only from large-scale cooperative effort. River damming and channeling to reach bedrock required heavy investments of time and labor, with no guarantee of returns, as Hogan learned to his sorrow. Efficient placer mining techniques used systems of ground sluices or riffle boxes tended by large crews. Like the Chinese miners who would soon take over many of these placer districts, the California Saints found their bonds of religion and communal experience an effective basis for banding together in mining companies. Hogan was fortunate to find a place within a company of battalion veterans who looked after the young man while providing him a society of like-minded souls to sustain him. Throughout his memoir Hogan makes apparent his reliance on the spiritual sustenance and social fellowship provided by Mormon brethren.

This lengthy excerpt from Hogan's autobiography begins in Great Salt Lake City, where his family had settled and begun farming in 1849.

GOUDY ERICSEN HOGAN, AUTOBIOGRAPHY, 1829–1898, LDS ARCHIVES.

In plowing the land, we selected damp ground around willows and spring holes, and much of it proved to be mineral, where crops would not grow. Then the crickets came down off the mountains, apparently on purpose, to destroy our crops that were growing. We made small wooden paddles, and with these, we all turned out for over one month, and worked as hard to fight crickets as in a field of battle. By our faithful struggle and the aid of the seagulls that came to our aid, there was a portion of our crops saved. When harvest time came, my father took sick and, having no reapers or cradles, my oldest sister, Caroline and myself took each a butcher knife to harvest wheat, all that was left after the crickets had done their work. When we had threashed the wheat with flails, we had 28 bushels.

The corn, beans, other garden truck was completely destroyed by the crickets. Brother Browning from Farmington came and stayed all night and said that his boys were going to start to California to dig gold. It had been councilled [by] President Young not to go to California but now after the crops were raised and gathered, he gave his consent. Two of the twelve, Charles C. Rich and Amasa Lyman, were going to preside over the brethren and receive the tithing. When my father found that out, he gave his consent for me to go, and fitted me out being very destitute of clothing and other things for the family, having been 3½ years since we left Nauvoo.

There were two brothers, Pomeroy, who were Gentiles, who had come to Salt Lake City with 100 wagons loaded with merchandise, with 3 or 4 teams of oxen to each wagon. After they had sold out they wished to get teamsters to drive through to California, the southern route. There were so many of our boys who wished to go through to California as teamsters, that we had to board ourselves and received no wages. The 3rd of November we started from Salt Lake City, south. There was a friend of mine that gave me some very good council before I started. Said he, "Attend to your secret prayers regularly. Do not associate with bad company nor drink strong drinks nor play cards, and pay your tithing regularly. If you will remember and observe all these things and be a good boy, I will promise to you, Goudy, that you will be blessed on your gold mission, and that you will come back being well satisfied with your trip."

During the large emigration [through Salt Lake] in the summer of 1849, I traded with one of the gold diggers for a new Stubentwist #1 Shotgun and one new knife. Before starting on my journey to California I gave for tithing, the shotgun and $25.00 although I had but very little property besides the rifle. When we started we expected to go there in two months, consequently, we ran out of provisions since we were nearly four months on the road. We lived on rations and poor beef that was given to us. We had to guard all the night through after leaving Provo, as there was no other settlement or fort until we reached lower California. Often the beef given us was so poor and tough that the guard could boil it all night and then in the morning it would be as tough as shoe leather, but our appetites were good for anything. The ox teams gave out and died very fast, having traveled through and across the plains in the summer. Very frequently, when we would camp there would be a wagon or more that had to be left so we chopped it up for firewood. When we came to the Muddy [River], the greater portion of the men left us and took a pack on their back. There was ten men of us that had run entirely out of flour and we asked Mr. Pomroy and brother to let us have some. The only way we could get it was to sign a joint note of $1,000,00, payable in California. I was one of that number that had to sign, and I also paid on the note. If we had not been Mormon boys there would have been mutiny in camp, but having just lately been driven from our homes in the United States because of the Gospel of Christ, we had learned to be patient in times of tribulation. After a long and tedious journey, we arrived in lower California, Los Angeles or San Bernardino on Feb. 27th. We found lower California the finest country that we had ever seen. Most of the boys went to upper California by land. Ten of us took a ship at San Pedro and sailed up the coast on a barge [brig], Fremont, to upper California, some 800 miles. Our fare was paid out of the $1,000 joint note previously spoken of. We landed alright.

We worked one month on the road for $5.00 per day, boarding ourselves, then we took steamboat and went to [Sacramento] and there we bought our outfit for mining and went to Greenwood Valley and commenced to work the surface digging with rockers to separate the gold from the dirt and sand. We made from $5.00 to 10.00 per day each, working in small companies. Very frequently we heard of companies making large wages in other places. After 5 weeks we concluded to go on the north fork of the American Fork. We paid $25.00 per hundred to have our provisions and tools packed up over some high mountains, laboring hard to turn the river out of it's channel, suffered great exposure by laboring in the cold water, building a double rock wall dam and filling in dirt between, to stop the water. By turning the stream in a race so to get in to the head of the river to work, we expected to find gold because there was thousands of dollars taken out of the same place the year before. After 6 weeks labor as a company, we found no gold in the bottom of the river. That labor cost us over $2,000. We were all broke and had to leave our tent and some tools. I left my double barrel shotgun and some clothing because we could not hire it packed back out. We were somewhat discouraged and each one went on his own hook. I made it a matter of prayer to know what to do. I was impressed to go where there was a company of ten men of the Mormon Battalion, who had been working a little above the place known as the Mormon Island on the American River.

After I worked a few days up and down the river with a shovel and pick and pan surface digging, I camped at night where this company were. I got acquainted with Abraham Woolf and when he took sick he offered me half of his share if I would work for him. I did for 6 weeks during this time he was very sick. He called on me often to administer to him. He had great confidence in me as a good boy and gave me charge of his sack of gold dust, something near $2,500.00. . . .

After I had worked 6 weeks, I took sick also. Charles C. Rich, one of the twelve apostles, was going to start in a few days, for Salt Lake. I began to be very anxious to go home, so I offered to sell out my share of what I had done to the company. Previously to this, I had a dream in which I dreamed that there came rain and washed our dam down, after which, we made no more money. At the time of this dream we were taking out from $500.00 to $1,000.00 per day, making my share $25.00 to $50.00. This dream made a great impression on me and though I did not tell any one of the company, for they were all well off, having been there before, it was in my mind. They wished me to stay and offered to work my share with theirs if I would be contented to stay until I was able to go to work again. They insisted that there was no doubt as to the amount of gold, and that I would make my independent fortune, but this could not persuade me if I could sell for enough to pay my debt and enough to fit me out to go home. They gave me $500.00, which satisfied me.

One night I dreamed that one of my family was dead and in a few days I received a letter from my father, in which it stated that one of my brothers, 3 years old, Charles Peter Hogan, had been poisoned eating wild parsnips by mistake. This gave me great sorrow and in the letter he wished me to send money if I could spare any. I had $100.00 at the time, that I had made previously. I read this letter to Brother Gordon Beckstead, remarking that I wished I had more money to send home.[39] He said that I might have all the money I needed in reason, so I received $200.00 and sent the $300.00 to my father.

I will now return to my preparing to go home, I bid farewell to my brethern on the old claim and went down to San Francisco where I bought a small mule and saddle, giving $50.00 for them. I got on the mule with the old saddle and got thrown off because the saddle turned with me. I then threw away the old saddle and went and bought a new one that I gave $80.00 for. George Boyd sent a mule by me to his folks in Salt Lake which I rode on through and delivered.[40] After we crossed the Sierra Nevada mountains we

[39]Gordon S. Beckstead, who served under Jefferson Hunt in Company A of the battalion, had reenlisted as one of the Mormon Volunteers. He reached Utah in January 1851 with five other Mormon miners, including three battalion veterans. See Ricketts, *Mormon Battalion*, 21, 266; and Davies, *Mormon Gold*, 268, 270.

[40]George Boyd was a veteran of the battalion's Company D. See Ricketts, *Mormon Battalion*, 26.

camped a few days and the Indians stole some of our horses, part of which belonged to Porter Rockwell, which made him feel out of patience with the red men. In crossing the 40 mile desert, there arose a terrible wind storm called a hurricane. We had to stop in the middle of the desert, and during the night a great many animals went off with the storm and never could be found. I lost my mule at that time, so I bought another pony from the Indians in Carson [Humboldt?] Valley. The natives were very hostile during these times, so much so, that we had to camp on open ground every night and had some very narrow escapes during the trip. Captain Charles C. Rich was a very good general. We thought Brother Porter Rockwell [was] a well known and brave man. While on guard one night there came a large Indian walking into camp with his gun on his shoulder, making out that he was a relief guard. As Porter spoke to him he ran. At this, said Rockwell, fired two shots with his drago[o]n pistol. In the morning we found the intruder about 300 yards from camp lying dead on his face. We all arrived safely home to Salt Lake Valley on the 6th of November 1850. I was gone from home one year and three days and was received with open arms.

I acknowledge the hand of the Lord in warning me in a dream to sell out so that I could pay my debt of $200.00 that I had borrowed to send home to my folks when they stood in need of things. When I left Calif. many of the boys told me that I was the luckiest boy that came from Salt Lake in 1849. I obeyed the advice given me by my friend before leaving, and had a very profitable trip in which I gained a great deal of experience. While in California I paid $50.00 to the tithing as well as the shotgun and $25.00. This was the beginning of paying tithing with me and I felt exceedingly well in so doing.

Edwin Pettit: We Were Not Very Successful at the Mines

One of the youngest Saints to accompany the Pomeroy train was Edwin Pettit, a native of Long Island, New York. A sturdy young man, Pettit had arrived at Salt Lake in September 1847, when he was thirteen years old, in the company of his sister and brother-in-law. His brief autobiography tells of the hard times the three of them faced together during the first two winters in the Great Basin. Because his brother-in-law, David Seely, was "a pretty good gunman," he could sometimes bring home from the hunt a quail or wild duck. Even so, they often had subsist "on thistle root or pig weed as our bill of fare." Pettit also mentions trading the brass buttons off his coat to Indians for sego lily bulbs. Like everyone in the country at the time, he was able to recall vividly the scourge of Mormon crickets that swept over grain fields nearly ready for harvest. Even with the famed arrival of seagulls to devour the insects, Pettit remembered, they could save only "a small portion of our crops."[41]

With no further explanation, Pettit's autobiography goes on to describe his experience as a cattle herder with the Pomeroy wagon train and, very briefly, subsequent mining in northern California. Although he and a few others left the Pomeroy party at Muddy River and packed on ahead, carrying their supplies on a two-wheeled cart drawn by an ox team, they were reunited with their LDS companions when the remnant of the Pomeroy train arrived at San Bernardino. Along with Thomas Morris, Goudy Hogan, and six or seven others, Pettit sailed from San Pedro to San Francisco aboard the brig *Fremont*, a trip arranged and financed on credit by the Pomeroy brothers for the mostly young and inexperienced Mormon travelers.

Pettit recalled being seasick about half the time while on this tedious voyage, and remembered also the excitement of catching a shark, which all the passengers helped eat. This excerpt describes their arrival in the City by the Bay, but gives only passing notice to their mining adventures, a topic Pettit was apparently willing to downplay in this account intended for his descendants.

> We landed in San Francisco after twelve days on the ship. Here we found friends who had sailed all the way from Brooklyn, N.Y. Some of the people here were from my old home in New York. Sam Brannan had fitted up a ship called the "Brooklyn." He was put in charge of a company of the Saints who traveled around Cape Horn down [*sic*] to San Francisco, and after arriving there he tried to induce President Brigham Young and associates to come to California, but he would never consent to this. One lady whom I met in San Francisco gave me and some other boy a calico shirt, as we were badly in need of them. We worked a few days in San Francisco to get a grub-stake to go to the mines. Went by steamboat up to Sacramento, and there met many friends. Here we engaged a team and took our mining tools out into the mines. On the 6th day of April, the day that the Conference convened in Salt Lake City, we had just reached the gold mines. We spent five months and four days making the trip from Salt Lake to our destination. We were not very successful at the mines and in the fall of 1850 we returned to Salt

[41]Pettit, *Biography of Edwin Pettit, 1834–1912*, 10–11.

> Lake. There were many who were discouraged, as they could not get any word from Salt Lake more than once a year. We went to Sacramento and bought two mules and fitted out for our return home, traveling by way of the Humboldt River—the northern route—in company with C. C. Rich and others. Crossing the desert we met a man who was selling water by the bucket. He had hauled the water out on the desert waiting for travelers to come along.[42]

In 1851 Pettit relocated with the Seelys to San Bernardino, but they were among the first to sell out and leave when Brigham Young recalled the Saints to the Great Basin six years later. Subsequently he spent many years as a teamster, driving freight wagons from Salt Lake to California, Montana, and elsewhere in the Intermountain West. He made his home in the Mormon capital, married in 1864, and raised a large family: ten girls and four boys. Pettit ended his autobiography, written after 1905, with a succinct retrospective statement about his life story that indicated the linkage in his mind between Mormon Utah and Mormon California.

> I have enjoyed the West. Have seen it under every condition, from the comparatively early days, and traversed it for the mere love of recreation. I finally settled in Salt Lake and made my home in the Fourteenth Ward for a short time, later moving to the present location, where I have spent the last forty years. I have crossed the desert between here and Los Angeles seventeen times by team and three times by rail. I am not only a Pioneer of 1847, but also of 1851, being one of those who went to fill the first mission in California.[43]

GEORGE W. HICKERSON: STILL LOOKING FOR THE MAIN PILE

Under the pressure of hard times in Great Salt Lake City, George Hickerson also signed on with the Pomeroy train. At age 36, he was somewhat older than most of the other Mormon teamsters, and he left behind a sick wife with young children. He probably relied on a senior church official, President Willard Richards, counselor and cousin to Brigham Young, to provide for his family during his absence, since Hickerson had an agreement that guaranteed Richards a share of his California mining profits.[44] These profits were not great. In 1850 a federal census taker found Hickerson, his brother Andrew, and his brother-in-

[42]Ibid., 13.

[43]Ibid., 22.

[44]Davies, *Mormon Gold,* 183.

law William Woolsey living in a mining camp named Louisville in El Dorado County, where they were identified as "gardeners" with $1,500 each in real estate.[45] Hickerson states that the three men were running a small store and boarding house at that time.

GEORGE WASHINGTON HICKERSON, FAMILY HISTORY, LDS ARCHIVES.

In the fall [1849] I started for California leaving my family in Great Salt Lake City and started in a train of old Pomroy, a gentile from Missouri on the 3rd of November. We traveled the southern route and on the 10 of March 1850 landed at Los Angeles, South California. Here four of us left the train in the premises and we walked on foot to the Mariposa Mine. Here we fell in company with several of the brethren from Salt Lake but being green miners and not striking gold by the shovel full we left and went prospecting and in this way spent the greater part of the summer.

In the fall I found myself on the Middle Fork of the American River. Here we might have done well if we had worked the banks, but we were still looking for the main pile but finally we began to work the banks and made a little money and in the month of October I had a severe spell of sickness. This used up the greater part of what I had made.

A little before I was taken sick my brother A. J. Hickerson came to me from Illinois and after my sickness he, myself and four others put our mites together, put up a house and kept goods and provisions and a boarding house. This we did until Spring when William Woolsey and myself sold out to the others and went out to Bear River and there kept a trading house until fall when we returned home on the 9th of October 1851.

In October 1850 Willard Richards deposited $202 in the church's gold accounts credited to Hickerson. After his return to Utah a year later, Hickerson opened a small store and started a farm at Kanosh, Utah. Following an interval as a missionary in Mississippi, Illinois, and Tennessee, he again settled in Kanosh and remained there until his death at age 71.[46]

SOLOMON CHAMBERLAIN: GOLD DIGGING WAS CRIED UP VERY MUCH

Solomon Chamberlain was one of the oldest Saints who ever ventured to the northern California placer diggings, and also one of the most dedicated church members to make this trip on his own, ignoring

[45]Ibid.

[46]Ibid., 184; and Hickerson, Family History, LDS Archives.

the counsel of church authorities. Like James Sly's account and some reports of the gold missionaries, Chamberlain's brief narrative of his placer mining experiences might also be taken as a cautionary tale for anyone who expected to find easy riches west of the Sierra Nevada.

Born in Connecticut in 1788 and orphaned at an early age, Chamberlain had learned the cooper's trade as a youth "and worked the most of my days at that." In his autobiography Chamberlain recalled that "till I was 19 years of age I lived a very wicked life." Then a series of visions shocked Chamberlain into repentance and led him to seek a religious faith consistent with his own developing beliefs. In time this search guided him to Joseph and Hyrum Smith in Palmyra, New York, where he gladly received instruction in *The Book of Mormon* and was baptized by Joseph Smith in April 1830, one of the first converts to the new religion.

Although he never attained a position of authority in the church, Chamberlain became an early missionary preacher for the LDS faith. He moved successively to Ohio and four different Missouri locations with the church, suffered physical attack and loss of property in the Missouri anti-Mormon persecutions, and relocated with his wife to Nauvoo. He joined the 1847 pioneer expedition that fixed on the Salt Lake Valley as the new LDS Zion, returned to Winter Quarters with Brigham Young, and prepared to make a permanent move to Utah the following spring. That winter his wife, "the wife of my youth," died, leaving Chamberlain totally bereft. "I said then," he wrote in 1858, "all my happiness as to the things of this world is gone, and so it has proved to this time."

Left with a young daughter as his only family, he traveled to Utah with Brigham Young in 1848, and perhaps first heard about the California gold discovery from Nathan Hawk on the overland trail that summer. His narrative gives no indication that he had any interest in California or its gold at that time, so we are left to imagine this aging, sorrowful, lonely Saint struggling to sustain himself and his daughter through the hardships experienced by all during the Utah colony's first years. Chamberlain describes almost casually his decision, apparently quite early in the 1850 traveling season, to make the journey to northern California. But very soon, as he relates, his lack of success in gold mining sent him home to Zion, again guided by a religious vision.

SOLOMON CHAMBERLAIN, A BRIEF SKETCH OF THE LIFE OF SOLOMON CHAMBERLAIN, HUNTINGTON LIBRARY.

Somewhere about the year 1850 I thought I would go to California as gold digging was cried up very much and get gold to make myself and family comfortable, as I was in poor circumstances. I accordingly went, the North Route, and made my stand this side of Sacramento on the Weber Creek. I went up this creek five miles and began to dig for gold. I made one dollar per day, but board was one dollar per meal in this place. The morning that I started out I found myself in the woods with but one mule to help me. I realized that if I stayed any longer I would have to sell my mule and live on the proceeds thereof. Digging was poor at this time, and the large streams were so high that there could be no digging on them for a month or more. I now thought I would ask the Lord what to do as I was alone and far from home. I knelt down and asked the Lord in faith what I should do. The voice of the Lord came unto me as plain as though a man spake, and said "If you will go home to your family you shall go in peace and nothing shall harm you."

I rose up and started with my one mule and left all I had, a chest of clothes and my rifle in a store, and said nothing to any man where I was going. I took the Lord at His word and put myself over the California mountains with no weapon but my pocket knife. This year the Indians were more troublesome than ever before or since. They were killing and being killed every night. I put my trust in God and in the power of the priesthood, and was carried safely through, although I came all the way alone—me and my one mule. So the Lord was a good as His word in bringing me safely through.[47]

THOMAS ORR, JR: POSSIBILITIES IN THE HOTEL BUSINESS

The parents of Scottish-born Thomas Orr had brought him from Glasgow to New York state as an infant. Successive moves in search of cheap land took the family to western Illinois near Nauvoo, where they joined the LDS church. Educated in Mormon schools, Thomas was thirteen years old when the Nauvoo Saints relocated to Winter Quarters.

[47]In addition to the Saints quoted in the foregoing sections, as future investigators will discover, at least three other LDS argonauts left a literary record of their California gold digging experience from 1849 to 1851. Moses Thatcher, a youngster in the gold fields, has a brief autobiographical statement in the Thatcher Family Papers, MS 22, Utah State University Library Special Collections. David Seely, the brother-in-law and older companion of Edwin Pettit, is the author of a manuscript autobiography found in the Bancroft Library. Henry Boyle's short account is in LDS Archives.

His father traded for cattle and took the family 125 miles upstream from the Missouri River refugee camps in fall 1846. The following spring they returned to Winter Quarters, where, Orr relates, "We found everyone there in a turmoil of excitement, making preparations to resume the overland trip to California." His father loaded a three-ox team with supplies for the trip, and they joined the westward movement, with Thomas Orr, Sr., serving as captain of the fifth "ten" in the second hundred of the main 1847 emigration under Edward Hunter, which reached Salt Lake at the end of September 1847.[48] Brigham Young, Orr recalled, acclaimed the place as Zion "and said no further progress of the caravan would be made that year if at all." The Orrs settled into the hard work of farm-making in a new country, becoming one of the first families to locate in Utah Valley, south of the Salt Lake. But, as Orr's account tells us, the family's desire to move on to California was not completely stifled by pronouncements from the church authorities.

This section of Orr's recollections describes the family's departure for California and a discovery of gold on the east side of the Sierra in 1850, while their company waited for the season to advance so they could take the Carson Pass Wagon Road to the Mother Lode region. Bill Prows, another Mormon Battalion veteran, later claimed to have made a first gold discovery in this area, near the extraordinarily rich Comstock Lode, while traveling to Salt Lake with the Ebenezer Brown company in 1848, but Orr's account is subject to a different interpretation. An exhaustive review of the evidence has led historian Will Bagley to conclude that the story of an 1848 discovery told by Prows, "if not an outright lie, could not possibly be true."[49] Their successful first experience with placer mining apparently encouraged father Orr and his sons to look forward to making their fortune in the gold fields of northern California.

---

[48]Carter, ed., *Heart Throbs of the West*, 8:424–27.

[49]Bagley, ed., *Frontiersman*, 134. As previously noted, Blackburn passed this way in spring 1849 and has a better claim to the distinction of first discovering gold in the vicinity of the Comstock. For an alternate viewpoint, see Townley, "Trail to the Comstock: An Accidental Bonanza," 22–30. William C. Prows had served in Company B, worked at Sutter's Fort, and mined at Mormon Island before joining the Ebenezer Brown company. After his return to California, Prows and his wife made their home on Dry Creek near Russian River in Mendocino County: Davies, *Mormon Gold*, 140. According to Norma Ricketts, he was one of thirty battalion veterans who later settled in Arizona. See *Mormon Battalion*, 23, 224, 328n4.

ORR, LIFE HISTORY OF THOMAS J. ORR, JR.,
PIONEER STORIES OF CALIFORNIA AND UTAH.

In the spring of '50 my brother, John, was anxious to proceed to California, the original objective. The gold discovery had been reported in Utah but there was little excitement among the Mormons as Brigham Young advised his followers to keep quiet and remain isolated from the Gentiles.

After much coaxing John finally prevailed on my father to make the trip, and with my mother, two brothers and two sisters, we started to California.

We left Provo and came to Salt Lake before the snow was off the ground and remained there until the grass began to grow. Thirty-five families joined our caravan to California and elected my father, Thomas Orr, as captain of the train.

Bill Prouse, who was working for General Sutter when gold was discovered at Coloma by J. W. Marshall, had gone back to Utah with pack animals to meet his folks. He said he was familiar with all the stopping places on the emigrant trail and after joining our train was made pilot. . . .

[*Omitted are details of the trip from Ogden to the Humboldt River and across the Forty-mile Desert.*]

We finally got across the desert and came to the Carson River. This river makes a bend around a desert twelve miles across and we reached the edge about noon. The locality is called Gold Canyon now, and is west of Virginia City. Prouse said the country there strongly resembled the California gold fields and a few of us went down with shovel and pan and dug a little pot hole the size of a post-hole and panned out two or three pans of dirt. Every pan showed color and we brought the gold for father's inspection. He was not much impressed with the find, so after our stock had a good feed on grass, we ate our lunch and started across the twelve-mile desert to avoid following the tortuous course of the river, out of our way a good many more miles. We came up with the Carson River again at dusk after a weary half-days journey and unyoked our oxen to feed. This location was later called Empire City. We stayed there all night and in the morning when we gathered the stock up to start out we discovered one horse missing and looked for it everywhere but to no avail until somebody saw it down in a whirlpool, floating around. It had fallen over a twenty-foot cliff and broke its neck.

Instead of going to where Carson City is now located, we cut across to Carson Canyon toward the Sierra Nevada range of mountains.

Half way across the plains below Carson we met three Indians going that way and they told us the oxen could cross the mountain but the snow was too deep for the wagons. We drove on to a little creek, with fine bottom land and stopped at a place near Lake Tahoe, now called Genoa. We were there three weeks waiting for the snow to disappear from the mountains. Some of us went up a canyon and felled trees. We used the poles in making a cor-

> duroy road across a creek and in other places bridges would be constructed by men in our company.
>
> My brother John, accompanied by men named Bill Prouse and Nick Kelly returned to prospect the place where Prouse had made a find of gold.[50] My brother was lucky in the first hole, panning out a nugget which later showed a value of $8.25. This was the first piece of gold ever found on that side of the mountains and my brother's sons living in Sonoma County, still possess this nugget, which has been handed down to them. . . .
>
> After this delay we left Mormon Station (now Genoa) and heard that the men ahead of us were exacting a toll from travelers on the three bridges we had built across the Carson River. When we arrived at that point, we put an end to that practice and left the bridges open for the travelers following us.
>
> We got into Hope Valley, followed up a canyon and camped over night. The next day we started out and had a time to get over the next summit. We bucked snow all day in getting up the grade and camped on the summit. The next morning we started down, negotiating snowbanks twenty feet deep. We could hear the water running beneath. We rough-locked the hind wheels of the wagons, took the lead cattle off and chained them to the hind wheels in order to hold back. That day we passed out of the snow belt and then followed the '49 [1848] trail to Leak Springs and came on through Sly Park to Pleasant Valley and arrived there the Fourth of July, 1850. The next day we continued on to Diamond Springs. The first man we saw this side of the summit was at Ringgold where he had a small trading post.[51]

Because the Orr family traveled together to California, we can infer that they intended from the start to make their home outside the Great Basin. The autobiographical statement of the younger Thomas Orr describes a process of settlement in northern California that moved them through the gold rush era into a subsequent period of commercial and agricultural development, without ever a thought about returning to Brigham Young's Zion. Incidentally, the younger Orr confirms the presence of Orrin Porter Rockwell in northern California during the height of the gold rush. After he guided Amasa Lyman's party to the gold country early in 1849, Rockwell had briefly tried his hand at placer mining, then found a surer method to make money. With various partners he opened saloon and hotel businesses at Murderer's Bar, Buckeye Flat, and

[50]George Kelley had served in the battalion's Company A and returned to Salt Lake in the Holmes-Thompson company in 1848. See Ricketts, *Mormon Battalion*, 28, 222.

[51]Ringgold was located in a narrow valley alongside Weber Creek west of Placerville, downstream from the Weberville site where Big Cut Road today crosses the stream. It was a small mining camp and trading center in 1850. Often flooded, the entire district has reverted to rough pasturage.

a roadhouse midway between the newly platted town of Sacramento and Mormon Island. This last establishment, known as the Halfway House, became his headquarters for nearly two years. He supplied these enterprises by running pack trains that hauled whiskey from Sacramento. Rockwell attempted to keep his true identity hidden, so far as possible, because his old enemy, former Missouri governor Lilburn Boggs, had also come to California and taken up residence in Sonoma, where he was elected as alcalde, the main municipal officer. Because he thought Boggs might take the first opportunity to have him ambushed, Rockwell not only assumed a different name but was constantly armed and had a guard dog always on the alert at his side.[52]

ORR, LIFE HISTORY OF THOMAS J. ORR, JR.,
PIONEER STORIES OF CALIFORNIA AND UTAH.

When we got to Shingle Springs we saw a man at a place above the present Planters House splitting shakes to build a cabin. We went on to Deer Creek. A man was keeping a trading post there and father had known him in Illinois and at Salt Lake. Father recognized him and called him by name, Porter Rockwell. He was alarmed and told father to call him Brown in the future because he was one of Brigham Young's destroying angels and his life wouldn't be worth much if people discovered his real identity. Father asked Brown where he thought the best place to settle and was told it was no use going further and that place was as good as any to locate.

In those days the underbrush of the present time was conspicuous by its absence and there were no annoying small ravines or washouts. One could cross the country almost any place. Big timber was found at every hand.

Father decided to profit by Brown's suggestion and turned around and went back half a mile in an open country where the feed was plentiful for our stock. We camped there three weeks and at the end of that time our train began to disintegrate and scattered in all directions.

Father and my oldest brother, John, went to Salmon Falls and met two old mountaineers. They had pitched a tent on New York Ravine and were keeping a trading post. Their biggest sales were in provisions and whiskey. Father took a liking to the place and made an offer of $500 for their two quarter sections secured by them on a squatters' right, and the deal was made.

About the time father went to Salmon Falls my brothers, James and John, secured a string of horses and established a stage line from Sacramento to

[52]Schindler, *Orrin Porter Rockwell,* 186–88, relates this chapter in Rockwell's colorful career. The establishment at Buckeye Flat, a mining camp a mile east of Shingle Springs, is noted in Cross, *The Early Inns of California,* 212. Cross states that the hotel at Buckeye Flat was kept by Peter King Rockwell, "a Salt Lake City man," who undoubtedly was Orrin Porter Rockwell's brother.

Marysville in competition with the California Stage Company and after running it for four years at good profits they sold out to Billy Hamilton.

In 1851 I met Sam Brannon in Sacramento. He and father were intimate friends in Illinois and at the time we started our overland trip, Brannon chose the water route and came around the Horn and arrived in California several years ahead of us.[53] He established a paper in San Francisco in 1846 and was considered one of the founders of the city.

After father had bought the place at New York Ravine we moved there from Deer Creek, and were accompanied by two or three families. We started the road from the old emigrant trail to Green Springs on the Coloma Road.

We started mining at Mormon Island and father rented the post at New York Ravine to McFarland. When we arrived in this country, men were mining up the American River from Mormon Island. Placerville had but a few tents and log cabins and was first known as Ravine City and then later Hangtown.

Father saw the possibilities in the hotel business and rented a hotel at Salmon Falls and added a log cabin to accommodate guests. He served the general traveling public with meals, costing $1 each. Mother secured some dried apples, which had been shipped across the Isthmus of Panama and made apple pies, which readily brought from $1 to $1.50 each. Barley sold for 25 cents a pound and hay cost $1 for a night's feed. Whiskey sold for 25 cents a drink. We had brought a dozen chickens with us from Salt Lake, carrying them in a coop, and they proved gold getters. Egg-nog sold for 50 cents and milk punch the same. Cigars sold for several dollars each and they were poor weeds at that. Nothing sold for less than two bits.

Father kept the hotel business running for two years and during that time brother John started mining, the popular diversion. Later he was put up for deputy sheriff with Henry Larkin and served in that capacity under Sheriff Dave Buell. I devoted most of my time upon arriving in California to freighting.

Our family raised the first barley in El Dorado County, planting out the seed in 1851 which we had brought with us.

The mining excitement was intense, and thousands of men were going up the Georgetown way.

The money used was Mexican silver quarters and half dollars and $50 and $10 gold slugs, but the principal medium of exchange was gold dust.

After father had gotten well established in the hotel and bakery business at Salmon Falls he bought the property from Henry Larkin for a consideration of $2,500. We had the only bakery, store, hotel and feed stable in

[53]No known contemporary source indisputably documents Brannan's presence at Nauvoo until his brief visit in May 1845, but Orr's comment supports the circumstantial evidence that Brannan lived in the settlement for a time in 1839 or the early 1840s.

town and made money rapidly. There were days when we would take in from $1,000 to $1,500.

It was an unwritten law of the country that if any man came around the Horn, across the plains or Isthmus he was to be grubstaked by the ones who had prospered and by this avenue father spent $85,000 in the twelve years he was in business, loaning money to miners, feeding the new arrivals and grubstaking them, and he never so much as received one penny in return.

Father rented the Salmon Falls business to the McKenzie boys, residents of French Creek now, and started farming at New York Ravine and I went back with him. James got married and took up a ranch nearby, devoting his time to farming.

Brother James and myself bought a threshing machine which we sold and later purchased the Georgetown stage line, operating it for eight years. I was one of the drivers on this line and our equipment consisted of four horses from Folsom to Georgetown and four more from Auburn to Georgetown. While in this service, James was twice held up by highwaymen.

Deciding to quit the stage business in 1869 upon my marriage to Margaret Walker in Auburn, we moved to Salmon Falls and engaged in farming; my five sons and two daughters being born on the old ranch there.

At one time father owned controlling interest in the Natomas ditch. Livermore, one of the promoters, wanted more shares for control, and we sold out to acquire more land adjoining our place.[54] We pre-empted one quarter section, homesteaded an additional quarter section, giving us 1340 acres all together.

We built a fine $7000.00 home and piped nice spring water to it, making everything as modern as possible. Reverses, however, began with a fire which completely destroyed the home. We mortgaged the place and rebuilt and later were compelled to forfeit, when unable to redeem the mortgage.

One of my last ventures was in the threshing business and I was inveigled into buying an expensive machine exhibited at the Fair. I still have the machine stored away in a shed next to my hotel, disabled when the boiler blew up and at one time I was offered $100.00 for it and rejected the offer, an action which I now regret. There isn't the grain in the county now as in the old days and I am afraid I shall never find a purchaser for the machine.

Along with his mining claim at Mormon Island and his hotel business nearby at Salmon Falls, his son relates, the senior Thomas Orr established a homestead above Salmon Falls on the road to Mormon Island,

[54]Horace Livermore was a partner in the Natomas Company and later a leading developer of the hydroelectric industry in northern California. His company built the first hydroelectric plant on the American River at Folsom and established a long-distance transmission line that carried the power to Sacramento. A Sacramento resident, he also was involved in real estate development and the city's first electrified trolley car system.

an area that came to be known as Mormon Hill. The family welcomed traveling missionaries and became principal leaders in a well-known LDS community in the Salmon Falls district. The Orr clan remained affiliated with the LDS church as long as the church was active in California.

Even considering the July 1850 report of Amasa Lyman and Charles C. Rich to Brigham Young, northern California Mormons of the gold rush era should not generally be categorized as fallen Saints. The widely varied nature of their experiences, while an immense mass migration was transforming the state, perhaps made it awkward to fulfill all their faith's requirements in California's chaotic gold rush society. Emphatically secular, bawdily immoral, frequently rebellious against authority in any form, life in California's gold camps was indeed, as Brigham Young declared, a polar opposite to the respectful and righteous ways Young intended for the faithful. In the gaudy, hastily built and easily destroyed canvas and wood boomtowns that sprang up to serve the miners, where commercialized sin was an essential growth industry and chance ruled all, an orderly faith-based social system was not easily sustained. Yet many observant Saints found it possible to live well and virtuously in California, at least for a season or two, without being swept from their religious and cultural moorings by worldly temptations.

For the most part, battalion veterans, *Brooklyn* Saints, and LDS sojourners who came to seek their fortunes in northern California successfully fashioned in this region a cultural and religious middle ground. For every one who went the way of Samuel Brannan into unrestrained self-indulgence, dozens remained true to their religion and its social and moral teachings. They lived as Mormon Californians without adopting the prevailing gold rush code of riotous excess. And in part they kept their faith, one may suppose, because leaders among the Latter-day Saints in the mid-nineteenth century at times demonstrated a practiced ability to tolerate behavior at odds with the church-mandated ideal.

Although California Saints were little governed by the institutions of church discipline and theocratic management which reigned in Utah, they tended naturally to maintain close ties with friends and family that fortified their sense of membership in a community of believers. These ties were further reinforced by a dense web of written and oral communication that linked California Saints with Utah and other locations, where loved ones were waiting to hear from them. Perhaps because of its New England roots, Mormon culture in mid-nineteenth century America retained an exceptional emphasis on written communication. A blessing for historians, the customary abundance of journals, diaries, letters, and other family records in LDS households further emphasized the bonds of family and friendship that sustained the Mormon value system for those who ranged far from home. Strong inner faith, association with fellow Saints, and continuing contacts with distant LDS family members and friends all helped restrain backsliding or apostasy among church members in gold rush California.

No one has yet compiled a record of apostasy among California Saints during the gold rush years.[55] Although Brigham Young might have disagreed, a reading of a great many contemporary documents and the few listings that account for the later careers of the gold rush Saints points toward an impressionistic conclusion that it was relatively uncommon for LDS church members to abjure their religion even in the gold fields. The documentary record may not give a fair picture, for these materials reflect primarily the literary output of observant church members, not apostates. Further, church leaders in Utah effectively abandoned California after 1857—terminating ties with those who did not heed the church presidency's recall to Zion—and ended missionary activities in California for more than thirty years. Nonetheless, even taking these circumstances into account, overall the enduring faith of the California Saints is impressive.

Whether they stayed for a few months, a few years, or for life, a good many California Saints of the gold rush era found it possible to be both Mormons and Californians. No matter their successes or failures in money making, they did not need to forsake their religion and its moral teachings during their time in the golden state. And for the families who remained in the gold country past the 1850s, like the Orrs, it might later seem that they did not leave the church, but that the church had left them.

---

[55]Using Larsen, ed., *A Data Base of the Mormon Battalion*, historian Edward Leo Lyman has tallied sixty-one veterans who remained or returned to the Pacific Coast to reside, while fifty-five others lived out their lives in states east of the Great Basin. No further information can be found for another twenty-five, and so they presumably abandoned Mormon country. While 324 of the total veterans remained within the centers of church influence, from Arizona to Idaho, Lyman observes, "the number that left Zion was almost a third of the march's survivors." Lyman, *San Bernardino*, 86–87n2. These data, of course, tell us nothing certain about faith or church membership. No similar investigation has been undertaken for the *Brooklyn* Saints or for the Utah church members who are known to have gone to the gold fields.

Chapter 8

"To Defend Yourselves Against All Our Foes"
The LDS Reformation, the Utah Way, and the Summons to Zion

By the mid-1850s the California gold rush was over.[1] Although gold mining was still the basis for the new state's economy, the heyday of independent, small-scale placer mining—poor people's mining—had passed by 1853. Placer mining accounted for an estimated contemporary value of $10.1 million in 1849, $41.3 million in 1850, $75.9 million in 1851, and $81.3 million in 1852. Mining returns declined substantially over the next three years but leveled off to the range of $43 million to $41.8 million between 1857 and 1861. By 1865, when hard rock mining had started to rival the production from placer mining, California's gold output fell to $17.9 million and held steady in that range for the next decade.[2] New methods for working placer deposits, like riverbed,

[1]Overland immigration boomed in 1849, peaked in 1850, then fell away to no more than a few hundred travelers in 1851 due to public reports about 1850's disasterous trail experiences. When it renewed with another surge in 1852, the demographic character of the overland companies had changed to a much more family-based movement. Rather than the gold-rush sojourners of 1849–1850, the newcomers often intended to relocate permanently and fashion an enduring life in the golden state. For those who could afford a quicker passage than the arduous overland routes, especially from the eastern seaboard and overseas, sailing ships and steamships offered an attractive alternative. Although we lack an exact statistical record of maritime travel, only about one-third of those bound for the West Coast between 1849 and 1860 came by way of South Pass, and historians commonly agree that a far larger proportion of the post-gold rush movement out of California was carried aboard ship. See Unruh, *The Plains Across*, 119, 401. The federal census counted California's population at 223,000 in 1850 and 308,000 ten years later, but the scholarly consensus is that the state's population peaked at about a half million in the early 1850s, before an outmigration of gold-rush sojourners reduced it to the 1860 total. Since that time, California has been the only state in the Union to record a population growth rate higher than the national average during each succeeding decade.

[2]Paul, *California Gold*, Appendix A, 345–48, provides the most authoritative record of gold production and discusses the statistical problems with this record.

SAN BERNARDINO IN 1857
This view shows the southern California LDS colony shortly before Brigham Young called on its Mormon settlers to return to Utah.
Courtesy LDS Archives.

hydraulic, and drift mining, placed a premium on cooperative efforts, requiring substantial investments for equipment and the labor needed to work large amounts of gold-bearing gravel with efficiency. Dredge mining experiments pointed the way toward still greater improvements in recovering free gold from deeper and more elusive placer deposits.[3]

Alongside mining, farming and livestock ranching were becoming the state's foremost industries. San Francisco, with a good many LDS entrepreneurs involved in its business affairs, had emerged as California's premier commercial metropolis and the principal American seaport on the Pacific Coast. The inland river cities Sacramento, Stockton, and Marysville served as mercantile and social centers for both the gold country and the developing agricultural districts of California's Central Valley.

In a real sense, the Mormon gold rush came to a definitive end in February 1853, when the church presidency issued its general epistle coun-

[3]Ibid., 124–70, provides a classic description of this transition. A skillfully detailed account of the development of placer technology is Spence, "From Gold Pans to California Dredges: The Search for Mass Production in Placer Mining," in Owens, ed., *Riches for All,* 296–316.

seling all Saints not to go to California unless under church direction. From this point forward, gold country Mormons were subject to a presumption on the part of their Utah brethren that by remaining in northern California they were in defiance of the LDS authorities. Moreover, as President Young had clearly stated, they were ostensibly placing in peril their salvation and eternal blessings. Church-approved alternatives were few. They could gather in Zion; or, less propitiously, they might move south to join the San Bernardino colony.[4] In either case, spiritual duty and conformity required observant Saints to follow the guidance of church leaders and the discipline of LDS institutions. In northern California, even in San Francisco where a framework of church organization survived frequent leadership changes, the substance of theocracy was lacking in the homes and community gathering places of the gold rush Saints. Clearly, those who remained after 1853 had determined to guide their public and private lives by imperatives separate from those which ruled in Zion.

Although seldom discussed, the doctrine of plural marriage and its practice were central to the differences between northern California Saints and Utah church members. By the time Brigham Young's vanguard company reached the Salt Lake Valley, this doctrine had become a matter of LDS orthodoxy, not publicly acknowledged until 1852 but openly practiced since at least 1847. Under church auspices, during the pioneer era plural marriage became integral to LDS society in the Great Basin. Few, if any, long-term northern California Saints advocated polygamy, and there is no documentary record of anyone arranging to take more than one wife while they remained in the gold country or its environs.[5]

[4]The San Bernardino Saints, like those in northern California, were also counseled to abandon California and gather in Zion in 1857. This directive came at a critical point in the life of that community, when land titles were being challenged and a strong anti-Mormon faction led by apostates was disputing LDS leadership in local politics. According to Leo Lyman's excellent history of the LDS experience in San Bernardino, "almost one-third of those who had once embraced Mormonism would choose to remain in the comfortable and prosperous location even though they would no longer associate with the church." Eventually some of these lingering Saints found a spiritual home in the Reorganized Church of Jesus Christ of Latter-day Saints, now the Community of Christ. Based in Missouri, the RLDS church had no allegiance to Brigham Young and rejected the doctrine of plural marriage. See Lyman, *San Bernardino: The Rise and Fall of a California Community*, 371. Others who remained in San Bernardino, like Abner Blackburn, joined long-established Protestant denominations. The broad historical outlines of polygamy as a political issue are fully discussed in the prize-winning study by Susan Barringer Gordon, *The Mormon Question: Polygamy and Constitutional Conflict in Nineteenth Century America*.

[5]In addition to local resistance in California, every plural marriage had to be performed by proper ecclesiastical authority, which was not present in northern California. Once permission was given, these marriages were usually solemnized in the Endowment House in Salt Lake or by Brigham Young in his offices.

Although polygamy violated California's common law legal code adopted in 1850, the issue was not simply a matter of law. The institution, so greatly at odds with mainstream Protestant custom and belief, simply failed to gain acceptance among California Saints. Polygamous husbands prominent in the church, like Amasa Lyman and Charles C. Rich, lived for a time in the San Bernardino LDS colony with more than one wife, but they kept their domestic arrangements in low profile.[6] Capt. Jefferson Hunt, another practitioner of "the principle," as it was called in LDS circles, served successive terms in the upper house of the California state legislature as a senator from the San Bernardino district; apparently his marital situation never occasioned public comment. Until the LDS theocracy's spectacularly unique system of belief and social policy emerged in the full light of national political controversy in 1857 and 1858, plural marriage was seldom a subject for discussion even in the private journals and letters of California Mormons. Through the 1850s, however, it clearly continued to be a sticking point among church members in the golden state. Like questions of hierarchical authority, differing viewpoints and beliefs about the practice of polygamy could fray the spiritual ties linking northern California Saints with their families, friends, and co-religionists in Utah. When they were directed to leave Babylon and hurry to Zion in 1857, plural marriage was still a troublesome issue as LDS families decided whether to go or stay.

Nelson Slater: Indignant at the Treatment They Received

As the flush times of the gold rush faded, northern California Saints were left largely on their own, beyond the range of church concern. The brethren in Utah did not entirely share their interests. The treatment that Great Basin Mormons had accorded some non-Mormon gold rush visitors to the City of the Saints had aggravated these differences and

[6]At San Bernardino, Amasa Lyman's brother-in-law, J. Henry Rollins, worried about his own marital situation with two wives who had both recently given birth to sons and about Lyman's more visible polygamous household. "I do not consider any man safe here," Rollins wrote Lyman, "who has more than one wife." Rollins to Lyman, 3 June 1856, in Lyman, *San Bernardino*, 334. Rollins was undoubtedly correct, states author Lyman, in assuming that public notice of polygamy on the part of an established California resident would have caused trouble for all the San Bernardino Saints.

brought Utah to the brink of serious conflict and even armed confrontation with the national government. In consequence, the Saints of northern California were compelled to make a hard choice between their loyalty to the Salt Lake hierarchy and the lives they had fashioned for themselves in the gold regions largely independent of church direction.

The impact of the California gold rush on the LDS church and people in Utah has been carefully examined by scholars, most recently and most fully by the distinguished historian Brigham D. Madsen, professor emeritus at the University of Utah. In 1849 and 1850, Madsen concludes, despite a few recorded incidents of sharp dealing by avaricious individuals, overall "the Mormon pioneers were generous and just in their treatment of the exhausted wayfarers."[7] The record is more controversial, he also relates, in evaluating LDS relations with the gold rush travelers who wintered over in the Mormon settlements during 1849–1850 and 1850–1851 before going on to the Pacific Coast. These sojourners found themselves subject to a government that operated under religious authority, with property taxes levied and collected by church-designated officials and with local courts and juries staffed by church members only. While Brigham Young preached against "swearing & other profane and such like immoral practices," according to common report these outsiders heard the national government damned and damned again by LDS leaders. Church authorities, witnesses stated, frequently denounced the federal administration and declared that the U.S. government should be overthrown. Prominent Saints, according to the same witnesses, asserted that LDS officials were collecting military supplies in preparation for a possible war against the United States.[8]

[7]Madsen, *Gold Rush Sojourners in Great Salt Lake City*, 79. A first extensive investigation of the economic ramifications of the gold rush in Utah is in Arrington, *Great Basin Kingdom*, 64–84, where Professor Arrington connects the gold rush "Harvest of '49" with subsequent LDS colonization efforts throughout the Great Basin and in southern California.

[8]Madsen, *Gold Rush Sojourners*, 120–21. These disloyal statements reflected both grievances fondly nurtured by LDS loyalists for past mistreatment at the hands of the national government and conflict over the issue of independent statehood for the Saints' Great Basin realm. In March 1849, by direction of Brigham Young, the Saints formed the State of Deseret, which remained in nominal operation until February 1851. Congress did not admit Deseret to the Union, of course, but instead formed Utah Territory under the Compromise of 1850 as a federal dependency, with the new government being initiated on 3 February 1851. Since Gov. Brigham Young of Deseret became the first governor of Utah Territory by presidential appointment, the effective authority did not change with this transition. Once the change took effect, the streams of anti-federal political invective in Utah dwindled for a few seasons.

In contrast to this hostile reaction, Mormon missionaries worked to convert the travelers with enough success to alarm some strong adherents to other creeds.[9] Most gold rush sojourners who wintered in Salt Lake, declares Professor Madsen, left with "a heritage of friendship and good feelings between the Saints and the majority of visitors."[10] But more than a few gold rushers who arrived in the Salt Lake Valley too late in the summer of 1850 to continue to the coast were outraged when they departed in 1851. These involuntary visitors in the city of the Saints expressed great anger against the Mormons for the mistreatment they felt they had experienced. Missionary Alvin Thompson Smith spoke with several such witnesses, including one who intended to take his case to the government.

> The emigrants this year have come in with less trouble than usual with the exception of a few of them who had trouble with the Snake Indians. Last year quite a number were obliged to winter at Salt Lake with the Mormons who treated them very harshly. Several who have got in have staid with us over night. The account they give of the Mormons is truly horrible. A gentleman put up with us last night who is a lawyer by profession who spent the winter with them who has developed more of their wickedness than any other individual. He but just escaped with his life. He tells of one young man a Dr who was a man of fine talents whom thay [*sic*] shot down without any provocation.[11] A great many facts which he related which I have not time to write he has written or is calculating to soon and inform our government of these facts. I know noι how these things will end. They [the Saints] may be considered a scourge where ever they go.[12]

Three other visitors left Utah early in 1851 with a searing sense of

[9]Among these travelers were some conversions of convenience. "Winter Mormons" joined the church, married women of the congregation, and enjoyed the benefits of LDS fellowship and the comforts of the marriage bed. But they abjured the religion and left for the California mines when the trails opened in the spring, many leaving behind a disillusioned bride and her aggrieved family.

[10]Madsen, *Gold Rush Sojourners*, 125. Professor Madsen attributes the criticisms of Langworthy, Goodell, and Slater, the "three principal reporters of alleged Mormon wrongdoing," to their mutual abhorrence of polygamy. Yet he also fully and fairly describes the other detailed complaints these authors made against their treatment and the evidence they provided to substantiate their charges.

[11]Madison Hambleton shot "Physician and Oculist" James M. Vaughn on 9 February 1851 in broad daylight after a church service at Manti, Utah, claiming Vaughn had seduced his wife. At a hearing the next month before the Supreme Court of Deseret, Brigham Young pronounced Hambleton justified. See Bigler, ed., *A Winter with the Mormons*, 74–75, 82–83.

[12]Thompson to Dear Brother & Sister, 20 October 1851, Alvin Thompson Smith Missionary Letters, Beinecke Library.

injustice over abuses they and fellow travelers had suffered and resolved to publish their experiences before the world. These three—Franklin Langworthy, Jotham W. Goodell, and Nelson Slater—found different outlets for their critical revelations about life as a gentile in Zion. In 1855 Langworthy, a Universalist preacher from Illinois, had a New York bookseller publish his 1850 travel diary, to which he added a stinging attack on LDS theology and a lengthy analysis of the Saints' disloyal activities against the U.S. government.[13] Goodell, a deeply religious Presbyterian minister, was on his way from northern Ohio to Oregon with his family when he decided to stay the winter in the city of the Saints. After making his escape the following spring, impoverished and angry, he dispatched nine letters to the Portland *Oregonian* newspaper that were published between April and June 1852.[14]

The third of these irate sojourners, Nelson Slater, was a seminary teacher from New York State also traveling with his family. Like Goodell, Slater originally intended to set down his embittered complaints against the Utah Saints in letter form for newspaper publication. Once he reached Carson Valley, however, he compared stories with other emigrants camping there who also felt they had been abused by Brigham Young's followers during their stay in Zion. Consequently Slater became the author of a work titled *Fruits of Mormonism* that described the tribulations and encapsulated the complaints of these aggrieved travelers. Published as a pamphlet of ninety-five pages, Slater's highly colored, sensationalist account was printed at Coloma later in 1851.[15] This excerpt from Slater's conclusion succinctly states the case that he and his outraged collaborators hoped to make as a political appeal to their friends, to all American citizens, and to the government of the United States.

---

[13]Langworthy, *Scenery of the Plains, Mountains, and Mines; or a Diary Kept Upon the Overland Route to California.*

[14]After lapsing into obscurity, Goodell's letters have recently been republished in a carefully prepared edition under the skilled editorship of David L. Bigler as *A Winter with the Mormons: The 1852 Letters of Jotham Goodell.* I am indebted to Bigler's work for much of my information not only about Goodell, but also about Langworthy and Slater.

[15]Slater, *Fruits of Mormonism: A Fair and Candid Statement of Facts Illustrative of Mormon Principles, Mormon Policy, and Mormon Character By More Than Forty Eye-Witnesses.* As noted by Gary F. Kurutz in his magisterial study of California gold rush literature, Slater's slender volume, a "bitter publication," was the first book entered for copyright in California. See *The California Gold Rush: A Descriptive Bibliography of Books and Pamphlets Covering the Years 1848–1853,* item 585, page 598.

N. SLATER, A.M., COMP.,
FRUITS OF MORMONISM, OR A FAIR AND CANDID STATEMENT OF FACTS ILLUSTRATIVE OF MORMON PRINCIPLES, MORMON POLICY, AND MORMON CHARACTER, BY MORE THAN FORTY EYE-WITNESSES, 95.

If it can in truth be shown that the principles, the policy, and the practices of the mormon people, as developed and enforced by its leaders, are not as bad as represented, we should be glad of it. But we believe we have given a fair representation of the legitimate Fruits of Mormonism, as exhibited in Salt Lake valley.

The emigrants are indignant at the treatment they received from the mormons this past winter and spring, and feel in duty bound to protest against such conduct towards United States citizens while passing through Utah territory. That their situations should be made uncomfortable, and almost intolerable, by abridging their rights of speech, by examining and destroying their letters deposited in the U.S. mail to be sent to their friends in the states, unlawfully taxing their property, threatening their lives, &c. &c., whilst the emigrants were peaceable, quiet, and law-abiding, was wanton and most iniquitous on the part of the mormons. It was a violation alike of the laws of hospitality and humanity.

We appeal to our friends in the states, to all United States citizens, and to Congress. We ask our government to protect its citizens in the exercise and enjoyment of their just rights and privileges in Utah territory against arbitrary and injurious encroachment.

The polemical writings of Langworthy, Goodell, and Slater had profound consequences.[16] More than any other events, the publication of these attacks on the LDS church and its hierarchy began a nationwide public debate about Mormon beliefs and practices. The discussion intensified due to the political circumstances in 1856, when the newly formed Republican Party established a national platform and nominated its first candidate for president. The LDS hierarchy, dissatisfied with Utah's territorial status, early in the year sent apostles John Taylor and George A. Smith to the U.S. capital with a proposed state constitu-

[16]For a well-informed discussion of the biases evident in Goodell's writing, see Ronald O. Barney's review of Goodell's letters in *Journal of Mormon History* (Fall 2002), 245–49. Goodell, however, noted that in Ohio he had denounced the expulsion of the Mormons from Nauvoo as "impolitic and unjust" and called Joseph Smith "truly a murdered man." In a further explanation, he stated "I make this remark that the reader may understand that I did not go into the valley with my mind overcharged with prejudice against the Mormons—that I was neither an actor nor sympathizer with those who drove them from Jackson county or Nauvoo." Goodell arrived in Utah believing "there was much exaggeration, if not misrepresentation" about Mormonism. His subsequent anger was born of experience. See Bigler, ed., *A Winter with the Mormons,* 61–62.

tion, seeking admission to the Union. Sen. Stephen A. Douglas of Illinois, a leading Democrat presidential hopeful and long-time friend of the Saints, convinced these Utah statehood advocates to wait until his popular sovereignty argument gained electoral endorsement, but merely their appearance in the national capital with a Mormon-written constitution was enough to set off a wave of newspaper comment.

Anti-slavery Republicans throughout the northern states immediately seized on the Mormon issue, seeking to broaden their base of political support by linking plural marriage in Utah with the threatened extension of black racial servitude into new western territories. Pressing the case for federal action, the 1856 Republican platform asserted "the right and imperative duty of Congress to prohibit in the territories those twin relics of barbarism—polygamy and slavery." To complete the anti-Mormon emphasis, the Republican convention named the former LDS antagonist John Charles Frémont of California as its presidential standard bearer.[17]

While Frémont's supporters chanted the slogan "free land, free soil, and free men," the 1856 presidential campaign focused mainly on the extension of slavery into the territories and the violent conflict between pro-slavery and anti-slavery forces in "Bleeding Kansas." By comparison, the controversy over LDS beliefs and practices in Utah was minor. Yet the subjects of polygamy and LDS theocracy continued to receive attention, particularly in the Republican press. As a result, a distinct anti-Mormon political faction, composed of New England and Midwestern Republicans, emerged in the nation's capital. Led by Sen. Justin Morrill of Vermont, this loosely organized group subsequently made its influence felt in Congress as the Democratic Party fractured over the slavery issue and lost its long-held majority power.

---

[17]Lyman, *Political Deliverance: The Mormon Quest for Utah Statehood,* 7–9, describes the LDS appeal for statehood in 1856. A general account of the 1856 election, magisterial in style and substance, is found in Allan Nevins, *Ordeal of the Union,* Volume II, *A House Dividing, 1852–1857,* 451–514. Frémont's role in the presidential contest is well covered in Rolle, *John Charles Frémont, Character as Destiny,* 162–77. Ironically, Frémont had his own issues of religious bigotry to contend against, since he had been raised in the Roman Catholic faith, was married to Jesse Benton by a Catholic priest, and reportedly had been observed making the sign of the cross while in Washington's Roman Catholic cathedral. His political handlers were able to make a persuasive case that he was in fact an Episcopalian, yet the issue had great resonance in the 1856 campaign. Still more ironic, in view of LDS arguments that polygamy strengthened domestic virtue, Frémont's Republican sponsors paid for an abortion and purchased the silence of a "servant girl," with whom the candidate had engaged in "disreputable conduct." This would not be the last case of his philandering.

The first sharp federal challenge to LDS church authorities, however, came not from Republicans but from James Buchanan, the successful Democratic presidential candidate in 1856. Mormonism received virtually no attention in Buchanan's campaign, but once in office, surprisingly, the new chief executive gave ear to a claque of embittered federal officeholders who had left Utah in 1856 and early 1857 full of threats against the LDS hierarchy. Making virtually no effort to weigh the merits of their complaints, Buchanan appointed a new territorial governor to replace Brigham Young—a customary procedure with every public office when a new administration took over during this era of political patronage and a party-based spoils system. To be certain his appointee would be able to enter into his duties, the president—acting through Sec. of War John B. Floyd, a fervent anti-Mormon—directed Brig. Gen. William S. Harney to lead a special force of 2,500 U.S. troops as an escort for the new governor from Ft. Leavenworth to Utah. This command, with Col. Albert S. Johnston replacing Harney in September 1857, also had instructions to ensure the enforcement of federal laws in the kingdom of the Saints. Buchanan compounded the possibility for conflict, as Brigham Young soon complained in defense of his own belligerent actions, by failing to notify Young officially that he was being replaced. As one scholar sums up the case, "In this fumbling fashion—swayed by public opinion, the correspondence of territorial officials, and other pressures—the Administration in 1857 finally groped its way to the conclusion that the Mormon people were in revolt against the United States."[18]

Brigham Young and his counselors determined to rally the people of Zion to battle what they viewed as an unwarranted and illegitimate federal invasion. To counter anti-Mormon arguments and influence American public opinion on behalf of their religion and their political position, they also set in motion what we might today call a public-relations campaign. They intended to justify LDS beliefs and practices, plural marriage in particular, and to sustain their political rights. Like the intransigent defenders of slavery in the southern states, they based their arguments on constitutional doctrines that favored local authority

[18]Furniss, *The Mormon Conflict,* 93. Buchanan's first appointee as governor declined the post, Furniss points out, and a replacement—Alfred Cumming of Georgia—did not accept the position until July. As he issued orders for the Utah Expedition in late May, however, Gen. Winfield Scott had noted that it was already too late for the army to reach Utah before winter set in.

and popular sovereignty against the exercise of arbitrary federal power. Prominent in this campaign was a young newspaper editor and publisher, George Q. Cannon, who made his San Francisco newspaper, the *Western Standard,* a literary clarion in defense of Zion.[19]

George Q. Cannon: Neither Unconstitutional Nor Unscriptural

Born in Liverpool, England, in 1827, George Q. Cannon was a model overseas convert to the LDS faith. He was introduced to the religion at an early age through the teachings of Apostle John Taylor, his uncle. Cannon's family migrated to Nauvoo, where he apprenticed in the newspaper business by working in Taylor's press room, helping print two Nauvoo gazettes that Taylor edited. Cannon followed the track of Brigham Young's pioneer company to Salt Lake in 1847, and in 1849, at age 22, he became a reluctant member of the Gold Mission to California. When relieved of this distasteful duty a year later, Cannon accepted an assignment to Hawaii, where his linguistic talents and literary gifts promoted the church's work. While taking part in a very successful proselytizing mission under Addison Pratt, he directed the translation of *The Book of Mormon* into the Hawaiian language.[20] Following his return to Utah in spring 1855, at Pratt's urging Brigham Young designated Cannon to return to California to complete the publication of his translation and start a church-authorized newspaper in San Francisco.

Cannon quickly became the most prominent and contentious public advocate for the Saints outside of Utah. He put into print 2,500 copies of his Hawaiian-language *Book of Mormon* and in February 1856 began publication of the *Western Standard,* a weekly journal that aggressively defended Mormon faith and practice. With Brigham Young's encouragement, he fought a colorful California newspaper war. The most heated battles came in a series of ill-tempered, ill-mannered exchanges with the

[19]Three other Mormon-owned newspapers preceded Cannon's San Francisco publication: *The Seer* published by Orson Pratt in Washington, D.C.; *The St. Louis Luminary,* edited by Erastus Snow; and *The Mormon,* edited and published by John Taylor in New York City. Editor Roger Robin Ekins describes Mormon journalism in the 1850s in *Defending Zion: George Q. Cannon and the California Mormon Newspaper Wars of 1856–1857,* 33.

[20]Although Cannon is widely credited with this achievement, Francis Hammond made major contributions to the translation.

GEORGE Q. CANNON
This youthful portrait shows the future apostle about the time he edited and published *The Western Standard* in San Francisco, where his ardent defense of the LDS leadership in Salt Lake City touched off a California newspaper war. *Courtesy Pioneer Memorial Museum, International Society, Daughters of Utah Pioneers.*

editors of the *Alta California*, by this time a well-established San Francisco publication that was beginning to print every available bit of critical news and opinion regarding Utah's Mormon leaders and their policies. This column written early in 1857, a justification of plural marriage as a religious doctrine and a defense of its practice by the Saints as a constitutional right, provides a classic example of Cannon's style.

GEORGE Q. CANNON, "THE 'ALTA CALIFORNIA' ON 'MORMONISM,'"
WESTERN STANDARD, 17 JANUARY 1857,
REPRINTED IN ROGER ROBIN EKINS, ED., *DEFENDING ZION*, 205–06.

The editors of the *Alta* think [polygamy] is a flagrant sin against God and nature, and that it should not be recognized as a portion of religion. They have equally as good a right to entertain this opinion, if they so wish, as we have to indulge in the opinion that the practice of monogamy is productive of misery, wretchedness and crime, and is in direct contravention of physiological laws. But Congress, in their legislative capacity, whether polygamists or monogamists, have no right to so express themselves; they are restricted by the Federal Constitution from making any law respecting an establishment of religion, or from prohibiting the free exercise thereof, and are expressly required to guarantee a republican form of government to every State. The question for them to decide, and the only question pertinent to the subject will be, is the constitution of Utah republican? If it be decided that it is, Congress *can not,* constitutionally, refuse her admission into the Confederacy. What her domestic institutions are, whether her inhabitants practice polygamy, monogamy, or the Shaker doctrines of non-intercourse of the sexes, is something that does not really concern Congress, or call for any action on their part. The moment they should assume the right to dictate to the inhabitants of a state or territory, what they shall believe and practice, and what they shall not, and remodel the constitution of such state or territory to suit their peculiar views, when it is already republican in every feature, they practically abrogate republicanism and institute an oligarchy in its stead. . . .

The editors say that we tell them flatly that we will come in "priestly tyranny, polygamy and all," or else we will not come in at all. Regarding it as we do, as a portion of our religious belief, are we not justified in saying that we will not submit to be curtailed or dictated to in these matters? The practice of this doctrine is neither unconstitutional nor unscriptural, why, then, should our form of belief in this point be dictated to us? The editors of the Alta say that this portion of it is revolting and horrible, that it is contrary to the laws of God, Man and nature. It may be contrary to the laws of some communities of men, who prohibit it, and sanction and legalize the diabolical crimes of prostitution and whoredom; but we have yet to be shown the law of God, or of nature, that is violated in its practice. . . .

We have noticed in our experience since the revelation of polygamy, that the honest, the pure, the virtuous of both sexes, when they hear it explained, never raise any objections against it; but the adulterous, the corrupt and the depraved, almost invariably protest in indignant terms against its proclamation or practice. They can see no propriety in such a principle, and they deride the most noble and holy of the ancient servants of God because they believed and practiced it. Whether the writer of the article to which we have alluded can be reckoned in the latter category or not, we do not pretend to say; but, whenever we hear such bitter denunciations of this doctrine and its believers, we set their author down as either ignorant or impure.

Six months later, while church authorities prepared a hard-hitting guerilla campaign to meet the federal forces heading to Utah, Cannon printed a column on the subject of Mormon patriotism. In style and substance, it may strike today's readers as a prime specimen of what some mid-nineteenth century critics called "windy buncombe."

So far as patriotism is concerned, the "Mormons" have never indulged in any other feeling. They have no need to resort to empty parades, orations or odes, to show to God and the world that they love their country and its Constitution. The patience and lofty heroism which they have exhibited in the midst of the severest trials, submitting to every indignity and making every sacrifice rather than assail or violate the Constitution of their country, will be embalmed in the archives of history, and be viewed by future generations with admiration. No man can point to a single act of the "Mormons," from the rise of the Church until the present time, that can be termed unpatriotic. And if that patriotism be measured by the style in which the fourth of July is celebrated, then it needs no future celebration to prove that they are patriots. The stories about the rebellion in Utah, circulated so extensively of late, are fast melting away. They are rapidly sharing the fate of those which have preceded them; the characters of their fabrication are becoming too well known for them to pass current long. Being false they must perish. Arrange it any way they please, as it is truly said, — Brigham has the inside track and knows how to keep it. But has it been or will it be by cunning? Did Governor Young and the "Mormons" depend on cunning alone they would have been worsted years ago. Shrewdness and cunning alone would have proved but poor auxiliaries in delivering them so frequently from the machinations of such hosts of crafty enemies. Nothing but eternal wisdom and Almighty power could have done it. By this aid they have kept *right* and *truth* on their side, and, therefore, have had the "inside track." By this aid they will continue to have the weather-gage of their enemies, and everything will be overruled for their good.[21]

An enthusiastic and dedicated man, George Q. Cannon believed he was doing the Lord's work as editor of the *Western Standard*, defending Zion and the LDS hierarchy with spirit and vehemence. Most modern authors who have examined Cannon's early career endorse this opinion.[22] Yet a cautious reappraisal is in order. Cannon was not simply preaching to the choir through the columns of the *Western Standard*. While he earnestly sought to justify every word and action of Utah's church authorities, his rhetoric roused latent anti-Mormon sentiments throughout California and elsewhere on the Pacific Coast.[23] For some gold-coun-

[21]"The 'Mormons' on the Inside Track," *Western Standard*, 10 July 1857, reprinted in Ekins, ed, *Defending Zion*, 270.

[22]In addition to Ekins's informative study, see particularly Flake, "George Q. Cannon's Mission to California, 1855–1857," *Regional Studies in Latter-day Saint Church History, California*, ed. David F. Boone *et al.*

[23]This conclusion is endorsed by Leo Lyman in his thorough study of the San Bernardino LDS colony. Until Cannon began publishing the *Western Standard*, observes Lyman, church members in California had received consistently positive press comments. But in May 1856, responding to Cannon's literary philippics, the editor of the *Alta California* first voiced his apprehensions about the problems generally posed by growing LDS numbers and power in Utah and southern California, a first volley in the subsequent California newspaper war. See Lyman, *San Bernardino*, 346–47. Cannon's columns were widely reprinted by other editors in California, Utah, and elsewhere, often as examples of Mormon extremism.

THE STAFF OF THE *WESTERN STANDARD*
Taken in June 1857, this photograph by R. H. Vance shows (*left to right*) Joseph Bull, David H. Cannon, George Q. Cannon, William H. Shearman, and Mathew F. Wilkie. *Courtesy LDS Archives.*

try Saints, Cannon's polemics made their religious beliefs and church membership for the first time a source of conflict with their non-Mormon neighbors.

The fiery young editor was not troubled by this fact. Upon leaving San Francisco for Utah in November 1857, Cannon confided to his journal that he was departing "without a sign of regret." He then reflected further on his services both as a writer and a church representative in northern California: "I feel clear from the blood of this people; I have labored diligently, labored to lay before them the principles of salvation by means of the press and public preaching, but to all the offers of salvation they have turned a deaf ear, and they have treated all our testimonies as idle tales."[24] He did not realize or perhaps he did not care

[24]Cannon, "George Q. Cannon: The Mission to California," 514, quoted in Ekins, *Defending Zion*, 402. A featured item in his last number of the *Western Standard* was an ill-informed report on stories just reaching California concerning the Mountain Meadows massacre. Characteristically, Cannon dismissed these reports as "reckless and malignant slanders" while urging the public to withhold judgment until all the facts were known: Ekins, *Defending Zion*, 369–72. The search for "all the facts" continues today, as demonstrated by Will Bagley's award-winning recent study, *Blood of the Prophets: Brigham Young and the Massacre at Mountain Meadows.*

that his diligent labors had intensified the predicament of those Saints who might remain in northern California.[25]

Frederick W. Hurst:
I Never Want to Be in a Greater Hell

Amid the developing newspaper war and the first reports of President Buchanan's preparations to confront Utah church leaders in early April 1857, twenty-four-year-old Frederick W. Hurst arrived in San Francisco with his younger brother Clement, returning from a mission in Hawaii. Hurst's detailed diary record of the following months as he traveled about northern California offers a rare personal view of missionary activities. From April until October, when he left with a company of Saints for San Bernardino and the southern desert route to Utah, Hurst described the situation of northern California Saints and his day-by-day experiences. The faithful, the backsliders, and the apostates alike he found generally vexed and unsettled by the Utah news and by instructions from church authorities to leave at once for the Mormon stronghold in the valley of the mountains. Each family had to determine, Hurst helps us understand, whether to obey authority or remain in the supposed California Babylon where faithful Latter-day Saints had lived well and happily for nearly a decade.

Hurst's diary begins with an account of his difficult voyage and his arrival in San Francisco. He expected to continue immediately to Utah, where his family was hoping to see the two brothers again. Instead, at a church conference in San Francisco's Philharmonic Hall, he and Clement agreed to remain and serve as missionaries in northern California. This agreement apparently came at the behest of George Q. Cannon, who, in addition to his editorial responsibilities, had authority over the San Francisco LDS branch and was serving as president to guide church affairs throughout northern California.

[25]Cannon published the newspaper for twenty-two months, from February 1856 until its final issue in early November 1857. Self-supporting after early struggles, the paper was able to return a modest profit largely because of a sizeable subscribership in Utah. Shortly after his return to Utah, Cannon became a member of the Twelve after Brigham Young proposed his name, filling the vacancy caused by Parley Pratt's murder in 1857. Arrington, *American Moses*, 303–4, describes the carefully managed selection process. Reviewing his later career, Arrington concludes that Cannon "was one of the most able, astute leaders the church produced in the nineteenth century."

FREDERICK W. HURST
A devoted young missionary who walked hundreds of miles to rally the Saints throughout northern California, Hurst became part of the LDS exodus in late 1857 and subsequently served in the Utah War militia. He later accepted missions in Australia and New Zealand. *Courtesy LDS Archives.*

DIARY OF FREDERICK WILLIAM HURST, LDS ARCHIVES.

San Francisco, April 3, 1857

For some months passed I have neglected my journal, the consequence is that I shall have to write from memory. On the 6th of last October, 1856, I was released from the Sandwich Island Mission. On the 8th of November following, I set sail, in company with my brother Charles C[lement]. Hurst, for San Francisco, California. Perhaps it will be necessary to say that we worked our passage before the mast, and when I look back and think of it I can truly say that the hand of the Lord was over us for good, although I realized that it was one of the greatest trials I have had to endure since I have been in the Church. To speak plainly we were in a perfect Hell. The first mate was the meanest scamp I ever saw, however, it did not last long for we arrived in San Francisco on the night of November 23rd. I will leave it to the imagination of the readers how glad we were to meet with the Saints after being with such a set of devils. My joy was so great that it knew no bounds. When we landed we were worth 37½ cents each. Owing to our clothing being very light and thin, and I must confess rather the worse for wear, we experienced the cold weather pretty severely till Brother John Baptist gave me a good cloth coat.[26] Sister Mowery gave me a pair of shoes, and Brother Everett kindly

[26]Hurst would have done well not to inquire where Australian emigrant Jean Baptiste, who advertised as a "Manufacturer of Trusses of all Kinds and Sizes" in the *Western Standard*, got the coat, for he later achieved fame as a grave robber in Great Salt Lake City. Morgan, *The Great Salt Lake*, 274–82, described the professional demise and disappearance of Baptiste.

took us in; in fact all of the Saints we met with behaved very kind.[27] We stayed in the city till the 3rd of December, then I accompanied Brother W. Whipple to the Redwoods [south of San Francisco near modern Redwood City]. He paid my fare. On the following Sunday Clement followed me.

It was some time before we could get work, in the mean time I helped do chores about the house, that is Brother Eli Whipple's. Bye the bye, his wife is very much opposed to Mormonism. We hired out at several places but could get no pay. In the beginning of March, Clement and I concluded we would work on our own account. We split 730 posts the first four days, then a Brother, newly baptized, came from the city. He having nothing to do we took him with us. I believe his name is Ingelsted, from Norway. Up to the end of March we split 3,000 posts and sold them all for $90. As to what was owing to us, we handed out some and left the rest in the hands of E[li] Whipple to collect though I hardly expect to get one cent. . . .

On the 3rd of April, four of us walked from the Redwoods up to San Francisco, a distance of 36 miles. We arrived at the [*Western Standard*] office at 3 o'clock P.M. and found all the brethren. April 3rd I gave Brother George Q. Cannon $10.00 for the paper. I gave Brother Mandle $3.00 etc. . . .

Sunday, April 6. We met in the capacity of Conference. . . . I can truly say I never attended better meetings before. The Spirit of the Lord was in our midst. I will state that it was my intention previous to the conference to accompany Brother W. Cooke to the [Salt Lake] valley, but the conference thought it best, as the field was large and the laborers few, to send us to the mines to preach under the presidency of Elder [William H.] Shearman.[28]

The Hurst brothers had reached California just as President Cannon was urging church workers to intensify their efforts to revitalize the LDS religion in northern California and persuade California Mormons to move to Utah. "A better feeling prevails throughout the Conference for some months back, than has at any previous time," reported the confer-

[27]Barton Mowry had arrived in California with his wife and two sons on board the *Brooklyn* in 1846. It was in Mowry's house that Parley Pratt conducted the meeting on 1 September 1851 that disfellowshipped Sam Brannan. See Bagley, ed., *Scoundrel's Tale*, 147, 233, 297. Mowry subsequently settled in southern Alameda County, although his wife, Ruth Walkup Mowry, returned to Utah in 1857 or 1858. In later life he became involved in spiritualism and left the church. See Biographical Register, LDS Archives. "Everett" is Dwight Eveleth, a wealthy merchant who arrived in San Francisco in 1852. See Eveleth to Brigham Young, 10 February 1855, Brigham Young Collection, LDS Archives. Eveleth became Young's main representative on the West Coast after the Utah War.

[28]His obituary in the *Deseret News*, 24 December 1892, reported that William H. Shearman joined the church in California in the 1850s and served as an editorial assistant to George Q. Cannon. Shortly after reaching Utah in 1857, he left on a mission to Great Britain. There he organized six hundred converts who sailed from Liverpool in 1865 for Utah. Shearman settled in Logan and at some point withdrew from the LDS church but subsequently returned and was a Seventy at the time of his death. He was noted for his skillful writing and for his unfailing generosity in aiding those in distress. See Biographical Register, LDS Archives.

WILLIAM H. SHEARMAN
Shearman in 1857 served both as editorial assistant for the *Western Standard* and director of northern California's Mormon revival movement. After relocating to Utah, he headed a mission in Great Britain and worked on the *Millennial Star.* He subsequently joined the Godbeite movement, but later reunited with the LDS church and became notable for his aid to other Saints in distress. *Courtesy LDS Archives.*

ence summary in the *Western Standard.* "The Saints are beginning to wake up, and to realize their true position and the necessity of giving heed to all the principles and obeying all the ordinances of the gospel instituted for the salvation and exaltation of the human family. The spirit of gathering prevails throughout the Conference; and it is likely a considerable number will emigrate this year. The Spirit of the Lord seems to be working with the people."[29]

During the next few weeks Hurst and one companion, Elder Henry G. Boyle, traveled from town to town about the region north and east of San Francisco Bay, attempting to hold meetings and preach, and visiting with church families they met along the way.[30] They traveled by foot, fre-

[29]Presumably clerk Charles W. Wandell reported the proceedings of this conference, which were printed in the *Western Standard* for 10 April 1857. During the conference, Elders D. M. Stuart and William H. Shearman summarized the work in "the Mines," the area organized as El Dorado Conference. "There are about 60 Saints scattered throughout the Mines. Some of them are not living as the gospel requires," they reported. Among other actions, the conference voted "Elders John D. and Aaron Thatcher, Frederick W. Hurst, and Charles C. Hurst labor in the El Dorado Conference under the Presidency of Elder Shearman."

[30]Henry G. Boyle had served as a private in Company C of the Mormon Battalion, then reenlisted for an additional six months in the Mormon Volunteers. After traveling to Utah, he returned to California in the 1851 company that established San Bernardino under the guidance of Amasa Lyman and Charles C. Rich. He left California late in 1857, but devoted himself to missionary work for most of his life, serving altogether in fourteen missions. He was president of the Southern States Mission from 1875 to 1878. He died in Arizona in 1908 at age 84. Andrew Jenson, *Latter-day Saint Biographical Encylopedia,* 4: 380.

quently walking twenty, thirty, even forty miles a day. Usually they found Saints or other hospitable souls who would give them a meal or two and a place to sleep. These mendicant missionaries spread the gospel as well as they could. Without purse or scrip, in the phraseology of Mormon missionary tradition, they gradually moved toward Sacramento and on to the LDS settlements near Mormon Island and Salmon Falls on the American River.

In this excerpt, Hurst describes a typical few days early in his California mission, sometimes enjoying success, sometimes meeting with a discouraging lack of response.

> Wednesday, April 15 [1857]. Elder Boyle and I started this morning for Russian River. We called at Mr. Mayfield's, three miles from Petaluma.[31] We rested a while and then pushed on until we got to Old Uncle Shelton's where we were treated kindly.[32] Spent the evening agreeably reading.
>
> Thursday, April 16. After breakfast, Brother Boyle and I went to Blacher Valley. Got liberty to preach in the school house. Gave out an appointment for tomorrow night at early candlelight.
>
> Friday, April 17. According to previous appointment we met this evening. The people turned out well. Brother Boyle preached, afterward I bore my testimony, etc. The few Saints here feel well at present.
>
> Saturday, April 18. We walked to the Dry Creek Branch, a distance of thirty miles. Found Brother Dramm well and feeling glad to see us. We spent the evening very agreeably.
>
> Sunday, April 19, Dry Creek. At 10:00 A.M. we met at Brother Q. D. Sparke's house. A few of the Saints attended, and to tell the truth they felt dull and sleepy. According to President George Q. Cannon's instructions we tried to find out who were going to Salt Lake and who to San Bernardino. In the evening we went home with Brother George W. Chick and wife, about four miles walk up in the mountains. I never saw such a beautiful variety of wild flowers before. Surely, as the scriptures saith, "This land is blessed about all other lands." The scenery in this Russian River district is really charming.

Hurst's diary provides evidence that substantially greater numbers of

---

[31]Hurst's host may have been Benjamin F. Mayfield, a private in Company A of the Mormon Battalion and third sergeant in the Mormon Volunteers. He was one of two men wounded slightly during a foray against Indian raiders in the mountains near Los Angeles in May 1847. See Ricketts, *Mormon Battalion*, 22, 151–52, 265.

[32]"Old Uncle Shelton" was probably Sebert Shelton, the quartermaster sergeant of Company D in the Mormon Battalion. His wife had once been married to Jackson Mayfield, so ties of kinship linked the Mayfields and the Sheltons: her two oldest children were Mayfields and her other four children were Sheltons. Although Sebert Shelton and his family had been among the Higgins family detachment that wintered at Pueblo, he arrived in California about the time of the battalion's discharge. See Ricketts, *Mormon Battalion*, 26, 32, 233–34, 346.

Saints were living in northern California in 1857 than historians have previously supposed. From the Russian River country the two missionaries moved to Petaluma, then walked thirty-five miles to reach Napa. His diary reports the meeting he and Boyle arranged at that place, and describes next their adventures on the way to the LDS community at the Buckeye branch in Yolo County. His story of a horse racing misadventure reminds us that he was still quite young and exuberant, capable of enjoying himself even while remaining dedicated to the work of the church.[33]

> Wednesday the 29th. We made out a quantity of hand bills and stuck them all over town informing the public that we would preach this evening at the courthouse. I might add that through the kindness of the Sheriff, Mr. Sparkes, we were permitted to hold meeting in the above mentioned house. About 50 attended. Brother Boyle spoke first, I followed. The people paid good attention.
>
> Thursday, April 30. Before starting this morning Mr. Mount gave us $1.00 each, besides lunch to eat on the road, for when we started we intended to walk to Buckeye, a distance of forty miles, but Brother Boyle thought it would not be wisdom.[34] We walked as far as Wilson's, 20 miles. Stayed all night.
>
> Next morning, Friday May 1st. We walked to the Putah River, 14 miles, where we met John and Moses Thatcher with horses.[35] After bathing we

[33]The Buckeye branch was in Yolo County, located a short distance east of the modern town of Winters. Henry Boyle and William Shearman organized the branch 31 December 1856, with Hezekiah Thatcher as branch president. Church records indicate nineteen members in the branch, all baptized between September 1856 and May 1857, and all but one baptized by Elder Boyle. See the Buckeye Branch, California Mission Historical Record, 1856–1857, LDS Archives.

[34]Hiram B. Mount had been a private in Company B of the battalion and subsequently served in the Mormon Volunteers as third corporal. See Ricketts, *The Mormon Battalion*, 23, 265.

[35]The Thatcher family was prominent in church affairs in northern California. The father, Hezekiah Thatcher, had been a member of the Nauvoo militia and brought his family from Winter Quarters to Salt Lake in 1847, only to leave for California with the family in June 1848. "Going to the mining regions near Auburn," according to author Andrew Jenson in the *Latter-day Saint Biographical Encyclopedia*, Hezekiah "became quite a capitalist, frequently receiving from travelers from one to five dollars for riding a horse to water." While his father ran an eating house on Auburn Road, Moses, the sixth of eight sons, attended school sporadically. By late 1856 the family had moved to Yolo County, where Elder Henry Boyle baptized Moses and other family members on 26 December 1856, when Moses was fourteen years of age. A month later he became a missionary under William Shearman's direction as Boyle's companion. Moses found himself moved by deep spiritual experiences on his mission, "often correctly quoting Scripture he had never read, the words and sentences, as he declared, appearing before his spiritual eyes were read, as from an open book." With his brothers John and Aaron, Moses Thatcher led the Mormon exodus from Yolo County, departing in mid-October 1847 and arriving in Salt Lake on 1 January 1858. Subsequently he married and became one of the first settlers in Cache Valley, where he entered the mercantile business in partnership with his father. Moses Thatcher served in the Utah territorial legislature, opened the successful mission in Mexico City, and was ordained an apostle in 1879. He enthusiastically promoted Mormon colonization in Mexico and became a leader in that effort. See Jenson, *Latter-day Saint Biographical Encyclopedia* 1:127–36.

> mounted and rode the rest of the way. Just before we reached our destination we had a race, and my saddle, not being girded on tight, slipped over one side, consequently I fell off, or rather let myself down. I escaped unhurt. We found the brethren and sisters all well and glad to see us. It was not long, in spite of my bashfulness before I felt quite at home. In the afternoon Brothers Cannon, Sherman, Steward, Higgins, and others arrived. We truly rejoiced together. On Saturday we held three meetings, received very much valuable instructions from Brother Cannon and others.
>
> The weather is very warm. The country is parched up for want of rain. This season is so dry it is thought that most of the grain in this district will fail.
>
> Monday, May 3rd. Buckeye Branch held three meetings, one a good testimony meeting. The evening meeting was kept up until half past 12 o'clock. The Saints feel better than I have witnessed for some time past. I really feel to love the Saints of Buckeye, and elsewhere, and may the Lord Bless them. Most of the Saints here are anxious to gather up to Zion.

The following day Frederick and Clement Hurst visited Sacramento, riding in a wagon in a party of twelve that included George Q. Cannon and W. H. Shearman, Cannon's assistant who headed the missionary effort in northern California. The Hurst brothers spent the night in a boarding house, their board and lodging paid for by Brother Joseph Thatcher, one of the Yolo County Saints from the Buckeye Branch. The following day the two young men walked twenty miles to Alder Creek east of Sacramento, where they made arrangements for a meeting the following evening. Hurst's description of that gathering illustrates a common peril in the career of a young missionary attempting to preach among strangers: an encounter with an elderly, self-designated expert on all matters religious who apparently was infatuated with the sound of his own voice. Hurst's account, complete with its retelling of a labored closing joke at the expense of the two young Mormon elders, indicates that he was not terribly taken aback by the encounter.

> I wrote out some notices. About sixty attended, paid good attention till I had done. Clem bore his testimony. Then a white headed old sinner, formerly a Methodist Preacher got up and said he wanted to ask a few questions. He asked me if I knew what the meaning of repentance was, and at what time the Kingdom of God would be established. He then said that I had pretended to preach Mormonism but I had not done it. Instead of me teaching them he could teach me, and then began telling what a good man he was. He did not swear or lie except in a joke to make fun, and I got up and told them that we understood repentance to simply mean a man turning away from his sins, etc., and forsaking them. And as to the Kingdom of God, if they would

> read their bibles they would see plainly many prophesies pertaining to the last days. For instance, Daniel, Isaiah, etc. Finally one got talking and another laughing, some shouting, some for us and the more part against us. The meeting broke up in disorder. However before leaving the house the old man said he would send twenty men up into the mountains and cut poles to fence in the cattle, or else (we were so green) the cattle would by mistake eat us up.

From Alder Creek the Hurst brothers walked twelve miles to Salmon Falls, amid the largest concentration of LDS settlers in the California gold country, and found lodgings in Brother Thomas Orr's hotel. By this time the *Western Standard* and other sources were informing northern California Saints that the church presidency had called all church members to Utah, to aid Brigham Young in defending theocratic rule in Zion. For the next five months the Hurst brothers and their missionary compatriots traveled around the district, holding meetings and preaching. Their duties included ministering to the sick, baptizing and confirming new converts and a few apostates who desired to rejoin the LDS fellowship, and helping to organize companies of Saints who intended to leave for Utah.

Beginning in 1856 a movement of spiritual rededication brought a heightened religious intensity to Utah's LDS communities. This Utah Mormon reformation, which some authors have interpreted as an emotional religious response to drought, plague, and a severe economic recession in 1855 and 1856, continued well into 1857. Led by Jedediah Grant, "Brigham's Hammer," reformation preachers called on the Mormon people to confess their sins individually and collectively and to rededicate their lives to the service of their religion under the Salt Lake City leadership. It was, in the words of one historian, "an all-engrossing movement that compelled the people to listen, pray, and search their souls."[36] With Pentecostal fervor, reformation evangelists exhorted apostates, backsliders, and the faithful to strengthen their spiritual ties to the church, be rebaptized, and reconsecrate themselves.[37]

---

[36]Furniss, *The Mormon Conflict*, 93. For Grant's career, consult Sessions, *Mormon Thunder: A Documentary History of Jedediah Morgan Grant.*

[37]This Utah Reformation, or Mormon Reformation, is well described in Peterson, "The Mormon Reformation of 1856–1857: Rhetoric and Reality," *Journal of Mormon History* 15 (1989); and the same author's "Brigham Young and the Mormon Reformation," in Black and Porter, eds., *Lion of the Lord: Essays on the Life & Services of Brigham Young.* The doctrine of blood atonement in reformation preaching is emphasized in Bagley, *Blood of the Prophets*, 49–53. Particularly strong in southern Utah, Bagley urges, the reformation set the stage in psychic terms for subsequent conflicts between LDS zealots and emigrants that led to the infamous Mountain Meadows massacre in September 1857. Among other accounts, see in particular Furniss, *The Mormon Conflict*, 91–94; and Bigler, *Forgotten Kingdom*, 121–40.

Added to George Q. Cannon's editorial fusillades in the *Western Standard,* Frederick Hurst's journal indisputably demonstrates that gold-country Saints were also experiencing an enthusiastic revival of religious dedication during this period. Long unnoticed by historians, the northern California Mormon reformation was strongly encouraged by the burst of missionary activity promoted by President Cannon.[38] As they traveled about the mining towns, the Hurst brothers were active agents in this movement, preaching the LDS faith and performing authorized church ordinances. A handful of journal entries from May 1857 show the two young men doing their best to build religious enthusiasm among the faithful, bring wayward Saints back to their faith, convert unbelievers, and, for all those who would go, help start them on the way to Zion.

> Monday [11 May] It rained this morning. We have been assisting Brother Raihes fix his wagon as they are going to start for San Bernardino next Thursday. Brother and Sister Johnston will accompany them, they will number, counting children and all, eight persons.[39] I wrote to Brother Aaron Thatcher and Elder Boyle in the Evening. I baptized and confirmed Brother William Johnston. He is one of the Battalion boys. He got up in meeting last night and confessed his faults and expressed a desire to live his religion. I will observe that I spoke very pointedly on renewing our covenants, etc. Clem and I laid hands on Sister Lunceford. She is better.
>
> Tuesday, Wall Diggings, May 12th. After breakfast we laid hands on Sister Johnston at her request as she was sick. She got up and went right to work. We bade them all farewell and after a walk of 14 miles reached this place. Found Mr. Outhouse and family well.[40] Although he is an apostate he is friendly to the Mormons. After resting a while we walked about one mile and a half to Wall City where we enjoyed a room. I wrote out and stuck up notices, much to the derision of the bystanders. We then went to a retired place and called on our Father to aid and assist us to get up in His Power and tell men the truth. A Mr. Goodenough got us a room. Mr. James Smith (they are both apostates) furnished lights. We had quite a large congrega-

---

[38]Cannon's writings about the Utah Reformation are discussed and reprinted in Ekins, *Defending Zion,* 208–42. See also Paul H. Peterson, "'Like a Fire in My Bones': The Reformation Correspondence between Brigham Young and George Q. Cannon," in *Regional Studies in Latter-day Saint Church History, California,* ed. David F. Boone *et al.*

[39]Most likely "Brother Johnston" is William Johnston, who was at Coloma with Henry Bigler, Azariah Smith, James S. Brown, and the other battalion veterans in January 1848.

[40]Born in 1820, Joseph Outhouse was an Illinois convert who had lived in Far West, Missouri, and Nauvoo. He had served a mission in Connecticut in 1843, and was captain of a wagon train that arrived in Salt Lake in September 1852. Apparently he and his first wife, Eliza Ann Allen Outhouse, broke with the church soon after arriving in Utah and resettled in northern California. See Biographical Register, LDS Archives.

tion. Clem spoke first, very fine and with spirit. I followed, etc. The people behaved well.

After meeting a Mrs. Bell, formerly a Mormon, came forward and shook hands with us. She commenced telling us how sorry she was for leaving the valley. I told her that she was not the only one that, Jonah like, had tried to run away from the Lord, and that they would be glad this day if they were back again. Although it was 10 o'clock and dark, we walked back to Mr. Outhouse's. All in bed.

Wednesday, Michigan Bar. We reached here about 3 o'clock P.M., introduced ourselfs to Mr. Lacklunt Tale Kemper. He is a kind of Jack Mormon.[41] He treated us very gentlemanly. I engaged Mr. Gray's Hall, as usual stuck up notices to the effect that we would hold meeting at early candlelight. From eighty to one hundred attended. I understand they tried to get a Methodist on the floor to oppose us but he declined. The meeting passed off quiet and peaceable. I spoke on the Kingdom of God and the kingdom of man.

Thursday, Drummersville ⌊Drummondsville⌋, May 14th. We arrived at this place about 11 A.M. Found Sister Simmons well and glad to see us. Sister Panel is sickly. I appointed a meeting and went around and told the miners, etc. We had quite a good meeting in the evening. Clem spoke first and I followed, etc.

Friday, Willow Springs, May 15th. After a walk of seven miles, we arrived here and put up at brother Thomas Hindley's. In the evening we held a meeting. Brother and Sister Rily live here. We are trying to sell of their stock to gather in San Bernardino.

Saturday, Dry Town, May 16th. Walked to Dry Town and put up at Brother Plunket's. We found them all well and glad to see us.

Sunday, Dry Town, May 17th. Held three meetings and organized a Branch consisting of nine members, to be called the Dry Town Branch. Also that Brother Thomas Hindley presides, and Brother John Carter act as Clerk. The best kind of spirit prevailed. I preached on the Book of Mormon.

Monday, Dry Town, Amador Co., May 18th. I wrote to Brother Cannon. Held meeting this afternoon. All the Brothers and Sisters bore testimony to the truth of Mormonism. Sister Plunket had the Spirit of Prophecy. She said that the Lord would bless us on our mission, that he would open up a way before us that we should overcome all difficulties, etc. We anointed and laid hands on Brother John Carter for his eyes are very sore, in fact he is not able to work. He has been to the Doctors but they have done more harm than good.

Tuesday, Cedar Ravine, Hang Town, May 19th. After a walk of 25 miles we arrived at Brother Bird's. Found them all well. I had not seen them for two years. They are anxious to gather to the valley but have not got the means.

[41]Although today the term usually refers to a lapsed or non-practicing Latter-day Saint, Jack Mormon originally referred to anyone sympathetic to Mormonism.

The presence of LDS missionaries in the small towns of the gold country did not escape general notice, nor did the flurry of activity as church members began to leave for Utah. California newspaper reports about LDS activities in Utah turned alarmist by the end of May 1857. In response, the editorials in Cannon's *Western Standard* became still more strident in defense of the LDS hierarchy in Salt Lake City. While public discussion turned shrill, Frederick Hurst experienced the consequences of a sharp polarization in opinion about the Saints' beliefs, practices, and policies. By the first of June, Hurst's journal indicates, opposition to their public preaching was making church work increasingly difficult for the Hurst brothers and other Mormon elders on missionary duty in northern California.

Sunday, May 31st. Held two meetings. One at French Creek and one in the evening at Father Lunceford's. We had a good time. On Monday, June 1st, we went to White Rock Springs but owing to so few coming together at their request we postponed the meeting etc. But such an evening I never wish to spend again as long as I live. Understand these had not renewed their covenants, they talked about Brother Brigham, the twelve, etc., concerning the evil that existed there. One of them said that if he met a certain Brother, calling him by name that he would put his knife into him.

Tuesday, June 2nd. We went to Prairie City. Saw Brother Rutherford. Stayed an hour or so and then walked to Wall's diggings. Ate dinner at Sister Bell's. Held meeting in the evening. Quite a number attended. Mr. Outhouse came over and after meeting we returned with him and stayed all night.

Next day, Wednesday, June 3rd, we went and visited with Mr. Pallick on the Casames [Cosumnes] River. He told us to make ourselves comfortable but not to mention anything about Mormonism.

Thursday, June 4th. We went to Michigan Bar. Preached in the schoolhouse in the evening to quite a large and attentive audience.

Next morning, June 5th. Went to Drummondville and as they could not keep us after dinner we walked to William Rering's. Found the Brethren well. Sunday we held four meetings. Organized a company to gather by way of San Bernardino. Eleven in number, namely Brother and Sister Royle and their boy, Brother Stanes and five sons, John Carter and L. Ball. I felt to talk plain to the Brothers and Sisters. They made a collection for us. Brother Stanes gave us $10.00, Brother Royle $5.00, Brother Plunkett $5.00, Brother Hindley $5.00, Brother Ball $2.50, Brother Carter $1.00. Monday I gave $10.00 for a coat, $6.00 for boots and shirts, and on Tuesday we walked to Volcano.

After a great deal of difficulty obtained a Baptist Chapel. About a hundred turned out to hear us but when I got through speaking Brother Aaron

[Thatcher] began but they would not hear him and the meeting broke up in an uproar.

We spent all but 50¢ for supper and bed, and next morning we started to Jackson Mines. Ate breakfast, Passed through Acquaduct City, found almost deserted. We ate dinner at the Pinecrane House after which we walked to Jackson City. Walked all over the town but could get no place to preach in. Consequently we bought 50¢ worth of bread and sausage and slept out in the mountains all night.

Next day, Thursday; set out for Dry Town. Ate dinner, then we went to Willow Springs. The brethren had all started for the South, however, we pulled out the staple [on the door of the meeting house] with a pick, then opened the other door from the inside and then replaced the staple and lock as before. We then looked around and hunted up some flour and butter, etc., and accordingly, while Aaron made a fire, I made some biscuits. However, shortly after breaking in a man came down to see who had broke into the house. We preached Mormonism to him and on the following Sunday, June 14th, we baptized him and confirmed him, etc. We held two meetings.

Monday, June 15th. We walked to Mud Springs. Got liberty to preach in the school house, however, in the evening we lighted up the place and rang the bell to no purpose. Two miserable cusses of apostates came out. Only at their request we returned home with them. They talked about how good they were. Also talked about the brethren of the Church, saying that Mormonism was true, and when the Church first started it was pure but now the head of the Church was like a man with a long stick and as long as they stirred up the mud the stream would be impure. However, they were so good that (although we had no supper) they neither asked us to eat or stay all night, leaving us to shift for ourselves, etc.

Tuesday the 16th. We walked to Jeany Town where we stayed until Friday. We did considerable fireside preaching but could not get a public place to preach in.

On Friday the 19th, came back to Diamond Springs. Got liberty to preach in Temperance Union Hall, but in the evening one of the trustees came up full of the spirit of the devil and as good as drove us out. Accordingly we left the city and slept under a bush all night. My mind was comforted much by dreams.

Frederick W. Hurst: We Might Get Mobbed Out

Soon after their unpleasant experience in Diamond Springs, Frederick Hurst and Aaron Thatcher, a Buckeye branch member, walked to Stockton. On 2 July 1857 President Cannon also arrived there, taking charge of arrangements for the Saints from Amador, San Joaquin, and Yolo counties who were organizing companies for the trip to Utah. "He gave us instructions," Hurst recorded, "to confine our labors here and not kill ourselves traveling all over the country." Yet Cannon then sent Hurst and Thatcher in belated pursuit of one company headed into the Sierra. Starting at eight o'clock in the evening, the two young men walked sixty miles in twenty-five hours to overtake a group of twelve Mormons from Yolo County. "They were all glad to see us," wrote Hurst, who now revealed something about his physical condition.

> I was so glad that I forgot all about being tired. Our feet were very much blistered, so much so that I could scarcely get about when I got cool. I realize that it is a treat to get among such good Saints that composed this company. To tell the truth, they are not often met with in the country. We held meeting in Mormon Camp at 3:00 P.M. Most of the Brethren spoke their feelings, myself among the number. . . . We have slept out of doors the last 10 or 12 days lately and I begin to feel the effects of the same. The Saints all tell me I look pale and thin. I weighed when I was in Stockton and instead of weighing 152 lbs I lack 20 of it. The most I could go, walking stick and all, was 132 lbs.[42]

For more than a week after reaching the LDS wagon train, Hurst and Thatcher rested nearby in French Town and conducted missionary meetings. Here Hurst met "Mr. Bigler," Henry William Bigler, the first of the battalion veterans to discover gold at Coloma in 1848. "He left Salt Lake in '53," Hurst wrote in his journal. "Has been trying to make money. He is a wiser man than when he first came here. So much for California." This encounter prompted a further comment from Hurst. "This is the testimony of all the Saints that have left Utah. When they reach here they find that it is not all gold that glitters."[43] But more than any other person in California, so Hurst failed to appreciate, Henry W. Bigler knew full well that sometimes what glittered was, indeed, gold.

"There are quite a few in French Town inquiring into the truth of Mormonism," Hurst recorded, his missionary goals firmly in mind. He was hopeful, he added, "that ere long we will be able to organize a branch in this place." The following week, while the wagon company at last headed toward Utah, Hurst and Thatcher walked back to Dry Town

[42]Diary of Frederick William Hurst, LDS Archives.

[43]Entry for 11 June 1857, Diary of Frederick William Hurst, LDS Archives. According to his biographer, Bigler arrived at Stockton on 11 July, having trekked from Carson Valley on his way to the Hawaiian Islands with a company of LDS missionaries. See Bishop, *Henry William Bigler,* 100–1.

and renewed their preaching in the small mining settlements. By this time opposition to the LDS missionaries was becoming extreme. Hurst reported on a Dry Town meeting on 21 July that ended in physical assault and general tumult.

> We preached in the public streets. We commenced by singing, "Come Let Us Anew." The crowd began coming together. Brother Thatcher opened meeting with prayer. I then mounted a box placed there for that purpose and boldly and freely preached on the first principles of the Gospel. After preaching for near an hour the people made such a noise that I was obliged to desist. Not long after I commenced speaking, some person threw a stone hard at my head. They threw it a little too high for it struck a cloth over my head which took its force. They also threw some mush melons or squash and struck me on the back of my head, but it did not hurt me. I can truly say I knew no fear, I really felt well. Brother A. Thatcher got up and spoke with power but they would not let him continue longer than five minutes. The meeting then broke up in an uproar.

On Saturday of the following week, Hurst and Thatcher joined other northern California missionaries and met for three days with President Cannon and mission director W. H. Shearman at Salmon Falls. Hurst's account documents the changing situation of the northern California Saints. Even in this long-established Mormon gold country stronghold, church representatives were meeting heightened public opposition.

> Met with President George Q. Cannon and Brother W. H. Shearman, my own brother Clem and others. Clem was sick with a bad cold, but all felt well. I can truly say that I rejoiced once more to see and meet with the Brethren. Father and Mother and Sarah Lunceford came over in their wagon with a number of others from different parts of the Gold Mines. We continued conference until Monday evening. The people began to get quite hostile. Brother Cannon said if we kept conference on a day or two longer we might get mobbed out. We received many valuable teachings from Brothers Cannon and Shearman. We had a good time. To tell the truth I was sorry when conference adjourned. The Brothers and Sisters Orr and Allred treated us very kindly and hospitably.[44]

Another missionary gathering took place at the Lunceford home the following Sunday, when Hurst summed up with some pride the situation of the northern California mission by early August.

---

[44]James Riley Allred was a battalion veteran who had remained in California until 1848. After spending a year in Utah, he returned to northern California with Charles C. Rich. He later lived in Spring City, Sanpete County, Utah. See Biographical Register, LDS Archives.

> I would state that the business that was done at conference was intended to get the Saints together, warm them up and lay before them the necessity to buy a Printing Press to send to the Sandwich Islands.[45] The various Elders gave in their reports in regard to the work in our respective fields of labor, the sum substance of which was that opposition was on the increase, that the work was slowly and steadily increasing. According to my report we had baptized 10 new members and rebaptized four old members, and others that are inquiring into the truth, that our field was too large, etc. I am thankful to say that both Brother Cannon and Brother Shearman were highly pleased with us boys.

Brigham Young: Secure as Much Ammunition as You Can

Intemperate declarations from Salt Lake and increasingly militant confrontations over LDS actions in both Utah and southern California sparked an explosion of anti-Mormon sentiment in the gold country by late summer 1857. On 21 June Brigham Young gave a speech in the Bowery that excoriated Senator Morrill and other anti-Mormon politicians in the nation's capital. He also roundly condemned any federal interference with Utah's territorial government under the church hierarchy's management as a violation of the U.S. Constitution. Young extolled Utah as the one true home for all Latter-day Saints, the only place where they could raise their children in peace and with a pure knowledge of their religion. In contrast, the church president declared, hell reigned for the Saints in California and every other region that had attracted Mormons. The time was now at hand, Young declared, for faithful Saints to leave each and every hellish place and gather together in Zion.[46]

In southern California meanwhile, a series of disputes between LDS leaders of the San Bernardino colony and a highly vocal faction of apostates had escalated into wrathful, violent conflict. Loosely organized under the label of Rakabites, the anti-Mormon extremists were a dissi-

[45] Sending a printing press to Hawaii was a fond project for George Q. Cannon, which he hoped the northern California Saints would finance.

[46] A corrected transcript of this speech, recorded by George D. Watt, is at the LDS Archives. Lyman, *San Bernardino*, 377–78, also refers to a version published in the *Deseret News*, which is not entirely consistent with Watt's transcript.

dent counterpart to the fervid exponents of the LDS reformation in Utah and California. They seized every possible opportunity to discredit and harass anyone affiliated with the church. Through letters in the Los Angeles and San Diego newspapers, they waged a campaign of calumny that more than offset George Q. Cannon's preachments in the *Western Standard*. The Rakabites' sole purpose, Charles C. Rich reported to the Utah authorities, was to spread anti-Mormon sentiment throughout California. But the intensity of their opposition also extended into disputes over money and property that made the local courts another battleground for this southern California version of religious warfare.[47]

In mid-August 1857 President Young determined to follow up his July speech by recalling all faithful Saints from California and other outlying localities. At this point, the church president was ordering a halt to every effort to sustain an LDS presence in the golden state. In Young's mind, his message indicates, "home" for the Saints could only be somewhere in the Great Basin. His directions to the colonists in Carson Valley also indicate his determination to defend this home with all necessary military force.

YOUNG TO CHESTER LOVELAND AND THE BRETHREN
IN CARSON CR [COUNTY], 15 AUGUST 1857,
LETTERBOOK 3, BRIGHAM YOUNG PAPERS, LDS ARCHIVES.

President's Office
G. S. L. City
Augt 15th 1857

Elder Chester Loveland, and the Brethren in Carson Cr.

Brethren

We have concluded that it is wisdom that you should dispose of your property as well as you can and come home. If you cannot sell to advantage, lease your places, and get your pay in advance.

We send this counsel to you by Express that you may avail yourselves of the present emigration to dispose of your property. We want you to secure as much ammunition as you can. Be wise "and not let the right hand know what the left hand doeth." A hint to the wise is sufficient. Make no noise about

[47]The Rakabites are identified and described in Lyman, *San Bernardino*, 321, 338–42, 361–62 *et seq.* Lyman states that the anti-Mormon agitation of this group became an important reason for the Saints' evacuation of San Bernardino in 1857. The name Rakabite, he also explains, came from an Old Testament reference to a group that meant to regenerate their religion.

your business, but let all things be done quietly and in order. You are aware that you can sell at better advantage if you can keep your own counsel.

The Express party will remain and assist you in fitting up and return with you on the Northern route. Br. Wm R. Smith, who went to California with Captn Hooper's stock, will, it is presumed, be ready to come with you.

Come in one company, and keep together so that that [*sic*] you can protect yourselves against the Indians who are said to be hostile. Come prepared to defend yourselves against al[l] our foes, both white and red.

We learn there is an army of from twenty five to thirty five hundred men now enroute for this Territory, besides Some ten or twelve hundred teamsters &c, Seven hundred wagons with ox teams loaded with Supplies; and about four hundred more mules and horse teams loaded with personal effects, camp equipage &c, Seven thousand head of beef cattle. The supplies are designed to last them fifteen months after they arrive in this Territory. We do not expect them to come *here*, although the last we heard from them, 160 of the wagons were 180 miles on the way, and a train of 30 wagons were Starting out every other day, and the troops were to Start on the 15th day of last month; they are to march on foot.

My counsel is for you to leave your farms with as good gentiles as you can, if you cannot Sell to advantage, for we would just as soon own the property as not. Buy all the powder, Lead, and Caps you possibly can, but do not tarry to go over into California, or at least to detain you any length of time.

Brigham Young

O. B. Huntington: On Gods Business for His People & Kingdom

To carry his directive to northern California, President Young appointed a small command of experienced LDS frontiersmen led by Peter W. Conover, a Nauvoo Legion colonel, with Oliver B. Huntington as guide. Huntington had explored a new direct route from Great Salt Lake City to Carson Valley for an army command led by Lt. Col. E. J. Steptoe in fall 1854, traveling past the Ruby Mountains and continuing south of the Carson River sink.[48] Early the following year Conover was part of an LDS detachment led by Porter Rockwell that set out to explore a route to Carson Valley for Steptoe, but ultimately Rockwell led the

[48]This journey is recorded in Oliver Huntington, Journal, 1854, LDS Archives. Poorly provisioned, the expedition members suffered starvation from the lack of game and subsisted a good part of the way on dried horsemeat.

army expedition west over the established California Trail.[49] Now Young entrusted these men not only with a critical message but with a highly sensitive and confidential assignment: to secure a cargo of guns and ammunition in San Francisco for delivery to Utah. For this purpose he supplied Conover with funds from the church treasury and authorized him to seek further financial support from the Saints in western Nevada and northern California.[50]

The start of the trip is described in graphic terms by Oliver Huntington, who explained it as part of Brigham Young's policy to stop the U.S. forces coming to Utah "with hostile intentions against an unoffending people."

O. B. Huntington, Incidents of Preservation by Inspiration in my Second Trip to Carson & Calafornia, BYU Library.

On the 1st of August 1857 I was hauling hay and had my last load in but had not unhitched the team when I was informed that General Daniel H. Wells wanted me at the Presidents office immediately.

I went immediately after unhitching. My residence was a mile N.W. from president Youngs office in the 19th Ward of Salt Lake.

I found the General waiting & he said that I was wanted to go as guide for a small express company to Carson and Calafornia by the direct west route which I had traveled once, and to start as soon as possible & wanted to know how long it would take to go. I studied a minute & replied 18 days if I had to go on my own work animals which I had found was the case.

Now the object of this journey was to send word for all the saints to come to Utah as soon as possible as there was an army of U.S. Soldiers enroute for Utah with hostile intentions against an unoffending people and President Young did not propose to let them come into our peaceful Settlement without asking them to stop and cool off a little and find out whether it was really right that they should come. It was deemed necessary that the whole Church of "Jesus Christ" should be called together to help look into this army business, and that the whole Church should help that army to make a halt and cool off, lest in their hot haste they should do something wrong.

---

[49]Schindler, *Orrin Porter Rockwell,* 217–18. The Utah Historical Society is the repository for a manuscript "Biographical Sketch of the Life of Peter Wilson Conover." George Bean had also been a member of this 1855 company with Conover. Bean's official report and map, never published, is in the LDS Archives.

[50]President Young also quietly sent directions to the San Bernardino Saints to secure arms and ammunition for Zion. News about the efforts of the southern Californians to bring these military supplies from San Francisco and send them on to Utah reached the southland newspapers, adding to the storm of controversy that surrounded the LDS leadership's abandonment of San Bernardino. Lyman, *San Bernardino,* 349–51.

At that time there was a large missionary settlement in Carson and adjoining vallies presided over by Chester Loveland, and our errand or Journey was to call them and all saints in the west, home to Utah.

Before I was called to the Presiding office by General Wells, he had sent from Provo ten men with orders to provide themselves with 15 days rations for the same Journey and to wait for others and written orders at a designated place in Rush Valley. The men sent from Provo were Peter W. Conover as Captain of the expidition, David Canfield, George Bean, Joseph Dudley, Geo. Daniels, Urvin Wilson, Lyman Carter, Evert Orsen, Wesley Wheeler, and William Hooper. Those from Salt Lake were O.B. Huntington, guide, Joshua Whitney, James Peck, Stephen B. Moore, James Frank Townsend and Simeon C. Dolton [Dalton]—We started from Salt lake on the 17th of August and reached our rendevous on the 18th where we found the men from Provo waiting.

The day of leaving Salt lake City I went [to] Pres Youngs Office for papers and instructions. Through me he promised the comp. that not a man should be lost if we would keep the commands of God be humble and stick together.

Printed instructions were given to us verbaly and written to President Loveland of the mission in Carson, for no man or company to come alone or separate from the main company "All come together in one company." The question was asked if, when on our return and directly west of Salt lake on our way up the Humbolt river, some one had better come across south of the lake and bring word how the company was getting along?

President Young studied a few seconds and replied, "There is no use of giving that instruction, some one will do it any how, without instructions.

The men from Salt lake Started with 20 days rations. I furnished 4 mules for the company & Josh Whitney and I messed together. Every man bore his own expenses or was furnished by his neighbor and not chargeable upon the Church.

Aug. 19 1857 our little company or "Express" left Rush Valley about noon and launched upon our wild ocean of desert but how wild & tempestious we little dreamed as we started full of life gayety and zelous energy on Gods business for his people & kingdom.

Huntington's mission quickly turned into a life-threatening ordeal. Traveling at the end of August in a year of extreme drought, Huntington led Colonel Conover (whom he called captain) and his company over a route he had seen under far better conditions in 1854. Predictably, they found no water where Huntington expected it. None of the men in this company would ever forget their desperate struggle for survival, but the expedition's two leaders, Huntington and Conover, each in his own fashion took full credit for their deliverance.

In this journal excerpt, Huntington narrates the men's arrival at the first Mormon outpost at the edge of the desert in western Nevada on the last day of August, and their urgent ride to reach the Saints of Carson Valley with the message from President Young.

> We ate bread and meat for supper, and traveled to Carson Lake that night where we arrived about eleven P.M. The next morning Sept. 2, 1857 we ate the last of our beef and not a morsel left to eat of anything. It was then 30 miles to Ragtown on Carson river, where the old emigrant road left Carson river to cross the 45 mile desert so renowned. The Captain and brother Simon Dalton started early for Ragtown with instructions for us to camp about 3 miles below the town and they would bring provisions if there was any in the town, which consisted of 4 or 5 houses inhabited. They brought us 50 lbs of flour with sugar coffee and bacon to correspond, and when we had finished our breakfast the next morning September 3rd we had nothing to eat again. When we had got to the town Captain Conover went to the same man and got more "all on time and had to be paid for when we came back" our bill was $20 which the brethern of the Carson mission paid as we came back. While in the town we learned that on the 5th which would be Monday a company of 15 was to start for Salt Lake from Carson.
>
> It was therefore necessary, in order to carry out the instructions of Pres. Young, i.e. "for all to come together;" for some of us to be there the next morning which would be Sunday, that the news of our mission might be had at all the meetings. It was 85 miles to Washoe and when we got ready to start from our noon ground, where we divided packs and lightened the horses that had to go through on fast time; it was afternoon. S. C. Dalton, Peter Conover, and I were picked to ride all night again and did it in 19 hours. Ate breakfast with President Loveland in Washoe Valley.[51] After breakfast I got onto a fresh horse and rode 25 miles to Genoa, Conover and Loveland rode in a wagon. We were not long going and by that time I had as much ride as I wanted.

In his reminiscences of the journey, Peter Conover described his effort to deliver the orders from Brigham Young to Mormon settlers in Carson Valley and seek their assistance in the other purpose of his expedition. He needed funds and volunteers to buy guns and ammunition and deliver these tools of war to the church authorities in Great Salt Lake City.

---

[51] Washoe Valley is between today's Carson City and Virginia City.

PETER W. CONOVER
This Nauvoo Legion colonel gained Brigham Young's gratitude for leading an 1857 expedition to northern California that summoned the Saints to Utah and brought back from San Francisco a badly needed supply of gunpowder and lead for LDS troops in the Utah War. *Courtesy Pioneer Memorial Museum, International Society, Daughters of Utah Pioneers.*

PETER WILSON CONOVER, REMINISCENCES, LDS ARCHIVES.

August 31st, we started and got to Congor's house [at Ragtown] about nine o'clock. There we met a man from Washoe Valley where we intended going. This man informed us that the President of that place was calculating to go with the company to Salt Lake to conference. I called the company together and told them what I had heard and that we must get there before they started, as my business was with the President. It looked like an impossibility as our horses were jaded and we had traveled so far without water and it was twenty miles away. We got food again at Congor's. About fifty pounds more flour and some coffee and other stuff. We traveled until about eleven o'clock then stopped for dinner. After dinner I called the guide [O. B. Huntington] and Samuel Dalton (who both had good mules) to accompany me. We traveled all that day up Carson river and came to a saloon kept by a man called Dutch John. There we got some crackers and cheese and ate supper about dark. After supper we mounted our horses, left the road and started over the mountains, through sagebrush etc. following an Indian trail. We traveled till midnight then lost the trail. We then dismounted, lay down until daybreak

September 1st I got up and found the trail then woke the others up. We saddled up as quickly as possible and started on over the mountain. We traveled about a mile and reached the top from there we could see Washoe settlement. As soon as we got to the top of the mountain my horse squealed as loud as he could acting like he knew there were people there. Under the edge of the hill was a log cabin. When the horse whinnied the inmates came to the door. We rode up and inquired how far it was to Washoe. They told us it was six miles and showed us what part of the settlement the President lived in. We then started on. The horses acted like they had new life.

We reached the President's house just as he was sitting down to breakfast. We called him out and he motioned us in at the gate. I gave him my message. In the express it asked for all the ammunition we could find, and for me to take the money and go to California. The President [Loveland] furnished me $5,000.00 that he had received for tithing and which he was going to take to Salt Lake with him. After breakfast we walked out into the town.

The President sent out four or five boys to tell the people to come to a meeting at nine o'clock. At the appointed time we met the people at the school house. Read the message to them, told them what was wanted, and to rally back to Salt Lake. The express told them there was difficulty between the Government and the mormons and that they were all requested to break camp and hurry back to Salt Lake as quickly as possible. After meeting was dismissed the President unloaded his buggy, took our horses and turned them into his wheat stubble. He then hitched his mules to the wagon and we started for Eagle Valley, twenty-five miles from Washoe.[52]

When we got to Eagle Valley we called the people together and held a meeting at two o'clock. We read the express to them, told the message of returning to Salt Lake, to furnish all the guns and ammunition they could, and if they could buy any powder, to do so. This was not a very large branch. They furnished $200.00 to buy ammunition. We were treated very kindly and after meeting ate dinner with them. The brethren were very thankful to have the chance to return. We then hitched up our teams and started for ____ City [Genoa] in Carson Valley, twenty five miles farther on. We arrived there after dark. Called a meeting and kept up till ten o'clock. That night we raised five [hundred?] dollars more.

The next morning at ten o'clock we called the people to meeting again and made arrangements to send after the ammunition. Rob Walker started for San Francisco with $12,160.00 in gold with orders to buy ammunition and to deliver it to Stockton by steamboat. The people agreed to meet them there with teams to bring it away. I waited four days to get teams. The people concluded that if they had to move to the Valley they would have no more teams than they needed themselves. We held a council to decide what to do.

Bob Walker was a clerk of Wm. Nickerson, a merchant of Genoa, and was

[52]According to Myron Angel's 1881 *History of Nevada*, Eagle Valley acquired its name from a trading post at the southwest end of the valley where the proprietor, Frank Hall, displayed a stuffed eagle. Carson City is located in Eagle Valley.

going to San Francisco to pay for some goods he had bought and to get some more. That was the reason I sent the money with him to buy the ammunition as he was well known there. At the council I decided to go with O. B. Huntington after the ammunition if the people would furnish horses, saddles, blankets, etc. and they agreed to. The next morning we got the horses and started on over the mountains. It was the sixth of September.

In his manuscript about the 1857 expedition, "Incidents of Preservation by Inspiration," Oliver Huntington was very guarded in describing the LDS effort to bring arms and ammunition from California. He stated only that Robert Walker and Henry Brazee "were dispatched to San Francisco on business to carry out instructions from Salt Lake." He added that he and Conover followed the two volunteer purchasing agents on a ride over the Sierra "by way of the Big Trees in a day and night constant riding 100 miles and were gone for a week—all returned with the business fully accomplished that we went for." He told much more of the story, however, in a journal of recollections. This account begins after the express reached the LDS settlement of Genoa in Carson Valley.

OLIVER B. HUNTINGTON JOURNAL, VOL. II,
UTAH STATE HISTORICAL SOCIETY.

I remained with Brother W. Nixon about a week and it became necessary to send an express to California to assist some brethren there in getting supplies of ammunition sent for the day after we arrived in Carson. Bro. Conover and I were sent with that express accompanied by Nelson Hollingshead and another young man from G.S.L. Valley as safeguard against Indians who were getting hostile in the mountains and had lately killed some whites while crossing.[53]

At Murphy in Calif. we found 4 or 5 of the brethren who took the Church Cattle over and were able to return to Carson the next day. Among them was my Nephew Lot Huntington but he and Y. Webb went by stage to Sacramento that night.

The next day the brethren all started back for Carson except Conover and I. We waited for the powder one week, hired teams to take it as soon as it arrived from San Francisco we packed it in the wagons and traveled with the teams 3 days then struck out leaving Robt. Walker and Henry Brazee in charge who also brought it up from the Bay. After leaving the teams we rode 60 miles in one day to Genoa from Murphy to Genoa 100 miles.

[53]Nelson Hollingshead was the patriarch of a large family, eventually numbering two wives and fifteen children, who settled in Parowan and subsequently relocated to Minersville, Utah. See Biographical Register, LDS Archives.

Sept. 22nd, 1857 a train of 130 wagons rolled out from Eagle Valley for G. S. Lake City embracing every good Mormon within our reach and time, either in the valleys about Carson or California.

Peter Conover: Determined to Take the Ammunition

Peter Conover provides a more detailed and entertaining account of the difficulties faced by the emissaries from Salt Lake in securing their cargo. They faced the threats of rowdy, belligerent anti-Mormons at a tavern in Angel's Camp, where he and Huntington had taken rooms while they waited for the guns and ammunition to arrive from San Francisco. This section of his account begins with the long, hurried ride from Genoa to the gold country.

Peter Wilson Conover, Reminiscences, LDS Archives.

Two young men volunteered to go with us as there were bad reports about robbers on the road. We rode all day and that night we stopped on the Sierra Nevada Mountains and built a fire to get warm. We stopped there to rest until daylight. When daylight came we saddled our horses and rode until about nine o'clock, when we came to a house and got breakfast and fed our horses. We paid $2.00 for a bushel of oats also $2.00 for our breakfast. We then mounted our horses and went on. About two o'clock we came to the big trees where we fed our horses and got breakfast. Then mounted and rode eighteen miles to a place called Angels Camp. Supper was very near ready when we fed our horses and called for supper.

I gave the tavern keeper a letter of introduction from William Nickerson. He received us very kindly and treated us very nicely that night. Next morning I got up very early and made a good many inquiries about [Robert] Walker. I told the tavern keeper I was very anxious to know about Walker and would give almost anything to hear from him. He told me he would tell me for two fifty. He went right in and telegraphed to Walker to know if he had got what he went for. The answer came back in about ten minutes, that he had got all he went for, and had it all ready to be shipped on the steamboat.

On the fourth day, I got up very early in the morning and went over to the tavern. The news boy came and threw the daily paper on the stand. I picked it up and started to read. The first thing that I saw was that Harney had started with fifteen thousand men to hang all the Mormons. That on the 22nd of July the Mormons and Harney had a fight. The paper said the Mormons had killed six hundred of his men and that Harney had gone back for reinforcements. Also that the Mormons had sent for $2,000 worth of ammunition and as many pistols and guns, and that the Mormons must be stopped at some point. I read this in the "Sacramento Bee."

This then was the point at which the Mormons must be stopped! I laughed for I knew that the ammunition had not even got there yet. Just then the tavern keeper came out and said "What's up now?" I said, "Oh, I was laughing at that damned lie that was in the paper," and he replied "How do you know that it was a lie?" I said "Because I started out on the 17th and at that time the Mormons were all at home minding their business." Just then I gave him the Masonic sign and he returned it. Said I, "John, two heads are better than one," and he called me into a back room and asked me again the particulars so we sat down on a sofa and I told him the whole truth, what we had come for and all about it. He said that it was a shame that we should be having such a time after we had paid for it, and that as we had paid for the ammunition we should have it if he could use his influence. He said "Why the idea! After you have bought it from the government and paid for it, for the government to try to take it away from you."

I had my team already hired and in the yard ready to load as soon as the ammunition should arrive. Walker had purchased 12,000 lbs. of other merchandise together with the ammunition.

The next morning Traverse handed me the key to his warehouse where the goods were consigned to. We had a tent pitched and slept in it to guard the warehouse and our horses were stabled near by. When we went in to breakfast the same paper came in with the same statement doubled. The miners that boarded at the tavern were determined to take the ammunition, etc. away from me as soon as it arrived. It arrived in the night of the 15th during a rain storm. We were at the warehouse waiting for it, and I opened the gate myself for the wagons to come in. As soon as the wagons stopped, I slid under and loosened the trail wagon which contained the ammunition, and we run it into the warehouse and locked it up. We then came out and took the hind end-gate out of the wagon which carried the 12,000 lbs of merchandise. Just as I got the end-gate out, about fifty men began to pour in with a big Missourian leading. I said, "Gentlemen, I am very glad that you came just now. I need help to unload so that I can get away from here as quickly as possible." The captain said that that is what they had come for, and they intended to get that ammunition. The first thing that presented itself in the hay wagon was a keg of whiskey. The captain lifted it out, set it on the scales and weighed it, and put it down on the platform. I took a big auger down from overhead, bored a big hole in the barrel and drew off a bucketfull. I called all the hands to come and sample the liquor. They came to a man. The Captain and I then got into the wagon and began handing out the goods, Walker weighing and loading into the other wagons with the others helping him. The Captain did not know anything about carrying powder in boxes so we handed out the cases of canister the same as the other goods, and kept on until we had it all unloaded and reloaded into the other wagons. It was now about 11 o'clock at night.

The Captain was very disappointed about not finding a single keg of powder in the wagons and got very mad about it. He swore that if he had the man that printed that newspaper that he would hang him in a minute, for there was not a pound of powder in the wagons, nor a gun or a pistol.

Then they began to go by twos and threes until there was not one of them left there with us. After they had left we sat down and rested as we were very tired and warm, it being very warm weather. After all was still, we rolled out the trail wagon. I had reserved two small wagons to haul the ammunition in. We weighed it and loaded it into these wagons. Then as the moon had just risen the boys hitched up their teams and started right out. Walker, O. B. Huntington and myself stayed until the morn of the 16th to settle up with the tavern keeper and get our breakfast. After breakfast the big Captain came to me and wanted to know what I was going to do with the guns and ammunition I had bought. I told him what I had bought was mine and it was none of his business what I did with it. "Well" he said "I will see you before you get to Carson." "Well," said I, "If you follow me I will kill you and bury you without a sheet." We started out but I never saw the Captain again though some of the miners did follow us but they caused us no trouble.

We did not overtake the teams until about noon that day. They were traveling along when we overtook them. We went about four miles farther, found some grass and stopped. We placed a guard about the horses and one in camp. O. B. Huntington and myself went back about fifty yards and slept beside the road under a big tree. Got up the next morning the 17th, and started on. That night we camped on the river.

On the 18th, we had to double our teams for seven miles right up a mountain. It took us nearly all day to get them up. Traveled about four miles farther and camped near the same house we camped by when we went over. The next night the 19th we camped at a lake about eighteen miles from Genoa. The 20th we got to Genoa about three o'clock in the afternoon. The camp had moved out about four miles on the road. We went on and overtook them that night. I went to the President and asked about getting wagons to haul the ammunition in the rest of the way. He said they had not a spare wagon. Everyone was loaded to the bows. I finally went to a teamster by the name of Luke Murphy and told him I wanted to ask a favor of him. He said, "Yes, yes, willingly, but how can I get home?" "Oh" said I, "Make a bargain there with Hart to take you home." "All right," said he, and that was settled.

There was a company of about twenty families came on with us. They had paid no tithing but were well able to pay theirs so I went to Zack Cheeny [Cheney], he being the head of the company and told him I had been to California and got ammunition, and now I had no team to haul it home with. That I had bought a wagon and team and wanted $500.00 to pay for them. While we were talking, Joseph Murdock came up and said he wanted to buy the little wagon for his family to ride in. I sold it to him for fifty dollars. Then I went back three miles to Genoa and bought a new wagon of Warren Smith. Paid $200.00 for it. I took the mules I had bought and went right up and bought the wagon. Then my lead was most too heavy for my mules so I called for more team. Joseph Murdock furnished a mule and a horse. The 21st day we started home. Evert Orsier drove the team into Salt Lake.

We formed our company in companies of fifties. We had five companies. There was from one to three men to every team. We started down the Carson river, traveled thirty miles then camped on the river that night.

That night the President called the company together to choose a Captain of the guard. They unanimously voted for me to be Captain of the guard. I then placed guard for the night. At twelve o'clock relieved guard.

Captain Conover's account of the return trip to Utah describes one other extraordinary episode, which took place after the expedition had crossed the Forty-mile Desert at night and reached the sink of the Humboldt River. While they rested in camp on 24 September, a small group of their avowed enemies who had pursued them from California caught up with Conover's men.

At 12 o'clock on the 24th, we came to the sink of the Humboldt. We had about three hundred head of horses and mules besides all the rest. We turned them all down on the sink to get water. They began in a hurry to get something to eat.

Before we got supper ready the [six] men who had been sent to take our ammunition away from us came to camp. They tried to stampede our horses but we were on our guard. I told the guard to holler every half hour or hour. This they did lustily. They could have been heard the world over it seemed to me.

When I went to relieve the guard at midnight, three of the [pursuing] men came and wanted to get their horses [which had now mixed with the Mormons' large herd of animals] as they would rather travel [back to California] in the night. I told them they could not get their horses or if they tried to catch them it would stampede all of the horses, and that was what they wanted to do. John Murdock said, "The first man that swings a lasso in that band of horses is a dead man." And he meant it too. I told the men to come back to camp and stay till morning, then we would get them all right. I put them under guard till morning. Then I went to Nickerson and told him that I wanted some liquor to treat the men to. I got a quart and called the six men to come up and we would settle the scrape about the horses. They left their horses and come up to get their bitters. I handed the bottle to their Captain and told them to drink hearty as we had plenty. The

> six men emptied the bottle then asked me if I would sell them some. I said, "Yes, I will sell you all you can find dishes for." The Captain sent for all the canteens and flasks they had.
>
> They had a canteen each and there were five flasks between them. The first thing they handed me was a pint flask. I filled it and they emptied it. I kept on until I filled all they had. I then asked if they would sell us some of their guns as they were going back. They had told us that they would never follow a Mormon again. They said yes, they would sell them. We bought all but one pair of revolvers which a young man said were his father's. They acknowledged that they had orders from the Missouri Captain to stampede our horses and run them back but they were sick of their job. They took their horses and left and we thought that we had got rid of them.

Captain Conover had a shrewd way of outwitting his opponents without the use of violence. On both occasions when his mission for guns and ammunition had been endangered, a liberal dose of free whiskey for his anti-Mormon adversaries ended the peril. His success in buying the guns of his pursuers in the middle of Nevada adds a final note of wry humor to the history of this encounter.

The rest of the journey back to Utah went without serious incident. "We reached home on the 25th October and went straight to the Presidents Office and reported our whole Journey, which was written by a short hand reporter," O. B. Huntington summed up the adventure succinctly. "Brigham and Heber were highly pleased."[54]

FREDERICK W. HURST: I CAN SHOULDER MY RIFLE WITH AS GOOD GRACE AS TO GET UP AND PREACH

While these events were taking place elsewhere, the Hurst brothers continued their missionary service in the gold country through August and well into September, traveling about the district from Salmon Falls to Placerville to Dry Town.[55] Then, as Frederick's journal records, in the third week of September instructions arrived by way of Carson Valley that abruptly caused all dutiful Saints to begin preparations for a hurried return to Zion according to President Young's directive.

[54]Huntington, Incidents of Preservation by Inspiration, BYU Library.

[55]Among other experiences, Frederick mentions in Union Town on 21 August 1857 a visit to "old father and Mother Wimmer," presumably Peter and Elizabeth Jane Wimmer who were with Marshall and the battalion veterans at Coloma when gold was discovered in January 1848.

DIARY OF FREDERICK WILLIAM HURST, LDS ARCHIVES.

Friday [18 September 1857]. Aaron [Thatcher] and I walked to Brother Miller's near White Rock Springs. There is quite an excitement among the Mormons. We hear they are all leaving Carson Valley. That all the Elders are called in.

Saturday the 19th. We walked to Salmon Falls. Stayed at Orr's. Next morning early we walked to Brother Cram's near Auburn. Met Clem, John and Brother Shearman. Held meeting in the morning and afternoon. In the evening President Cannon and James Orr arrived and confirmed the news we had previously. Brother Brigham started instantly for Carson Valley.

We were sent on a special mission to warn all the Saints to be ready to gather at a moments warning. Brother Cannon informed us that the troops ordered for Utah were abusing the Handcart Companies, ravaging their women, etc.[56] That 5 or 7 companies had left Utah to meet the Hell Hounds and give them what they justly deserved. My prayer is that the vengence of the Almighty may speedily overtake them. I cannot express how I feel. My blood runs cold. To tell the truth I hope and pray that if there is any fuss that the Lord will spare my life to gather to Zion, there to be one soul and body to defend the cause of truth. I have hitherto tried to do so and I do not count my life dear to me if it is necessary I believe I can shoulder my rifle with as good grace as to get up and preach, and with the self same spirit. Well, we started the same evening and walked to Brain Cram's, five miles. Brother John accompanied us on his way to Yolo County. Clem and Brother Shearman started for Grass Valley. We walked to Miller's, Thomas's, Joseph Outhouse's, Pollick's, etc. Brother Aaron's cousin paid him $104.00. We then walked to Dry Town to Brother Plunkett's, then to Father Lunceford's, then to Placerville to Brother George F. Hendry's, Taylor's, Bird's, then to Calama [Coloma] to Sister Plumtree's then back to Salmon Falls. By Friday noon Brother Aaron was there about given out, was sick all day Saturday. Brother Preston arrived Sunday Evening. Brothers Clem and Shearman arrived next day. Brother Aaron went to Yolo with Brother Preston. Brother Shearman went to Union Town, Clem and I went to Michigan Bar. Stayed all night at Brother Dancy's. He gave us $5.00 and I forgot to state that Brother Hendry gave me $10.00 to buy a rifle. Tuesday came back to Salmon Falls. Wednesday walked to Father Lunceford's. Met Brother Shearman.

[56]The tales told by LDS leaders in both California and Utah about vicious soldiers attacking defenseless Mormon emigrants were more than baseless. An army commissary train marched up the north bank of the Sweetwater River "sometimes close to the handcart company," emigrant James Jensen recalled. "Nothing of an unpleasant nature occurred." The army, of course, was well supplied, but the handcart companies "were often in dire distress." Despite the disaster that had killed some 250 Mormon emigrants the previous winter, church officials again failed to act responsibly and the parties were running out of flour before they reached South Pass. Jensen recalled how an army captain gave his handcart train "one of Uncle Sam's fat oxen" whose foot had been crushed. "You can have that ox," said the officer. "I guess you need it." See Biography of James Jensen by J. W. Tanner, quoted in Journal History, 13 September 1857, 21–22.

> Saturday. Brother S. Henry and I went to Salmon Falls. Bought a span of horses for $300.00 off Brother Orr. Brother Hendry paid cash $250.00 and gave a note for $50.00. I have been helping the Lunceford's fix their wagon. I have been carpenter, painter, in fact, Jack of all Trades. We were to have started today, Sunday, October 9th, but there is so much hanging back. However, if all is well we will start tomorrow.
>
> I do not know what the Pharisees around here will think of us Mormon men. Preaching one day and working another. This is Sunday and I have painted a wagon, in fact, worked hard all day. I have been trying all I can to get the folks off. I have received two letters from Brother Shearman informing me that the Company will not start till the 20th of October. I went over to French Town this evening. Mr. Waters (who has been friendly with us) was very much excited. Said if he could sell out he would go by water and meet us at San Bernardino. Quite a mob of fellows got together here drinking and swore vengence regarding us young Elders. However, we escaped out at the back door. When we got nearly home I fell into a deep hole, escaped injury.

The Hurst brothers actually started for Utah on 12 October. With eleven other people, three wagons, eleven horses, and three large dogs, their company began moving toward San Bernardino and the winter desert crossing. Frederick kept his journal as they traveled southwest to Stockton and San José, headed to an ocean-side route past San Luis Obispo, slowly traveled southward along the coast to Santa Barbara, then turned inland, detoured around Los Angeles, and reached San Bernardino a month after leaving the gold country. On the way their small party was joined by a larger group from San Francisco, and the combined company then organized under the leadership of John B. Thatcher as captain, with W. H. Shearman serving as chaplain. The trip through California was relatively uneventful, though at times the travelers were guarded about their identity as Saints, and they bypassed larger towns where they supposed they would risk a hostile demonstration.[57]

[57]The Hursts and their companions had good reasons to avoid Los Angeles. In October 1857 the first reports of the Mountain Meadows massacre reached southern California, with stories appearing in the Los Angeles *Star* on 3 October and 10 October. Shortly afterwards William M. Wall, a senior LDS missionary returning from Australia, stopped for the night in Los Angeles because his lame horse needed to be shod. He ran into an excited band of anti-Mormons, led by well-known Rakabite apostates from San Bernardino, who threatened him with hanging. A gang of twenty-five or more men tried to drag Wall from the hotel room where he had barricaded himself, then spent most of the night drinking whiskey outside his lodging while "shouting the most furious oaths and threats and . . . firing their revolvers." They finally left just before dawn. After paying his bill and leaving the hotel, Wall again found himself confronted by some of the same foes, but made his escape after warning that he "made it a practice to kill all dogs that took hold of me." Until he left San Bernardino for Utah, he relied on the security of his "splendid double barrelled shotgun, three revolvers, a good bowie knife, and legging knife all in plain sight" and only visited public (*continued*)

The rest of Hurst's account belongs to the history of Utah. In good time the two brothers reached Zion, where both served briefly as volunteers in LDS militia companies, shouldering their rifles and standing guard in the snow at Echo Camp through winter and spring 1858. Discharged at the end of May, Frederick and Clement started walking toward Provo, covering one hundred thirty miles through rugged country in only three days to rejoin family members and friends after a three-year absence. Recording their arrival and their reception with "a hearty welcome from all the family," Frederick wrote a fittingly pious conclusion to his record of missionary adventures: "I feel thankful that we have got home once more. I realize that the hand of the Lord has been over us for good all the time we have been away."

Eli Bell: The Returning Missionary Company

The Hurst brothers were not the last LDS missionaries to leave California. Arriving from Hawaii, Eli Bell landed in San Francisco with a few other returning elders on 26 December 1857. "We found that Bro's Cannon, Smith, & others have gone to Utah," he recorded in his journal, "leaving us to follow on as soon as posiable acording to order from the President Young."[58] After spending a day with a hospitable LDS family in the Bay city, Bell and his companions went twenty-five miles south to Redwood City. Here they found a substantial community of Saints preparing to make the trip to Utah by way of San Bernardino as soon as traveling conditions improved.

Although jobs were scarce, Bell and one companion went to work lumbering and cutting fence posts and rails, "which is very hard work to new beginers."[59] On 2 March he recorded, assuredly with satisfaction, "To day we finished makeing 1,000 Posts & 1,000 Rails & quit work about 1 P.M." That same evening he and another young Saint began preparation for the trip east: "bro [William] King & I . . . need to fix up a wagon for us to go cross the plains in. We are going to join to gether with four more of the brethren & go with one wagon." Nearly two weeks

(*continued*) places with companions who were similarly prepared to defend themselves. Statement of W. H. Wall, Historian's Office, 12 December 1857, reported by Leo Hawkins, Journal History, 12 December 1857, LDS Archives.

[58]Eli Bell Journal, 27 December 1857, LDS Archives.

[59]Ibid., 25 February 1858.

passed while preparations continued. Bell carefully described how the entire company met and selected officers with a care that would have done credit to many larger outfits.

> Saturday 13 met to day to organise the companey present of the breathern 19 in number. J.A. Kelting, Eli Whipple, Wm King, Sixtus E. Johnson, Elemuel Sawtell, Franklin Young, Wm W. Cluff, John A. West, George Speirs, S. M. Molen, Hans Carlson, Peter Williams, Jerod Sutson, T.S. Setson, Eli Bell, John Brinley, Nelson P. Beebe, S. B. Thurston & Broth Kelting was called to preside over the meeting. the officers of the companey was then chosen & elected unanimousley. Broth Whipple was voted in as the Captain of the Company, E. Sawtell as Secretary, J. R. Young, Chaplain, & S. E. Johnson Sargent of the gard. Resolved that the companey be called the Returning Missionary company under the care of bro Whipple. Meeting was dismissed by prayer from the Chaplain. The wether is butiful.[60]

The Whipple company began moving out on 17 and 18 March, first heading to Gilroy, then traveling over Pacheco Pass and turning southward. They made the trip through the San Joaquin Valley in easy stages, pausing frequently to rest their draft animals while Bell and others went hunting or fishing. Their journey was through open country, well away from settlements. The company crossed Tejon Pass in mid-April and soon joined other travelers from San Bernardino to make the desert trip eastward. Aided by mild spring weather, Bell and his traveling companions reached Cedar City, Utah, at the very end of May 1858. "Met with several of my old acquaintances," Bell reported, "who made me welcom to my home again & on to the valey of the Mountains."[61] The following day, a Sunday, Bell went to the Cedar City church meeting. "Was called on to speak," he reported, "don the best that I could, also in the afternoon." That same evening he made a last visit to the company. "We settled up in our mess & I come of 2,75 Cts in dept to the companey." He ended his journal account with a curious observation: "so fare so good."[62]

With the exit of George Q. Cannon and William Shearman in late 1857, followed by the departures of the Whipple company and other small groups the following spring, the Church of Jesus Christ of Latter-day Saints went inactive in northern California. At the same time, the withdrawal of the Saints from San Bernardino finished the church's activ-

[60]Ibid. [61]Ibid., 29 May 1858. [62]Ibid., 30 May 1858.

ities in the south. In February 1858 Ebenezer Hanks sold the remaining San Bernardino ranch lands, finally retiring the debt that had hung over the property ever since Amasa Lyman and Charles C. Rich acquired it. Following Brigham Young's mandate, Hanks was compelled to close out the dream of owning a fabulously valuable property that had been nurtured so long by the community of Saints in southern California.

As in northern California, a significant number of San Bernardino Saints remained behind, preferring to hold onto their California way of life and their individual homes, farms, and businesses rather than sell at sacrifice prices. Over the next few years others in the 1857–1858 exodus returned from Utah. Some families were caught in dilemmas of separation. Addison Pratt, for example, remained in southern California because of concern for his failing health, even though his wife Louisa insisted on making the move to the Great Basin. He agreed to join her in 1863, but after suffering through two Utah winters, the ailing Pratt returned to Anaheim to live with a daughter. Jefferson Hunt went to Utah; his three daughters stayed in California; his son moved to Utah, then briefly back to California before relocating his family permanently in Utah in 1863.

For northern California Saints, whether to stay or leave was usually a community decision. Virtually all the Mormons near Redwood City, in San José, and at the Buckeye branch in Yolo County left for Utah by early 1858, with community members usually traveling together. In western El Dorado County, Salmon Falls and along Green Valley road and adjacent districts, on the other hand, very few Saints left in response to Brigham Young's orders. The Thomas Orr family remained at the center of a lively settlement of church-related families, with ties of friendship, kinship, and marriage that linked the community even after church authorities abandoned California. In this area too, some Saints who had rushed to Zion at the emotional height of the northern California LDS reformation later returned to live once more among friends and relatives in the gold country. In later years as well, a few newcomers arrived from the Great Basin and settled into this unofficial Mormon colony.[63]

[63]Melinda Peak, president of Peak & Associates, Inc., affirms this impressionistic conclusion. Based on her company's twenty-five years of research in the area, Ms. Peak has expert knowledge of the archeological and historical resources of eastern Sacramento County and western El Dorado County. For a report on one Mormon-related property, see Peak, *An Evaluation of the Rolling Hills House, El Dorado County, California,* a Cultural Resources Management report available at the North Central Information Center at California State University, Sacramento.

For church authorities in Utah, there was no early reconciliation with the remaining California brethren. Those Saints who stayed in the gold country or in San Bernardino were left unchurched. Although the Reorganized LDS church began missionary activities and organized branches in California beginning in the late 1860s, for more than thirty years the Utah-based church had only a shadowy presence in the golden state.

A singular exception could be found in Sacramento, where the young British converts Aaron and Mary Garlick had just arrived when the 1857 exodus began. Poor and exhausted from their overland trip, and because Mary was pregnant, they did not join the movement to Utah but remained in Sacramento, where the Garlicks rose to modest prosperity and a position of respect. After a brief association with the Reorganized LDS church, in 1871 the Garlick parents and their two sons were rebaptized by Elder Philip Leuba, who was traveling through the area as an LDS missionary on the way to his native Switzerland. With appointment from Leuba, Garlick formed a six-member branch that grew to twenty members by 1880. Job Taylor Smith, a traveling businessman from Ogden, lodged overnight with the Garlicks in December 1876 and reported favorably on their efforts to keep the LDS faith alive. During this same trip, Smith climbed to the top of the new California state capitol building, knelt, and prayed to God that confusion would enter the counsels of the state's lawmakers who were plotting measures for "the injury, downfall or disadvantage of thy Saints."[64]

The revival of the Latter-day Saint church in California was begun unintentionally by an unanticipated new migration of refugees from Utah: polygamists who were fleeing to the Pacific Coast to avoid arrest and prosecution on federal charges under the 1882 Edmunds Act.[65] After President Chester A. Arthur appointed an anti-Mormon chief jus-

[64]Cowan and Homer, *California Saints*, 218, 225. Before returning to Ogden, Smith attempted with limited success to organize a small group of Oakland Saints. Encouraged by the First Presidency, Smith went back to Oakland in 1877 and formed an LDS cooperative to run a boarding house, a green grocery, and a chair caning business. With few members and shaky finances, this organization dissolved by the end of the year and Smith again returned to Utah. See ibid., 225–26.

[65]This severe measure made "unlawful cohabitation" with an alleged plural wife a misdemeanor, punishable by a $600 fine and up to six months' imprisonment for each separate offense. To assure that plural marriages would not be protected by LDS juries, the act disqualified polygamists and cohabitants from basic civil rights under the U.S. Constitution. Anyone so identified lost the right to vote, to hold public office, and to serve on a jury. Moreover, the law transferred control of voter registration and local election boards to a federally-appointed Utah commission, a further effort to end theocratic control over politics and governmental operations in Utah Territory.

tice of Utah Territory in 1884, federal officials joined in a crusade against polygamy based on the assumption that all high church officials not only practiced plural marriage but they were part of a criminal conspiracy to defy the law. Supported by most Utah Mormons, church leaders went into hiding "underground" rather than submit to harsh sentences and the biased proceedings of unfriendly judges, juries, and court officers.[66] While no prominent members of the Salt Lake City hierarchy took refuge in California, at least a few local church officials came to the golden state temporarily to escape the federal marshals and judges who threatened their freedom. Other polygamous families also found it prudent to move to the Pacific Coast on extended visits. In Oakland and a few other areas, these newcomers brought the LDS faith with them, returning the church to California if only on an interim basis.[67]

Further changes in Utah led the church authorities to disavow the practice of polygamy and soon expedited an LDS revival in northern California. After President John Taylor's death in July 1887, continuing Edmunds Act prosecutions in Utah Territory and sweeping new federal legislation that confiscated church property challenged Wilford Woodruff, the new prophet. Further, an 1890 U.S. Supreme Court decision, upholding an Idaho anti-Mormon enactment, threatened wholesale disfranchisement not merely for polygamists but for all church members. Several prominent Utah Saints accompanied President Woodruff on a railroad trip to California in April 1889, where they met twice with Sen. Leland Stanford, a powerful national politician and railroad president. Although details of these meetings were never fully revealed, Woodruff's journal indicates that the LDS leaders were seeking the aid of Stanford and his associates in pressing for Utah statehood, as they had done two years earlier. Stanford declared, according to Woodruff, that President Harrison "is bigoted and too much wedded to the Presbyterian Church," but the senator "spoke in the kindest manner concerning us and our circumstances, and is evidently willing, as he has been for a long time, to do everything in his power for our good."[68]

---

[66]The history of the 1882 Edmunds Act and its enforcement in Utah is ably summarized in Lyman, *Political Deliverance,* 21–26.

[67]Cowan and Homer, *California Saints,* 226–28.

[68]Woodruff, Journal, 24 April 1889, 9:26–27. I am indebted to historian Norman Tutorow and to Sandra L. Tidwell, General Reference Librarian at Brigham Young University, for the research (*continued*)

Proceeding "under the necessity of acting for the temporal salvation of the Church," President Woodruff announced in September 1890 that he would submit to the anti-polygamy laws "and to use my influence with members of the Church over which I preside to have them do likewise."[69] From this decisive beginning, the disestablishment of plural marriage as an LDS sacrament soon prepared the way for Utah statehood and the end of federal prosecutions aimed at church authorities.

The issues that for so long had kept apart northern California Saints and the Utah hierarchy thus became moot. In 1892 the church's first presidency, which included George Q. Cannon, determined to reopen a mission in northern California. The designated California president, Luther Dalton, arrived in August and two months later organized the Oakland branch. At the end of November Dalton officially reorganized the Sacramento branch with Aaron Garlick as president. By the end of the year four LDS missionaries were traveling through California, two in the south state and two in the north, based in Sacramento.[70] After an absence of thirty-five years, the Latter-day Saints were reentering the social, cultural, and religious life of the golden state.

(*continued*) and the transcription of Woodruff's journal. Alexander Badlam, Jr., arranged these meetings. Samuel Brannan's nephew and a well-known San Francisco businessman, Badlam was closely involved in lobbying ventures both with Stanford's Central Pacific Railroad and with George Q. Cannon and other LDS authorities. President Woodruff had first met the Badlam family many years before in Saco, Maine, the scene of Woodruff's early missionary success, and he had helped persuade the senior Alexander Badlam to move to Kirtland, Ohio, taking along young Brannan. See Lyman, *Political Deliverance*, 56, 73, 79, 85–87, 109, 169; Cowan and Homer, *California Saints*, 230–31; and Alexander, *Things in Heaven and Earth: The Life and Times of Wilford Woodruff*, 249–54.

[69]Diary of Wilford Woodruff, 25 September 1890, LDS Archives; "Official Declaration," Doctrine and Covenants, after sec. 136, in Arrington and Bitton, *The Mormon Experience*, 183.

[70]Cowan and Homer, *California Saints*, 234–35.

HENRY W. BIGLER

The Mormon Battalion veteran, pioneer California miner, Hawaiian missionary, and devoted Saint as he appeared in his later years, soon after he was honored as one of the "Companions of Marshall" at California's 1898 Gold Rush Jubilee. *Courtesy LDS Archives.*

Chapter 9

"We Are the Men That Developed the Resources of the Pacific Coast"

The Forgotten Heritage of California's Gold Rush Saints

Brigham Young and other senior church spokesmen in Salt Lake put forward the first broad interpretations of the Mormon role in California during the gold rush. In keeping with Young's concerns, they initially portrayed the gold country as Babylon. As their fears that Saints might abandon Zion began to subside, Young and his colleagues boasted that LDS pioneers deserved the nation's gratitude because they had made possible California's growth under American sovereignty. According to this interpretation, the daring, sacrifices, and hard work of the *Brooklyn* colonists and the Mormon Battalion laid the foundation for California's greatness.

Brigham Young: Some of You Will Be Off to California

As church president, Brigham Young did not easily give up his worries about losing Saints to the powerful attraction of the gold fields. Long after the heyday of placer mining, Young continued to preach about the dangers of abandoning Zion. But as he stated in an 1860 address to Utah newcomers, the danger was not simply that those who left would be drawn into the iniquitous ways of California's profane and sinful non-Mormon society. Rather, Young identified the golden state as a stronghold of backsliders and apostates; he predicted that it would attract more such weak-kneed Saints trying to slip away from the true religion practiced by sanctified LDS church members, whose moral and doctrinal compass was oriented toward the Lion House.

> I wish to inform you, brethren and sisters, who have just arrived in these valleys, that all your trials hitherto are but trifling in comparison to the trials you will now be called to meet and pass through. How many of you will continue faithful—preserve yourself in your integrity and in the faith of the Lord Jesus Christ? You have come here expressly to be assembled with the Saints; your object in gathering was to forsake the wickedness that is in the world and to mingle with those who serve God with an undivided heart, and you expect to be faithful; but let me inform you that you will not all prove faithful; some of you will apostatize. Can you tell who? You reply, "No:" but the first you are aware, some of you will be off to California, perhaps, with the words—"To Cache or Carson, we don't care a d— which," on your waggon-covers, as they were on the waggon-covers of some who started for Carson last spring. Some of you will be tempted above what you will bear—will tamely submit to darkness and its powers—to the evil influences of wicked spirits—will forsake the faith, and the Devil will get the advantage of you.[1]

Church leaders devoutly believed the LDS exodus from Nauvoo and subsequent settlement in the Great Basin was divinely inspired. In hindsight, President Young professed to see God's hand as well in the recruitment of the Mormon Battalion and the discovery of gold in northern California by its veterans. Before the gold rush began, he vehemently urged the true people of God to gather in Zion and maintain complete isolation from the non-Mormon world. Only by remaining separate and secluded, he declaimed, could the Saints avoid the persecution that had driven them from previous gathering places. By 1863, however, the church president had altered his view. The gold rush, he now asserted, had been a benefit to the people of Zion, since it brought thousands of non-Mormons through Utah, where they could learn the truth about the LDS people and their religion.

> We had anticipated, when we came into these distant valleys, that we should be entirely secluded from the world—that we should trouble no person and that no person would trouble us. The "Mormon" Battalion had been dis-

[1]Brigham Young, "Trials and Duties of the Saints," 2 September 1860, *Journal of Discourses*, 8:162

banded in California, and some of that body first discovered gold there; the news of that discovery quickly reached the eastern States, and thousands were soon upon our track. Instead of being secluded, we find ourselves in the great national highway. We must be known, and we could not be in a better situation to be known than where we are.[2]

George A. Smith: We Are the Pioneers of the Great West

By the close of the American Civil War in 1865, a broad spirit of reconciliation began to soften national policies toward the Latter-day Saints. In Zion the perfervid oratory of the Utah Mormon reformation and the Utah War period was past, and church authorities quietly moved to muffle discussion of the controversial Mountain Meadows massacre. Utah's Saints had been unenthusiastic in expressing their allegiance to the federal Union during the war. For his part, the wartime military commander in the Great Basin, Brig. Gen. Patrick E. Connor, was deeply suspicious of Brigham Young's motives and critical both of polygamy and the Saints' resistance to federal management of the territory. But President Abraham Lincoln and his cabinet realized the strategic importance of Utah for maintaining Union control over the western territories and states, and so practiced a *laissez-faire* political strategy that averted serious conflicts between the Saints and non-Mormon territorial officials.[3]

After Lincoln's death in April 1865, LDS authorities took a more cooperative attitude toward the U.S. government and non-Mormon society that had many expressions. In an address of October 1865, George A. Smith, a good friend and adviser to Brigham Young and a well-liked preacher, asserted that the Saints should be credited for opening California and all the lands west of Zion for the American people. In this fashion, he claimed approval from the non-Mormon world while reinforcing among the Saints a conviction of their entitlement to a share in the postwar blessings of peace and growing economic prosperity.

---

[2]Brigham Young, "Discourse," 8 July 1863, *Journal of Discourses,* 10:229–30.

[3]This period in Utah's history is well described in Long, *The Saints and the Union: Utah Territory during the Civil War.* A valuable summary is found in Chapter 17 of Eugene E. Campbell's fine work, *Establishing Zion: The Mormon Church in the American West.* The career of James Duane Doty, a Wisconsin politician who became Utah's conciliatory wartime governor, is the subject of Smith, *James Duane Doty, Frontier Promoter.*

GEORGE ALBERT SMITH, 8 OCTOBER 1865, *JOURNAL OF DISCOURSES,* 11:178.

California is indebted to the Latter-day Saints for its present greatness. We opened its gold mines, explored its country, explored and made the three principal roads leading there, and ran the first ship load of American emigrants into the port of San Francisco, then called Yerba Buena. We are the men that developed the resources of the Pacific Coast, and then we fed those tens of thousands passing through to that land, who would have starved and perished on the deserts had we not provided them with bread while they traveled the roads we made, to go to the mines.

The passengers on board the ship Brooklyn not only brought to the Pacific Coast their valuable library, but a printing press. . . . We are the Pioneers of the great west.

ORSON PRATT: WHERE WOULD HAVE BEEN THE GOLD MINES?

The conviction that the Saints in California had made a great contribution to the welfare of the nation very soon became received opinion in Utah's church circles. In 1868 Orson Pratt, one of the first LDS apostles and a noted church theologian, restated this opinion in a self-congratulatory address to the Saints at the regular fall conference.

> If it had not been for the "Mormons" where would have been the gold mines of California? They might not have been opened for fifty years yet, if it not had been for the Mormon battalion, which went forth to fight the battles of the nation in her war with Mexico. Had it not been for this the world might still have been in ignorance of their existence unless God, for the accomplishment of His own wise purposes, had revealed them in some other way.[4]

Through frequent repetition over the next few decades, an orthodox historical interpretation emerged in Utah that depicted the California experience as a boon for the Saints of the Great Basin as well as a benefit to the American people. While Brigham Young and his successors guided the LDS church toward greater growth and material success—and toward more convenient, broader accommodation with the non-Mormon world—a Zioncentric perspective solidified in Utah. According to this reading of Mormon history, the trials and triumphs of the *Brooklyn* colonists and the battalion boys in California were significant because of what they meant to the Utah Saints and their inspired leaders.

[4]Orson Pratt, "Discourse," 6 October 1868, *Journal of Discourses,* 12:304.

Brigham Young: California, California, California, California

By 1874, more than a quarter-century after the Mormon people began their move to California and Utah, the golden state's attractions were no longer a danger to the LDS Great Basin settlements. The millennial ardor of the early days was fast fading as a new generation arose in the church. These younger Saints had not known firsthand the persecutions in Ohio, Missouri, and Illinois; they had not thrilled to the vibrant voices of Joseph Smith, Parley Pratt, Jedediah Grant, and other charismatic young preachers of the Mormon vanguard. Yet even looking back on a career of epic accomplishment, Brigham Young could still be bothered by a nagging sense of unease over the spiritual condition of the Mormon people. At this distance in time, he recalled the gold rush commotion over California, and he spoke to the Saints of a dream that had once come to him. It was a dream of Joseph Smith and his sheep and goats, he explained, which brought him to understand that even California's gold rush Saints, though they might not have appeared so pleasing as the faithful in Zion, had been in the right place. President Young had referred to this dream previously in public addresses, but never so eloquently and to such good effect as on this occasion, three years before his death.

Brigham Young, "Discourse," 21 June 1874, *Journal of Discourses*, 18:243–44.

Now we come to our present condition. You know the past. These children who were born in this city or Territory, know what they can remember and many of them are old enough to have many reflections and can see and understand a great many things; but the older ones know that this people have drifted just as far as they can without a reformation. Every spiritual mind knows this. I will now say to my brethren and sisters, that while we were in Winter Quarters, the Lord gave to me a revelation just as much as he ever gave one to anybody. He opened my mind, and showed me the organization of the kingdom of God in a family capacity. I talked it to my brethren; I would throw it out a few words here, and a few words there, to my first counselor, to my second counselor and the Twelve Apostles, but with the exception of one or two of the Twelve, it would not touch a man. They believed it would come, O yes, but it would be by and by. Says I, "Why not now?" If I had been worth millions when we came into this valley and built what we now call the "Old Fort," I would have given it if the people had been prepared to then receive the kingdom of God according to the pattern given to Enoch. But I could not touch them. One would say, "I am for California," another one, "I am for gold," and I am for this and I am for that; and some used their influence in trying to persuade others to go to California. They said—You can't stay here, you can't raise anything here, it is too cold, too frosty, these mountains are not fit to live in, this is not the place for white people, let us go to California and get some gold," etc.

Now I am going to tell a dream that I had, which I think is applicable, to the people today—the 21st of June 1874, as when I had it. There were so many going to California, and going this way and that way, and they did not know what they wanted, and said I—"stay here, we can raise our food here, I know it is a good stock country, a good sheep country, and as good a country for raising silk as there is in the world, and we shall raise some of the best of wheat" . . . Said I, "We can raise all we want here, do not go away, do not be discouraged." That was when the pioneers came; the next year, it was California, California, California, California. "No," said I, "stay here." After much thought and reflection, and a good deal of praying and anxiety as to whether the people would be saved after all our trouble of being driven into the wilderness, I had a dream one night, the second year after we came in here. Captain Brown had gone up to the Weber, and bought a little place belonging to Miles Goodyear. Miles Goodyear had a few goats, and I had a few sheep that I had driven into the Valley, and I wanted to get a few goats to put along with the sheep. I had seen Captain Brown and spoken to him about the goats, and he said I could have them. Just at that time I had this dream, which I will now related. I thought I had started and gone past the Hot Springs, which is about four miles north of this city. I was going after my goats. When I had gone round the point of the mountain by the Hot Springs, and had got about half a mile on the rise of ground beyond the Spring, whom should I meet but brother Joseph Smith. He had a wagon with no bed on, with bottom boards, and tents and camp equipage piled on. Somebody sat on the wagon driving the team. Behind the team I saw a great flock of sheep. I heard their bleating, and saw some goats among them. I looked at them and thought—"This is curious, brother Joseph has been up to Captain Brown's and got my goats." There were men driving the sheep, and some of the sheep I should think were three and a half feet high, with large, fine, beautiful white fleeces, and they looked so lovely and pure; others were of moderate size, and pure and white. Then I saw some that were dark and spotted, of all colors and sizes and kinds, and their fleeces were dirty, and they looked inferior; some of these were a pretty good size, but not as large as some of the large fine clean sheep, and altogether there was a multitude of them of all sizes and kinds, and goats of all colors, sizes and kinds mixed among them. Joseph stopped the wagon, and the sheep kept

> rushing up until there was an immense herd. I looked in Joseph's eye, and laughed, just as I had many a time when he was alive, about some trifling thing or another, and said I—"Joseph, you have got the darndest flock of sheep I ever saw in my life; what are you going to do with them, what on earth are they for?" Joseph looked cunningly out of his eyes, just as he used to at times, and said he—"They are all good in their places." When I awoke in the morning I did not find any fault with those who wanted to go to California; I said "If they want to go let them go, and we will do all we can to save them; I have no more fault to find, the sheep and the goats will run together, but Joseph says, "they are all good in their places."

ABNER BLACKBURN: WE STARTED AN EMPIRE IN THE WEST

Those Saints and former Saints who took part in the California gold rush put forward a different interpretation of their experience in later years. Henry Bigler and Azariah Smith in particular found that their two journal records of the Coloma gold discovery gained them substantial attention and appreciative public acclaim in California. Bigler, Smith, James S. Brown, and William Johnston were the only surviving members of the Coloma mill-building crew by 1898, when the Society of California Pioneers organized a massive parade and celebration to mark the golden anniversary of Marshall's gold discovery. These four men received invitations to attend, with the sponsoring committee paying train fares from Utah and all expenses during their visit. The four aged Saints took part in a series of public appearances, signed autographs, and rode in the parade in a special carriage that bore on each side the prominent legend "THE COMPANIONS OF MARSHALL." They would never pontificate on issues of historical significance; but, together this one last time, they enjoyed the event and the attention immensely.[5]

In his *Life of a Pioneer*, written a few years later, James S. Brown provided the fullest (and most longwinded) statement about the Golden Jubilee Celebration and their experiences at Sutter's mill a half century earlier. "Like my Mormon Battalion companions who were with me on the memorable 24th of January 1848," he wrote, "I could not but feel

[5]The celebration and parade is admirably described in David L. Bigler's "Epilogue" in *The Gold Discovery Journal of Azariah Smith*, 147–51. See also Gudde, ed., *Bigler's Chronicle*, 134–35; Brown, *Life of a Pioneer*, 511–19; and Bigler and Bagley, eds., *Army of Israel*, 447–56.

highly gratified at the courtesy extended, and look forward with pleasure to the commemoration, under so favorable circumstances and with such marvelous progress as California had made in civilization, of the fiftieth anniversary of a notable event, which at the time of its occurrence, came to us in the midst of hardships, fatigue, and almost exile from home and relatives, yet was a world-wonder in its results which followed the announcement to the world of California's great gold discovery."[6]

Abner Blackburn, living in San Bernardino in his old age and no longer in fellowship with the Saints, was invited to none of the celebrations. He attended local historical society meetings as long as his health allowed, and he relished his distinction as a pioneer settler of the San Bernardino area. But by 1894 he was "totally disabled from the performance of manual labor," and his resources were insufficient to support himself and his family "with the necessities of life." Like many veterans of the gold rush, he expressed a certain bewilderment at how he could have experienced such flush times only to arrive at old age so impoverished.

Sometime after the centennial year Blackburn expressed a broader and certainly a more romantic perspective than James S. Brown on his experience and the role of the Saints in their great California adventure. His deep-seated nostalgia is evident in these rhymed four-line stanzas.

ABNER BLACKBURN, "EARLY DAYES IN CALIFORNIA,"
IN BAGLEY, ED., *FRONTIERSMAN: ABNER BLACKBURN'S NARRATIVE*, 109–10.

We loved this country at first sight
When first our flag was raised,
And saw the ocean in its might,
Bathed in her angry waves.

Over 55 years have come and past,
Since that eventful time.
Can see the stars and stripes at last,
Wave over this tropic clime.

[6]Brown, *Life of a Pioneer*, 513–14. Brown also remarked, a trifle peevishly, that Utah's historical commemorations extended only brief, summary recognition to the veterans of the Mormon Battalion, in strong contrast to what he experienced in California. The effect, he stated, "was to enhance greatly, in the minds of those who participated in the California and the Utah celebrations, the admiration for the California managers in their broad and thorough comprehension of the amenities of such historic public events." See *Life of a Pioneer*, 510–11. The history of California's 1998–2000 Gold-Rush-to-Statehood Sesquicentennial Committee, finally scuttled and abandoned in a crossfire of partisan bickering and backstage maneuvering, points out that times certainly do change.

Such balmy winds blew over the plains,
With sun sets gorgeous sight,
And cattle on a thousand hills,
It was lovely day and night.

The noble elk here stalked the plains,
It was astonishing to see,
Never molested and so tame,
With wild horses to be seen.

Jolly times we had then,
The natives good and kind.
To change a horse with one of them,
Until another ranch you find.

There were no fences there to climb,
We roamed at our sweet will.
To take a bullock was no crime,
And manny a one was killed.

And lay upon the ground at night,
It was softer then than now.
The insects [g]nawed until daylight,
Some times a grisley grould.

At every door a horse did stand,
His owner a basking around,
Ready to coral his broncho bands,
When ever a trade was found.

Chele colorow [chile colorado] beside every door,
And dogs to greet you there.
The houses had no us[e]less floors,
We were welcome as the air.

The caty dids sang us to sleep,
With the coyotes dismal howl.
A sentinal we did not keep,
And snakes a crawling around.

The lizards twined around our necks,
And slumberd safe and sound.
We scraped the rocks from round our beds,
With the broncoes staked around.

With tooly boats to cross the streams,
And naut to bar the way.
While fishes in the rivers team,
In this land we[']re bound to stay.

Stories in books were filled,
  The half it was not told.
With oats on top of all the hills,
  And mountains seamed with gold.

To New Helvetia we were bound
  The best place in this land.
The gold then it was not found,
  It was buried in the sand.

It slumbered quiet under ground,
  And did not know its power,
And sho[o]k the world around and around,
  From that eventful hour.

We started an empire in the West,
  From the war with Mexico.
Our brothers from the East come next,
  To this Ophir whose sands were gold.

The Richest People on Earth: History, California, and the Mormons

James W. Marshall, "a wreck of his former self," launched a lecture tour in September 1871 to recoup his vanished fortunes. His first appearance was in Salt Lake City, where he was reunited with several of the men who had been present at the gold discovery. James S. Brown took Marshall to visit Brigham Young, introducing him as the discoverer of California's gold. Young disagreed and claimed the honor instead for Sidney Willes of Mormon Island fame, based on the record in the Church Historian's Office. After hearing Brown's "vivid account" of Marshall showing him the first nugget, "President Young concluded that he had been misinformed." Reportedly he had the error corrected the very next day.[7]

Twenty-seven years later, the golden anniversary celebration of the 1848 gold discovery took place just as Californians were codifying their state's history through the publications of Hubert Howe Bancroft and Theodore H. Hittell. In their multi-volume narratives published in the

[7]Gay, *James W. Marshall,* 354–55, citing the *Reno State Journal,* 13 May 1871, 3:3; *Deseret Evening News,* 16 September 1871, 3; and an undated news clipping.

1880s and 1890s, the two master historians provided a version of the state's past that met the needs of the well-educated, book-buying public, who were proud to celebrate the accomplishments of the pioneer generation. Compendiums of historical fact, the works of Bancroft and Hittell came to be regarded for at least half a century as the definitive description of California's early years and the state's development through the gold rush era and the subsequent Gilded Age of great commercial and industrial growth. Other authors added bits and pieces to their thematic narrative as time passed, but such subsequent works all stayed well within the conceptual and topical boundaries defined by Hittell and especially by Bancroft.

Both men, in keeping with the historical spirit of the era, made it a priority to document the first gold discovery in northern California. In 1885 Hittell's older brother, lecturer and journalist John S. Hittell, first reclaimed from obscurity the journals of Henry Bigler and Azariah Smith, proving that it was indeed James Marshall who made the first discovery but that the event actually did not take place between 18 and 20 January 1848, the approximation supplied by Marshall in his dictated reminiscence.[8] Bancroft and Theodore Hittel both followed John Hittell's description. In particular, Bancroft made effective use of Henry Bigler's journal transcription that Bigler had prepared and sent to him in installments during the 1870s, at the historian's request.[9]

Except for the story of the gold discovery, the Saints in California received scant attention in Bancroft's writings. He described very briefly the arrival of Samuel Brannan and the *Brooklyn* colonists, and their enterprise in San Francisco and at the New Hope settlement.[10] He gave wide currency to the story of Brannan's dramatic San Francisco appearance in early May 1848, when the Mormon preacher and promoter announced the gold discovery by striding up the city's main street waving a sample of American River gold and excitedly yelling out the news to one and all.[11] On the authority of Bigler's transcribed journal, Bancroft also supplied a brief account of gold mining by the battalion veterans in the

[8]As noted in Chapter 3, this controversy is documented in Paul, ed., *The California Gold Discovery*. Hittel's contribution is featured in Richard Dillon's introduction to Hittell, Marshall, and Waite, *The Discovery of Gold in California*. On John Hittell's career, see not only Dillon's biographical sketch but also the entry in Hart, *A Companion to California*, 189.

[9]Bancroft, *History of California* 6:49–51.

[10]Ibid., 5:544–54.

[11]Ibid., 6:56.

spring of 1848. But when Bigler left California for Utah in July 1848, the Mormons took their leave permanently from California's historical record, so far as one might discover from Bancroft's writings.[12]

Like both his brother John Hittell and Hubert H. Bancroft, Theodore Hittell came to California during the gold rush. He found work as a newspaper editor in San Francisco, then opened a legal practice, specializing in land law. With this preparation, he undertook to write and publish a four-volume *History of California* that rivaled Bancroft's seven-volume work in its attention to detail and surpassed Bancroft's volumes in its focus on governmental and legal affairs to the exclusion of social and cultural history. His account of Brannan and the *Brooklyn* Saints took only a terse two and a half pages. Hittell confined notice of "the so-called Mormon Battalion" to three sentences tucked into an account of General Kearny's Army of the West in California. Most remarkably, he completely obscured the role of the battalion veterans in the gold discovery and early mining activities at Mormon Island.[13]

Following the model provided by Bancroft and Hittell, historians during the next decades generally ignored the activities of the Saints in California. Beginning in 1943 with Paul Bailey's *Sam Brannan and the California Mormons,* a few books resurrected this remarkable character for the history-reading public.[14] Because of Brannan's exciting and scandalous life in California—his gold rush adventures, his leadership of the 1851 vigilante movement, his break with Brigham Young, and his personal trajectory from Saint to hard-drinking, womanizing California millionaire and finally to financial and personal ruin—Brannan offered an attractive subject for popular biography that did not demand from authors any

[12]In fine print, as part of his chronicle of county history, Bancroft makes very brief mention of the LDS founding of San Bernardino, an account that conveys only skeletal bits of information. See Bancroft, *History of California* 5:520. Bancroft's life and career are summarized in Hart, *Companion to California,* 26–27.

[13]Passive voice enabled Hittell to avoid any mention of the Mormons in Sutter and Marshall's employment. After describing the agreement between the two men to build and run a sawmill at Coloma, Hittell writes, "Men were employed and ox-teams, carts and pack-animals engaged to carry machinery, tools and provisions." See Hittell, *History of California,* 2:684. For a sketch of Theodore Hittell's career, see Hart, *Companion to California,* 189.

[14]Bailey, *Sam Brannan and the California Mormons,* was soon followed by Reva L. H. Scott's fictionalized *Samuel Brannan and the Golden Fleece: A Biography* and Louis J. Stellman's *Sam Brannan, Builder of San Francisco: A Biography.* Bailey also published an altogether forgettable novel based on Brannan's life, memorably titled *The Gay Saint.*

great scholarly research. But except for this sort of journalistic or tabloid reporting on Brannan, gold-rush Saints were neglected and all but completely forgotten in California history.

In Utah, Brigham H. Roberts was virtually an LDS counterpart to Bancroft. He composed a six-volume tome titled *A Comprehensive History of the Church of Jesus Christ of Latter-day Saints, Century I,* published with church authorization by the Deseret News Press in Salt Lake City in 1930. While Roberts filled out the published record for both the *Brooklyn* voyage and the march of the Mormon Battalion, he added no significant factual information in his account of the Saints in gold-rush California. He relied exclusively on Bancroft's work for a summary of Mormon involvement in the gold discovery and the earliest placer mining, never consulting potential sources in the church's archives. He did publish a photocopy of the one-page gold discovery record in Henry Bigler's journal but made no further use of that source. His rendition of Brannan's San Francisco announcement of the gold discovery was another tribute to Bancroft's history: he simply reworded slightly the California historian's account. Roberts's most original passage relating to the gold-rush Saints is found at the end of his description of the Thompson-Holmes party's July 1848 departure for Utah. The decision of these veterans to leave California, he sanctimoniously declared, was an "example of fidelity to duty . . . which is not over-matched in any of the records written by men."[15] And like Bancroft, Roberts ends his account of the Saints in northern California with the 1848 trek of the LDS trail-makers over Carson Pass.

With the approach of the centennial of the California gold discovery, two new works introduced the modern scholarly era in gold-rush historiography. Rodman Paul completed a dissertation on the California gold rush at Harvard University and had it revised and ready for publication by 1942. Wartime interruptions, as Paul phrased it, delayed publication until 1947, when his study reached print with the title *California Gold: The Beginning of Mining in the Far West.* A work of remarkable reach, demonstrating a masterful command of primary sources for a young scholar, *California Gold* quickly became the new standard authority for the technological, economic, and social history of the California gold rush. Unfortunately,

[15]Roberts, *A Comprehensive History of the Church of Jesus Christ of Latter-day Saints,* 4:368.

Paul's narrative skipped past the Saints with no hint of Mormon involvement in any of the events he explained so well. Although Paul's later documentary work, *The California Gold Discovery,* gave appropriate attention to the battalion veterans at Coloma, its restricted subject left entirely obscure the larger role taken by the Saints in the first weeks and months of the great rush for riches in northern California.

John W. Caughey, a talented member of the UCLA history faculty, brought out his popular work on this period with the title *Gold is the Cornerstone* in 1948, retitling it more prosaically *The California Gold Rush* for a paperback reprint in 1975. Caughey had written a textbook history of the state named simply *California* in 1940, in which he provided a bare summary of Bancroft's brief notices of the LDS role in the events of 1847–1849.[16] The gold rush book, however, demonstrated the author's familiarity with the unpublished Henry Bigler journal, which he found either in the Bancroft Library version or, more likely, in the transcription available at the Huntington Library. He may also have made use of James S. Brown's published recollections. Although not by any means extensive, his acknowledgment of the Mormon presence at the beginning of the gold rush made Caughey the first author since Bancroft to record accurately the Saints' participation in California history.

The reappearance of the Mormons in the golden state's historical consciousness was aided by Paul Bailey's 1954 publication *The Mormons in California,* a literal transcription of William Glover's autobiographical account from the Bancroft Library collections. Glover described the *Brooklyn* voyage, the New Hope settlement, his experience mining at Mormon Island, and his departure overland for Utah with the Thomas Rhoades company in 1849. Although editor Bailey added little in the way of documentation or historical detail, the publication of this work substantiated the presence of the Saints and their involvement in central events at the beginning of the gold rush.

Bailey's edition of Glover's memoir was followed in 1962 by a more ambitious work, Erwin G. Gudde's substantially modified transcription of Henry Bigler's California journal. The volume appeared as *Bigler's Chronicle of the West: The Conquest of California, Discovery of Gold, and Mormon*

[16]By the time Caughey completed his third edition of the textbook in 1970, he had pared the LDS material even a bit further.

Settlement as Reflected in Henry William Bigler's Diaries. Closely based on the Bancroft Library version of the journal, Gudde's publication added abundant explanatory material while often altering Bigler's exact language. The difficulty with this work, apparent to anyone familiar with modern editorial techniques, is that the editor did not clearly distinguish which passages were solely Bigler's, which passages were an altered version of his original, and which passages were added by the editor. Nonetheless, with *Bigler's Chronicle* and Glover's *Mormons in California* both in print, the LDS presence in California's gold rush history could no longer be ignored.

From this point in the 1960s, with rich documentation available, the record of California's gold rush Saints might soon have been fully investigated. The interested and the inquisitive would then have had an array of journal articles and scholarly monographs for study, all with appropriate academic trappings. But history—the doing of history through original scholarly research and writing—is a chaotic enterprise, without committees of oversight or significant funding to push along a comprehensive, well-designed research program. Scholarship on the history of the American West is fostered and sustained principally in a score of major university graduate programs, each totally independent, with few if any external influences directly shaping topical priorities or interpretive themes. This is as it should be, since it guarantees an independence of scholarly thought and inquiry that is intrinsic to our pursuit of historical truth. On the downside, the passion of young scholars and their mentors to be positioned on the cutting edge of inquiry—to be thought *au courant*, "high concept" historians—creates a tendency for intellectual fads and abstruse theoretic formulations to set the style and subject matter of graduate-school scholarship.

Outside of Brigham Young University, Mormon history has not often been a subject of scholarly inquiry among academics in recent years, nor have the achievements of Anglo-American males like the gold-rush Saints been a trendy topic. For these reasons, if no other, it has been left to scholars thinking outside the graduate school box—scholars not directly associated with academic history—to do the necessary investigations.

A few recent studies related to Mormons in gold rush California stand out. J. Kenneth Davies, a professor of managerial economics teaching in the fields of labor and economics at Brigham Young University, in 1984 published *Mormon Gold: The Story of California's Mormon Argonauts.* This work was the first to make extensive use of the outstanding manuscript resources at the LDS church archives and the Lee Library at Brigham Young University. Understandably, the issues addressed by Davies and the volume's narrative tend to represent the Zioncentric viewpoint inherent in those documents.

A second major study is Norma Baldwin Rickett's *The Mormon Battalion: U.S. Army of the West, 1846–1848,* published in 1996. Following her career as a publicist, newspaper columnist, and music critic, Ricketts devoted six years to compiling an extraordinarily detailed record of the battalion's service and the activities of the veterans after they were mustered out at Los Angeles in July 1847. Her painstaking investigation and narrative skills established a new scholarly baseline for all further studies of the battalion boys in California.

Third in this series of recent accounts of the California Saints in the gold rush era is Edward Leo Lyman's *San Bernardino: The Rise and Fall of a California Community* (1996). Lyman's volume offers a substantial, well-written study of the southern California LDS colony, which began with grand expectations in 1849 but was unable to survive local anti-Mormon opposition, factional conflict, and Brigham Young's disapproval. A professional educator and educational administrator, Lyman writes with clear sympathy for the colonizing venture—due in part, one suspects, to his descent from Amasa Lyman, the colony's organizer and foremost champion. His work, however, like those by Davies and Ricketts, is most distinguished not by sentiment but by the high quality of scholarship that underlies the historical narrative.

The same year that Lyman's *San Bernardino* appeared, the Religious Studies Center at Brigham Young University published *California Saints: A 150-Year Legacy in the Golden State* by Richard O. Cowan, professor of Church History and Doctrine at BYU, and William E. Homer, a businessman, educator, and writer based in northern California. A work intended primarily for a readership of church members, Cowan and Homer's *California Saints* devotes two hundred of its four hundred pages to the period before 1857, including coverage of the San Bernardino colony and San Francisco-based early missionary activity in the islands of the South Pacific. The authors make effective use of a large variety of published sources, primary and secondary, with limited use of unpublished documentary materials. Despite its tendency to indulge in filiopietistic celebration of the Saints' accomplishments, *California Saints* provides valuable coverage of the wide sweep of LDS activities during the gold rush period, never before recognized as part of a coherent historical narrative.

Still more recently, three volumes in the Kingdom in the West series under the general editorship of Will Bagley, in which this work appears, have made further contributions to the study of California Saints from 1846 through 1857. Bagley's *Scoundrel's Tale: The Samuel Brannan Papers* (1999), a documentary history of Brannan and his California career, clears away a century and a half of mythmaking started by Brannan himself and enthusiastically carried on by others. *Army of Israel: Mormon Battalion Narratives,* edited by David L. Bigler and Will Bagley (2000), includes a substantial chapter on the battalion veterans in California.[17] Built on the foundation of Norma Baldwin Ricketts' narrative, *Army of Israel* admirably addresses the larger military, political, and cultural issues in this remarkable story while its authors carefully avoid rehashing *The Mormon Battalion.* Most recent is *Defending Zion: George Q. Cannon and the California Mormon Newspaper Wars of 1856–1857* (2002) by Roger Robin Ekins, a fifth-generation LDS church member and professional educator who is currently Dean of Instruction at Butte College in Oroville, California. Ekins's work documents Cannon's prominence in the public controversy over the policies and actions of Mormon authorities prior to the Utah War. A firebrand journalist who was fiercely loyal to Brigham Young, Cannon promoted the LDS exodus, urging gold country Saints to uproot their lives and head east across the Sierra. Ekins's volume gives evidence for a conclusion that Cannon's defense of Zion assured the departure of the church from the golden state.

A scholarly freshet rather than a torrent, this stream of publication flows into the history of northern California's gold rush Saints. Samuel Brannan and the *Brooklyn* Saints were first on the scene. Henry Bigler,

[17]David Bigler earlier signaled his entry into western Mormon history writing with the publication of *The Gold Discovery Journal of Azariah Smith* (1990), demonstrating his strong skills as an editor and analyst of documentary narratives. Smith's journal provides a significant documentary record of the Mormon Battalion's march to California as well as the gold discovery at Coloma.

Azariah Smith, and their companions from the ranks of the Mormon Battalion arrived at what appeared to be a fortuitous moment for John Sutter. All these historical actors were significant in beginning the California gold rush, an event that pervasively and deeply influenced western America, with impacts felt around the world. Even Brigham Young came to regard the accomplishments of these first California Saints as beneficial for the LDS church and its leadership. Too long forgotten or ignored, they made contributions to California's most famous moment in history and, at least indirectly, to the prosperity of Zion.

Without the Mormons, James Marshall's gold discovery would have been someone else's gold discovery at a different time and almost certainly in a different place. Lacking a capable workforce of battalion veterans willing to labor on Sutter and Marshall's sawmill, it would likely have been many months or even years before chance excavation along some stream in the remote Sierra Nevada uncovered a small gold treasure. The start of intensive placer mining would presumably have been delayed even longer, until the fortuitous detection of some site with the amazing extent and richness of the Mormon Island diggings. John Bidwell set aside stories about placer gold in 1844. Could we not expect that most other preoccupied newcomers, during the early period of the American conquest, would replicate his inaction?

The gold discovery story represents only one aspect of the Saints' record in the larger narrative of this world-changing event. Latter-day Saints sustained a process that opened California to Anglo-American occupation and made it a valuable part of the American Union. Without the Mormons both in San Francisco and southern California, this province would not have been conquered and pacified so quickly by U.S. military forces.[18] Latter-day Saint trailblazers and road makers helped end California's landlocked isolation between 1846 and 1848 by opening three major wagon routes connecting California with New Mexico, the Great Basin, and the older regions of the United States. One of these, the Carson Pass Wagon Road, became the most traveled trans-Sierra route for overland emigrants during the early gold rush years.

While counterfactual speculation never yields conclusive results, it

[18]The Mormon Battalion's role in securing the U.S. conquest and occupation of both New Mexico and Alta California by the Army of the West, we should note, may not be viewed as a positive accomplishment by irredentist-minded descendants of Hispanic *Nuevo Mexicanos* and *Californios.*

seems clear that without the 1848 gold discovery and the rush for riches that followed, the development of the LDS church and community in the Great Basin must certainly have taken an alternative course. The difficult economic challenges the Saints faced in their valley in the mountains would have intensified, and Brigham Young's people would have lacked an impetus to join fortunes with the broader American society. For a short while, church authorities created an isolated Zion in the Salt Lake Valley, but the California gold rush brought the world by their doorstep. The parade of overland travelers and sojourners offered opportunities the Saints could not ignore: opportunities to profit that would enable them to unite the faithful, aid the poor, look after the weak, and sustain the ever-expanding mission of the church.

"Get rich," President Young wrote to the California Saints in 1847, "for the Lord designs that his should be the richest people on earth." Like the Saints who joined the rush to California, Young and his associates in the Great Salt Lake Valley followed this dictum. They seized the economic main chance the gold rush offered, modified their policy of isolation, engaged with the wider world, and directed the LDS church toward a far broader calling as the most successful Christian evangelical institution in modern American society. The issues of plural marriage and theocratic authority made the path of conciliation a rocky one, but the first steps were taken as a result of events in northern California. That too became a long-term service to their religion and to the Mormon people, rendered surely if unwittingly by the gold-rush Saints.

Just as a Zioncentric tradition has permeated LDS historical writing, the master narrative assembled by Theodore Hittel and Hubert Howe Bancroft has continued to color if not dominate our interpretation of California's history.[19] One result has been to place heavy emphasis on

[19]These remarks are not meant to slight the strong influence of Herbert Eugene Bolton's interpretation of the Spanish and Mexican periods of California history. But that is another story, told most effectively by historians Albert Hurtado, David Weber, Russell Magnaghi, and James Sandos, who have all contributed to a critical reappraisal of Bolton's work. Their publications have reaffirmed Bolton's reputation as the preeminent twentieth-century interpreter of early California history, seen through a prism that privileged the Franciscan missionaries and upper-class *Californios*. During his long career as a professor at the University of California, Bolton became a mentor to a generation of Mormon and Western frontier historians. Bolton and his students, these authors point out, readily joined a grand interpretive schema concerning the colonial Spanish borderlands with data on the post-colonial West they extrapolated from Bancroft's works and the materials in the Bancroft Library at Berkeley. Bancroft's influence, it may further be suggested, was in fact extended and reinforced through the teaching and writing of Bolton and two generations of his students.

the preeminence of Salt Lake City and San Francisco as commercial and cultural capitals in western America. Another consequence has been to portray Utah and California as stand-alone historical entities, each somehow unique and set apart from the common past of other western regions. Our historical vision has seldom fitted Zion and Babylon, to use Brigham Young's terminology one last time, side by side in the same conceptual frame. Attention to California Mormon history should prompt us toward a wider perspective and a surer focus.

Embedded in the long-standing versions of our history is a persistent tendency toward geographical, cultural, and class-biased forms of parochialism. For decades, dominant historical canons have slighted the lives of ordinary people, especially those in the hinterlands, and especially if they were tagged with an ethnic, gender, racial, or religious identity that conceptually isolated them from the elite leadership in metropolitan centers of power. In a society devoted to democratic ideals, history should not serve power. Yet our predecessors in scholarship have frequently displayed a lamentable though unthinking inclination to kowtow in the direction of the mighty.

The gold rush Saints—Henry Bigler, Melissa Coray, Abner Blackburn, Mary Ann Cheney, Goudy Hogan, Frederick Hurst, and their many compatriots in northern California's placer diggings—could never be counted among the nineteenth century's elite. The course of their lives set them apart from the well-known figures who signed papers at ornate desks in richly appointed offices in Salt Lake City or along San Francisco's Montgomery Street. The records they left for posterity never fit easily into the Zioncentric LDS tradition or California's Hittell-Bancroft master narrative. Still, they, not Brigham Young or John Sutter or even Samuel Brannan, were the main actors in the day-to-day dramas of northern California's LDS history during the gold rush era. Reclaimed from obscurity, the stories of their lives and the substance of their concerns deserve a prominent, secure place in the more spacious historical structures being fashioned by scholars of the present generation.

BIBLIOGRAPHY & INDEX

Bibliography

This bibliography is organized into:

- Secondary Sources: Books
- Secondary Sources: Articles and Book Chapters
- Published Primary Sources
- Unpublished Primary Sources

Secondary Sources: Books

Alexander, Thomas G. *Things in Heaven and Earth: The Life and Times of Wilford Woodruff, a Mormon Prophet.* Salt Lake City: Signature Books, 1991.

Arrington, Leonard. *Brigham Young: American Moses.* New York: Alfred A. Knopf, 1985.

———. *Charles C. Rich, Mormon General and Western Frontiersman.* Provo: Brigham Young University Press, 1974.

———. *Great Basin Kingdom: An Economic History of the Latter-day Saints, 1830–1900.* Cambridge: Harvard University Press, 1958.

Arrington, Leonard, and Davis Bitton. *The Mormon Experience: A History of the Latter-day Saints,* 2nd ed. Urbana: University of Illinois Press, 1992.

Bagley, Will. *Blood of the Prophets: Brigham Young and the Massacre at Mountain Meadows.* Norman: University of Oklahoma Press, 2002.

Bagley, Will, ed. *"A Bright, Rising Star": A Brief Life of James Ferguson, Sergeant Major, Mormon Battalion; Adjutant General, Nauvoo Legion.* Collector's Edition Keepsake for volume 4 of the *Kingdom in the West* series, *Army of Israel.* Spokane, Washington: The Arthur H. Clark Co., 2000.

Bailey, Paul. *Sam Brannan and the California Mormons.* Los Angeles: Westernlore Press, 1943.

———. *The Gay Saint.* Hollywood, Calif: Murray & Gee, 1944.

Bancroft, Hubert Howe. *History of California,* 7 vols. San Francisco: The History Co., 1886–1890.

Barry, Louise. *The Beginning of the West: Annals of the Kansas Gateway to the American West, 1540–1854.* Topeka: Kansas State Historical Society, 1972. Foreword by Dale L. Morgan.

Bennett, Richard E. *Mormons at the Missouri, 1846–1852: "And should we die—"* Norman: University of Oklahoma Press, 1987.

Bigler, David L. *Forgotten Kingdom: The Mormon Theocracy in the American West, 1847–1896.* Spokane, Washington: The Arthur H. Clark Co., 1998.

Bigler, David L., and Will Bagley, eds. *Army of Israel: Mormon Battalion Narratives.* Spokane, Washington: The Arthur H. Clark Co., 2000.

Bishop, M. Guy. *Henry William Bigler: Soldier, Gold Miner, Missionary, Chronicler, 1815–1900.* Logan: Utah State University Press, 1998.

Bitton, Davis. *George Q. Cannon: A Biography.* Salt Lake City: Deseret Book Co., 1999.

Black, Susan Easton, and Larry C. Porter, ed. *Lion of the Lord: Essays on the Life & Services of Brigham Young.* Salt Lake City: Deseret Book Co., 1995.

Blodgett, Peter J. *Land of Dreams: California and the Gold Rush Decade, 1848–1858.* San Marino, California: Huntington Library, 1999.

Boone, David F., *et al.*, ed. *Regional Studies in Latter-day Saint Church History, California.* Provo: Department of Church History and Doctrine, Brigham Young University, 1998.

Campbell, Eugene E. *Establishing Zion: The Mormon Church in the American West.* Salt Lake City: Signature Books, 1988.

Clark, William B. *Gold Districts of California.* Sacramento: California Divison of Mines and Geology Bulletin 193, 1963.

Cowan, Richard O., and William E. Homer. *California Saints: A 150-Year Legacy in the Golden State.* Provo: Religious Studies Center, Brigham Young University, 1996.

Cross, Ralph Herbert. *The Early Inns of California, 1844–1869.* San Francisco: Cross & Brandt, 1954.

Davies, J. Kenneth. *Mormon Gold: The Story of California's Mormon Argonauts.* Salt Lake City: Olympus Publishing, 1984.

Dillon, Richard H. *Fool's Gold: The Decline and Fall of Captain John Sutter.* New York: Coward McCann, 1967; reprint ed., Santa Cruz, California: Western Tanager, 1981.

Furniss, Norman F. *The Mormon Conflict, 1850–1859.* New Haven: Yale University Press, 1960.

Gates, Paul W. *History of Public Land Law Development.* Washington, D.C: Government Printing Office, 1968.

Gay, Theressa. *James W. Marshall, The Discoverer of Gold: A Biography.* Georgetown, California: Talisman Press, 1966.

Gillis, Michael J., and Michael F. Magliari. *John Bidwell and California: The Life and Writings of a Pioneer.* Spokane, Washington: The Arthur H. Clark Co., 2002.

Gordon, Susan Barringer. *The Mormon Question: Polygamy and Constitutional Conflict in Nineteenth Century America.* Chapel Hill: University of North Carolina Press, 2002.

Gudde, Erwin G. *California Gold Camps: A Geographical and Historical Dictionary of Camps, Towns, and Localities Where Gold Was Found and Mined, and of Wayside Stations and Trading Centers.* Ed. by Elisabeth K. Gudde. Berkeley: University of California Press, 1975.

Hafen, LeRoy R., ed. *The Mountain Men and the Fur Trade of the Far West,* 10 vols. Glendale, California: The Arthur H. Clark Co., 1965–1972.

Hammond, George P. *Who Saw the Elephant? An Inquiry by a Scholar Well Acquainted with the Beast.* San Francisco: California Historical Society, 1964.

Hansen, Lorin J., and Lila J. Bringhurst. *Let this Be Zion: Mormon Pioneers and Modern Saints in Southern Alameda County, California.* Salt Lake City: Publishers Press, 1996.

Harlow, Neal. *California Conquered: War and Peace on the Pacific, 1846–1850.* Berkeley: University of California Press, 1982.

Hart, James D. *A Companion to California.* New York: Oxford University Press, 1978.

Heizer, Robert F., F. Fenenga, and Aubrey Neasham. *California Gold Discovery: Centennial Papers on the Time, the Site, and Artifacts.* San Francisco: California Historical Society, 1947.

Hittell, John S., James W. Marshall, and Edwin G. Waite. *The Discovery of Gold in California.* Palo Alto, California: Lewis Osborne, 1968.

Hittell, Theodore H. *History of California,* 4 vols. San Francisco: N.J. Stone & Co., 1885–1897.

Holland, S. Dennis. *Sierra Saints: A Brief History of the Mormons in Western El Dorado County, 1847–1997.* Placerville, California: S.D. Holland Publishing, 1997.

Holliday, J. S. *Rush for Riches: Gold Fever and the Making of California.* Berkeley: Oakland Museum of California and University of California Press, 1999.

Hoover, Mildred, et al. *Historic Spots in California,* 4th ed., rev. Dougles E. Kyle. Stanford: Stanford University Press, 1990.

Hunt, Rockwell D. *John Bidwell, Prince of California Pioneers.* Caldwell, Idaho: Caxton Printers, 1942.

Hurtado, Albert L. *Indian Survival on the California Frontier.* New Haven: Yale University Press, 1988.

Jenson, Andrew. *Latter-day Saint Biographical Encyclopedia,* 4 vols. Salt Lake City: Andrew Jenson History Co., 1901.

Kemble, Edward C. *A History of California Newspapers, 1846–1858.* Ed. by Helen Harding Bretnor. Los Gatos, California: Talisman Press, 1962.

Kurutz, Gary F. *The California Gold Rush: A Descriptive Bibliography of Books and Pamphlets Covering the Years 1848–1853.* San Francisco: The Book Club of California, 1997.

Lamar, Howard R., ed. *The Cruise of the Portsmouth, 1845–1847: A Sailor's View of the Naval Conquest of California by Joseph T. Downey, Ordinary Seaman.* New Haven: Yale University Press, 1958.

Larson, Carl V. *A Data Base of the Mormon Battalion.* Providence, Utah: Keith W. Watkins and Sons Printing Co., 1987. Second Edition, *A Database of the Mormon Battalion: An Identification of the Original Members of the Mormon Battalion.* Salt Lake City: U.S. Mormon Battalion, Inc., 1997.

Long, E. B. *The Saints and the Union: Utah Territory during the Civil War.* Urbana: University of Illinois Press, 1981.

Lyman, Edward Leo. *Political Deliverance: The Mormon Quest for Utah Statehood.* Urbana: University of Illinois Press, 1986.

———. *San Bernardino: The Rise and Fall of a California Community.* Salt Lake City: Signature Books, 1996.

Madsen, Brigham D. *Gold Rush Sojourners in Great Salt Lake City, 1849 and 1850.* Salt Lake City: University of Utah Press, 1983.

Morgan, Dale L. *The Great Salt Lake.* Indianapolis: Bobbs-Merrill, 1947.

Nevins, Allan. *Ordeal of the Union,* Volume II, *A House Dividing, 1852–1857.* New York: Charles Scribner's Sons, 1947.

Orsi, Richard J., and James J. Rawls, eds. *A Golden State: Mining and Economic Development in Gold Rush California.* Berkeley: University of California Press, 1999.

Orsi, Richard J., and Kevin Starr, eds. *Rooted in Barbarous Soil: People, Culture, and Community in Gold Rush California.* Berkeley: University of California Press, 2000.

Owens, Kenneth N., ed. *John Sutter and a Wider West.* Lincoln: University of Nebraska Press, 1994.

Owens, Kenneth N., ed. *Riches for All: The California Gold Rush and the World.* Lincoln: University of Nebraska Press, 2002.

Paul, Rodman. *California Gold: The Beginning of Mining in the Far West.* Cambridge: Harvard University Press, 1947.

Peak, Melinda. *An Evaluation of the Rolling Hills House, El Dorado County, California.* El Dorado Hills, California: Peak & Associates, Inc., 1987.

Ricketts, Norma B. *Historic Cosumnes and the Slough House Pioneer Cemetery.* Salt Lake City: Daughters of Utah Pioneers, 1978.

———. *The California Star Express.* Sacramento County Historical Society, *Golden Notes* 28:1 (Spring 1982).

———. *Tragedy Spring and the Pouch of Gold.* Sacramento: Ricketts Publishing Co., 1983.

———. *Melissa's Journey with the Mormon Battalion—The Western Odyssey of Melissa Burton Coray: 1846–1848*. Salt Lake City: Daughter of Utah Pioneers, 1994.

———. *The Mormon Battalion: U. S. Army of the West, 1846–1848*. Logan: Utah State University Press, 1996.

Roberts, Brigham H. *A Comprehensive History of the Church of Jesus Christ of Latter-day Saints, Century I*, 6 vols. Salt Lake City: Deseret News Press, 1930.

Rogers, Fred Blackburn, ed. *Filings from an Old Saw: Reminiscences of San Francisco and California's Conquest by "Filings"—Joseph T. Downey*. San Francisco: John Howell, 1956.

Rohrbough, Malcolm J. *Days of Gold: The California Gold Rush and the American Nation*. Berkeley: University of California Press, 1997.

Rolle, Andrew. *John Charles Frémont, Character as Destiny*. Norman: University of Oklahoma Press, 1991.

Rowland, Donald E. *John Rowland and William Workman: Southern California Pioneers of 1841*. Spokane, Washington: The Arthur H. Clark Co; and Los Angeles: Historical Society of Southern California, 1999.

Schindler, Harold. *Orrin Porter Rockwell: Man of God, Son of Thunder*, 2d ed. Salt Lake City: University of Utah Press, 1983.

Scott, Reva L. H. *Samuel Brannan and the Golden Fleece: A Biography*. New York: Macmillan, 1944.

Sessions, Gene A. *Mormon Thunder: A Documentary History of Jedediah Morgan Grant*. Urbana: University of Illinois Press, 1982.

Slaughter, William W., and Michael Landon. *Trail of Hope: The Story of the Mormon Trail*. Salt Lake City: Shadow Mountain, 1997.

Smith, Alice E. *James Duane Doty, Frontier Promoter*. Madison: State Historical Society of Wisconsin, 1954.

Soulé, Frank, John H. Gihon, and James Nisbet. *The Annals of San Francisco, Containing a Summary of the First Discovery, Settlement, Progress and Present Condition of California, and a Complete History of All the Important Events Connected with Its Great City: To Which Are Added, Biographical Memoirs of Some Important Citizens*. New York and San Francisco: D. Appleton & Co., 1854.

Stellman, Louis J. *Sam Brannan, Builder of San Francisco: A Biography*. New York: Exposition Press, 1953.

Tyler, Daniel. *A Concise History of the Mormon Battalion in the Mexican War, 1846–1847*. Salt Lake City: Juvenile Instructor Press, 1939.

Unruh, John D., Jr. *The Plains Across: The Overland Emigrants and the Trans-Mississippi West, 1840–1860*. Urbana: University of Illinois Press, 1979.

White, David A., ed. *News of the Plains and the Rockies, 1803–1865*, 8 vols. Spokane, Washington: The Arthur H. Clark Co., 1996–2001.

SECONDARY SOURCES: ARTICLES AND BOOK CHAPTERS

Bagley, Will. "Lansford W. Hastings: Scoundrel or Visionary?" *Overland Journal* 12 (Spring 1994).

———. "'Every Thing Is Favourable! And God Is On Our Side': Samuel Brannan and the Conquest of California." *Journal of Mormon History* 23 (Fall 1997).

Cowan, Robert Ernest. "The Leidesdorff-Folsom Estate, A Forgotten Chapter in the Romantic History of Early San Francisco." *Quarterly of the California Historical Society* 7:2 (June 1928), 7–105.

Davis, Richard M. "The Walker River–Sonora Crossing." *Overland Journal* 6–3 (Fall 1988).

Dillon, Richard H. "Introduction." John S. Hittell, James W. Marshall, and Edwin G. Waite, *The Discovery of Gold in California.*

Dockstader, Julie A. "California Peak Named in Honor of Wife of Battalion Member—Melissa Coray's Honeymoon: Trudging 1,000 Miles in Southwest." *LDS Church News,* 13 August 1994.

Fifield, Allen. "Wagons East Across the Sierra." *Historical Society of Southern California Quarterly* 43 (September 1961).

Flake, Lawrence R. "George Q. Cannon's Mission to California, 1855–1857." *Regional Studies in Latter-day Saint Church History, California.* Ed. by David F. Boone *et al.*

Fleming, L. A., and A. R. Standing, "The Road to 'Fortune': The Salt Lake Cutoff." *Utah Historical Quarterly* 33 (Summer 1985).

Hansen. Lorin. "Voyage of the *Brooklyn.*" *Dialogue: A Journal of Mormon Thought* 21 (Autumn 1988).

Hittell, John S. "The Discovery of Gold in California." *Century Magazine* 41 (February 1891).

Korns, J. Roderic. "The Salt Lake Cutoff." *Utah Historical Quarterly* 19 (Summer 1951).

Owens, Kenneth N. "Begun by Gold: Sacramento and the Gold Rush Legacy after 150 Years." *Riches for All: The California Gold Rush and the World.* Ed. by Kenneth N. Owens.

———. "The California Gold Rush in History." *Riches for All: The California Gold Rush and the World.* Ed. by Kenneth N. Owens.

———. "Gold-Rich Saints: The Mormon Beginnings of the California Gold Rush." *Riches for All: The California Gold Rush and the World.* Ed. by Kenneth N. Owens.

———. "The Mormon-Carson Emigrant Trail in Western History." *Montana The Magazine of Western History* 42–1 (Winter 1992).

Paden, Irene D., ed. "The Ira J. Willis Guide to the Gold Fields." *California Historical Quarterly* 32 (September 1953).

Peterson, Paul H. "The Mormon Reformation of 1856–1857: Rhetoric and Reality." *Journal of Mormon History* 15 (1989).

———. "'Like a Fire in My Bones': The Reformation Correspondence between Brigham Young and George Q. Cannon." *Regional Studies in Latter-day Saint Church History, California.* Ed. by David F. Boone *et al.*

———. "Brigham Young and the Mormon Reformation." *Lion of the Lord: Essays on the Life & Services of Brigham Young.* Ed. by Susan Easton Black and Larry C. Porter.

Rohrbough, Malcolm J. "We Will Make Our Fortunes—No Doubt of It": The Worldwide Rush to California." *Riches for All: The California Gold Rush and the World.* Ed. by Kenneth N. Owens.

Spence, Clark C. "From Gold Pans to California Dredges: The Search for Mass Production in Placer Mining." *Riches for All: The California Gold Rush and the World.* Ed. by Kenneth N. Owens.

Stanley, Reva Holdaway. "Sutter's Mormon Workmen at Natoma and Coloma in 1848." *California Historical Quarterly* 14 (September 1935).

Townley, John. "Trail to the Comstock: An Accidental Bonanza." *Overland Journal* 9:1 (Spring 1991), 22–30.

Watson, Douglas S. "The Great Express Extra of the *California Star* of April 1, 1848." *California Historical Society Quarterly* 11 (June 1932).

Published Primary Sources

Anonymous [Samuel John Bayard]. *A Sketch of the Life of Com. Robert F. Stockton.* New York: Derby & Jackson, 1856.

Bidwell, John. *Life in California Before the Gold Discovery.* Palo Alto, California: Lewis Osborne, 1966.

Bagley, Will, ed. *A Road from El Dorado: The 1848 Trail Journal of Ephraim Green.* Salt Lake City: The Prairie Dog Press, 1991.

———. *Frontiersman: Abner Blackburn's Narrative.* Salt Lake City: University of Utah Press, 1992.

———. "'To the Tops of the California Mountains': The 1848 Carson Pass Journal of Elijah Elmer." *Crossroads: Utah Crossroads Quarterly Newsletter* 4:3 (Summer 1993), 4–7.

———. *The Pioneer Camp of the Saints: The 1846 and 1847 Mormon Trail Journals of Thomas Bullock.* Spokane, Washington: The Arthur H. Clark Co., 1997.

———. *Scoundrel's Tale: The Samuel Brannan Papers.* Spokane, Washington: The Arthur H. Clark Co., 1999.

Bigler, David L., ed. *The Gold Discovery Journal of Azariah Smith*. Salt Lake City: University of Utah Press, 1990.

———. *A Winter with the Mormons: The 1852 Letters of Jotham Goodell*. Salt Lake City: The Tanner Trust Fund, J. Willard Marriott Library, University of Utah, 2001.

[Bigler, Henry W.] Henele Pikale. "Recollections of the Past." *Juvenile Instructor* 21 (1, 15 December 1886).

Brown, James Stephens. *California Gold—An Authentic History of the First Find, With the Names of Those Interested in the Discovery*. Salt Lake City: James S. Brown, 1894.

———. *Life of a Pioneer*. Salt Lake City: Geo. Q. Cannon & Sons, 1900.

Brown, John. "An Evidence of Inspiration." *Juvenile Instructor* 16 (1881).

Cain, Joseph, and Ariah C. Brower. *Mormon Way-Bill to the Gold Mines from the Pacific Springs by the Northern and Southern Routes*. Salt Lake City: W. Richard, Publisher, 1851.

Campbell, David. "Pioneer of 1846: Sketch of Hardships Endured by Those Who Crossed the Plains in '46." *Porterville Recorder*, 11, 12, and 13 August 1910.

Cannon, George Q. "Twenty Years Ago: A Trip to California." *Juvenile Instructor* 4–2 (16 January 1869), 13

Carter, Kate B., ed. *Heart Throbs of the West*, 12 vols. Salt Lake City: Daughters of Utah Pioneers, 1939–51.

———. *Our Pioneer Heritage*, 20 vols. Salt Lake City: Daughters of Utah Pioneers, 1958–1977.

Crocheron, Augusta Joyce. "The Ship *Brooklyn*." *Western Galaxy* (March 1888).

Dmytryshyn, Basil, E. A. P. Crownhart-Vaughan, and Thomas Vaughan, eds., *To Siberia and Russian America, Three Centuries of Russian Eastward Expansion: The Russian American Colonies, 1798–1867, Volume Three, A Documentary Record*. Portland: Oregon Historical Society Press, 1989.

Downey, Joseph T. *The Cruise of the Portsmouth: A Sailor's View of the Naval Conquest of California*, ed. Howard Lamar. New Haven: Yale University Press, 1958.

Egan, Howard. *Pioneering the West, 1846–1878: Major Howard Egan's Diary*. Ed. by William M Eagan. Richmond, Utah: Howard R. Egan Estate, 1917.

Ekins, Roger Robin, ed. *Defending Zion: George Q. Cannon and the California Mormon Newspaper Wars of 1856–1857*. Spokane, Washington: The Arthur H. Clark Co., 2002.

Ellsworth, S. George, ed. *The Journals of Addison Pratt: Being a Narrative of Yankee Whaling in the Eighteen Twenties, a Mormon Mission to the Society Islands, and of Early California and Utah in the Eighteen Forties and Fifties*. Salt Lake City: University of Utah Press, 1990.

Glover, William. *The Mormons in California*. Ed. by Paul Bailey. Los Angeles: Glen Dawson, 1954.

Gordon, Mary McDougall, ed. *Overland to California with the Pioneer Line: The Gold Rush Diary of Bernard J. Reid.* Stanford: Stanford University Press, 1983. Revised second printing, 1985.

Hafen, LeRoy R., and Ann W. Hafen, eds. *Journals of the Forty-niners.* Glendale, California: The Arthur H. Clark Co., 1954.

Hammond, Francis Asbury. "In Early Days: My Introduction to Mormonism." *The Juvenile Instructor* (June–September, 1894).

Hammond, George P., ed. *The Larkin Papers: Personal, Business, and Official Correspondence of Thomas Oliver Larkin, Merchant and United States Consul in California,* 10 vols. Berkeley: University of California Press, 1951–1964.

Hawk, Nathan Hawk. Interview. *The [Sacramento] Evening Bee,* 4 January 1906.

Johnston, William G. *Experiences of a Forty-Niner.* Pittsburgh, 1892; reprint New York: Arno Press, 1973.

Journal of Discourses, 26 vols. London: Latter-day Saints Book Depot, 1854–1886.

Kemble, Edward. "Flag of the Twelve Stars." *Sacramento Daily Union,* 22 May 1858.

Kemble, Edward. *A Kemble Reader: Stories of California, 1846–1848 by Edward Cleveland Kemble, Early California Journalist.* Ed. by Fred Blackburn Rogers. San Francisco: California Historical Society, 1963.

Landon, Michael N., ed. *The Journals of George Q. Cannon, Volume 1: To California in '49.* Salt Lake City: Deseret Book Co., 1999.

Langworthy, Franklin. *Scenery of the Plains, Mountains, and Mines; or a Diary Kept Upon the Overland Route to California.* Ogdenburgh, New York: J. C. Sprague, Bookseller, Hitchcock and Tillotson, Printers, 1855.

Marshall, James W. "Marshall's Own Account of the Gold Discovery." *The Century Illustrated Monthly Magazine* (February 1891).

May, Richard Martin. *A Sketch of a Migrating Family to California in 1848.* Fairfield, Washington: Ye Galleon Press, 1991. Also published as *The Schreek of Wagons: 1848 Diary of Richard M. May.* Ed. by Devere Helfrich and Trudy Ackerman. Hopkinton, Massachusetts: Rigel Publications, 1993.

Orr, Thomas J., Jr. *Life History of Thomas J. Orr, Jr., Pioneer Stories of California and Utah.* [Shingle Springs, Calif:] Lillie Jane Orr Taylor, 1930.

Patterson, Lawson B. *Twelve Years in the Mines of California; Embracing a General View of the Gold Region, with Practical Observations on Hill, Placer, and Quartz Diggings; & Notes on the Origin of Gold Deposits.* Cambridge, Massachusetts: Miles & Dillingham, 1862.

Paul, Rodman, ed. *The California Gold Discovery: Sources, Documents, Accounts and Memoirs Relating to the Discovery of Gold at Sutter's Mill.* Georgetown, California: Talisman Press, 1966.

Pettit, Edwin. *Biography of Edwin Pettit, 1834–1912.* Salt Lake City: The Arrow Press, n.d.

Riter, W. W. "Statement of W. W. Riter, January 10, 1917." Kate B. Carter, ed., *Heart Throbs of the West,* 7:402–6. Salt Lake City: Daughters of Utah Pioneers, 1946. Original in Levi E. Riter Documents. MSS 114 Bx 6, Fd 20, Joel Ricks Papers, Utah State University.

Sherman, William T. *Memoirs of General William Tecumseh Sherman,* 2 vols. New York: D. Appleton and Co., 1876.

Slater, Nelson. *Fruits of Mormonism: A Fair and Candid Statement of Facts Illustrative of Mormon Principles, Mormon Policy, and Mormon Character By More Than Forty Eye-Witnesses.* Coloma, California: Harmon & Springer, 1851.

Spence, Mary Lee, and Donald Jackson, eds. *The Expeditions of John Charles Frémont,* 4 vols. Urbana: University of Illinois Press, 1970.

Smith, Jedediah. *The Southwest Expedition of Jedediah S. Smith: His Personal Account of the Journey to California.* Ed. by George R. Brooks. Glendale, California: The Arthur H. Clark Co., 1977.

Sutter, John A. "General Sutter's Diary," ed. Kenneth N. Owens. *John Sutter and a Wider West.* Ed. by Kenneth N. Owens.

———. *Sutter's Own Story: The Life of General John Augustus Sutter and the History of New Helvetia in the Sacramento Valley.* Ed. by Erwin Gudde. New York: G. P. Putnam's Sons, 1936.

Sutter, John A., *et al. New Helvetia Diary: A Record of Events Kept by John A. Sutter and His Clerks at New Helvetia, California, from September 9, 1815 to May 25, 1848.* San Francisco: Grabhorn Press, 1939.

Tanner, Myron. *Biography of Myron Tanner.* Salt Lake City: Deseret News, 1907.

Woodruff, Wilford. *The Discourses of Wilford Woodruff.* Salt Lake City: Bookcraft, 1969.

Unpublished Primary Sources

Bates, Joseph W. Autobiography. MS 11748, LDS Archives

Bell, Eli. Journal. LDS Archives.

Bigler, Henry William. Daybook of 1848, Bancroft Library, University of California, Berkeley.

———. Diary, Book B. Henry E. Huntington Library, San Marino, California.

Borrowman, John. Journal from Dec. 23, 1846 to Mar. 1870. LDS Archives.

Bullock, Thomas. Thomas Bullock Papers. LDS Archives.

Chamberlain, Solomon. A Brief Sketch of the Life of Solomon Chamberlain. Huntington Library, San Marino, California.

Elmer, Elijah. Journal, 1810–1878. Photocopy of original handwritten journal. MSS SC 1572, Lee Library, Brigham Young University.

Glover, William. The Mormons in California. CD 238, Bancroft Library, University of California, Berkeley.

Henrie, Danile. "Biography &c of President Daniel Henrie." South Sanpete Stake, 48th Quorum of Seventies Records, 1857–1928, LDS Archives.

Hickerson, George Washington. Family History. LDS Archives.

Hogan, Goudy Ericsen. Autobiography, 1829–1898. MS 7445, LDS Archives.

Huntington, Oliver Boardman, 1823–1909. Autobiography, ca. 1880. MSS SC 2219. Special Collections and Manuscripts, BYU Library.

Holmes, Jonathan Holmes. 1848 Trail Journal. MS 1673, LDS Archives.

Journal History of the Church of Jesus Christ of Latter-day Saints. LDS Archives.

Hurst, Frederick William. Diary of Frederick William Hurst. MS 1861, LDS Archives.

Judd, Zadock Knapp. Reminiscences of Zadock Knapp Judd, Senior. Manuscript A 462, Utah State Historical Society.

List of Brethren from California, 14 July 1849. LDS Archives.

Lyman, Amasa. Journal, Typescript. MS 2757, LDS Archives.

May, Richard Martin. A Sketch of a Migrating Family to California. Bancroft Library, University of California, Berkeley.

Miles, Samuel. Autobiography and Diary. LDS Archives.

Morris, Thomas. Memorandum Book. LDS Archives.

Naegle, George C. Life Sketch of John Conrad Naegle. Lee Library, Brigham Young University.

Pace, James. Autobiographical Sketch. LDS Archives.

Pixton, Robert. Autobiography. MS 5474, LDS Archives.

Rogers, Samuel Hollister. 1848 Diary. MS 883, LDS Archives.

Skinner, James Horace. Reminiscences, 1915. MS 6587, LDS Archives.

Sly, James C. Journal, June 1849 to March 1850. LDS Archives.

Smith, Alvin Thompson. Missionary Letters, 1840–1852. WA MSS S-1157 Sm515, Western Americana Collection, Beinecke Rare Book and Manuscript Library, Yale University.

Smith, Edward. A Journal of Scenes and Incidents on a Journey from Missouri to California in 1848. Typescript in California DAR, Genealogical Records Committee Report: Series 2, Volume 4, Miscellaneous Records of Several States and Counties. Copy at California State Library, CS 68 C 34 v. 4.

Salt Lake Stake. Minutes, 25 June 1848. LDS LR 604 109, LDS Archives.

Salt Lake Stake. Proceedings of Stake Presidency and High Council in Executive, Legislative and Judicial Capacity, Great Salt Lake Stake 1847–48, Minutes of the High Council, Albert Carrington—Clerk. LDS Archives.

Sirrine, Warren LeRoy. A Little Sketch of the Life of George Warren Sirrine. MS 1377, LDS Archives.

Skinner, James. Autobiography. MS 6587, LDS Archives.

Sutter, John A. Personal Reminiscences of General John Augustus Sutter. Bancroft Library, University of California, Berkeley.

——— to Mariano G. Vallejo, October 21, 1847, New Helvetia. Box 312, folder 10, Sutter Collection, California State Library. Translation from Spanish by Nellie Van de Grift Sanchez. (The original letter, written in Sutter's rudimentary Spanish, is in Mariano G. Vallejo, *Documentos para la historia de California, Tomo XII, 1844–48*, manuscript no. 315, Bancroft Library, University of California, Berkeley.)

——— to A. P. Collin, 12 June 1879, John Sutter Folder, Sacramento Pioneer Association Papers, Membership, Individual, Box I: A. Tingman, 3:03, Sacramento Archives and Museum Collection Center.

Thurber, Albert King. Journal. Bancroft Library, University of California, Berkeley.

Tiffany, Pardon Dexter. Journals and Letters, 1849. Originals in Tiffany Family Papers, 1779–1967, AMC94-001159, Missouri Historical Society. Typescript in OCTA Manuscripts, Mattes Library, National Frontier Trails Center, 99–103.

Willis, Ira J. "Ira J. Willis Guide to the Gold Mines." Huntington Library, San Marino, California.

Young, Brigham. Collection. MS 1234, LDS Archives.

Jefferson Hunt *et al.* to President Brigham Young, 14 May 1847.

Amasa Lyman to President Young and Council, 6 July 1849.

Amasa Lyman to Brigham Young, 19 September 1849.

———. To the Saints in California (Draft), 7 August 1847. Lee Library, Brigham Young University.

———, Heber C. Kimball, and Willard Richards. General Epistle to all Latter-day Saints, 19 February 1853. Journal History, LDS Archives.

INDEX

The Editor

Ken Owens is Professor Emeritus of History and Ethnic Studies at California State University, Sacramento, where he taught the history of the American West, Native American history, and public history. The founding director of the CSUS Capital Campus Public History Program, he has also been a consultant for public and private agencies in cultural resources management and historical resources interpretation. In addition, he held an appointment as adjunct professor in public history at the University of California, Santa Barbara.

As author and editor, his publications include *Riches for All: The California Gold Rush and the World* (2002); *John Sutter and a Wider West* (new ed. 2002); *The Wreck of the Sv. Nikolai* (new ed. 2001); and *Perilous Passage: A Narrative of the Montana Gold Rush, 1862–1863, by Edwin Ruthven Purple* (1995). He has been project manager and principal author for more than twenty CRM historical investigations. Among them, in collaboration with archaeologist Al Farber, he completed in 1990 the two-volume *Archaeological and Historical Investigation of the Mormon-Carson Emigrant Trail, El Dorado and Toiyabe National Forests* for the U.S. Forest Service, the project that began his research on California's Gold Rush Saints.

He has also written a series of the articles on the history of fly fishing in western America that have appeared recently in *Montana The Magazine of Western History, California Fly Fisher*, and other periodicals.

Ken has been a Woodrow Wilson Graduate Fellow, a Danforth Teaching Fellow, and a Penrose Fellow of the American Philosophical Society. Among his awards are the American Association of State and Local History's Certificate of Commendation, the local history prize of the Association for Northern California Records and Research, the Distinguished Faculty Award of the CSUS Alumni Association, and the Western History Association's Award of Merit. He and his wife, Dr. Sally Owens, make their home in Sacramento.